THE ADOLESCENT
IN THE
AMERICAN NOVEL
SINCE 1960

THE ADOLESCENT IN THE AMERICAN NOVEL
SINCE 1960

Mary Jean DeMarr
and
Jane S. Bakerman

UNGAR/NEW YORK

1986

The Ungar Publishing Company
370 Lexington Avenue
New York, New York 10017

Printed in the United States of America

Designed by Gene Garone

Library of Congress Cataloging-in-Publication Data

DeMarr, Mary Jean, 1932–
   The adolescent in the American novel since 1960.

   Bibliography: p.
   Includes index.
   1. American fiction—20th century—History and criticism. 2. Adolescence in literature.
3. Youth in literature. I. Bakerman, Jane S., 1931–
II. Title.
PS374.A3D45   1986   813'.54'09352055   86-235
ISBN 0-8044-3067-5

In memory of our fathers
William Fleming Bailey and Clarence Calvin Schnabel

Contents

Acknowledgments

We are grateful to the capable people who contributed to the preparation of this book. Karen Chittick Stabler, Mary Ann Phillips, Carol Chapman, and Richard Collins, the indefatigable and extraordinarily competent staff of the Indiana State University Interlibrary Loan Department, located literally hundreds of books for our use, and this project would have been impossible without their aid. Sonia Martin, Mary Ann Wallace, and Betty Harstad, members of the secretarial staff of the Department of English, were also very helpful. We extend warm thanks to all these folk as well as to Marilyn Meads, ever patient and accurate. We also give special thanks to Louise Richards, Mary Lu McFall, and William C. Schnabel, who were extremely generous in helping us to prepare the manuscript, and to the Indiana State University Research Committee for the grant that helped support our research during one of several summers devoted to this study.

Though the responsibility for any errors or omissions in this work rests, of course, with us, we appreciate the efforts of all who have participated in its development.

From the time we were all graduate students together, W. Tasker Witham has been our friend and colleague. His *The Adolescent in the American Novel, 1920–1960* is widely recognized as an important, useful contribution to the study of American literature; it paved the way for our own work, and in many ways, we see our book as a symbol for over twenty years of warm friendship and stimulating exchange. We thank him.

Mary Jean DeMarr
Jane S. Bakerman
Indiana State University

Introduction

If that element of folk wisdom holding that all human beings "have at least one novel in them" is correct, it may also be true that the vast majority of those potential novels are stories treating adolescence. The process of moving from dependence to independence, almost always a difficult progression, is one of the very few experiences all adults share and one of the even fewer—perhaps the *only*—universal experiences everyone remembers. This very universality, then, may well account for the popularity that stories of adolescence enjoy among writers and readers.

This book is a companion volume to W. Tasker Witham's *The Adolescent in the American Novel, 1920–1960* and to our own *Adolescent Female Portraits in the American Novel, 1961–1981: An Annotated Bibliography*. This new volume aims to provide, within the bounds of practicality, the broadest possible view of treatments of adolescent characters in American novels published between 1961 and 1982. In order to achieve that goal, we have examined titles selected from both "high" and popular culture, some paperback originals, and novels written for young adults. Some 4200 novels were examined, read, and evaluated, and approximately 600 titles are treated in this volume.

Because of the proliferation of recent novels featuring adolescent characters, it was, of course, essential to set some boundaries. Accordingly, only novels depicting American youths in American settings and written by American authors were included. From among the novels thus singled out for study, we have tried to present a cross section of authors, themes, tones, attitudes, and modes of treatment. Not every American novel treating adolescence and published during the pertinent time period is discussed here, but those included represent, we believe, the kinds of materials readers will find throughout the range of titles available.

In order to make the discussions of selected subject-novels as useful as possible, we have tried to strike a balance between very well-known works and rather more obscure works, as well as among examples of the types of novels identified for consideration. We have generally defined adolescence as the period between ages twelve and nineteen, though, as the Annotated Chart indicates, many of our subject-novels depict characters' lives for much longer periods, even from childhood through maturity. In those instances, the discussions and the annotations focus upon the adolescent years. For the most part, characters' college years (or the period that would parallel college years) have been omitted from discussion in the interest of unity. These years might indeed be a very fruitful subject for a separate study.

The sources of our original list of potentially useful titles were *Book*

Review Digest (1961–1982), *Adolescence in Literature* by Thomas West Gregory (New York and London: Longman, 1978), and a list Professor Witham created for his own use in teaching. Because of our long-term interest in this subject, we also drew upon personal knowledge of novels stressing adolescents' experiences. The extensive working list of novels that emerged from analyzing these sources was then evaluated according to the books' potential usefulness in indicating and analyzing the roles and functions of their American adolescent characters.

From our study of the novels covered in this book as well as from reading and analyzing many not included, several patterns depicting adolescence have emerged; these patterns tend to hold true for both major and minor characters. Sometimes the adventures of fictional adolescents seem to be a means of authors' coming to terms with the tests imposed upon the young person striving for emancipation and self-determination. The large audience attracted by novels of adolescence suggests that they may serve the same purpose for many readers. Certainly in the traditional *Bildungsroman* this motif of trial and tempering is dominant. Such titles as Philip Roth's *When She Was Good* (1967), John Knowles's *Peace Breaks Out* (1981), and Carolyn Doty's *A Day Late* (1980) come immediately to mind.

Other authors, perhaps most frequently the writers of books for young adults, appear to perceive their work as cautionary or preparatory. That is, they discuss problems and difficulties that modern teenagers may well have to face, and they address them with a youthful audience in mind. Useful examples are *Domestic Arrangements* (1981) and *Breaking Up* (1980), both by Norma Klein, and *The Son of Someone Famous* (1974) by Marijane Meaker (pseudonym, M. E. Kerr).

Still other authors—such as Kenneth Millar (pseudonym, Ross Macdonald) in *The Underground Man* (1971), Maureen Howard in *Before My Time* (1974), Joyce Carol Oates in *them* (1969), and Curtis Harnack in *Limits of the Land* (1979)—see their adolescent characters as useful symbols of American social attitudes and practices and treat them accordingly. Often this treatment offers a family or several families as microcosmic representations of a social class, of a professional group, or of the culture as a whole.

These patterns of usage often blend and combine, especially, it seems, in novels that describe the lives of American minority-group members, as Kristin Hunter's *Lou in the Limelight* (1981), Toni Morrison's *Sula* (1973), and Sylvia Wilkinson's *Moss on the North Side* (1966), clearly demonstrate. Combined patterns lend universality to the plots and help indicate the pervasiveness of the social patterns (usually injustices) upon which the novels focus.

As we read and analyzed our subject-novels, seven areas of interest to both authors and their adolescent characters were revealed as basic subjects for authors, crucial concerns of their teenaged characters: love and sexuality, family relationships, friendships, crises, social institutions, environment (setting), and fate. These subjects and concerns are dominant—either individually or in combination—throughout the time span (1961–1982) covered in our study, the only significant variations being frankness in the treatment of some topics (masturbation, homosexuality, violence, for instance) or explicitness of language in a few (but far from all) novels of recent date.

We have therefore organized this study thematically according to these subjects and concerns rather than chronologically according to the publication dates of the subject-novels. Each basic area of interest is discussed in a chapter dealing with fictional adolescent females and in another chapter dealing with males. As a means of further examining the interrelated ways in which some subject-authors employ these seven basic subjects and concerns, we have discussed a number of particularly thought-provoking subject-novels such as Mendal Johnson's *Let's Go Play at the Adams'* (1974), Gretchen Sprague's *A Question of Harmony* (1965), and Jessamyn West's *The Massacre at Fall Creek* (1975) in several chapters of this book. Readers interested in doing a chronological study of novels of adolescence written between 1961 and 1982 or of one of the basic subjects or concerns will find helpful information in the Annotated Chart.

In our thematic study, Part One deals with young female characters; Part Two considers male adolescents. The concerns of both female and male characters, as they are addressed by the authors of our subject-novels, are strikingly parallel topically, though often divergent in emphasis and attitude. To illustrate both the similarities *and* the differences, we have made the division between discussions of female and male characters but have organized Parts One and Two in parallel fashion. Thus, readers seeking comparisons and contrasts between characters of either sex will find them immediately at hand yet will readily be able to locate the same types of information about both sexes. Individual chapters (which are numbered consecutively throughout the book) discuss the major concerns reflected in the subject-novels.

Brief introductions to each chapter appear in the texts of Parts One and Two, and these are followed by a series of paragraphs that describe, discuss, analyze, and often evaluate the treatment representative subject-authors have given the specific concern in individual, representative novels. The intent here is to give an overview of the concern and then to illustrate the various modes in which it is approached, the various functions it serves, the various means by which authors reveal its importance in the maturation process. We have also incorporated an overview of the novel and whenever possible indicated its place in the author's canon. For the convenience of our readers, novels intended for young adult readers have been identified in Parts One and Two by the characters "YA" following the date.

Some subject-novels do not appear in either Parts One or Two. Part Three, however, the Annotated Chart, does include every novel treated in this study. Here the novels are grouped according to year of publication and then listed in alphabetical order according to author's last name. Complete information is given under the author's true name and cross references with pseudonyms are provided as necessary here as in the index. The chart is designed to give readers a very quick summary of the plot, characters, setting, and focus of each subject-novel (see key to Annotated Chart); the Chart also directs readers to appropriate chapters in the text and identifies the major subjects and concerns addressed in the novel.

The Index to this volume lists all titles, pseudonymns, and authors included in all three parts as well as all the major subjects and concerns discussed in Parts One and Two. Important topics that are not *major* subjects and concerns are also listed in the index, for instance, rape, incest, crime.

It is our hope that these means of selection and organization will help general readers, librarians, teachers, and scholars to identify and locate novels treating adolescence that will be useful to them.

Part One

CHAPTER I
Female Love and Sexuality

Fairly or unfairly, a good many adults perceive adolescents as essentially selfish beings, though sometimes this judgment is softened by an awareness that the youngsters' preoccupation with self often arises directly from the emotional, psychological, physical, and social changes that confront them. While most fictional adolescents seem to welcome these changes and challenges, others fear them. In either circumstance, their perceptions that they must change, must begin making vastly important decisions, absorb almost all of their attention.

As adolescents struggle to define themselves and to gain some measure of autonomy, they are also coping with their awakening or developing sexuality, and in the minds of many of the young characters included in this study, these three central goals are very closely allied. Common attitudes, desires, or goals appear in almost every novel considered here, no matter how early or how recently it was published.

One of the most basic questions in novels about adolescents is that dealing with sexuality. And for the young women under consideration here, two important social attitudes complicate their interest in, their experimentation with, and their comfort with their sexuality. Almost every author who deals with this question (and most do) reflects these attitudes—that it is the female partner who must determine the degree of intimacy a heterosexual couple establishes and, as a corollary, it is primarily (very often, solely) the young woman's problem if she becomes pregnant.

Closely allied to these positions is another at least equally important. The young women in these novels, whether they are heterosexuals or lesbians, want very much to love and be loved. No matter how openly sensual they are, no matter how comfortable or uncomfortable they may be with their sexuality, most of these girls keenly desire the love relationship as much as—or even more than—they desire sexual union. Underlying this yearning is another attitude that, in most instances, sharply separates female characters from male fictional adolescents. Loving—and, sometimes even much more importantly, *being loved*—is, for the majority of these girls, absolutely essential to the development of a positive self-image. It is as if they cannot be *anyone* if an important love-object, peer or elder, does not ratify their sense of self by loving and desiring them. For their male counterparts, however, giving or imposing love or sexual activity is central to their self-images. The need to be loved or at least desired in order to be able to accept oneself makes it seem imperative for a girl to be conventionally pretty (or beautiful if she can manage it or has been "lucky") and also complicates enormously the responsibilities of regulating relationships and dealing with possible pregnancies.

Adolescent lesbian love affairs are, of course, no less complex or perplexing. Though the lesbian characters who appear in this study are gratified by being the chosen love-objects of desirable partners, the girls' self-acceptance can still be threatened by their keen awareness that generally society disapproves of or at best only tolerates their relationships. And always, as with their heterosexual peers, the threat of rejection and the dread of undesirability can be debilitating factors in their search for self-realization.

When youthful premarital heterosexual relationships result in marriage, the success or failure of those unions is still, very often, dependent in good part upon whether or not the young wife feels made whole, feels that she's been granted adulthood, feels ratified as a person by her new role. If she does not and so seeks identity through motherhood, she frequently remains dependent upon the perceptions of others for her sense of self.

As a result of consciousness-raising by the Women's Movement, these observations will not seem new to many readers, but they must be made for two important reasons: as a reminder that these attitudes still persist (as witnessed by even the most recent novels studied here) and as the groundwork for noting an important difference among the sexually active female adolescent characters discussed in this chapter. Their sexual experience damages some girls and benefits others. Those who do benefit (even if the love affair founders, even if they suffer during or after it) are almost always those youngsters capable of abandoning the destructive habit of defining themselves according to the perceptions of their partners. Instead, they use their youthful love affairs as educative experiences in the process of self-definition. In short, they mature; they learn to possess themselves, often, their creators suggest, to be far better partners in either the current or future relationships.

For adolescent female characters, the inception, conduct, and resolution of a love affair frequently substitute, at least in part, for the initiation journey of the traditional *Bildungsroman*. The inward journey toward self-realization and self-confidence is vastly important, usually much more important than the actual physical journey of the *Bildungsroman* hero and the actual romance of the female adolescent, which both function both as symbols of progress toward self-realization and maturity. Consciously or unconsciously, the female adolescents depicted in many modern American novels are aware of the importance of the educative process; they understand or intuit its link to their concept of self-realization.

Perhaps, then, it is not surprising that these fictional adolescent girls, like the living people they represent, sometimes seem to readers or to the characters who surround them to be selfish and preoccupied with their own desires. Some, of course, are self-seeking in the standard, negative meaning of the term. But even the most blatantly, unappealingly self-centered are selfish also in another sense: they are preoccupied with creating the selves, the adults, they hope to be. In doing so, the girls must constantly ratify and accept, alter, or reject the expectations imposed upon them—and often internalized by them—by the adult society they passionately desire to join. Whether female adolescents succeed or fail in this important, absorbing, hard work, their love relationships are often considered important, even determining, factors in that success or failure.

The question whether or not a girl should allow—or welcome—intercourse, as we have said, is central to every novel that discusses young female characters' awakening heterosexuality, whether the girls are simply dating or are considering serious affairs with adolescent males. The question becomes even more difficult, as a rule, when the girls are involved with older men. Most authors address this decision very seriously, reflecting the societal attitude that "going all the way" or refusing to do so can be a determining factor in any young woman's life. Sometimes this puzzlement is employed as a fairly obvious, but very useful, symbol of the generalized confusion of adolescence.

A mixture of comedy and sentiment characterizes B. L. Barrett's story of sexual awakening, *Love in Atlantis* (1969). Set in a California beach town in the 1930s, it tells of Virginia, an innocent middle-class girl who, at fourteen and fifteen, knows the facts of sex but does not really understand them. She is still virginal at the end of her story but has grown greatly in awareness. Two loves, one in each of the summers covered by the narrative, dramatize her maturing. Her uncertainties, her embarrassments at her ignorance, her attempts to pretend sophistication, and her yearnings after love are described with both nostalgia and amusement by the adult Virginia, herself now the mother of a daughter just a little younger than she was then, in a long flashback that comprises most of the novel.

Other authors use one partner's restraint—interpreted as "good sense" or wise practicality—as a cautionary signal to young readers. Jeanne Blake is first drawn to Dave Carpenter when the two are trapped in a sticky social situation with college students whose behavior doesn't meet the high-school couple's standards. Later, when Jeanne, the protagonist of Gretchen Sprague's *A Question of Harmony* (1965, YA), and Dave begin to play together in a string trio, the relationship deepens, and they learn that they have much in common. The infrequency of their social dates frustrates Jeanne, who slowly becomes aware that she cares for Dave much more than for the other youths she dates from time to time, but she is puzzled by his refusal to "get involved," until she discovers that he is benefiting from the negative example of his older brother who has dropped out of college to support a wife and infant twins. Ultimately, the couple work out their problem, aware that they are very special to one another but that each has educational and professional demands to meet. One of the many lessons the author intends to teach here is that going steady is not a wise step for many adolescents.

When their female characters do engage in actively sexual relationships, many authors use the affairs—even despite periods of turbulence or pain—as positive evidence of the girls' evolving maturity and independence. Sometimes this motif is only one of many in a novel. For example, Mynette Hancock, a beautiful eighteen-year-old who leaves home in search of adventure and finds a brief but enriching affair with Lenny Lewis, a young truck driver, is one of a number of characters whose lives briefly touch J. W. Pickett, the almost legendary trucker facing a moment of decision who is the protagonist of Phillip Finch's *Haulin'* (1975). Here, though Mynette's experiences are positive, they are used primarily to flesh out the plot.

The experiences of the protagonist of Alice Hoffman's *Property Of* (1977) are more painful, but the greater strength of that young woman enables her to survive and to overcome the compulsion which had bound her to an unworthy lover. *Property Of* follows the love of the nameless seventeen-year-old narrator for a New York City gang leader over the year from its inception until she finally leaves him. In the course of that year she sees him commit murder, lose his concept of "honor," become addicted to heroin, serve a brief prison term, and become a drug pusher. She takes drugs because that is the only way to be close to him, she helps him commit crimes, she betrays friends for him, and she is raped by members of an enemy gang. But she maintains her self-awareness and finally frees herself of her compulsive love for him. His self-destructiveness is believably depicted, as is her concentration on him to the exclusion of all else.

Even when female sexuality is a major focus of the plot and sexual activity is clearly a symbol of growth, readers cannot be fully assured of a clear, detailed characterization. When authors do employ rather cloudy treatments of sexually active girls the novels still can be informative and interesting. Although readers tend not to identify with poorly realized characters, they may find their situations recognizable, moving, or amusing.

Rosalyn Drexler's *I Am the Beautiful Stranger* (1965) is the diary of Selma Silver, kept in the late 1930s, as she ages from thirteen to sixteen. It deals with many of the problems of growing up in a city (New York

City) in a family that the protagonist sees as unstable and unloving. Selma has little respect for herself, even occasionally considering suicide. But her main concern is with her sexual maturation. Early in the novel she has a hopeless crush on her friend's older brother, and she rejoices that she has begun to menstruate and that her breasts are developing. We see her carry on a correspondence with a pen pal who is a juvenile delinquent in reform school, then go through a period of sexual promiscuity, until at the end she seems to be considering a real commitment to a young man. But her introspection is shallow, and key episodes in her development are skipped over so that the reader never really gets to know her—nor does she seem to know herself. The novel, nevertheless, is a funny and insightful treatment of the struggles of female adolescence.

Though Pam Sheehy is a major character in Arthur Roth's *The Caretaker* (1980), she is depicted only through the eyes of the male protagonist and, perhaps as a consequence, emerges as flat and a trifle unconvincing. Having run away from family and school, Pam hides out in her parents' summer residence where she meets and conducts a brief affair with Mark Cooper, the protagonist. Both Pam and Mark have had intercourse before; neither is surprised nor feels guilty; they seem, in fact, to take sexual activity for granted. Mark becomes infatuated with Pam, and there is some question of her having deliberately seduced him in order to ensure his secrecy about her whereabouts; her true feelings are not fully clear. The point that the encounter has been beneficial to both youngsters, however, is clearly stated if not persuasively demonstrated.

In *Now Molly Knows* (1974), Merrill Joan Gerber recaps the sexual codes of the 1950's—carefully orchestrated stages of petting, dormitory lights-out and curfew rules, for instance—through the story of Molly's long, often frustrating pursuit of Joshua. Often at odds with her own parents during her early teens, Molly cannot understand Joshua's ties (based on money and emotional blackmail) to his parents; she believes him to be frustratingly slow to mature, and his parents' refusal to accept her leads to a fairly brief but trying rupture in their long romance. For Molly, their courtship, which parallels her sexual development, is the extended prelude to the true beginning of her life, which is her first experience of intercourse: "Though Molly has always known it is this act which creates life, she never knew it would be her reward for having to live it." Throughout the novel, Gerber's portrait of Molly never expands much beyond the girl's preoccupation with her sexual development as symbolized by her struggle to possess the lad she loves, to achieve sexual maturity.

Clearly delineated, carefully detailed, and very compelling, the portraits of most protagonists who are enriched by their sexual awakenings contrast sharply with that of Gerber's Molly. Though these girls find both problems as well as gratification in their love affairs, their sexual development is treated as only one element of their advancement toward fuller understanding of themselves and of human relationships, rather than as an end in itself.

The theme of dating (including the "rules" for progressive sexual permissiveness, and the tensions and jealousies that can arise between even close friends when male attention is at stake) is an important concern in *The Cheerleader* (1973), which, like *Now Molly Knows*, also reflects the 1950s. For protagonist Henrietta Snow, her prolonged affair with Tom Forbes, athlete and "Big Man on Campus," is a social triumph, a physical delight, and a torment. Snowy and Tom really care deeply for one another, and their sexual experiments are never taken lightly by either of them or by author Ruth Doan MacDougall. Considered cool, poised, and confident by others, Snowy is prey inwardly to all the usual doubts and worries of adolescence, and her relationship with Tom—first capturing his attention, then garnering his letter sweater and ring, and finally coping with breaking up—is a major generator of plot tension. The couple deal surprisingly well, at first, with their divergent interests: Snowy is intellectual, Tom interested in sports. But without fanfare and without a great deal of verbalization, those differences (along with Tom's wish to be free to date other girls and be sexually active during his first year of college) contribute to their parting. Even a passionate reconciliation cannot heal all these differences, and Snowy's final decision about their relationship symbolizes her maturity.

Urania Bishop, the protagonist of Daphne Athas's *Entering Ephesus* (1971), forms an intense friendship with Zebulon Walley; together the two experience the excitement of learning. As the children grow older, they begin their sexual experimentation together, but this process is interrupted by the appearance of Edmund Bostwick, a naval officer. When Urie falls in love with Bostwick and has an affair with him, the chief complication is the disruption of her relationship with Zebul. For Urie, Zebul represents one constant in her hectic childhood. Bostwick represents the outside, adult world, particularly the advent of World War II. The affair signifies Urie's transition into greater maturity and independence, and though she fully understands neither the relationship with Bostwick nor its implications, Urie is able to cope with it and with her grief when Bostwick's orders take him away. She has become mature enough to assume an altered but again meaningful friendship with Zebul; like Snowy in *The Cheerleader*, Urie has grown up.

Her own immaturity alarms Winnie Simon, protagonist of Winifred Rosen's *Cruisin for a Bruisin* (1976, YA). She speaks of herself as a "true maniac," and her early comment that "not only was it difficult to be a girl, but it looked like it was going to get worse," seems, for most of Winnie's thirteenth year, to be right on target. Her early romantic experiences are awkward and unpromising until she begins to date John Miller; their mutual explorations of sexuality are comfortable and natural. During a summer at the shore, however, Winnie misses John, is restless and prickly—and launches herself into a reckless adventure. She takes up with Timothy, who is mysterious and somewhat older, the personification of exploitation; their meetings are secret and could be very dangerous. The Timothy affair explodes into a gigantic family crisis which ultimately proves redemptive by bringing Winnie better understanding of her family, helping her to be wiser about her sound affection for John. Sometimes funny, occasionally foolish, but never silly, all in all, Winnie is a satisfactorily maturing protagonist.

In contrast to Winnie, the protagonist of *Domestic Arrangements* (1981, YA) by Norma Klein overestimates her maturity. When her father insists that age fourteen is still "extremely young," Rusty Engleberg protests that "It *isn't*. . . . It used to be, but it isn't anymore." The point at issue is Rusty's request for a diaphragm (as a Christmas present) because she wants freedom from the fear of pregnancy during her affair with Joshua Lasker. Both Rusty and Lionel, her father, are correct in their estimates of Rusty's immaturity. She *is* still too young to conduct a long-term liaison comfortably, but she is also startlingly sophisticated. Rusty and Joshua genuinely care for one another, devoting, for example, considerable frank discussion to her lack of orgasm during intercourse; he frets about it; she reassures him. They strive to behave responsibly and tend to measure their relationship against those of their peers and their parents, in which they both consciously and unconsciously perceive flaws. Seemingly worldly, experienced, "enlightened," Rusty and Joshua learn that it takes more than joyous sexual experimentation and true concern for one's lover to build and to protect a fulfilling relationship.

A strong, vital subplot in *The Massacre at Fall Creek* (1975) underscores one of Jessamyn West's recurring themes: that the ability to handle one's sexuality wisely and generously is a sign of true maturity. Here, Hannah Cape's youthful affair and courtship with the slightly older Charlie Fort serves as her initiation into womanhood. Hannah makes several errors in her quest for adulthood; she is uncertain of the moral code by which she wishes to live; she withdraws from Charlie when he needs her most; and she nearly allows pride to stand in the way of genuine love and potential happiness when Charlie, hurt and bewildered, takes another mistress. But like the true *Bildungsroman* hero she is, Hannah emerges sadder and wiser but stronger at the end of her quest and accepts Charlie as he is rather than as she wishes him to be, assuming, rightfully in West's view, some of the responsibility for his "other" affair as well as for their own.

A brief affair with an older man and a longer and more meaningful relationship with a college classmate are important parts of Susannah Ellison's maturation, narrated by herself in Harriet Hahn's *The Plantain Season* (1976). At seventeen, Susannah feels inferior to her beautiful mother, but she succeeds in asserting her independence and striking out on a life of her own. The affair with Jim, her classmate, is a particularly liberating experience, and at the end of the novel she is able to look ahead to a possible life with Jim or to a separate existence. She thinks about "making my own, separate plan. For that, there's a full world of possibility."

Sometimes a nurturing affair ends tragically. In her mid-teens, Vyry, a mulatto slave, the daughter of her owner, John Morris Dutton, and his long-term slave-mistress, Hetta, falls in love with Randall Ware, a free black; their love story is one of Vyry's many tests of courage and endurance in *Jubilee* (1966) by Margaret Walker. According to Georgia law, a slave could marry a free man, given her owner's consent, but that consent is never acquired, and Vyry becomes Ware's lover, counting on his promise to buy and free her. In his arms, she can forget, briefly, the horrors of her life, and thus he represents relief from present pain as well as hope for the future. Circumstances—primarily the bitter willfulness of others—part the couple, however, and at the end of her adolescence, Vyry, the mother of two, is left to remake her life, to achieve full personhood, even in the face of slavery. Though the loss of Ware's supportive love and the added burden of trying to protect her very young children from the horrors of slavery are additional complications for Vyry, the overall consequences of their relationship are positive, for she is stronger, more determined, even tougher as a result of it. Ware has confirmed her sense of worth, taught her much, helped harden her will to survive.

As Elizabeth Allen illustrates in *The Loser* (1965, YA) even unsuccessful relationships can have positive results. "Deitz" Ames becomes far more sensitive to her own capabilities as well as to the world around her through caring for Denny Hawks. By dating Denny over almost everyone's objections, she learns a good deal about both accepted and acceptable social norms, expanding her mind as well as her experiences. Most important, she learns to value Denny for what he has taught her and for his potential; the immature Deitz would have rejected him completely.

Pati Hill's *One Thing I Know* (1962, YA) makes a similar point. At sixteen, Francesca Hollins is thoughtful and introspective. As a result of dating several young men and briefly being infatuated with Graham, with whom she actually has little in common, she is disillusioned about human relationships and begins to recognize the isolation that is part of the human condition. When she sees Graham some time after their relationship has ended, she is surprised to discover that she now feels nothing for him.

> It was about the worst thing that ever happened to me in my whole life, realizing that who I cared most for in the whole world had not changed at all and that it did not mean a thing. . . .

> After a while I began to cry the way you do when you are
> very young and it is dark and they have gone out leaving you
> . . . , only then there is always the chance they will come back and
> I knew that in this case there wasn't anyone *to* come back.
> The person I loved was just an idea and for all I knew that's
> all any of us were to each other. Just something we dreamed to
> keep ourselves from facing the nothing around us.

The "one thing" she knows is that she "will never be in love again."
Nevertheless, she does not isolate herself, and she seems to grow in
strength and maturity as a result of her new knowledge. Narrated by
Francesca and containing some malapropisms and clumsy grammar
which help characterize her, this brief novel is suitable for young readers.

One of a large number of important characters in Edwin Lanham's
Speak Not Evil (1964) is Vera Blaine, who is not pretty and has not been
especially popular in high school. She is, in fact, distinguished only for
her large and beautiful breasts. We learn that she had been enticed, by
an older woman who is made to represent almost pure evil, into a sex
ring whose orgies become to Vera the most real and only important part
of her life. When, however, two acquaintances become briefly involved
and are horrified at what they learn, Vera is able to see herself and her
activities through their eyes. Appalled, she briefly tries to form a relationship with a simple but honest young man as well as to assuage her
guilt by confessing to the Congregational minister. When these attempts
just intensify her sense of alienation, she resolves to leave her small
town: "They all owed her a little something. . . ; they owed her a chance
to start over again. In New York, in a new environment, she could be a
different girl, a new Vera Blaine. She couldn't stay here in Sagamore,
not possibly, and there was one thing about this big world, there were
always new people." The resiliency of youth, Lanham leads us to believe, will carry her through this troubled time in her life, and Vera's
story reaffirms the importance of both self-assessment *and* an awareness
of others to a character's ability to survive even potentially disastrous
youthful sexual encounters.

In *The Watchman* (1961), Davis Grubb plays one sister's unhealthy,
dangerous manipulation of her sexual attractions against the other's
clear-eyed awareness that sexuality is only one facet of the human personality. Initially, Jill Alt, nineteen, believes herself to be in love with
Cole Blake and takes pride in limiting their sexual experimentation. She
explains that she is a "good girl" whose life contrasts sharply with that
of her sister, Cristi, seventeen, who openly conducts an affair with Jason
Hunnicutt. When Cole is murdered, however, Jason transfers his affections to Jill and learns that there are very dark elements to her convo-
luted personality. In contrast, Cristi, supposedly promiscuous, reveals
ever deepening levels of maturity, compassion, and love. Grubb uses
the sisters' love for the same lad to demonstrate that social codes can dis-

guise goodness as well as evil, that sexuality can symbolize both destruction and redemption, maturity and crippling childishness.

When, like Davis Grubb's Jill Alt, a girl perceives her sexuality as *the*
defining factor of her character and abuses her appeal in order to reassure herself of her worth, the results can be disastrous. Occasionally,
the resulting damage is inflicted by a young woman scorned or even
merely disappointed. Paul Covert's *Cages* (1971), in which Barbara Gar-
ret also represents a hostile, uncaring society, is another good example.
Bob Ward's attention and affection are depicted as the saving factors in
Barbara's transformation from ugly duckling into acceptable date. They
seem to share an almost idyllic love until another boy invites Barbara to
the prom, triggering a crisis in their relationship. When Bob is impotent
during their reconciliation, Barbara is humiliated, furious, and vengeful.
Her unfounded claims that he attempted to rape her and that he is a homosexual destroy Bob's faith in himself.

In Marianne Hauser's experimental novel *The Talking Room* (1976),
the thirteen-year-old narrator, known only as B (all characters are identified only by initials), is both fat and pregnant, having become sexually
active at the age of ten. However, her feelings about herself and her situation, particularly her self-hatred and insecurity, are implied rather than
clearly stated, for the focus of the novel is on her observations of others.
Here, as in *Cages*, a girl's acceptability is linked to her appearance (and
thus to desirability), but B seems bent upon self-destruction rather than
upon the destruction of others.

At times, youngsters simply drift into sexual alliances because it
seems to be time to do so, and wasteful dissatisfaction rather than overt
destruction results. In Lisa Alther's *Original Sins* (1981), the Prince sisters, Emily and Sally, begin their sexual experimentation with the Tatro
brothers, Raymond and Jed, who are the girls' cousins and best childhood buddies. Neither Emily nor Raymond finds much pleasure in the
obligatory hugs and kisses they manage on their strained dates, and
they date one another because each feels too out of step with the high-
school crowd to attract anyone else. A later, more physically satisfying
affair with a college student leaves Emily still vaguely seeking something better. Sally also tolerates rather than enjoys Jed's use of her body,
though they are supposedly Newland, Tennessee's, "ideal couple," perfectly suited to one another, perfect examples of southern teenagers,
popular and beautiful. When Sally yields to Jed's importunities to "go all
the way," she becomes pregnant, and the couple drop out of high
school and into a dreary married life. Once confident they could do anything, not one of these four youngsters achieves happiness though they
continue to influence one another's lives forever.

When sexual activity joins with or stems primarily from rebellion
against parental restriction, the results are hardly more satisfying for
young females, even though they may strive to make decisions more in-

dependently than Emily and Sally Prince (*Original Sins*). At sixteen, Sarah Green, protagonist of Patricia Welles's *Babyhip* (1967), is bright, frank, and eager for experience. The novel, a modern female picaresque story, tells of her sexual initiation and experimentation, her crushes and lusts, and her unfocused rebellion against her middle-class Jewish parents and their way of life. She follows her "fiancé" to Harvard, where immersion in the counter-culture leads only to disappointment.

Well realized, humorous flashbacks to Ginny Babcock's adolescence comprise about a quarter of *Kinflicks* (1976), by Lisa Alther. Reared by parents who take their "own vulnerability seriously" and are keenly aware of mortality, Ginny rebels by "going with" disapproved high school classmates—a football hero and the local tough—in efforts to assert her independence and reaffirm her sense of being alive. In these sexual alliances, Ginny tends to become the person her loved one expects her to be; thus Alther uses the motif of sexual initiation to indicate that experience alone does not generate maturity.

Though the creators of characters such as Ginny Babcock (*Kinflicks*), Sarah Green (*Babyhip*), Emily and Sally Prince (*Original Sins*), and B (*The Talking Room*) acknowledge the girls' active participation in creating their own unhappiness, other authors depict girls' negative early sexual experiences as imposed upon them. In these cases the young men who exploit them often reflect social attitudes that allow for or encourage such abuse. As the following examples illustrate, these attitudes appear in novels set in both modern and earlier times.

A grim picture of men's sexual exploitation of young women and its consequences in the women's views of themselves and in the life patterns they create for themselves is given by Alix Kates Shulman in *Memoirs of an Ex-Prom Queen* (1972). Sasha Davis is repeatedly seduced and sexually used by a succession of men of various ages, types, and professions. Having internalized the values of her society that teach that a woman's primary goals are personal beauty and success achieved through her relationships with men, she compares later experiences to the moment of glory when she was chosen queen of a high-school prom. Presented graphically in flashbacks, the memories of her adolescent sexual adventures help the reader—and Sasha—understand why her two marriages have failed and why she has accomplished little of value despite her great talents. The novel's cryptic ending may suggest that in her thirties she has finally freed herself from the baneful effects of an all-American girlhood. An important feminist novel, *Memoirs* effectively depicts many of the insights of the Women's Movement of the 1960s and 1970s.

In *Kindred* (1979) by Octavia E. Butler, adolescent Alice Greenwood Jackson, born a free black in antebellum Maryland, is enslaved partly because of her efforts to aid her husband, a slave, to escape. Her freedom also is sacrificed to Rufe Weylin's sexual obsession—he must have her;

in his mind, her marriage counts for nothing and as a slave, she is fair prey. Alice's physical and emotional recovery from the horrors of seeing her husband maimed and sold south and from her own vicious beating is limited by her status as Rufe's mistress-slave. Dozens of conflicting pressures assail her: dependence upon, hatred of, and grudging tolerance of Rufe; love for her children and terror about their futures (because Rufe refuses to free them); the disdain and jealousy of her peers; and her own self-disgust and pragmatic acceptance. Denied autonomy, Alice becomes manipulative and distrustful. Ultimately, as a young woman, she takes final, tragic, assertive action. *Kindred* compares and contrasts Alice's development with the changes undergone by Dana, the contemporary black protagonist who is repeatedly drawn back in time to the Weylin plantation.

In *Kindred*, sexual exploitation is linked clearly with the fact that Alice Jackson is a black and a slave; yet the consequent extreme psychological and emotional damage is horridly similar to the effects suffered by Sasha Davis in *Memoirs of an Ex-Prom Queen*. Other results of damaging relationships between heterosexual adolescents range from cynicism through the death of one of the partners.

In Ellen Douglas's long novel *A Family's Affairs* (1962), approximately the middle third is given over to young Anna McGovern and her introduction to the pain and uncertainty of love. As a high-school girl, of a "rigidly idiosyncratic background," she falls in love with a boy her family considers unsuitable. Through their love she gains in confidence, and she becomes almost obsessed with looking forward to their eventual marriage. The relationship endures for a number of years, ending finally when Anna is in college. In her bitter disappointment, she knows she has been changed for all time:

> Her second self had been born—the dissenter who would always stand by, detachedly watching from the wings, making ironic reservations. . . . Her life loomed up, and she felt that she could never be involved again. What man could make her forget that love dies? Every word she spoke in love again would remind her that she had spoken it before, once and forever, with her whole soul, and it had proved untrue.

In *Blade of Light* (1968) by Don Carpenter, Carole Weigandt, the most beautiful girl in Quinton High School, dates Harold Hunt, the leader of the tough boys' crowd. Their relationship is based primarily on their sexual explorations, and the tensions engendered by Carole's refusal to have intercourse trigger a series of many serious quarrels that culminates in the girl's death. Though she is puzzled by her own desires and tormented by Harold's importuning, Carole does understand that "it was not so much her virginity she was attempting to protect but her right to determine when and how it was to be taken, to not be forced by circumstance or emotion into an act she had decided must wait." One of the book's several tragic ironies is that these are precisely the factors that eventually precipitated Carole's fate.

May-December affairs between adolescent girls and older men are much more consistently depicted as destructive experiences than are relationships between teenagers. *Umbrella Steps* (1972) by Julie Goldsmith Gilbert is a rare exception. By the time she is seventeen, Prudence Goodrich has conducted an affair with and is planning to marry Nate Spitz, forty-five. She perceives Nate as a man who "rescued me from being my own age, which I was never good at anyway." Not surprisingly, this relationship alters Prude's entire life: "Not that I went around with a scarlet letter on my forehead. I still had friends, but very casual ones. After all, I was a woman of affairs, with little time for pillow fights and making fudge." By and large, however, Prude finds the affair nurturing and sustaining, for Nate is not only (though primarily) her lover but also a substitute for Prudence's own rather distant father and for her mother who has slipped out of family life and into madness. Largely recounted on the eve of the couple's wedding, *Umbrella Steps* describes Prude's responses to—and rationalizations for—her accelerated transition from childhood to adulthood.

When Jessica Brewer of *The Impermanence of Heroes* (1965) by Eunice Cleland Fikso (pseudonym, C. F. Griffin) hears that paralyzed Joe St. George, a Korean War veteran, is coming to town, she idealizes him into a hero, a dragon-slayer. Her steadfast friendship includes elements of both love and hero worship, as Jessica realizes at seventeen, when she recalls her eleventh year, for she still measures her boyfriends against her image of Joe. His moodiness and only partially controlled fury teach her that love is a complex emotion: "I can't recall ever liking him an awful lot, but liking didn't have anything to do with how I felt about him." Though Jessica's crush is far different from Prudence Goodrich's affair, it, too, serves to move Jessica beyond adolescence, toward adulthood. The overall repercussions of these two relationships are largely positive.

Other youngsters salvage good from the initial disruption generated by their affairs, as in *A Sudden Woman* (1964) by Heida Huberta Freybe Loewengard (pseudonym, Christine Lambert). Seventeen-year-old Doro Tenant, in some ways idealistically naive and in other ways wise beyond her years, falls in love with a disillusioned, embittered man of forty-five. Knowing he does not love her, she seduces him. When she later discovers that he, who had thought he could not love, has fallen in love with her mother, she breaks with her mother, destroying what had been a close and trusting relationship. Her anger and new-found cynicism lead her to reckless actions, but eventually she comes to understand herself and to forgive her lover and her mother. To her mother she says,

> Lisa darling, and I don't mean it ironically either, everybody has to grow up. You always said so. But everyone can only do it his

own way. Remember what you said that night when I slept in your bed because I couldn't even be alone with myself, because I was so desperate that he should find it in his heart to love, and not to love me? I quoted Dash then. Dash Brown, the painter. You always forget who he is, and that he said there were only two kinds of women—those for whom the first man was the end and those for whom he was just the beginning. And when I asked you, you told me—that it was just a beginning for me. And, as usual, you were right.

Like Doro Tenant, several other young women among the characters studied here initiate their affairs. Sometimes, an older lover represents security or refuge to these girls, and often these novels reflect male viewpoints more clearly than female attitudes. Only seventeen years old but experienced far beyond her years, Charlotte Harkin seeks respite from worry over her alcoholic father, a famous playwright, by seducing the protagonist and title character of Sloan Wilson's *Georgie Winthrop* (1963). Troubled by her rootless past and yearning to live through passion (her symbol is the Bird of Fire of Russian folklore and ballet), she at first wants only to be George's mistress, but she discovers in herself a need for greater commitment and permanence. The story, however, is seen through the eyes of her reluctant lover, a respectable college administrator and a happily married man.

Though she has reached a major turning point of her life, Sandy MacKenzie of Edward Abbey's *Black Sun* (1971) is hardly characterized at all. At nineteen, she is at an emotional impasse, for her young fiancé is reconsidering their engagement. With Will Gatlin, thirty-seven, divorced, and withdrawn from the academic world which was once his life, she undertakes her first affair. Abbey portrays Sandy simply as a means of dramatizing Will's brief summer of hope and rejuvenation.

Other adolescent seductresses are more vividly portrayed, indicating the importance of the May-December motif as a central motivational factor both for male and female characters. Still, however, even when the relationships are not wholly destructive, damages outweigh benefits.

The complicated relationships of Hardy Brewster (a thirty-seven-year-old divorced man), his friend Jim Long, his occasional mistress Fauna Mayo, and his fourteen-year-old foster daughter Delilah Jean Sampson are observed by Hardy's landlord, Victor Ramsey, a prissy but sympathetic English actor, in James Leigh's *Downstairs at Ramsey's* (1968). The novel is replete with echoes of *Lolita* and *Romeo and Juliet*, as Delilah, living up to her name, seduces Hardy. A complex mixture of child and woman, she seems to care deeply for Hardy, and, when he refuses to marry her, she calls down upon him the forces of both church and state, as represented by a boyfriend's priest and the police. While Hardy's point of view is more clearly conveyed than Delilah's, she is nevertheless well depicted as an intense, sometimes selfish and arrogant, sometimes kind and loving young woman, wise beyond her years in some ways, but exceptionally vulnerable in others. Although the novel's ending lacks the impact of classical tragedy, it achieves much power; the pity and sense of loss and waste felt by Mr. Ramsey, and thus by the reader, are strong.

At the beginning of *Where Love Has Gone* (1962) by Harold Rubin (pseudonym, Harold Robbins), Luke Carey, the protagonist, is informed that the dearly loved daughter whom he has not seen for several years has just killed her mother's lover and is in the custody of the California juvenile authorities. Her story, which her mother supports, is that she committed the act on impulse and to save her mother from the lover during a violent quarrel. The father gradually learns, however, that fourteen-year-old Dani was no innocent, and that she too had been intimate with and become obsessed by her mother's lover. The character of the mother (an almost stereotypical sexual piranha and castrator of men) and the troubled relationship of mother and daughter also seem central to what Dani has become, though the causes of Dani's behavior are not actually examined in any real depth.

Novels in which girls are pursued by powerful men suggest that young females are potential victims simply because they are female. Cassie Keen's story is one good example. Cassie's gradual introduction to the tawdry sexuality of Hollywood in the 1930s and 1940s is the subject of Sandra Berkley's *Coming Attractions* (1971). Her stepfather early makes sexual overtures that puzzle and dismay her. There follows a series of misadventures as this lovely and intelligent but stardom-dazzled girl dreams of becoming famous and tries to fend off the predatory males who surround her. She sees the world in terms of grade-B movies; her naive (even ignorant) view of sex contrasts with the exploitative view of the men she meets, and the novel closes with her clearly ill-fated marriage at seventeen.

A good portion of Shylah Boyd's *American Made* (1975) is devoted to the adolescence of Shylah Dale. Though Shylah undertakes the usual sexual experimentation with boys of approximately her own age, her adolescence is marked—and she is damaged—by the unwanted attentions of an older man, a friend and associate of Shylah's unloving, sometimes brutal, hard-drinking father. Uncle Bobby Jay's relentless pursuit culminates when he takes Shylah to a business party where the only other women present are prostitutes. Though Bobby Jay is perfectly willing to take Shylah to such a gathering, and though he is eager to browbeat her into having intercourse with him, he is shocked that Shylah should have liked the prostitutes and have enjoyed their attention, their short lessons in how to dress her hair. Bobby Jay's hypocrisy and his exploitativeness are typical of the attitudes of almost all of the male characters in this sexually explicit novel.

With very few exceptions, young women characters who conduct affairs with older men are victims even when they are also victimizers. For the majority, femaleness is their identity, and their youth increases their vulnerability even when it also intensifies the vulnerability of their partners. Like fictional girls who are damaged by affairs with adolescent boys, most fail to mature, and many carry emotional scars forever. Both groups of characters share an inability to evaluate their experiences usefully, and they are certainly unable to generalize wisely as a result of their encounters. Instead, they persist in defining themselves according to the perceptions or needs of others, exploiting or surrendering to others, surviving, if they survive at all, crippled and in pain.

The same absence of self-definition apparent in young females who survive destructive premarital affairs without becoming pregnant also sadly marks most of those whose maturation tests result from unexpected and unwelcome pregnancies. Generally, these girls suffer, at least initially, from the sense of confusion that is the defining characteristic of the protagonist of *Phoebe* (1970, YA). This novel, based on a Canadian film but written by American author Patricia Dizenzo and set in the United States, covers several weeks in the life of sixteen-year-old Phoebe Altman, the period in which the high-school senior becomes certain she is pregnant. Her confusion and fears of revealing her condition to her parents or her boyfriend are convincingly conveyed, but the book's treatment of her options is both simplistic and incomplete. Abortion is discarded simply because it is illegal (the novel was published in 1970), and deeper moral questions are never dealt with. The option of giving up the child for adoption is briefly suggested and seems likely to be the choice Phoebe will eventually make. The possibility of bearing and keeping the child (either with or without the benefit of marriage to the boy) is hardly mentioned.

For some girls, the obvious answer to their dilemmas is permanent union with the father of the expected child. As *Fair Day, and Another Step Begun* and *A Long and Happy Life* illustrate, these characters are unlikely to define themselves except as questers or accommodators; love, fear, social pressure, and traditionalism impose roles upon them.

Although suitable for young readers, Katie Letcher Lyle's *Fair Day, and Another Step Begun* (1974, YA) is an extraordinarily spare yet paradoxically poetic study of the relationship between a sixteen-year-old pregnant girl, Ellen Burd, and John Waters, the father of her coming child. She is a mountain girl, filled with a mixture of superstition and scientific knowledge of nature, naive and loving and strangely certain of herself and her love. He, a twenty-two-year-old Yale graduate, is much the less mature of the two. After being told of her pregnancy, he deserts her; she follows him, certain that he must only be persuaded of the truth of their love. The novel is a retelling in modern setting of the English ballad of "Childe Waters." While the symbolic meaning sometimes becomes a bit obvious (John's refuge and Ellen's goal is a plantation called

Fair Day near the town of Avalon!), it curiously strengthens the lean force of the narrative. Lyle's interest was in her characters' motivations, and the result is a tender and sensitive novella.

Reynolds Price examines the impact of southern social conventions, sex-role stereotyping, and fundamentalist Protestantism in *A Long and Happy Life* (1961). After an extended courtship, Rosacoke Mustian finds herself pregnant by Wesley Beavers, who has steadily failed to make any satisfactory commitment to her. Fearful of the burden of parenthood, Rosacoke is also reluctant to marry simply because of the pregnancy. Ultimately, she accepts Wesley, and her assumed maturation is signified in very traditional fashion—by her accommodation to the fate imposed upon her.

Traditional values very similar to those of Rosacoke Mustian prompt Maryalyse Tyler, central character in the subplot of Elizabeth Savage's *Happy Ending* (1972), to attempt to rear her child alone, despite social disapprobation and the economic pressures of the Depression. Maryalyse feels she has been "betrayed" by the father of her illegitimate baby, a teenager whose parents refuse to allow the youngsters to marry. Determined to protect Timmy, the baby, Maryalyse takes work as cook and maid to elderly Carrie and Thomas Russell, whose sensible, open acceptance of her and her infant son helps her to reconstruct her self-image and confirms her determination to keep and support her child.

Adolescent expectant mothers who plan to keep their infants and to rear them as single mothers are, however, more often characterized as unrealistic or impractical. A useful example is Jill, one of several major adolescent female characters in *Baby Love* (1981) by Joyce Maynard. Though Jill, who is sixteen and pregnant, finds some acceptance and support from three friends, Tara, Sandy, and Wanda, themselves teenaged mothers, Jill dreads her parents' reactions and finds her young sexual partner unresponsive to her situation. Her life becomes a round of anxiety and confusion; her days are marked by do-it-yourself pregnancy tests, secret acquisition of maternity clothes, and a disastrous trip to an abortion clinic. Though she eventually joins her friend Tara in fleeing home, family, and friends, Jill's problems are far from over at the close of the novel. Their destination—a southern commune—is only dimly known to them, and Jill's pregnancy, rather than being a means of her maturation, seems to be only a symbol of her continuing immaturity. Desperation and vague hope are the factors which unite her and Tara in their journey; the commune perceived by them as Edenic and supportive is a distant, perhaps unachievable, goal.

Just as Jill's decision to run away to a supposedly better place marks her as immature, the bizarrely ironic outcome of B. J. Chute's *The Story of a Small Life* (1971) suggests that Anna will remain dependent. Certainly, her chances of achieving any sort of self-definition are meager indeed. As Jill is sustained by hope (no matter how slim), so Anna is sustained by another's perceptions of her. Anna, weak, illiterate, and fearful, has run away from home to live with Mig, a tough street nomad who has no intention of making their relationship permanent. When she becomes pregnant, Anna dreads his abandoning her. "She—who had wanted a kitten of her own since childhood, who ached for every lame pigeon, every hungry sparrow—now prayed, through all her waking hours, for a baby's death." Eventually, Anna turns to an abortionist whose work nearly costs Anna's life, but her terror and pain are changed to a timid happiness when Mig at last assumes responsibility for her—the abortion, instead of freeing him, convinces him of her value.

In the novels read for this study, pregnant girls who choose abortion almost always mature as a result of making and implementing that decision. In some ways, this pattern is not surprising; most of them have been exploited by and then rejected by others, usually by the most significant figures in their lives, and they make their decisions alone. But though they are forced to act independently, they also generally elect to contemplate and assess their situations, the consequences, and their own reactions. Each knows what she is doing and what it is doing to her, even when she must reassess her vision of herself as well as of the man she loves, as in the case of the title character of Rosa Guy's *Edith Jackson* (1978, YA), whose situation remains tragic.

When Edith Jackson becomes pregnant by a much older man, she believes she has found love and security. "His arms were strong around me, and I knew this was the way folks were supposed to feel. Warm. Warm and together. Loving. Really, really loving. We orphans had sure found each other between earth and sky." She discovers her mistake, however, when she flees to him, hoping for marriage, only to have him offer her to a buddy for a fee, and Edith is forced to turn for aid to a woman who is glad to offer it on her own terms. In deciding to seek an abortion, Edith violates her original self-definition, for she has devoted her life to caring for other children. The novel is an unsparing account of the destruction of Edith's world.

Other protagonists, however, recognize the strength they have gained and are able to face the future chastened but hopeful. For the heroine of *Bonnie Jo, Go Home* (1972, YA) by Jeannette Eyerly, obtaining an abortion "was the only way out she could think of for herself. The only way." But this solution is complicated by many difficulties. Because her pregnancy is further advanced than she thought, Bonnie Jo finds herself a lonely stranger in New York City searching for a doctor who can legally and safely perform a "salting-out process." Though her search is successful, the price is high, for strangers do not hesitate to judge her, and the staff at the hospital often speak and act harshly toward her. "Leaving New York eleven days after she arrived, her face seemed to have aged a year for every day she had been there." Though Bonnie Jo has found the inner resources to complete her quest, she recognizes that her real girlhood is now forever behind her.

Nineteen-year-old Vida Kramar, in Richard Brautigan's *The Abortion: An Historical Romance 1966* (1971), has a marvelously endowed body, which distracts men and causes consternation among women wherever she goes. She hates her body and feels it is not truly her own. Her affair with the novel's nameless protagonist and narrator reconciles her to the hated body but also leads to pregnancy and thus to the abortion of the title. Vida's effect on her lover is as healthy as his effect on her; from being a timid, but gentle recluse he is returned to society and social involvement. The abortion itself is treated objectively, as little more than a brief interruption to their lives, though one which accidentally becomes a turning point. The brief novel consists of many very short chapters which are filled with aphoristic insights; though it has a certain charm, it lacks depth.

Miscarriage is rarely treated, but in *A Day Late* (1980), Carolyn Doty explores Katy Daniels's reaction to her unexpected and unwelcome pregnancy, which does abort spontaneously. At seventeen, Katy "falls in love" with another teenager, Kurt Edwards, largely because she is lonely and he is at hand. When he "vanishes" as soon as she reveals her pregnancy, she knows that she must face her situation on her own and begins a difficult journey home to tell her parents. She doesn't want a baby, dreads her family's reaction, and feels angry, confused, and trapped. The miscarriage, which occurs en route to her California home, is glibly dubbed "a blessing, really," for the "malformed fetus" by the doctor, and though Katy feels some guilt for not having wanted the child, Doty suggests that she will be strong enough to accept the loss and to resume her life as a wiser, more mature—though probably less trusting—person. Like Bonnie Jo Jackson (*Bonnie Jo, Go Home*), Katy Daniels has faced her situation squarely; like Anna (*The Story of a Small Life*), she has also found value in the eyes of another. But in accepting a lover after her child's father has abandoned her, Katy has succored as much as she has been comforted, and she moves beyond both men's vision of her toward her own.

Contrary to the beliefs of many adolescents, extended premarital alliances are not necessarily guarantees of popularity. Sometimes they can be bizarrely exploitative as is demonstrated by the story of Barbara Anne Greene, who engages in long-lasting but basically frustrating relationships with two men in Al Hine's satiric *Lord Love a Duck* (1961). She is beautiful and bright but shallowly materialistic and clever at manipulating others so she can achieve her own ends. She meets her match, however, in brilliant Gooney Bird Musgrave, a high-school classmate, who gains control of her through hypnotism. Their relationship is highly erotic and continues for several years, but it never goes so far as sexual intercourse. Indeed, her sexual morality is thoroughly practical:

> If she was the kind of girl who did what they all worried about, she'd have done it long ago. But she wasn't that kind; she was too smart.

> Barbara Anne knew very well and without any coaching from [her parents] that a smart girl waited till she had something in the balance that was really important before she did. Girls who gave in under the influence of fraternity pins or full moons or just letting boys carry on till they got too excited to hold out, these girls who started didn't seem to stop and the word got around mighty fast, no matter what promises boys might make. Darn near all these girls, unless they got married right away quick, lost out one way or another.

She retains her "purity" until her marriage, shortly after graduation from high school, to Bob Barnard, a handsome but dull college graduate also under Gooney Bird's domination; but that marriage is less important to her than her dreams of Hollywood stardom. At the end of the novel she has escaped from Gooney Bird's power and gained control over Bob. The author describes his characters as "largely mindless," but their story is amusingly told and delightful to read.

An adolescent's attitude toward marriage is also a theme of *Happy Ending* (1972) by Elizabeth Savage, which suggests that an early, unhappy affair can endanger later, stronger relationships. Abandoned by her first lover and committed to the support and care of her illegitimate son, Maryalyse Tyler is slow to trust Bud Romeo, the hired hand at the ranch where she has found work. Bud's reliability and his growing affection for the baby as well as for Maryalyse attract her greatly, but the girl distrusts her own judgment and her own worth. Both Bud and Maryalyse see their employers, the Russells, as model marriage partners, and the confidence that Carrie and Thomas Russell display in both youngsters gives them the courage to establish a new family in the face of earlier disappointments.

Unlike the Russells, most adults discourage marriages between adolescents. Occasionally, however, early union proves to be exactly the right choice, as it is for fifteen-year-old Milly Slaughter, in David Wagoner's *The Road to Many a Wonder* (1974). She follows Ike Bender when he leaves his Nebraska home to seek his fortune in the Colorado gold fields of 1859. She loves Ike and knows he loves her, and she is certain she can manage him and cope with any adventures they may have. Their marriage, which surprises him, is precisely what she had anticipated, and their success along the trail can often be credited to her spunk, assertiveness, and inventive intelligence. Although she always insists on calling her new husband "Mr. Bender," because "it seems more respectful," she manages him quite capably. Her good humor and youthful certainty make her an appealing character; we see her through the eyes of Ike, the narrator, who is continually struck into wonderment by her competence and her love for him. Wagoner's earthy and comic novel depicts a marriage of two youngsters facing dangers of all sorts who manage both to find the gold they had come to seek and to remember always that the greatest wonder they have seen or experienced is their love for each other.

An unexpected, usually unwanted, pregnancy often impels a young woman into marriage. Almost uniformly, these youngsters discover that the titles "wife" and "mother" do not necessarily bestow self-confidence, security, or maturity, goals which must be achieved by growth rather than by mere change of status. While accommodation to married life is often a symbol of earned adulthood, dissolution of the marriage occasionally serves the same symbolic purpose.

For sixteen-year-old Callie Wells, marriage represents both rescue and the surrender of her dreams. Pregnant and unwed, she marries her employer, Henry Soames, protagonist of John Gardner's *Nickel Mountain* (1973), to give herself and her child secure futures and because she recognizes that gentleness and honesty lie beneath Henry's unattractive appearance. Henry, almost a figure of fun to some of the townspeople, is also confessor and sustainer for several of them. Callie, learning to be wife and mother during her late adolescence, is sometimes annoyed, embarrassed, or dismayed by the very traits which motivated Henry to marry her. Both deeply devoted to Callie's child, both seeking some sort of understanding of their world and the people who inhabit it, Callie and Henry must make peace with their lives as individuals, as a couple, and as parents.

One of several plot lines in Edwin Lanham's *Speak Not Evil* (1964) deals with a brief sexual contact between Faithful Zybioski, high-school valedictorian in a small town, and Earl Dexter, a troubled newcomer. The episode was instigated by Faithful; immediately after, to Earl's confusion, she rejects him. Later we learn that she has become pregnant, and she briefly considers having an abortion. Eventually she gives in to her feelings for Earl and they decide to marry and have the child. The novel is basically a study of the manners, morals, and politics of an old New England town. Faithful's attitudes toward both Earl and her pregnancy seem deeply affected by the fact that she is the daughter of a woman from a leading family and a Polish sailor, now dead, as well as by the social attitudes toward illegitimacy of the late 1960s, but her motivations are not always clear and believable. Nevertheless, the reader is led to believe that the marriage of Faithful and Earl indicates their achievement of mature adulthood.

Anne MacLorne, protagonist of *The Flowers of the Forest* (1981) by Ruth Doan MacDougall, marries for love at seventeen, and her courtship and initial experiences as a wife are compared to those of her eldest daughter, Janet, whose story serves as an important subplot. Though Anne's marriage is not what she expected, being marked by poverty, desperately hard work, and a lack of demonstrated affection, Janet's marriage is far worse, marked by physical abuse, mental torture, frequent, debilitating pregnancies, and finally horror. Because she has been the victim of multiple rape, adolescent Janet, pregnant, has married the only available man (one of the rapists), a youth totally unsuited to her. Because she feels a loyalty to him for giving her first child a surname and because she feels bound by her wedding vows, Janet endures the hatred and abuse imposed upon her by his demented mother. She remains, in fact, a child in the hands of husband and mother-in-law, guilt over the rape seemingly having frozen her into immaturity. Only her mother-in-law's final mad violence and the death of her husband free this young wife to take her life into her own hands, to behave as an adult.

Salvation from an unwanted pregnancy is not the only reason married life seems alluring to troubled young women. Many perceive marriage as a refuge from difficult family situations, thwarted ambition, or the fear of seeming unattractive and undesirable. In these instances, the dual symbolic pattern also holds true. With the wife's personal growth, marriage can be sustaining, can represent maturity; without growth it can be very repressive, locking her into immaturity.

The narrator of Elizabeth Savage's *The Girls from the Five Great Valleys* (1978) is Doll, a motherless, loving girl who keeps house for her father and brother, both of whom are defeated by life and sometimes surly. Affectionate, lonely, and aware that, unlike her friends, she must support herself without benefit of college training, she determines upon early marriage: "Doll's own wants were simple. She wanted older beaux, because they could afford more. By older, she meant about twenty-two. After that men seem to have other things on their minds." Doll's search for a proper husband teaches her just what is "on their minds," but good luck and her own decency and charm lead her into a sustaining, supportive, touchingly humorous courtship. This relationship is an important symbol for the fact that Doll is a survivor; her marriage will be sound.

The childhood and adolescence of Cordelia Miller, in *Chez Cordelia* (1980) by Kitty Burns Florey, are shadowed by a sense of failure because she is a non-reader. Everyone else in the Miller household is not only a devoted reader but also a writer by profession, and to escape these influences, Cordelia takes refuge with her friend, later suitor, still later adolescent husband, Danny Frontenac, a fellow remedial-reading student. At Danny's home, above his family's grocery store, Cordelia finds relief from her family's subtle pressures, and she falls in love with and marries Danny at least partially as an act of gentle rebellion. At first, their union seems happy and fulfilling, a final escape from the Millers, but Danny's flawed personality and difficulties with his own parents eventually motivate his desertion of Cordelia; ultimately he commits murder and is imprisoned. Cordelia's growing understanding of and support for her young husband is one important symbol that as a young adult she has painfully but successfully faced the fact that identity as Mrs. Danny Frontenac is not enough; she has had to establish her own personality and her own goals.

In sharp contrast to Kitty Burns Florey's use of learning as negative motivation, Jessamyn West twice links the desire to marry with the love of learning. When the heroine of *Leafy Rivers* (1967) falls in love with and marries her young teacher, she is really falling in love with the education that has been denied her, and though the affection between the couple is genuine and binding, their sexual relationship is unsatisfactory for this young wife. Leafy, however, is unaware of the precise nature of the problem, knowing only that something seems to be missing. Several men make overtures to her during the Rivers' first year on the Indiana frontier, but until she is rescued from danger by a young drover, Leafy remains faithful to her marriage vows. In the arms of Cashie Wade, however, Leafy learns what sexual satisfaction can be. Much of the action of this novel takes place in flashbacks triggered during Leafy's difficult first labor, and it becomes clear to readers that she is fighting the delivery because of doubt over the identity of the child's father. When Leafy resolves her feelings toward her affair, she is able to deliver her baby, and the infant daughter is Jessamyn West's symbol that Cashie Wade has helped Leafy mature into the wife Reno Rivers needs. This view of marriage is not conventional, perhaps, but it is most convincingly presented.

It is love of learning and of books which ostensibly first attracts young Orpha Chase (considered an "old maid" at eighteen) to her teacher, Lon Dudley; these interests mark their courtship and marriage, depicted in an important passage in *The Life I Really Lived* (1979) by Jessamyn West. Other distinguishing features of the relationship—Lon's preoccupation with his own body and his dedication to "teaching" a young boy—are noted but not understood by the innocent, love-dazed, trusting young bride. Only when Lon resorts to murder and suicide in order to keep the boy's father from accusing him of homosexuality does Orpha allow herself to begin to examine their marriage honestly, but for many years, she submerges even this limited confrontation with reality in motherhood, her own teaching, and a new, equally ill-advised courtship. It is this book, told in the first person by Orpha, which finally helps her to face the full truth about herself and the extended family surrounding her. West suggests, as she has in other novels, that until a woman understands her adolescence, she doesn't understand herself.

Though self-interest (or self-protection) may be an important factor in a troubled girl's decision to marry, the novels read for this study do not generally identify that motive with sheer manipulativeness. Outright manipulation, either on the part of others or on the part of a young woman herself, generally foreshadows an uneasy relationship or total disaster. It almost always suggests an absence of fruitful personal growth and development.

In *The Moonflower Vine* (1962) by Jetta Carleton, Jessica Soames's impulsive, forbidden marriage to Tom Purdy is largely engineered by her little sister, Mathy: "Please, Tom! We love you so much!" Though Tom and Jessica do love one another dearly, neither would have felt at all prepared for marriage without Mathy's prompting. A long flashback recounts the story of their swift courtship and brief married life, which enrich Jessica's maturation with both great joy and terrible sorrow. Her marriage is the first break in the family circle and has a lasting emotional effect upon her parents and sisters.

Portrait in Brownstone (1962) by Louis Auchincloss describes the complex lives of two cousins, protagonist Ida Trask and Geraldine Denison. The culminating episode, a long flashback to Ida's adolescence, is the girls' competition for the same man, Derrick Hartley. Geraldine, pretty, flirtatious, confident, entrances Derrick, who has been courting quiet, insecure Ida. When Geraldine marries another man, Ida's maternal relatives, people of great force, promote the original courtship. They succeed; the marriage takes place, and Ida thereafter identifies herself as a respected but unloved wife, while Geraldine perceives herself as the victim of thwarted love for Derrick. Each girl's definition of herself springs from these family manipulations and colors her entire life.

Lora Bowen, a well-developed, crafty nineteen-year-old in *The Inkling* (1965) by Fred Chappell, comes into the Andersons' strange household as a housekeeper and accelerates what has been slow degeneration. Her successful plan to take over the home includes marrying middle-aged Uncle Hake and seducing his teenaged nephew, Jan. When Lora's adultery is discovered, the household erupts into open violence, and the Andersons' precarious control over their lives is shattered.

The Last of Eden, The Talking Room, Ruby, and *Happy Endings Are All Alike* are representative treatments of lesbianism in the novels considered for this study; it is notable, perhaps, that all were published after 1975. Whether the author is assessing the impact of the relationship upon an observer or upon the lovers, she generally emphasizes its importance to character growth or revelation and takes into account not only both the joys and pain within the relationship itself but also the impact others' social attitudes may have upon it.

Lesbianism appears twice as a theme in Stephanie S. Tolan's *The Last of Eden* (1980, YA), which describes life at a boarding school for girls. Bits, hurt and angry, strikes out at Marty, a classmate, and a woman teacher by falsely accusing them of a lesbian relationship, but the school silently smoothes over that situation. Later, however, Marty is enticed by a new, and very dishonest and corrupt, classmate into an actual lesbian affair. This does not become public, for only Marty's roommate, the protagonist and narrator of the novel, knows for sure of their sexual involvement; sensitized by the earlier situation, she conceals the knowledge. Marty eventually leaves the school, and her experiences, including the lesbian affair, are important primarily because of their disillusioning effect on the narrator, an entirely likable young woman.

A lesbian marriage observed by the daughter of one member of the pair is the central subject of Marianne Hauser's *The Talking Room* (1976). B, the thirteen-year-old narrator, is the daughter (perhaps by artificial insemination) of J, whose drinking and erratic behavior she offhandedly describes. Aunt V, J's lover, has been first to desire a child, apparently in order to preserve the lesbian relationship, but she was herself unable to bear a child; possessiveness is her most significant quality. Little happens in the novel, and B's problems (always obese, she also becomes pregnant) are never clearly related to her situation and experience. Told through disjointed memories and observations, the novel has some sharply observed scenes and is technically interesting.

In *Ruby* (1976) by Rosa Guy, despite the taunts of schoolmates, familial opposition, and bewilderment over the attitudes of her lover, Ruby Cathy is utterly obsessed by her secret affair with classmate Daphne Duprey, and both youngsters find comfort and satisfaction in their passion: "Holding, touching, fondling, body intertwined with body, racing around the world on rays of brilliant color, roaring into eternity on cresting waves of violence, returning to tenderness, a gentle, lapping tenderness." Several times the girls' varying levels of sophistication, their selfishness, and their youth create ruptures, but their final parting arises from Daphne's ambition and her decision to "go straight." Because she has defined herself solely by Daphne's love and by seeking Daphne's respect, Ruby is so devastated that she attempts suicide. The attempt fails, and the novel concludes with the suggestion that Ruby will seek solace with a long-time male admirer.

For Jaret Tyler, a high-school senior in Sandra Scoppettone's *Happy Endings Are All Alike* (1978, YA), her affair with Peggy Danziger marks her initiation into her true sexual identity; she has had one male lover and has found heterosexual love unfulfilling. Peggy is less certain of her sexual identity, but nevertheless, the pair are happy lovers who sustain and support one another despite the stress generated by the necessity of keeping their love a secret. As members of their circle—Peggy's sister, Jaret's mother, a close female friend—discover the affair, Jaret and Peggy learn to cope with well-intended but wounding reactions as well as with outright persecution. The whole town learns of their love, however, when a violent youth rapes Jaret, planning to blackmail her into silence. Jaret's staunch resolve to prosecute her attacker may be more than Peggy can face. Scoppettone reveals both the values of this love affair and the price the young women must pay. The tone of the novel is cool and precise; the conventions of society as well as the feelings of the lovers are fairly and honestly portrayed, but these strengths are a bit undercut by a failure to dramatize rather than to report.

In serious fictional treatments of both heterosexual and lesbian sexual relationships (ranging from dating through serious affairs and marriage), then, authors clearly assess female adolescents' abilities to love and be loved as central to the characters' growth and development. Repeatedly, the love and sexuality motif appears as a test of a girl's ability to develop her own sense of self-worth, even if doing so necessitates a break with the loved one. In a very significant number of novels, the authors stress the theme that being loved is not enough; knowing (and valuing) oneself is far more important to genuine maturity. Because maturity—active, gratifying participation in the adult world—is the chief goal of almost every adolescent female in the subject-novels, the characters' responses to this crucial test of their readiness is as important on the symbolic level as it is necessary to any attempt at a realistic reflection of the major preoccupations of real-life young women.

CHAPTER II
Females within Families

Just as adolescents often perceive moving *into* sexual relationships as indicative of growing up, so do they frequently view moving *away from* or altering family relationships as vital to their maturation. At this juncture, as seems true on many levels of the process, young people often get conflicting signals from authoritative adults: grow up, be self-sufficient, behave responsibly, and—simultaneously—slow down, you *are* dependent, don't trust your own judgment. Such seemingly contradictory advice does little to help solve the ever-difficult problem of striking a proper balance between selfishness and self-realization.

If the object of family life is its eventual dissolution—or at least its redefinition—as young folk make new lives for themselves as adults or establish new families of their own, then the original family situation can be seen as a laboratory where youngsters evaluate the behavior of other family members (especially, perhaps, older relatives), deciding which habits and attitudes to emulate, which to spurn. In that laboratory, they also should be able to learn how to manage not only interpersonal relationships but also how to face threats imposed upon the family unit by outside circumstances such as death, financial disaster, or relocation.

Authors of the subject-novels under consideration here give no clear, overall formula for a youth's successful completion of familial laboratory work, but all recognize its importance and its difficulty. All suggest that family relationships, enduring or broken, are crucial influences upon the young for good or ill. Most also stress the necessity for young people to put self-realization above acquiescence to relatives' expectations. Almost all recognize that gratifying maturity and independence are very often earned by the pain of separation or realignment.

Because adolescent females so keenly desire to love and, especially, *to be loved*, it may be particularly difficult for them to press for independence or to alter their bonds with parents, guardians, and siblings. Fear of rejection, of being unloved, can limit girls' willingness to risk rebellion or even change. When their own needs or circumstances force them to take that risk, they are facing yet another severe test on their maturation journeys.

No matter how earnestly elders try to protect their young, they cannot ensure that fate in the form of various disrupting factors will not endanger the family, will not, consequently, threaten the children. Perhaps the most terrifying and devastating of those outside forces are illness and death. In *Birch Interval* (1964) by Joanna Crawford, the anguish caused by illness is exacerbated by society's misguided disapprobation. In the early chapters, Jesse is part of a large family including grandparents, aunt, uncle, and cousins. When her uncle is dragged away to the state asylum and her favorite cousin's reactions cause him to be sent away to be "strictly disciplined" at school, the family begins to disintegrate. Jesse faces the harsh judgments the community has made about her "crazy" family and draws her own conclusions about humane behavior and loyalty. She learns some difficult lessons: that one *can* undertake almost impossible tasks and that running away is no solution.

For some young women, awareness of their mothers' death during childbirth can generate long-term problems. In Mary Astor's *The Image of Kate* (1962), Kate Martin's mother dies as a result of the girl's birth, and Kate is reared by adult members of her family who are not only busy running a California ranch but also are very undemonstrative. Kate constantly feels "in the way," unwanted, and guilty, and so she teaches herself not to care for other people. "I've learned not to need people. I think everybody's got his own life to live—the way he wants to live it—and the heck with everyone else." This self-imposed alienation (even from the ranch she loves) is sealed in adolescence when no one —neither father, friends, lover, nor suitor—can truly penetrate Kate's loneliness, and Mary Astor demonstrates that this pattern, hardened during girlhood, precipitates tragedy in adulthood.

The story of Maidie Chapman, in Margaret Gray Blanton's *The White Unicorn* (1961), moves from her mother's death in childbirth toward her own first delivery. Having seen the accident that caused her mother's death, she observes, without understanding, the sordid life of dancers at a fair and finally forms a close tie with a young man hopelessly in love with her older sister. Headstrong, gifted, curious, marked by her unfortunate brushes with death and violence, she is fortunate to have the support of a loving family. As she grows from nine to sixteen, the timespan of the novel proper, she learns to overcome some of her fears, but many remain. The white unicorn of the title becomes a symbol for her, and her willingness to let it go, when her child is born in the later scene which frames the novel, shows that she has finally been released from the youthful fears and compulsions started by her mother's death. Both comic and poetic, Blanton's treatment shows Maidie to be a very real and believable girl and effectively evokes her turn-of-the-century Tennessee milieu.

Always stressful, usually tragic, the death of a parent can also impose enormous responsibility upon a trustworthy daughter. This theme is stressed in Vera and Bill Cleaver's *Where the Lillies Bloom* (1969, YA). When Roy Luther dies, his second daughter, fourteen-year-old Mary Call, sets about fulfilling the promises she has made him: to maintain the family's independence and unity and to prevent her older sister,

Devola, eighteen, from marrying their landlord. One crisis follows another as the four Luther youngsters try to support themselves by gathering and selling useful roots and herbs native to the Great Smoky Mountains, but Mary Call is determined to keep the vows made on her "highest word of honor" and to live up to her own potential: "My name is Mary Call Luther, I thought, and someday I'm going to be a big shot. I've got the guts to be one. I'm not going to let this beat me. If it does, everything else will for the rest of my life." Throughout the hard winter depicted in the novel, Mary Call is aware that she is growing up too fast, and she achieves her greatest maturity when she learns to distinguish between the possible and the impossible goals her father set.

Even when one parent survives or when well-intended guardians move immediately to offer support and comfort, the complexities of adjustment are never easy. Indeed, according to Margaret Boylen, surrogate parents can sometimes cause as much pain as they assuage, and Anne Bernays suggests that the presence of a guardian does little to mitigate an orphan's grief. Adjustment to a new balance within the reorganized family puts great stress upon both youngsters and their elders.

In part an updating and a parody of the best-selling nineteenth-century children's book *Five Little Peppers and How They Grew*, the plot of Margaret Boylen's *A Moveable Feast* (1961) is set in motion by the deaths, in a grotesque farming mishap, of the parents of two girls and three boys. Part of the novel shows their growing up and part reveals what they have become as adults and, in a sudden reversal at the end, explains unsuspected truths about both the parental deaths and the children's adolescent behavior. As a youngster, Jessica, the elder girl and second child, seems more mature than her years and acts as a little mother to the others, while Eleanor is particularly talented and imaginative. All four of the surviving children leave their home village, which has self-righteously adopted them, just as soon as they are able, and the reasons for their rebellion become clear only at the end of the novel. They have become emotional cripples of various sorts, and yet all four are happy and successful. The novel is an interesting and complex work, comic and symbolic and philosophical, gradually peeling away the poses and concealments of the young people and revealing the truth of what the parents were and how they died which the children half knew and half denied.

The deaths of her mother and her stepfather catapult Sally Stern, protagonist of Anne Bernays's *Growing Up Rich* (1975), into crisis, and Sally, confused, grieving, lonely, is aware of the impact both emotionally and intellectually:

> I want to cry but I am as dry as an unlicked stamp. My mother's death has already begun to alter me. I find I can now do something I have never been able to do before: stand outside myself and watch what I'm doing. With a terrible wrench I have been

torn apart. One half suffers, the other half stands aside and marvels.

This duality of vision and feeling both complicates and cushions Sally's difficult adjustment to a new life, even as it symbolizes her divided feelings toward almost every significant adult who now influences that life and foreshadows her ability to tell her story.

Another novel dealing with a family in crisis is L. T. Lorimer's *Secrets* (1981, YA). Narrated by sixteen-year-old Maggie Thompson, it tells of her gradual discovery of the "secrets" that lay under her family's apparent happy placidity and led to the death by suicide of her minister-father. Told with restraint and sympathetic but objective maturity, this juvenile novel effectively shows Maggie and her mother gaining in strength as they compensate for and try to understand the weakness of Maggie's father.

Loss of a parent, itself a major blow, seems frequently to be coupled with other shocks which also impose demands upon the young person's ability to understand and to cope with change. For example, Sally Courtland, a pampered, loved, and apparently happy wife and mother in Mary Ellin Barrett's *Castle Ugly* (1966), bears the scars of two youthful experiences, told in flashbacks which occupy the bulk of the novel. In the summer of 1938 when she was eleven, she became aware of the infidelities of her parents and their friends. Just when her security seemed restored, her mother and the mother's cousin were murdered in an apparently random act of violence. Then, less than ten years later, her first idyllic love was shattered by another violent death growing from the earlier episode. The girl, just awakening to life, was scarred by these events, and the mature woman is haunted by them. The novel, narrated in an understated way by Sally, sensitively conveys her youthful fear and confusion and her adult sense of lost innocence.

When death of a parent couples with the relocation of the orphan or of all the surviving family, young women must learn courage in the face of a growing sense of the impermanence of all things, while they also adjust to new intrafamily demands, sometimes to new regional customs. The death of Phyllisia Cathy's mother brings turmoil to an already strained household in *The Friends* (1973, YA) by Rosa Guy. Ruby and Phyllisia, sixteen and fourteen, are preoccupied with making the transition from the West Indies to Harlem and have been rivals for their mother's affection. Calvin, their father, is preoccupied with making his restaurant a success. Thus estranged, the three do not share their grief or their thoughts, and Calvin is not able to cope with his daughters' needs, resorting too often to threats and violence. Phyllisia's struggle for independence and selfhood is thus complicated by her turbulent family life.

The search for a permanent place, a home, is the central theme of Ruth Wolff's *I, Keturah* (1963). Keturah Brown, a foundling whose name was chosen at random from a telephone book, has been reared in an orphanage. At sixteen, she is fortunate to find a home with the Dennys, an elderly farm couple, who take her in—rather to their own surprise. She lives happily with them, finding the first affection and security she has known and resolving to stay with them forever. Several traumatic experiences (being jilted by the young man she thought she loved and escaping a near rape as her assailant is accidentally killed) temporarily scar her, but the Dennys and her friends in their farming community comfort her. When the Dennys die, however, she must again seek a home. She finds employment with a wealthy elderly woman and her small ward, and once again her qualities of warmth, openness, and nurturance enable her to make a place for herself. And this time, though deaths again intervene, her place is permanent. In some ways, Keturah's story recapitulates Jane Eyre's, though Keturah is never forced to plumb the depths of despair and degradation that her predecessor experiences. Her repeated losses seem to strengthen her, and the reader never really doubts that she will eventually achieve her ambition to "become a lady."

Divorce and separation as well as death, of course, can banish a parent from the family unit. Young women who feel guilty because of their parents' alienation from one another or who feel unwanted are particularly slow to adjust—if, indeed, they adjust at all; sometimes they substitute angry, even violent, reaction for adjustment. Here, too, the coupling of family disruption with relocation seems to impose especially severe problems. All these factors exacerbate female teenagers' already profound concern with questions of self-worth. If her parents don't want her, who does? Who will? If the social unit which is forming her (no matter how much against her will) is badly flawed, what, then, is she?

Connie, one of two protagonists of Marjorie Lee's *The Eye of Summer* (1961), is the child of divorce; her father has now disappeared from her life, and her mother sees her as little more than a hindrance to remarriage. The only stability in her life comes from her relationship with her cousin Spence, two years younger than she, and the summers they spend together on an island resort. The novel treats three special summers, when Connie is ten, eighteen, and twenty-one, revealing her dependence on Spence, her growing awareness of her sexuality, and ultimately their need to free themselves from each other.

The characters of Harold Rubin (pseudonym, Harold Robbins) move in a world of wealth and power with little stability. *Where Love Has Gone* (1962) centers around a broken family. Luke Carey, a former war hero, and Nora Hayden, a prominent sculptor and member of a powerful California family, are divorced, with Nora gaining custody of their daughter Danielle (Dani). Almost destroyed by the experience, Luke only gradually escapes and rebuilds his life. Deeply loving her father, Dani sees his leaving as desertion of her and is hurt again when (because of Nora's manipulations) he ceases even coming to see her. The divorce following her mother's second marriage compounds her sense of rejection by men. She never receives love from her mother though she strives for recognition from her. Attractive and brilliant at school, she has little sense of self-worth. Her observation of her mother's promiscuous sexuality is yet another factor in her troubled development. All this is shown in flashback, largely through her father's viewpoint, as Dani is in the hands of the juvenile authorities, accused of having killed her mother's current lover. The substance of the novel is the unraveling of the tangled threads that have brought Dani to that plight and the disintegration of the characters of the three persons most closely involved —Dani's parents and Dani herself. But the truly operative character is Nora, who is presented as a genuinely destructive person who uses her wealth and power as well as her personal appearance and ability to manipulate others and achieve her own ends; the solid marriage and rebuilt life which Luke achieved since meeting his second wife contrast markedly with his experience with Nora. The reader is left to assume that the child being born to that second marriage, despite Luke's straitened circumstances, will have a much better chance than Dani ever had.

A disturbed thirteen-year-old girl, Renata, in Caroline Blackwood's *The Stepdaughter* (1977), comes to live with her putative father and stepmother. Grotesquely fat and withdrawn, she repulses the stepmother, whose imaginary letters comprise this epistolary suspense novel. The stepmother eventually learns that Renata had her own sort of bravery and honor, that being transplanted to New York was only one of a series of shocks she had suffered. The real center of the novelette, however, is the stepmother and the deterioration of her marriage and life.

In *The Iron Peacock* (1966, YA) by Mary Stetson Clarke, the story of Yaweta, an Indian girl living among the Massachusetts Bay colonists, forms the subplot. When Yaweta's father converts to Christianity, he puts aside Indian life, and he expects his daughter to learn white ways along with her new faith. Constantly torn by the local Indians' scorn for her father, grieving over the separation from her mother (who remains with the tribe), despairing over her disrupted courtship, and tormented by the racism of the whites, Yaweta strives to obey her father with grace and good will. In this effort, she is sustained by her friendship with protagonist Joanna Sprague, even during the crisis of an Indian attack.

Even when a family stays together, relocation can be a serious problem for young women. In some cases, it exacerbates their already complex problem of reassessing family standards and behaviors. In *Entering Ephesus* (1971) by Daphne Athas, the Depression drives the Bishop family from their ocean-side home in the North into Ephesus, a Georgia university town. The three daughters, Irene, Urania, and Sylvia (called Loco Poco), are aware of their poverty and of their parents' unusual attitudes, but as children, they glory in "Bishopry against the world." Yet the girls must contend with the local conventions and thus become somewhat sensitive about their differences—though white, they live in the black section; they are always oddly dressed; their father is unable to earn a living; and Mrs. Bishop resorts to stealing food for the family. A good measure of courage and an awareness of their own ability help the girls face a key question: Must they relinquish their sense of superiority? "Was life the losing of Bishopry?" Daphne Athas answers with a qualified "yes." The girls must modify some of their parents' ideas. The family's ideals, however, are worthy, and the author indicates that the surviving Bishop sisters will successfully cope with tragedy and continued poverty.

That disruption of a family by death, divorce, or relocation—all obvious indicators of potential trouble—can cause trauma comes as no surprise, and American folk wisdom tends to suggest that a contrary situation, the active presence of a well-established, extended family, offers stability and comfort. Multitudes of interested relatives can serve as buffers against insecurity, we like to think. But sheer numbers do not guarantee good nurture. *The Reason for Roses*, *The Keepers of the House*, *Portrait in Brownstone*, and *Whipple's Castle* are representative examples of novels that point out the strengths and the weaknesses of extended families and the impact they have on their young female members.

In Babs H. Deal's *The Reason for Roses* (1974), Spencer Howard nostalgically remembers her Alabama girlhood of the late 1930s. Trying to understand why she has survived and been able to succeed in both marriage and career, unlike her cousins, she recalls "that summer we trembled on the edge of discovery . . . happiness . . . fear" (Deal's ellipses), a summer with the "feeling that all of life was changing too fast." Little actually happens, but relationships within Spencer's large extended family are sensitively drawn. It is highly matriarchal, as young Spencer had been quite aware. She loved her grandmother, aunts, and cousins, and the adult Spencer looks back fondly on that old time, sometimes portraying both family and town almost idyllically. But the adult also knows that "the damages inflicted in that small closed world were psychic, and most of them didn't show up for a long long time." In puzzling over it all, she realizes, "I had spent a summer involved with all the real things of life: love, marriage, death, betrayal, desertion, farewell." She, unlike the others, had a stubborn love and belief in roses, which have no excuse for being but simply are—and this optimism is apparently what has brought her through.

The Keepers of the House (1964) by Shirley Ann Grau recounts the tragic results of Margaret Carmichael's rejection of her black family and its heritage. When Margaret turns eleven, she asks her great-grandmother about her parentage and learns that she is the child of a white father and a black-Indian mother.

> She had always thought of her body as solid, one piece. Now she
> knew it was otherwise. She was black outside, but inside there
> was her father's blood.
>   She thought about this carefully. And her body seemed to
> expand, to swell, growing like a balloon. She thought of all the
> distance between the two parts of her, the white and the black.
> And it seemed to her that these two halves would pull away and
> separate and leave her there in the open, popped out like a kernel
> from its husk.

The new knowledge estranges her from her mother's large, complex
family, who have reared her, and she leads a strange and solitary life
during adolescence. When her great-grandmother dies, Margaret declares, "I buried my blood with you. . . . I'm using only the other half
now." This decision gives her the courage to become, at eighteen, the
beloved mistress of a wealthy white farmer, Will Howland.

Ida Trask, the protagonist of Louis Auchincloss's *Portrait in Brownstone* (1962), is profoundly affected by her insecurity, her lack of self-
worth, and her desire to please her mother's family. Ida's maternal relatives, the Denisons, are assertive, confident people accustomed to
achieving their own ends. A long flashback depicts Ida as a teenager
who twice, perhaps quite innocently, sets the Denison machine in motion—once to disrupt a romance between cousins and once to press her
reluctant grandmother into a second marriage. As a result of these
events, Ida, impressed by the force of Denison will, becomes adept at
"transmuting the mere tastes of my forebears into moral principles,"
and she lives much of her life according to these falsely constructed
ideals.

Thomas Williams's *Whipple's Castle* (1968) is a long, sprawling family novel, centered around the growing up of four children of a prominent small-town family; a number of other adolescents play important
roles. Kate Whipple, the only girl of the family, is both lovely and talented; she undergoes fewer highly dramatic experiences than do her
brothers, and she seems to escape some of the traumas they must face.
She is contrasted with two other young women, both from appalling circumstances very different from her material ease. Susie Davis, a born
victim, is destroyed, while Peggy Mudd, a servant in the Whipple
home, eventually becomes a member of the family through marrying
into it. While the family is deeply flawed, its members in their various
ways can care for others—for Peggy that love and concern mean salvation, but for Susie they are not sufficient. Kate, meanwhile, achieves a
prosperous but sterile adulthood.

Whether the immediate family remains intact or whether it has
been reorganized, one of its major purposes is to provide its children
with a sense of nurturing love. Numerous parents depicted in the novels considered for this study recognize the responsibility of this charge
(frequently because their children accuse them of failures of love). One

frankly confesses the difficulty. The question of parental love, its effectiveness, value, and expression, is central to Robb Forman Dew's *Dale Loves Sophie to Death* (1981). During a summer spent in her home town, Dinah Howells recalls her youth as she sees one of her children through a serious illness and reevaluates her responses to her own parents. Feeling that her parents have loved her inadequately and have sometimes behaved badly, Dinah recalls and contemplates their relationship, comparing and contrasting it to her own successes and failures in motherhood and to friends' attitudes toward their children. When she confronts her father with her dissatisfaction, Dinah is not comforted but is informed by his comment: "it's not easy . . . to know that you can't love your children the way they want to be loved. You can only love people however you happen to love them. . . . I hoped you'd know that I wished you well." The message finds its mark and helps Dinah toward a new level of maturity, a new understanding of her adolescence.

Another major purpose of the immediate family is the guidance and development of its young. When family elders are themselves chronic seekers of guidance, the habit may be contagious, as in Josephine Lawrence's generally comic, sometimes satiric novel *I Am in Urgent Need of Advice* (1962). The Carpenter family, consisting of fourteen-year-old Amanda, her parents, her maternal grandmother, and their maid, are comfortably situated. All are goodhearted, but all except Amanda's father (who clearly provides the stable strength of the family) are reliant on others with varied claims of expertise to validate or support their attempts at coping with the problems, sometimes real and sometimes imagined, which confront them. While Amanda's mother regularly consults a marriage counselor and her grandmother lives by her horoscope and the advice of her astrologer, Amanda herself rejects the ideas of her parents and relies on the wisdom of Mirabelle Marilyn Meeks, writer of a newspaper column of counsel to teenagers. Each of these characters is ultimately failed by her mentor, and Amanda in particular shows herself to have more strength of character than either she or her parents might have suspected.

Beneath the comedy of this novel lies the same message as in the more serious *Dale Loves Sophie to Death*: love and guidance must both be present, both be perceived by the daughter or she will be disappointed, perhaps stunted, or will seek support and counsel elsewhere. Occasionally, a young woman who does not perceive her parents' concern nevertheless manages to find some kind of mature balance, as *Limits of the Land* demonstrates, but these instances are rare.

The already troubled life of August, the protagonist of *Limits of the Land* (1979) by Curtis Harnack, is further disrupted by the tormented adolescence of his daughter Sheila. Sheila's responses to the ordinary tensions of adolescence (she is very tall, for instance) and to the special problems which beset her (assault, family illness, deaths, parents' preoccupation with their own serious problems, her stint as a carnival performer) range from sullen rebellion to violent tantrums. Her final emergence into maturity, self-control, and independence seems to be more a matter of instinctive survival than of nurture or genuine development. Perhaps because Sheila's life is reported by her father who observes but does not fully understand her, her story is interesting but distanced; she is revealed quite fully but never excites empathy.

Even when parents are confident dispensers of guidance and especially when they are stern or overbearing, the situation is complex, for they are conveying information designed to serve two purposes. First, they are establishing rules and standards for their daughters to follow while the girls remain well within the family circle. The underlying purpose of parental instruction, however, is its eventual absence; that is, mothers and fathers depicted in these novels (like their real-life counterparts) also intend to teach their daughters to conduct themselves well as emancipated adults free of parental supervision. To the youngsters, always observing, always evaluating, it sometimes appears that the code for the present and the code for the future are not wholly congruent, indeed may seem sharply divergent.

Generally, the young women are straining for emancipation, impatient to be free of parents' restriction and tutelage. When this impulse joins with the perception that parents are holding their children to one standard and are themselves obeying another, especially one of which the daughters disapprove, the girls suffer considerably. The incongruity is too great and they resent it. Not only does it seem unfair to be denied proper counsel, reinforced by good example, it also seems vastly unfair to be led by an unworthy mentor. This situation always causes pain; sometimes it leads to outright rebellion.

A grim picture of a middle-class New Jersey family in the early 1950s is presented in Patricia Dizenzo's *An American Girl* (1971). The unnamed protagonist is very aware of family problems (her parents' regular fighting, her mother's alcoholism, the fact that only she cares about the cleanliness and appearance of their house, etc.), but she seems to accept them almost as noncommittally as all the other aspects of her daily life which she records in great detail. Indeed, much of the impact of this short novel comes from the juxtaposition of her circumstantial retelling of movie plots with descriptions of her mother's drunken behavior.

Indemnity Only (1982) by Sara Paretsky contrasts the relationships within two families, comparing both to the story of King Midas. Anita McGraw, daughter of a powerful union leader, has grown up envisioning her father as the champion of exploited workers, and her ambition is to follow in his footsteps. Jill Thayer's relationship with her father, a senior executive with a large insurance corporation, is less idyllic, for she has seen his coldness and anger toward her brother, his disdain for some of her own standards, and his eagerness to present a smooth, unblemished façade before his wealthy, sophisticated peers. Anita, however, learns that Andrew McGraw's nobility doesn't reach much below the surface, and Jill discovers that corruption as well as pretense defines John Thayer's life. Their fathers' schemes endanger the lives of both girls; both mature as a result. Paretsky compares and contrasts the McGraw and Thayer families to suggest that honor, rather than social class or wealth, is the true measure of success and that the younger generation need not emulate their parents' failures.

The tonal and stylistic realism of *The Weedkiller's Daughter* (1970) adds to the novel's great irony. In the most matter-of-fact fashion, Harriet Arnow depicts Susan Schnitzer's double life. Totally at odds with her repressed mother and her father, a racist right-winger, Susan appears to be obedient but actually operates by her own ethical, political, and moral codes, nurtured by her school friends and by members of her extended family with whom she secretly lives while supposedly at camp. By keeping the reader's sympathy totally with Susan, Arnow underscores her point that a debased society must either corrupt its young or drive them underground.

Two teenagers, Martha Carson and Sherry Loomis, figure prominently in Sam Ross's *Hang-up* (1968), and both become endangered because they seek refuge from home problems in the Sunset Strip teen scene of the 1960s. Martha seems to feel abandoned and alone because her single-parent mother works nights and is not home to care for her, and though she disapproves of her mother's lovers, the girl emulates Laura Carson's sexual freedom, evidently as a kind of revenge. Martha's last, ironic sexual experiment leads to her murder, the inciting action of the plot. Though Sherry survives her brief but dangerous sojourn on the Strip, and though she returns home, readers have only marginal hope for her future welfare, for her mother is an abusive alcoholic, and the mother's lover, a wino, has already made sexual overtures toward the youngster. Sherry and Martha serve primarily as symbols of adolescent disaffection and dislocation, and the portraits are types rather than fully developed characterizations.

Parents who do not or cannot make their love felt or their guidance seem useful can, according to Joyce Maynard, complicate their daughters' lives in another, rather different, fashion. The absence of effective parental influence impels some daughters to substitute love of children for love from parents. In *Baby Love* (1981), Maynard examines the theory that many adolescent mothers retain and cherish their babies partly in order to acquire love objects who are uncritical, dependent, wholly theirs. In this way, often unconsciously, they hope to fill voids in their own emotional lives. *Baby Love* recounts the stories of three young women—Wanda, Sandy (who has married her child's father), and Tara —all of whom attempt to keep and rear their infants. The girls' experiences are far from idyllic, however, and the babies' demands, a spouse's unfaithfulness, parents' disapproval, and social pressure all combine to complicate their lives, sometimes almost unbearably. Suffering, loss, and bitter compromise are the results of their well-intended but immature efforts to be good mothers, to parent better than they were parented. The limited hope allowed Tara is found only through escape from their small New Hampshire home town, and like her readers, Maynard questions the viability of even that slim chance for peace and security.

If some adolescent daughters turn to their own children for the acceptance and love they miss from their parents, yet others, equally troubled, are expected to parent their own parents. These young women, still very young, still subject to parental control, must nevertheless function as putative adults. Often they must exercise power and authority in an almost secret fashion, function as heads of households without seeming to do so. Forced to behave maturely even though they may feel immature, parenting daughters are well aware that they are being tested and fear they will be found wanting.

The Limner's Daughter (1967, YA) by Mary Stetson Clarke skillfully blends historical fact with fiction as it records the slow resolution of tension between Amity Lyte and her father. Darius Lyte's affections have been frozen three years earlier by the deaths of his wife and two older children. Because her father is so absorbed in his own pain, Amity is not only the real guardian of her small brother but also acts as head of their family. The Lytes' situation is exacerbated by the long-lasting hatred directed against Lyte; neighbors suppose him to have been a Tory, and this false charge drives him further into himself. Clarke effectively depicts Amity's bewilderment, loneliness, and sense of loss during the estrangement. It is Amity's loyalty and energy which bring the family safely through the dramatic events which restore Lyte's balance and his ability to function as a parent.

Long before she has completed high school, Amelia Lacey, in Elizabeth Savage's *The Girls from the Five Great Valleys* (1978), has been complying with her dead father's last instructions, to "fill his shoes," a demand which includes "mothering" her own mother, a cold, self-destructive woman:

> The worst of it was that Amelia was never sure of what bad thing she was afraid. She was afraid of her mother's silence and of her recklessness. She might be lying in a darkened room with her eyes fixed on the ceiling, planning something desperate. But what? . . . Up at the cottage at the lake there was a gun, and anyone can get hold of razors. And, with a little difficulty, she supposed sleeping pills. But it was the Pierce Arrow of which she thought most often.

But though her mother's dependence and selfishness are burdensome at the outset of the story, they become intolerable for Amelia when she discovers that Anne Lacey has so criminally neglected Amelia's retarded little sister that the younger girl falls ill and dies. This knowledge and Amelia's awareness that Anne feels no guilt account for the despair which destroys the younger woman at the climax of the novel.

Norma Klein twice describes situations closely allied to those presented in *The Limner's Daughter* and *The Girls from the Five Great Valleys*. In both the Klein novels, daughters are, apparently, fully dependent upon their parents. Yet both young women are well aware that they are partially responsible for maintaining the balance within their parents' relationships; an injudicious word or act could trigger serious consequences. Wishing not to choose between their mothers and fathers, both these adolescents attempt to discharge an almost overwhelming responsibility.

From the outset of *Domestic Arrangements* (1981), by Norma Klein, narrator "Rusty" Engleberg is aware that her parents' marriage requires massive doses of restraint and manipulation to keep it serene. Rusty contrasts her similarity to and easy relationship with her open, relaxed mother, an actress, to her differences from and more rule-bound relationship with her intellectual, protective father, a producer of television documentaries. The same characteristics which dominate the Englebergs' relationships with Rusty and her sister Deel also strain their marriage. The changing quality of the love between her parents and their decisions about their marriage complicate a crucial period in Rusty's maturation.

In another novel, *Breaking Up* (1980, YA), Norma Klein scrutinizes the modern American family with the story of Alison Rose's progress toward adulthood. Many of Ali's initiation experiences stem from conflict between her father and his second wife and her mother and her mother's lover, Peggy. Alison feels a bit uneasy with Eileen, her stepmother, who is "nice in some ways, but not lovable." By contrast, Ali is quite comfortable with Peggy, "a very calm, down-to-earth person with a good sense of humor." When Harold Rose realizes that Cynthia is a lesbian, he seeks custody of Ali, who dreads being forced to choose between her parents. Though tempers flare and tension mounts among the adults, Howard and Cynthia are, finally, both governed by their love for Ali and her brother Martin. The Rose family's ability to strike a reasonable compromise based on their children's wishes is hopeful and is convincingly portrayed.

Garet Rogers's *The Jumping Off Place* (1962) details in a key subplot the ironic results of the machinations of Caddy Bartholomew, who delays her own maturation for a good while because of loyalty to her dead mother and a keen desire to dominate the affections of her father. In a sense, all of Caddy's other emotions are twisted while she persists in this fixation. She is jealous of her brothers, she resents her aunt, and she tries to thwart her father's growing love for a colleague. Each of these reactions denies her useful support and nurturing affection. Feisty and talented, Caddy must, however, eventually mature, whether she is willing or not. Initially, Caddy's responses seem much more childish than those of Rusty Engleberg (*Domestic Arrangements*) and Alison Rose (*Breaking Up*), but in some ways they may be more realistic, for she reflects an understandable if fruitless reluctance to redefine an already reorganized family unit. Caddy is a good example of a child who uses her dependence to control a parent, thus reassuring herself of his love. She also exemplifies the daughter who wishes freedom to change without being willing to grant the same freedom to her parent.

Generally, however, it is parents who legislate—or are perceived by the children to legislate—against their daughters' self-definition. Naturally, parents' inability to allow genuine maturation (or their misguided, selfish, or vicious action to foreclose it) generates conflict within their daughters and their families. Conflict grows from the girls' desire to make their own decisions, to be free of parental control, to be independent. It also stems, however, from girls' fear—acknowledged or unacknowledged—that resistance to parents' wishes could mean disapprobation, the loss of love and approval. Because immature adolescents' self-images seem to be so dependent upon the approval of others, upon the sense of being loved, this conflict can retard, limit, or even prohibit their true maturation.

Either daughter or parent may exacerbate these natural tensions. In Toni Morrison's *Sula* (1973), for instance, problems within two families go unassuaged because, from childhood through adolescence, two young family members conceal their reactions. Children of essentially fatherless households, Nel Wright and Sula Peace are particularly influenced by their mothers. Nel's mother represses her daughter's sense of fun and teaches her to be strictly conventional. Further, Nel learns to be hard and cold when she witnesses her mother's servility to a white railway conductor on a trip south. Nel thinks her mother turns to "custard" and resolves never to be softened, defeated, by any other person. In contrast, the Peace household is chaotic and totally unconventional. Sula learns from her mother's promiscuity to take sex wherever she finds it, and her sense of her own worth is badly damaged when she overhears her mother admit that she *loves* Sula but does not *like* her. Though both mothers intend to do well by their daughters, they fail, and Sula and Nel, as a result, grow up to be limited women, unable to cope successfully with life.

Similarly, a parent's perceptions can be dimmed by flaws in his or her own personality which preoccupy or mislead him or her, and it is often those very personality traits which cause their daughters serious trouble. Luther Alt's (*The Watchman*) willful naiveté motivates one daughter to exploit him, the other to protect him. Mrs. Chase's (*The Life I*

Really Lived) jealousy and unease with sexuality cripple her child's ability to evaluate others and to value herself.

In the eyes of the townsfolk of Adena, West Virginia, setting of Davis Grubb's *The Watchman* (1961), Luther Alt, the sheriff, is correct in prizing his elder daughter, Jill, over his younger daughter, Cristi. Jill keeps house for her widowed father, conducts a sedate courtship according to his wishes, and helps him preserve the "beautiful" memory of her mother. Even Cristi, who says that Jill is their father's "all and everything," seems to endorse Luther's preoccupation with Jill, and though she lives separately from her father and sister and seems to be estranged from them, she is really demonstrating her affection for parent and sister as well as her loyal daughterhood. Grubb casts Jill as a symbol for the head, Cristi as symbol for the heart, and suggests that examined emotions are central to the examined, healthy life—a fact Luther and Jill Alt learn too late, for he has allowed possessive protectiveness to color his relationships with both his daughters.

Early portions of *The Life I Really Lived* (1979) by Jessamyn West recount the youth and adolescence of Orpha Chase who tells her own story as she looks back over a long, successful career as a writer and a somewhat less successful career as a woman. As in many of West's other novels, a key theme here is the impact of a mother-daughter relationship upon the later life of the daughter. The Chase family were never overtly affectionate toward one another, and Orpha believes that her mother was particularly suspicious of any display of affection between father and daughter—partly because Mrs. Chase's own nature demanded the drama which extreme jealously lent to her life, partly because Mrs. Chase understood and feared the sexual aberrations which seem to have abounded in their area of northern Kentucky early in the twentieth century. Both Orpha and her father come to realize that Orpha's difficulties in finding a suitable mate stem in part from Mrs. Chase's restrictive influence. These lessons also stand Orpha in good stead when her own teenaged daughter loves and steals Orpha's lover.

The parents in *The Watchman* and *The Life I Really Lived* are unintentionally damaging to their daughters; indeed both parents engage in considered action intended to benefit their young. In her first novel, *The Bluest Eye*, Toni Morrison—like Bryant Rollins in *Danger Song* and Lois Gould in *Necessary Objects*—depicts families in which parents' unconsidered self-interest is a major force contributing to daughters' inability to achieve emancipation. In all five of these examples, the young women's failure to define themselves is closely tied to sexual exploitation or unfulfillment.

Pecola Breedlove, protagonist of Toni Morrison's *The Bluest Eye* (1970), is introduced at the onset of menstruation, and, like other girls her age, she wonders what intercourse is, what love is like. For Pecola sexual initiation is a horror, for her father rapes and impregnates her, actions which contribute to her eventual madness. Devastating in itself, the act also epitomizes society's destructiveness toward a child denied strong, protective familial support.

The story of Arla McMahon serves as frame for the main plot of Bryant Rollins's *Danger Song* (1967), and the portrait of this helpless, manipulated youngster is designed to reveal the corruption hidden in seemingly genteel white Bostonians. Arla is little more than a puppet in the hands of her father, a violent, barely balanced social climber who embraces all the "right" causes (here, primarily racial justice) in order to gain his own ends; he wishes to penetrate the upper echelons of Boston society, and to this purpose, he devotes his considerable financial means and his daughter's youth, beauty, and talents. Arla lives in fear of her father's dreadful temper and intense ambition and can find little comfort from her mother, who seeks her own relief in alcohol. Though Arla develops enough independence to become angry and to rebel briefly against her father's destruction of her two love affairs, assertiveness comes too late to avert the bloody confrontation which is the novel's climax.

Lois Gould's *Necessary Objects* (1972) is the account of the destructive force wielded by the Lowen sisters, mature women who seem incapable of tenderness, love, or commitment. The stories of two of the Lowens' daughters form important subplots and demonstrate the devastation wreaked by mothers who do not understand—and do not really want to understand—anything about parenting. Jill Landau, fourteen, recognizes her mother's coldness and fears that it will reappear in her own personality; her parents' divorce has exacerbated this dread as does the dissolution of her mother's second marriage: "Maybe if the real father goes away, then no other man has to stay with you, either. . . ." Cathy's mother, Mai, like her sisters, substitutes possessions and psychiatrists for maternal love. Cathy is well aware of this, in both her conscious thoughts and her fantasies, just as she knows that at eighteen (and probably forever), she cannot respond to her baby. This portrayal of family life among wealthy New Yorkers is grim but compelling.

Other authors concentrate on young women's efforts to overcome psychological and emotional limitations imposed by their parents' attitudes and behavior rather than on the damaging circumstances themselves. Whether problems result from long-term tensions or from temporary conflicts, these youngsters not only survive intact but also gain strength, even, occasionally, resiliency, from the struggle. Less passive than the Alt sisters (*The Watchman*), Orpha Chase (*The Life I Really Lived*), Pecola Breedlove (*The Bluest Eye*), Arla McMahon (*Danger Song*), or the Lowen cousins (*Necessary Objects*), these angry daughters act—sometimes foolishly, sometimes self-destructively, sometimes heroically—

and they continue to act until they learn behaviors which strengthen them.

In *Summer of My German Soldier* (1973, YA) by Bette Greene, Patty Bergen's relationship with her parents is always difficult, sometimes strained almost beyond endurance. Because of her mother's constant, voiced disappointment with her daughter's looks, interests, and behavior, Patty has little confidence in her own potential. Repeatedly, Mr. Bergen rejects Patty's overtures, and when he is angered, he beats her. "Sometimes I think it's because I'm bad that my father wants to do the right thing by beating it out of me. And at other times I think he's beating from my body all his own bad." When Patty aids an escaped German prisoner of war, her parents are not only horrified by the act itself, but also, in a sense, they seem to feel that their abuse and rejection have been validated. Nevertheless, Patty emerges as a relatively strong young woman with potential as a survivor. Patty's development of greater self-reliance is chronicled in *Morning Is a Long Time Coming* (1978), which is set primarily in Germany and thus outside the limits of this study.

In *Lessons* (1981) by Lee Zacharias, the relationship between Janie Hurdle and her mother remains strained throughout Janie's youth and into her adult years; neither can seem to please the other. Part of the difficulty stems from Janie's reluctance to come to terms with her father's death, which has occurred before the opening of the action, but most arises from the daughter's rebellion against her mother's rules, her mother's affection for a young grandson, and her mother's efforts to impose a "safe," conventional lower-middle-class life style upon her daughter. Though it has been the mother who suggests that Janie take up the clarinet (she wants to wean her daughter from "tomboy" activities), Mrs. Hurdle resists Janie's preoccupation with music and her determination to study at Indiana University. Janie feels that her accomplishments always seem inconsequential to her mother, and she believes that she can find personal satisfaction only through estrangement. Though these tensions are never really resolved, Janie comes, in time, to understand them, and they contribute to her growth and maturation.

A triangle consisting of Doro Tenant, her mother Lisa, and a mature man is the subject of *A Sudden Woman* (1964) by Heida Huberta Freybe Loewengard (pseudonym, Christine Lambert). Doro, at seventeen, falls in love with Mike, enters into an affair with him, and then feels both enraged and betrayed when she learns that Lisa and Mike are in love with each other. Doro and Lisa had previously had a close and understanding relationship, and their rivalry over Mike destroys it for a time. Doro's anger and Lisa's guilt must both be overcome before, at the novel's end, they can be reconciled. The novel examines various kinds of love and their effects, the final lesson being, as Lisa says to a stronger and wiser Doro, that "to let yourself be loved is a much more difficult obligation than to love. Only little children, and some adults who haven't grown up, accept love indiscriminately." Though Doro still doesn't quite comprehend this lesson, she is now able to listen to her mother and to promise to think about it.

Shirley Eclov's *My Father's House* (1962) is primarily about middle-aged Rena Morrison's attempt to understand her relationship to her father. Important to the plot and to the revelation of Rena's character, however, is the tension between her and her daughter, Lydia. Lydia loves a boy the Morrisons find dull, and so she is defensive about her feelings, especially when her grandfather accuses her of wantonness. When Lydia's grandfather dies almost immediately after the girl's failed attempt to elope, she blames herself, and mother and daughter are drawn together through mutual need and shared feelings of guilt. Eclov clearly conveys the tensions between generations without recourse to cliché or sentimentality.

Often, as we have noted, intrafamily conflict is not evident to observers, and, indeed, parents themselves may be unaware that trouble is brewing despite fairly clear evidence that a daughter is unhappy. Several authors link this obtuseness to parents' belief that their modern, progressive concepts of nurture are by definition sound, quite possibly, the best, as *Chez Cordelia, Dinky Hocker Shoots Smack*, and *It's OK If You Don't Love Me* demonstrate. These analyses can be compared and contrasted with Ella Leffland's depiction of a very traditional nuclear family (*Rumors of Peace*) in which similar problems arise. But in all four novels, a very significant factor—that the family situations seem almost ideal —separates these treatments from novels such as *The Watchman, The Bluest Eye,* or *Summer of My German Soldier.* These four novels are disconcerting by virtue of the fact that their intent is to indicate that very real trouble often does exist in familial paradise.

Books dominate the Miller household in *Chez Cordelia* (1980) by Kitty Burns Florey: Jeremiah Miller is a popular poet; his wife writes elegant biographies of little-known literati; their three older children become writers, and these five Millers read omnivorously. The youngest Miller, Cordelia, the protagonist, however, dreads reading and cannot do it well in school or at home. Because her inability is regarded as a handicap, perhaps a disgrace, by her parents, Cordelia is uncomfortable with them; she loves them dearly (though she doesn't always know that) and believes that their affection for her is sharply limited because of her disability. This thinking is exacerbated by Cordelia's belief that reading is an escape from the real world. Cordelia is a young adult before she—and her parents—realize that differences do not necessarily deter love and that family members can bond strongly even when their standards and behaviors vary markedly.

A sense of the dramatic and an angry use of irony inform Susan

("Dinky") Hocker's most overtly rebellious action in *Dinky Hocker Shoots Smack* (1972, YA) by Marijane Meaker (pseudonym, M. E. Kerr). Though Dinky's parents are presumably sensitive, aware people, and though Dinky's close friends (including her foster sister Natalie, also a troubled child) seem to be maturing nicely, no one responds effectively to Dinky's growing dissatisfaction and panic. Signs of trouble—sullenness, obesity, isolation, irresponsibility—are largely ignored as growing pains until Dinky turns a very public, triumphant moment in her mother's life into a special kind of confrontation. Meaker demonstrates that serious disquiet can affect the children of even the most stable, most socially responsible parents.

Jody Epstein, in *It's OK If You Don't Love Me* (1977, YA) by Norma Klein, handles most relationships with her varied parents handily. She gets along nicely with Elliott, her mother's lover, and tries to be maturely understanding when the couple break up for a brief period. Phillip, her mother's former second husband, is one of Jody's dearest friends; their affection for one another is firm and deep, probably strong enough to withstand Phillip's growing interest in a woman well-suited to him. Jody's father and his second wife have two daughters, and the standards and values of that branch of the family differ sharply from Jody's. She reports that the tension between her father and herself is easing a bit, though his male chauvinistic attitudes still antagonize and belittle her. Because Jody lives with her mother, that relationship is very important. They discuss many topics—such as sex, sexual alliances, and preferences—far more freely than do most mothers and daughters, and Ms. Epstein frequently treats Jody as an equal; indeed, sometimes, Jody seems more mature and composed than her parent. Given these attitudes, it is difficult, then, for Jody to understand her volatile mother's anger over small matters such as Jody's beloved but worn winter coat or larger matters such as Jody's choice of a college. Modernity, openness, and candor do not, Klein suggests, guarantee completely smooth parent-child relationships.

The Hansen family of *Rumors of Peace* (1979) by Ella Leffland are a firmly knit, supportive unit. Suse Hansen, the protagonist, loves her parents, knows she is loved by them, trusts them, is trusted by them. Nevertheless, Suse lives a chilling secret existence of which her parents remain unaware, for she believes that she and her family are unlikely to survive World War II, and she conducts her life according to a dark philosophy: "You should always expect the worst, because it always happens." The complex process of maturation is further complicated for Suse not only by her belief in the animosity of fate but also by the need to protect her mother and father from knowledge of her bitterness and fear. When she finally does learn to allow herself hope, the lesson comes not from her parents but rather from a young man, a victim of the war. Ella Leffland's portrait of a seemingly sound, solid family who do not really understand one another is grounded in realism and is also a bit disquieting. Mr. and Mrs. Hansen mean well and they do well—yet it's not enough; like all youngsters, Suse must find her own way, suffer her own torments, and she must do so alone, despite the love which surrounds her.

Happily, despite the almost universal perception that female adolescence is a troubled period marked by tensions between parents and daughters, suportive, nurturing families who consistently help their daughters achieve independent maturity also appear. Treatments of these situations range from realistic to fanciful, evidence, perhaps, that sustaining relationships are really very common, just overshadowed, one likes to think, by the human impulse to write about conflict more frequently than about peaceful association.

In a series of loosely connected sketches, Sally Daniels's *The Inconstant Season* (1962) presents scenes from the girlhood of Peggy Dillon, a middle-class resident of a small town in New York. Various aspects of her experiences are narrated with nostalgia by the mature Peggy: deaths in the family, school experiences, birthday parties, her first boyfriend, her older brother's wedding, for example. But almost always, the warmth of her generally loving and supportive family is felt, and it is largely this that makes her growing up relatively easy. Themes of change and growth of the individual within the continuity of the family and human experience are stressed. Though the work has no single clear plot line and even the individual chapters lack sharp narrative focus, it is nonetheless an effective presentation of a happy, and in many ways representative, adolescence.

Though she doesn't, at first, think much about it, Hilary, the chief protagonist of *The Girls from the Five Great Valleys* (1978) by Elizabeth Savage, has very strong parents (especially Myra, her mother, the stabilizing factor within the family) who have taught her worthy values. Early in the story, Hilary, selfish and ambitious, seems ready to exchange her parents' standards for the social prominence she so determinedly seeks. But when Myra can no longer conceal the ravages of a progressive, fatal illness, Hilary responds instantly, abandoning her shallow goals and living without bitterness according to the pattern of caring and concern for others which Myra has established. "Link arms and stand together. The rest is poppycock," Myra's code, becomes Hilary's and is the theme of the novel.

In *A Sea-Change* (1976), Lois Gould uses the maturation of Diane Waterman, thirteen, as a means of underscoring the development of her protagonist, Diane's stepmother, and of complicating her plot. As Jessie Waterman slowly abandons her traditional wife–sex-symbol female role and assumes a stronger, more androgynous stance, her new attitudes and behaviors influence both Diane and Jessie's younger daughter, Robin. When Jessie, Diane, and Robin are marooned at the family beach house during Hurricane Minerva, Diane is caught out in the storm, and her maturation and androgynous transformation are symbolized by the physical trials she endures in order to survive; she manages this triumph because of Jessie's example. Mythic and powerful, *A Sea-Change* is, among many other things, an intriguing treatment of the mother-daughter relationship.

If relationships between parents and their adolescent daughters can be difficult, then it must follow that many relationships between foster parents and their charges may also be turbulent. Foster-parenting can be further complicated (as in *Edith Jackson* and *Growing Up Rich*) by young women's prickly awareness that their guardians *are* only substitutes. Generally, however, the same problems of overprotection, misperception, inattention, or exploitation and the less dramatic (if sometimes equally painful) tensions rising from the generation gap as well as loving nurture and consistent support figure in novels dealing with foster parent–child relationship as they do in novels centering upon the relationship between a child and her biological parents.

Virulently wicked stepmothers (and stepfathers) are notably missing from these novels, but one book tentatively suggests that the bond between a group of foster parents and their informally adopted daughter is not strong enough to generate loving gratitude—or even, should it have been called for, forgiveness. In John H. Culp's *A Whistle in the Wind* (1968), Cesre is a symbol of hope and decency to the adults (her foster parents) in the primitive frontier camp for Indians' prisoners where she grows up. When, in her late teens, she surrenders herself to an Indian to save the camp and her husband, however, she is denounced by the white women as a traitor and a whore.

Conversely, an equally informal bond does sustain a sister and her brother in *Orphan Jim* (1975) by Lonnie Coleman. When Trudy and Jim Maynard lose their parents and are emotionally brutalized by an aunt and uncle, they run away, eventually finding shelter and affection with black Hazel Fay and her white lover, Mr. Harris. The children come to love Hazel as a firm and affectionate older sister and to regard Mr. Harris as a kindly benefactor. These two are the first adults to treat the children decently since the death of their mother and represent a turning point in the plot.

Also, an informal motherly-daughterly relationship, which the dominant society—as depicted in Bette Greene's *Summer of My German Soldier* (1973, YA)—would be most reluctant to acknowledge for what it is, functions very positively. Though Patty Bergen's parents seem unable to love her and though they are certainly unable to accept her for what she is, the youngster is sustained through her initiation into adulthood as she has been sustained throughout her childhood by Ruth Hughes, the family's black maid. Ruth offers counsel and comfort, avoiding easy untruths, and paying Patty the compliment of treating her as a thinking being who can—and will—survive sorrow and difficulty. Somewhat reminiscent of the relationship between Berenice, her mentor, and Frankie Addams in Carson McCullers's *The Member of the Wedding* (1946), the Ruth-Patty bond is a brightening element in a grim story.

Anne Bernays depicts, in *Growing Up Rich* (1975), a foster family whose structure has been well and truly legalized and demonstrates that it is human strength and weakness rather than formality which determines the tone of the foster parent–child union. Here, Sally Stern is expected to behave maturely by allowing for her guardians' foibles even as she is expected to remain childish by surrendering her own opinions and decision-making powers. Remanded to their care upon the deaths of her mother and stepfather, Sally has trouble adjusting to life with Sam and Judy London. To Sally, Sam London, her guardian, seems inordinately preoccupied with her family's wealth, what he calls her "marzipan life," and his interest surprises her and makes her uneasy. There are different problems in adjusting to Judy London's attitudes. "Judy doesn't get along with Germans. As a matter of fact, she can't stand them. . . . she lost a lot of relatives during the war . . . they just disappeared along with about five million other Jews." Because of Sally's own German heritage (she's been taught to look down upon Russian Jews, to assume that German Jews naturally enjoy a higher status) and because of her little brother's extreme dependence, especially now that he is orphaned, upon his German governess, Sally anticipates trouble with Judy. These stresses complicate an already difficult situation, and Sally's gradually developed tolerance of Sam and Judy is a mark of her maturation.

Even within blood-tie foster families, some young women resist guidance and others must parent their foster parents, situations parallel to some parent-child power struggles. Useful examples appear in *The Rivers of Eros* and *Grandpa and Frank*. In both instances, female adolescents manipulate their elders, one for selfish, the other for unselfish purposes. In both instances, elder and youth must come to terms with the guardians' varied motives (some admirable, some less admirable) which have set the tones for the relationships.

In Cyrus Colter's *The Rivers of Eros* (1972), sixteen-year-old Addie learns that, because of a guilty secret in her guardian's past, she can defy Clotilda, the grandmother who has reared her. Addie is bored and frightened by the dullness of life in their middle-class neighborhood.

> "Oh, Grandma," she cried, "didn't you like to have a good time when you were young?—didn't you? Didn't people that just plodded and plodded along, no life in 'em, no fun, just bore you till you wanted to scream? Didn't they? They do me. . . . in the movies and on television things're so different, exciting, people doing things, things they never did before and probably'll never

do again, not just getting up in the morning, going to work, coming home, eating supper, going to bed again. Didn't real happy
people do more than just that? . . . Just staying on one *same, same,
same* old level all the time is awful! . . . It's really wasting your life,
that's what it is."

In her search for excitement and happiness, Addie has an affair with a
much older, married man, and thus loses her grandmother's affection
and disrupts Clotilda's sanity, for her grandchildren have been her life.
When Clotilda finally takes steps to control the teenager, the result is a
tragic climax.

In *Grandpa and Frank* (1976) by Janet Majerus, orphaned Sarah
MacDermott has two foster fathers, her grandfather, George, whom she
loves, and her uncle, Frank, whom she fears and distrusts. When Frank
attempts to have George MacDermott declared mentally incompetent,
Sarah determines to thwart his plan. She is motivated by a sense of fair
play and by her loyalty to her grandfather who has nurtured her for
many years. With the help of Joey Martin, a neighbor, Sarah runs away,
taking George to Chicago in search of a physician who can confirm his
sanity. Their journey not only marks Sarah's maturation but also creates
an interesting role reversal, for now Sarah must act as parent to her
grandfather, guarding, protecting, and guiding him. The novel abounds
with echoes of both Mark Twain's *The Adventures of Huckleberry Finn*
(1884) and William Faulkner's *The Reivers* (1962).

Sometimes tenuous family ties evolve into guardianship, and
though early encounters may be awkward (*The Amiable Meddlers*) or
frankly acrimonious (*Hearts*), goodwill can overcome, according to these
authors, circumstance and anger. Josephine Lawrence's quietly amusing
tale of the relationship between fifteen-year-old Jenny Faler and her
guardians, Belle and Zinnia Bruell, forms one of many plots in *The Amiable Meddlers* (1961) and demonstrates that parenting even an obedient,
biddable teenager can be worrisome. Jenny is foisted on the Misses
Bruell, and the women at first fear that the youngster will disrupt their
orderly, peaceful lives. Instead, shortly after Jenny's arrival, the Bruells
find themselves worrying because the girl is so intensely studious, so
buried in her books that she seems hardly to be alive apart from them.
Gradually, without much tension and with a good deal of understated
affection, the three learn to appreciate one another's value systems, and
Jenny teaches her elders several important lessons.

In *Hearts* (1980) by Hilma Wolitzer, the death of Wright Reismann
shortly after his second marriage leaves his thirteen-year-old daughter,
Robin, in the care of his young widow, Linda, who plans to surrender
the sullen, prickly girl to blood relatives. Wright's family, however,
are harsh, materialistic anti-Semites, and Linda cannot bear to leave
Robin with them. Robin herself refuses to remain with Miriam, her own
mother. An important step in Robin's maturation is her realization (not

without melodrama) that her childish, secret plan to murder her mother (who abandoned her at the time of her parents' divorce) is useless, and from that moment there is hope—strained though it sometimes is —that she and Linda can form the nucleus of a genuine family. Both Linda and Robin mature during their cross-country trip in search of new lives, and their decison to remain together, achieved only after numerous tests and trials, is the climax of *Hearts*.

Just as the seemingly temporary nature of Robin and Linda Reismann's foster family structure initially exacerbates problems of adjustment and accommodation, so does it complicate the situation in *Edith Jackson*. At other times, however, the very brevity of the proposed association heightens acceptance and understanding (*Kinds of Love*) or makes the relationship more precious (*Happy Ending*).

Edith Jackson (1978, YA) follows *The Friends* and *Ruby* in Rosa Guy's trilogy about the successes and failures of a group of young black women. Alternately accepting and rejecting the aid of Mrs. Bates, who is eager to substitute for Edith's own dead parents, Edith resents her sponsor's bluntness and her unswerving belief that education is the only solution for Edith's problems:

> I picked my words. It wasn't easy, telling someone trying to be nice that what they wanted and what you wanted was different. Book learning was not my thing. I didn't dig sitting in a room, door closed, my mind in deep torture. "I sure appreciate you wanting to help and all like that. But I just want to stay on here till I find me a job."

The two exploit one another, each seeking her own ends, until Edith, pregnant and abandoned, must surrender to Mrs. Bates. In the book's closing passage, Guy suggests that both women may have learned something about themselves and about the other and that now, perhaps, their relationship can be more fruitful.

With some reluctance but also a good deal of eagerness, elderly Christina and Cornelius Chapman, of May Sarton's *Kinds of Love* (1970), set aside their plan to spend a quiet winter alone and welcome their granddaughter, Cathy, to live with them. Cathy has been having difficulty with her parents, who do not, she believes, understand or appreciate her, and she thinks her grandparents will be more tolerant and perhaps more exciting to live with: "You don't seem so safe. My parents are so damned safe!" The arrangement is useful for all parties: Cathy brings youth into a household where Cornelius, who has recently suffered a crippling stroke, is working his way back into a restricted but still vital life, and the Chapmans are able to offer Cathy support and unobtrusive guidance as she falls in love for the first time. Though *Kinds of Love* concentrates primarily on the ongoing vigor and complexity of life for the elderly, the Cathy subplot is a useful and appealing device.

In *Happy Ending* (1972) by Elizabeth Savage, Maralyse Tyler, orphaned by the death of her father, seeks love and comfort from a young man and almost immediately becomes pregnant. Abandoned by the child's father, she finds work with Carrie and Thomas Russell, elderly Montana ranchers. The Russells are themselves lonely and soon become substitute parents for Maryalyse and foster grandparents for her infant. With them, Maryalyse finds stability and love, conditions which help her to rebuild her life. She also finds the courage to extend daughterly love again, despite the clear fact that the Russells' age and growing infirmities mean that the relationship will be brief. When Maryalyse says, "Mrs. Russell, there isn't anything you or Mr. Russell might like I would mind," she means it wholly. The portrait of this unusually constituted family is warm, sustaining, and unsentimental.

In some of the most unhappy of situations, foster homes are institutions in which yet another type of parent-daughter alliances may develop, that between therapist and client. In these instances, it is the hope (dim though it may be) that the relationship may be brief which sustains doctor and patient during very difficult periods. In the representative examples discussed here, the authors are unsparing in depicting the complexity and tension within this bond, showing its artificiality (in that it is imposed by outside authorities) and its absolute necessity. For the adolescent females of *Like the Lion's Tooth* and *I Never Promised You a Rose Garden*, redemptive support, if it comes, must come from outside any family circle they have heretofore known.

Like the Lion's Tooth (1972) by Marjorie Kellogg presents grim, despairing portraits of several inhabitants of a school for abused children. Julie Williams, strong, furious, and rebellious, seems to be one of the hopeless cases:

> Julie could not or would not remember her mother's name or where they had lived, or anything, for that matter, about her life before she came to the School. It was as though the part of her brain which had contained those facts had dried up and blown away, for all the information she was able to recall. A face maybe, here and there; a lightbulb swinging from a ceiling; a man intervening. He wore a hat. Or did he? A moustache? It had been too dark to see.

Julie invests her time in brilliant, ruthless, well-organized acts of rebellion and destruction against the school and in searching for the vaguely remembered person called "the Man." Yet, in a moment of crisis, Julie turns to the school psychologist. Though her gesture begins cynically, it ends with the only symbol of hope Kellogg allows her characters.

In *I Never Promised You a Rose Garden* (1964), Joanne Greenberg (pseudonym, Hannah Green) presents a remarkably sensitive portrait of the relationship between psychiatrist and patient. For Deborah Blau, Dr. Fried (whom Deborah calls Furii) becomes a kind of third parent as she helps Deborah uncover the secrets of her early life and thus reconstruct her self-concept; she presides at Deborah's rebirth and nurtures her growth. The doctor's first gift is an honest recognition of Deborah's illness coupled with her acceptance of Deborah for what she is and for what she can become. "Now Furii was giving a second gift, a little piece of herself. Its delicacy meant more than a small respite from the probing or an unsaid message to 'take heart'; it said, 'I will trust you with one of my memories as you have trusted me with yours.'" This gesture signifies acceptance as an equal, and Deborah values it highly. The relationship between the two women is never sentimentalized, and Deborah's progress is never depicted as easy—for instance, the doctor's long absence during the therapy results in dreadful setbacks. But Dr. Fried's skill at offering restrained support and at encouraging helpful if painful insight creates a steady pressure toward Deborah's recovery. For Deborah, Dr. Fried's refusal to promise a rose garden is an important token of her therapist's honesty and strength.

Siblings are another group of family members who are very nearly as important as parents or parent substitutes to adolescent females' development. When all siblings in a family are struggling toward selfhood at the same time, a certain amount of jostling for position within the family usually occurs simultaneously with each youngster's efforts at self-realization, and consequently many of the same patterns which appear in parent-child and foster parent–child relationships appear in the interactions between sisters or sisters and brothers.

Occasionally, as in Maureen Howard's *Before My Time* (1974), it is a sibling relationship which a youth tries to exploit in an effort to cling to girlhood. At twelve, Cormac and Siobhan Cogan move into adolescence despite Siobhan's heroic efforts to retain childhood ways. The twins are startlingly alike in appearance and have almost always been able to play tricks on teachers, merchants, and other casual acquaintances by exchanging identities. To Siobhan, this similarity represents a kind of marginal security unavailable in the twins' family life which is damaged by their father's gambling and their mother's alcoholism. Because she has no one to depend upon but her twin, Siobhan forces him to run away with her despite Cormac's reluctance—he is eager for maturity, for a life more independent of both his parents and his sister. The children's odd, brief idyl in a sterile, incomplete housing development is thus doomed from the start, for not only Cormac but also the adult world disapprove of Siobhan's attempts to avoid maturation. Howard compares Siobhan's rebellion with those of several other youngsters to suggest that reluctant and unsatisfactory compromise with reality is sometimes an adolescent's only option.

In contrast to Siobhan, who fends off adulthood for a time, other adolescent females are catapulted into adult roles because they are expected to mother their siblings. Sadly, for some of these young women, the great responsibility of parenting so preoccupies the "mother" sibling that she misses most of the joys of sisterhood or else she submerges herself in the role of substitute mother to the point that she misses experiences important to her own self-realization. This motif appears in *The Girls from the Five Great Valleys*, is established in *The Friends*, and made explicit in *Edith Jackson*, the latter pair being two of the three novels in Rosa Guy's series about a circle of young black women.

Amelia Lacey, a major character in Elizabeth Savage's *The Girls from the Five Great Valleys* (1978), is almost solely responsible for the protection and well-being of her retarded sister, identified only as "the child." Because Amelia is so preoccupied with protecting "the child," she is unaware of her love for her sister until the younger girl is dead, and because Amelia has had to discipline "the child," she has also remained unaware of her sister's true feelings: "She didn't know Amelia was her sister, but she had small impressions that fitted into a good thing: a gentle voice, a tallness, a warm firm hand. And she knew where that tallness slept and had a long warm back and wasn't cross." Instead, Amelia believes that "the child" has lived her whole life fearing her. Though Amelia has coped stalwartly with the death of her father and the total inadequacy of her mother, the death of her little sister precipitates an unmanageable crisis in Amelia's own life.

The situation in the Lacey household compares with the equally tragic circumstances of the Jackson family. In *The Friends* (1973, YA) by Rosa Guy, fourteen-year-old Edith Jackson bears primary responsibility for the welfare of her sisters, often staying home from school to care for them and trying to manage on their shadowy father's slim earnings. The entire pattern of Edith's life is structured around her promise to care for her sisters and to keep the family intact. When Mr. Jackson disappears, the children, at Edith's insistence, do not appeal to the authorities for help because she fears, rightly, that city officials will split up the family. At the novel's close, she has only her limited friendship with Phyllisia Cathy to sustain her.

Edith, in another volume of Rosa Guy's trilogy, *Edith Jackson* (1978), remains determined to keep herself and her three younger sisters—Bessie, thirteen; Minnie, eleven; and Suzy, twelve—together until she turns eighteen and can get a job to support them. The children have lived in a succession of foster homes, and their stay in the most bearable ends abruptly when Bessie runs off with their foster mother's suitor. Back in "The Institution," social workers place Minnie happily and Suzy very unhappily in separate homes, blasting Edith's dream. Perhaps a worse blow, however, is her realization that she has been so preoccupied with being tough enough to hold them together that she hasn't really known her sisters: "Guess I'd been too busy looking after the kids ever to really see them good." Trying to cope with Bessie's death, Minnie's acceptance into a white family, and Suzy's disappearance leaves Edith too weakened and vulnerable to handle her own life wisely.

Shirley Jackson extends this pattern dramatically in *We Have Always Lived in the Castle* (1962), in which love, duty, and circumstance combine to make one sister sacrifice almost everything for another. The Blackwood sisters, Constance and Mary Katherine ("Merricat"), the central characters, live in the shadow of a crime, the poisoning of several relatives, which was committed about six years earlier. Jackson depicts Merricat's possessiveness toward her sister and Constance's loyal forbearance toward Merricat, qualities which endure in the face of neighbors' growing antagonism for the family. Though the courts have determined that Constance is not a poisoner, the local folk believe her to be guilty and undertake her punishment. Readers, however, come to understand the true solution of the mystery, as the Blackwood girls' characters are revealed. Questions of honor, decency, sacrifice, and individual and societal guilt are, as is usual in Jackson's work, raised most effectively, and though the portraits of Constance and Merricat are full and moving, they are designed to reveal theme more than characterization.

Though bonds of sibling love and loyalty are emphasized in almost all of the novels treated in this study, the authors do, quite naturally, also depict sibling tension and rivalry. These strained relationships range, as they do in life, from warm alliances sometimes troubled by relatively brief periods (even moments) of stress to relationships which are seriously flawed.

In *The Loser* (1965, YA), Elizabeth Allen portrays the Ames sisters —Deitz, sixteen, and Lee, fifteen—with realism and insight. Though there are tensions between the girls arising from their differing interests and Lee's occasional jealousy of Deitz, the two are essentially loving friends. The portrait of Lee's developing poetic skill and awakening social poise is contrasted with protagonist Deitz's growing awareness of her intellectual capability.

Two major factors strain the bonds between the teenaged sisters featured in Norma Klein's *Domestic Arrangements* (1981). Protagonist Rusty Engleberg is a beauty, particularly notable for her stunning red hair and her aura of innocent sensuality. Deel Engleberg is not conventionally pretty, is less successful at school, and, unlike her younger sister, is still a virgin who, early in the novel, claims "she's just going to go out and find someone, in cold blood, sort of, and do it to get it over with." Rusty's rather unexpected success as the star of *Domestic Arrangements*, a film, heightens the tension between the sisters. Klein uses their relationship (and most others in this novel) to illustrate the concept that enlightened modernity, open discussion, and even love do not solve all the problems that beset what Mrs. Engleberg dubs "a typical New York family."

In *The Friends* (1973, YA) by Rosa Guy, Phyllisia Cathy's relationship with her sister, Ruby, is difficult. Phyllisia, like Deel Engleberg in

Domestic Arrangements, believes herself to be plain, and she envies her sister Ruby's beauty; she also envies Ruby's seemingly easy adjustment to life in Harlem, for Phyllisia sometimes yearns to return to the West Indies. During their mother's long terminal illness, Phyllisia is often scornful of Ruby's care for Mrs. Cathy, partly because she does not know how to express her own concern. The girls are not united by grief but are driven to protect one another from their father's rages, which worsen after their mother's death. When, at the conclusion of *The Friends*, Phyllisia struggles through to a degree of maturity, Rosa Guy allows a bit of hope that the sisters' relationship may improve.

In *Chez Cordelia* (1980) by Kitty Burns Florey, love and hatred for reading and writing divide a family. Juliet, Miranda, and Horatio Miller all read constantly (as do their parents who are writers) and steadily nag their little sister, Cordelia, the protagonist, who does not enjoy reading, cannot do it well, and resents the pressures her siblings bring to bear upon her. Because the family reverence for literary activity and academic excellence makes Cordelia feel inferior and because she resents being patronized by her older siblings, some distrust, submerged quarrels, and lack of understanding result. It is only late in adolescence that Cordelia learns that she, too, is a person of value, and as a young adult she asserts herself to pull Juliet out of a dangerous situation. These factors help her to understand that though her siblings, like her parents, have become writers, they have made serious professional compromises and have failed to achieve much personal happiness. Florey uses Cordelia's distrust of the printed word as an original and effective symbol of the tensions often present between siblings.

Claire Danziger of Sandra Scoppettone's *Happy Endings Are All Alike* (1978, YA) is an unsympathetic auxiliary character who refuses to face her problems squarely. Because she is not conventionally pretty, Claire feels unlovable and presents a hostile front to all the world, including her family, especially her sister, Peggy, who is pretty and who is, Claire believes, favored. Scoppettone depicts Claire as a victim of society's standards of conventional female beauty, but makes it clear that Claire is also a victim of herself, for she has no charity toward others and thus assumes that none will be extended toward her. Ironically, it is Claire's bitter denunciation of Peggy and Jaret Tyler as lesbians which causes the younger girls to confront their real feelings and actually triggers the beginning of their love affair. One of Peggy's great problems is managing a decent relationship with Claire, who frequently threatens to reveal Peggy's secret to their father. Ultimately, Claire emerges as the loser in this sibling battle.

In all forms of family relationships, then, according to these authors, good intent can be as damaging as outright destructiveness if it is not informed by awareness of an adolescent female's need to become her own person. It matters very little whether a restrictive bond is maintained by mother, father, foster parent, sister, or brother; it is unreasonable restriction that torments young females by stunting their emotional growth and by invoking the threat of being unloved. Further, a too rapidly imposed maturity, forcing a young woman to behave as if she were the parent of her own parent or of a sibling, can be just as limiting as abuse or demeaning overguidance.

What is vital in family relationships (as in sexual relationships) is that adolescent women be given or demand or take the freedom to define themselves, to create a sense of self which will allow them to be active, useful adults who are aware of their own worth. They must be able to function beyond the boundaries of their original families in the larger society and in the new families which those who become wives and mothers must help establish. Cautionary portraits of fictional adolescents who fail, such as Ida Trask (*Portrait in Brownstone*), Sula Peace and Nel Wright (*Sula*), Pecola Breedlove (*The Bluest Eye*), or Amelia Lacey (*The Girls from the Five Great Valleys*), warn readers to avoid mistakes made by the fictional relatives or by the girls themselves. The stories of female adolescents who are guided toward or win through to positive adulthood, such as Mary Call Luther (*Where the Lilies Bloom*), Amanda Carpenter (*I Am in Urgent Need of Advice*), Deitz and Lee Ames (*The Loser*), or Suse Hansen (*Rumors of Peace*) suggest various modes in which youngsters can seize the day and the future.

None of these authors even momentarily overlooks the difficulty of maintaining fruitful family relationships; few depict parents or siblings who are willfully destructive, and most recognize that the responsibility for a young woman's maturation must be her own far more than her family's. Her ability to establish a code of ethics and a mode of behavior that will serve her well in the adult world (and will be the measure by which she is judged as an adult) is one of the most crucial obligations of her inward journey to maturity. Happy is she whose family encourages that development; strong is she who manages it singly. Without it, she will never live as a fully realized, independent being.

CHAPTER III
Female Friendships

Because the search for selfhood is a lonely quest, most adolescents actively seek companions who will support them during the journey toward adulthood. Many youngsters consider friendship as protection from the rigors of any necessary, unfamiliar social interaction, as a barrier against intrusive adults, and also, often, as a means of confirming one's worth to oneself and to the world. The presence of friends in one's life signals acceptance beyond family, suggests that one has been *chosen* (rather than accepted by virtue of birth or adoption), and implies the possibility of equality between partners. To adolescents, who so often feel themselves to be pawns of powerful adults—parents, other relatives, teachers, for example—the idea of a significant, *equal* other, a friend, represents the power of unity and solidarity. In bonding, they may feel, lies strength.

For the many female adolescents who tend to value themselves because others value them, friendship often appears to be the obvious, most readily available means of acquiring the social acceptance they deem essential. Whether young women judge their own worth according to the opinions of others because society teaches them to do so or because they misperceive social messages, the habit, according to the novels studied here, strains friendship, just as it complicates adolescent love affairs and family relationships.

There tends to be, then, in the friendships of adolescent females, as in most of their relationships, an element of self-interest, and quite often conflict develops when the friends' needs are not—or are no longer —congruent. Also, though females are traditionally considered to be more passive than males, passivity seldom defines both partners, and in friendships between females, true equality (and hence balance of power) rarely exists, much as adolescents might wish it, and tensions can thus develop because of power struggles very similar to those between family members, lovers, or mates. Finally, young female friends discover that though they may perceive friendship as a sanctuary from the pressures and complexities of society, the very social attitudes and demands from which they seek protection or relief are often present in the friendships themselves.

It is important to note that the complexities of adolescents' friendships are almost no different from those in friendships between adults. Difficulties and benefits arise from the same human needs, weaknesses, and strengths in both cases. For adolescents, however, their very youthfulness can make healthful solutions to problems between friends more difficult to reach. Teenagers haven't, after all, a large fund of experience on which to draw; most do not yet realize that human relationships are very seldom untroubled, wholly supportive, or ideal. Disruptions or dissolutions of friendships between young women can be particularly disturbing, suggesting to the youngster that she is inept or unworthy and possibly making her wary of others, distrustful, and unwilling to extend friendship again. These risks inform adolescents' efforts to maintain unwavering friendships with a particular irony, for the very refuge they construct against adults and against adult society is, in fact, one of the tests they must undergo to achieve their passionately desired goals: admission to and effective activity within that very society. These goals mean everything to young women, no matter if adulthood also sometimes seems to them as mysterious and as dangerous as it seems alluring.

When friendship between adolescents shuts out the adult world, one consequence frequently stems from youngsters' sense of enclosure in a separate society of their own: they support and protect one another in activities carefully kept secret from the adults who supervise them. Two authors extend this fairly common habit dramatically, using it to strengthen the symbolism in their plots. Blunt, cheerful, and open, Amy Hertz is the loyal friend of Adam Farmer, the shy protagonist of *I Am the Cheese* (1977, YA) by Robert Cormier. The pair share their first limited sexual experiences, and Amy enlists Adam's aid in her "numbers," practical jokes engineered in local supermarkets and parking lots. Though these stunts hurt no one, they disrupt the normal order of everyday life, both contrasting with and underscoring the extreme abnormality of Adam's existence.

Susan Schnitzer of Harriet Arnow's *The Weedkiller's Daughter* (1970) not only leads a secret life herself but also helps two young male friends delude their families, though the boys' motives and escapades are questionable. These two subplots reveal Susan's slowly developing maturity and the boys' schemes contrast with her own need to deceive her bigoted family in order to preserve decent standards.

Neither Robert Cormier in *I Am the Cheese* nor Harriet Arnow in *The Weedkiller's Daughter* depicts the deceitful overtones of these friendships as particularly enriching elements in the lives of their characters; both, however, indicate that the youngsters' behavior is dictated—or at least prompted—by flaws in the larger society. Similarly, a number of characters show how flaws within friendships reflect or result from faulty adult thinking or negligence. Cha'Lou Moonlight and Irma Renner (*Sundays*) are forced into companionship by mere proximity whereas Sula Peace and Nel Wright (*Sula*) freely choose one another's company. In the first instance, the girls are expected to understand and abide by the hypocritical class distinctions their elders practice; in the second, they are expected to nurture one another in the absence of adult guidance. Neither expectation is fulfilled in any beneficial way.

The two female adolescents who inhabit the central household depicted in *Sundays* (1979) by Cynthia Applewhite are expected to be friendly with one another without becoming friends. Both girls are the angry recipients of the "charity" of protagonist Cha'Lou Moonlight's aunts, and neither girl is allowed to forget it for a moment. Irma Renner, the aunts' maid of all work, is humiliated at every turn. Cha'Lou is constantly reminded that she is "lucky" to have a place to stay when her parents' marriage falls upon hard times. Perhaps not unnaturally, then, the girls turn to—and against—one another. For Irma, earthy and possibly truly evil, the corruption of Cha'Lou would be splendid vengeance upon her employers. For Cha'Lou, lonely, emotionally battered, and immensely curious about sex, exploration of Irma's side of town and Irma's apparently unfettered sexual activity would not only assuage some of her own longings but also be a means of defying her aunts. In no way are Cha'Lou and Irma good for one another, but each is almost all the other has.

Their intense friendship is the one constant in the girlhoods of Sula Peace and Nel Wright in *Sula* (1973) by Toni Morrison. "They found relief in each other's personality" from the pressures of puberty and the awkwardnesses in their homes. "In the safe harbor of each other's company they could afford to abandon the ways of other people and concentrate on their perceptions of things," and this preoccupation with their own feelings and desires sets the tone for the girls' entire lives. Morrison depicts Sula and Nel as incomplete personalities, indicating through their friendship that if the two characters could but merge, a whole, effective woman would result.

Even the presence of an older mentor who represents certain social attitudes or values can prove unfruitful, perhaps even damaging. The complex relationship of a nineteen-year-old girl, Delia Wright, and an older woman is depicted in Harris Downey's *The Key to My Prison* (1964). Caroline Atherton takes the orphaned Delia into her home, trying to guide her to culture and maintain her in her gentility. But Delia, intensely subjective and always seeking her own free identity, resents any curbs on her freedom. Leaving Miss Atherton, she returns to her own home, ironically drifting further into isolation and alienation. Thus, partly, is motivated the decision to commit suicide on which the novel is based.

Alix Kates Shulman takes this pattern one step further and makes older friends the symbols of a teenager's desperate straits, closely linking setting and character as a background for her grim plot in *On the Stroll* (1981). The Stroll, Broadway, Hell's Kitchen, Times Square, the fast track, are among the various names applied to "the small circle of Midtown New York surrounding the Port Authority Bus Terminal for a radius of half a dozen blocks." Shulman describes Robin Ward, an adolescent prostitute; Prince, her pimp; and Owl, Robin's bag-lady friend, as fairly typical examples of denizens of the Stroll, their individual stories and interrelationships representing the bitterness and desperation of thousands of lives lived in the dark holes behind the bright lights. Details of grisly hotels, vagrants' "shelters," temporary "homes" in abandoned buildings, characterize the area and the protagonists' lives, leaving little hope that Robin's final escape from New York City will lead her to anything but another Stroll at the other end of the continent, to another set of debilitating acquaintanceships.

All too often, adolescent females themselves reflect and embrace shoddy social attitudes. These girls are very sensitive to class distinctions, for example, and plan either to exploit friendship as a means of upward mobility or to avoid friends deemed socially unworthy. *The Girls from the Five Great Valleys* (1978), by Elizabeth Savage, centers upon the friendship between five high school students. Hilary, their leader, is determined to break into whatever "high society" exists in Missoula, Montana, in the midst of the Depression. She sees her friends as aides in her campaign, believing that their various skills, looks, and talents can help her crash the barriers raised against them all. This ambition so preoccupies Hilary that for many months, she is insensitive to the pressures that threaten various of her friends and undermine their unity. While Hilary assures herself that she is working for her friends' advantage, as well as using them to promote her own, Phillisia Cathy (*The Friends*) intends to avoid even the possibility of encouraging a schoolmate's movement "up."

Despite the fact that Phyllisia Cathy is the scapegoat of her class —the other children resent her brains, her manners, and her West Indian accent—she is disdainful of Edith Jackson's friendly overtures. But Edith is not daunted. "Edith ignored my snub. She always ignored my snubs. Edith had made up her mind, from the first day I entered this class, that she would be my friend whether I wanted it or not." Phyllisia, the protagonist of *The Friends* (1973, YA) by Rosa Guy, is a snob, and she is put off by Edith's poverty and personal carelessness, even after Edith defends her against the other youngsters, protects her during a race riot, and introduces her to the mysteries of New York City. The girls do manage a kind of restrained alliance until family pressures and Phyllisia's biases cause a serious rupture. When Phyllisia resumes the friendship, it is very nearly too late, but the gesture represents hope to Edith and symbolizes Phyllisia's maturation. *The Friends* is the first of a trilogy, including *Ruby* and *Edith Jackson*, which traces the lives of Phyllisia, Edith, and their families.

Fortunately, not all youngsters from differing social groups allow their backgrounds to deny them friendship. Although herself the daughter of artists considered Bohemian, the narrator of Nancy Hale's brief and nostalgic *Secrets* (1971) had for closest friends the four children (two boys and two girls) of a very proper and upwardly mobile Bostonian. The novel is her recollection of their growing up together, first their childish games and shared secrets and then the debutante year experienced together by the narrator and Jinny, the elder of the two sisters.

Two novels for young adults by Kristin Hunter, *The Soul Brothers and Sister Lou* and *Lou in the Limelight*, feature Louretta Hawkins, an appealing, talented young woman. During the initial action of *The Soul Brothers and Sister Lou* (1968, YA), Louretta feels almost friendless. At school, long-term white girlfriends now avoid her as the girls grow up and allow racism to supersede loyalty. In her neighborhood, there is no place for youngsters to congregate safely, and, furthermore, her mother and older brother, the heads of the Hawkins household, disapprove of every adolescent for blocks around. Lou finally persuades her brother, William, to allow a gang of neighborhood boys (teetering on the edge of lawlessness) and their female hangers-on to meet in his newly established printing shop. She sticks with them, "Because I have to. There isn't anybody else." Despite interpersonal tensions and outright persecution from the local law, the youngsters unite in supportive friendships. Lou discovers that she is a very good musician, and the soul group that organizes itself in the clubhouse achieves some degree of success. Perhaps even better, Lou finds a new sense of herself through her friends and their newly defined black pride.

Though the clubhouse and her singing group sustain Lou at first, even these associations lead to temptation and serious trouble when the group moves among adults. Too young to make good judgments, too inexperienced to assert control over their talents, they fall prey to fakery, exploitation, and dissent. In the sequel, *Lou in the Limelight* (1981, YA), Kristin Hunter uses Louretta Hawkins's various friendships to dramatize a major theme: Lou's search for identity. The open, healthy friendship between Lou and her colleagues, Ulysses, David, and Frank, is badly strained by the schemes of their manager, Marty, and Charles, their campy "Imagist," as the singing group attempts to break into "the big time." Marty and Charles suggest major changes in the group's structure; they want to feature Lou as lead singer and use the Soul Brothers as a flashy but secondary "back-up." Equally threatening are their efforts to transform Lou from a teenaged soul singer into a bold, seductive sex-object. Loud, tight clothes, outrageous wigs, distasteful public appearances, and pleas for her to "be nice" to various influential men confuse Lou's perceptions of who she is and what she wants, confuse Ulysses, David, and Frank about her goals and attitudes. Only by regaining control of her own personality and by reassessing almost all her friendships and the obligations they engender can this talented young black woman hope to have a valuable, enjoyable life.

Lou's dilemma introduces another theme common among the novels studied here. For talented young women, the effort to maintain a good balance between attention to friends and attentiveness to their disciplines often creates tensions and calls for decisions they find very hard to manage. Frequently, these problems are exacerbated by one friend's jealousy of the other. The difficulties of building and maintaining friendships are movingly studied in Stephanie S. Tolan's *The Last of Eden* (1980, YA). Michelle ("Mike") Caine, the fifteen-year-old narrator and protagonist, is a popular and well-adjusted boarding school pupil. She has one group of friendships based on common activities and another particularly intimate friendship with Martha ("Marty") Sheffield based on mutual commitment to artistic and poetic goals. But the group never accepts Marty, and Mike discovers within herself a rather surprising jealousy when Marty achieves artistic success and recognition beyond anything she herself can claim—or has even striven for. Other forces ultimately destroy the friendship, and Mike is forced to acknowledge the fragility of relationships, but she is comforted by having friends who have remained loyal, even though their relationships lack the depth of intimacy she has treasured with Marty.

Jeanne Blake is accustomed to discussing her triumphs and troubles with a close friend, Marjorie Terry, and *A Question of Harmony* (1965, YA) by Gretchen Sprague details Jeanne's confusion, irritation, and pain when, during their senior year in high school, the girls become estranged. To Jeanne, it seems that Marjorie is pulling away from their friendship from jealousy of Jeanne's newly defined commitment to music (an interest they have heretofore shared) as a profession, for Marjorie considers the violin her avocation, not a potential career. To Marjorie, however, Jeanne's sudden preoccupation with a string trio which excludes Margy, a new friend, Dixie Thorne, and a new boyfriend seems to indicate that Jeanne has little time for old friendships. When the girls learn to communicate on a more adult level, their problems are not solved, but they *are* shared, a development the author considers a key ingredient to true friendship.

Sometimes juvenile competitiveness and jealousy go unresolved for many years, as Dinah Howells's story, told in *Dale Loves Sophie to Death* (1981) by Robb Forman Dew, demonstrates. In flashbacks and memories, Dinah tries to assess the impact her best youthful friends, Isobel and Lawrence Brooks, siblings, have made upon her life. Though Lawrence was her first lover, their sexual relationship arose primarily from lifelong friendship rather than romance; at least that is the awareness which Dinah allows herself. Isobel, older and more glamorous than Dinah, was role-model and competitor; Dinah both did and did not want to be like Isobel, wished to surpass her friend in vaguely defined ways, and resented Isobel's ability to please Dinah's father. Memories of Dinah's weekend reign as Homecoming Queen are especially useful in her reassessment of herself and her friends, and through those reflections, Dinah realizes that "old friends are just like creatures from dreams. They are so elusive because they are made up of memory that isn't always reminiscent of reality but only of one's past ambitions, hopes, and necessities." Dinah's new awareness helps her to grasp the fact that no matter how enduring adolescent friendships remain, the human condition is aloneness (if not loneliness).

In her sprawling first novel, *Coming Attractions* (1981), which is a compendium of themes important in stories of female adolescence, Fannie Flagg pulls together the themes of snobbery, competitiveness, and jealousy by comparing and contrasting two friendships—one artificial, a matter of proximity, the other real and, for a time, vital to both youngsters—which complicate the life of her protagonist. Two girls, Pickle Watkins and Kay Bob Benson, figure in the adolescence of Daisy Fay Harper and both have important, if commonplace, functions in the novel's structure. Kay Bob, Daisy Fay's competitor, stands for the snobbery which money and position generate, and Daisy Fay's ultimate defeat of Kay Bob is meant to demonstrate that genuinely nice people sometimes triumph, a lesson undercut considerably by the duplicitous efforts of Daisy Fay's friends who ensure the victory. Pickle, Daisy Fay's friend, who marries to escape a terrible home life, represents compromise, the failure of ambition, and when Daisy Fay discovers that she and Pickle no longer have much in common, Flagg is signaling her protagonist's readiness to move up and out. Daisy Fay is on the verge of maturity, and life has more to offer to her than to Pickle or to Kay Bob.

Because young female friends seldom mature at exactly the same rate, one youngster's developing sexuality can also threaten a friendship by arousing jealousy in her comrade. This pattern, of which *Breaking Up* and *Umbrella Steps* are interesting examples, is far more common than are instances of two fictional girls competing for the same young man, which appear with surprising infrequency. To Alison Rose, in Norma Klein's *Breaking Up* (1980, YA), returning to California for the summer means returning to the shelter of her relationship with Gretchen, her best friend. Though she has buddies in New York City where she has recently moved with her mother, Ali does not feel especially close to them. She considers Gretchen to be a major stabilizing factor in her life, and despite their differences in attitude, appearance, and levels of maturity, both girls greatly value their relationship. When Ali's casual friendship with Ethan, Gretchen's brother, turns into love, Gretchen feels angry, threatened, and abandoned, and the fact that both girls' families are facing other crises only complicates matters. Gretchen learns that jealousy is a limiting emotion, and Ali learns that personal gratification sometimes causes others pain; both friends discover that their bond can grow and develop, that change is not necessarily destructive.

Best friends Prudence Goodrich and Lolly Spitz are never quite equal in their relationship. Prude, the narrator of *Umbrella Steps* (1972) by

Julie Goldsmith Gilbert, reports, for instance, that "I never corrected her [Lolly]. I let her be superior to me. She needed to be. . . . I was afraid of losing her." Prude does lose Lolly, however, when her friend withdraws, an act Prude attributes to Lolly's early-developing sexuality. Despite what Prude regards as her own slower maturation, she engages in an affair with Lolly's father, learning only much later that Lolly has been Prude's father's lover for the last two years. As Prude moves toward marriage with Nate Spitz, Lolly and Marvin Goodrich terminate their affair. The girls' friendship, a bit tentative and certainly altered, resumes, but Prude now has rather different ideas about her own and Lolly's respective levels of maturity and dependence.

Though Gretchen and Alison (*Breaking Up*) and Prudence and Lolly (*Umbrella Steps*) mature in ways which allow them to redefine and retain their friendships, some friends such as Daisy Fay Harper and Pickle Watkins (*Coming Attractions*), as we have seen, must relinquish their alliances. Other authors also use the dissolved friendship motif, as Fannie Flagg does, to indicate their protagonists' developing maturity, their greater strength, or their difference from their comrades. Underlying this usage is the awareness—of author, character, reader—that though good friendships are sustaining and helpful, everything changes, even friendship, and that, eventually, each young woman must move ahead, alone, on her inward journey toward selfhood. In these pilgrims' progress, some friends must be left behind.

Doll, one of a circle of friends in *The Girls from the Five Great Valleys* (1978) by Elizabeth Savage, is the first among her crowd to realize that their closeness cannot last. Very much aware that the girls are drifting apart, Doll understands that when the others go on to the university and she takes a job, their paths will diverge permanently. Amelia, with a dependent mother and little sister, is so laden with family responsibilities that the other girls already seem distant, and Kathy and Janet, lesser characters in the group, are quietly undermining the authority of Hilary, the dominant friend, by making their own decisions. Even Hilary, slow though she is to realize that the five can't function much longer as one unit, is being conscripted, unawares, into a new role by growing family obligations. How wisely and responsibly the five handle their redefined roles is Savage's major subject. Early in the novel, the authorial voice observes, "Take five girls anywhere, at any time. Three will be all right, and one will make it. One won't." The novel details that pattern in the lives of these Montana girls.

A small town in northern Alabama is the microcosmic setting for Babs H. Deal's *It's Always Three O'Clock* (1961), which characterizes three decades—the 1920s, 1930s, and 1940s—as seen by Eileen Holder from her vantage in the era of space exploration. The novel's first third deals with the adolescence of Eileen and her friends—school, parties, dates, loves. Eileen marries while still in high school, has a child, and soon loses the husband she has loved since childhood. Her strength and love of life carry her through, while most of her friends are less successful in controlling their lives. Alone of her generation she has the attitude of the old captain, grandfather of one of her friends, who had fought for the Union in the Civil War because "That's what I happened to believe." "Captain Simms loved life. It was that simple. He liked to get up in the morning and go to his room at night. And he wanted to live a century because he wanted to know what was going to happen next." Deal's adolescents and their children face many sorrows and often fail—but through Eileen and the strength she shows from girlhood, and through the symbolic presence of the captain, her book affirms the possibilities of joy and life.

Suse Hansen, protagonist of Ella Leffland's *Rumors of Peace* (1979), at first believes she has found an almost perfect friend in Peggy Hatton, but as the girls grow older, they also grow apart. Not only does Peggy fail to respond to World War II as seriously as does Suse (who is obsessed with it), but she also, having introduced Suse to the pleasures of learning, abandons intellectual seriousness in favor of popularity, cliques, and glamor. Suse is then taken up by Peggy's older sister, Helen Maria, considered to be a genius by her family (she is a senior at the University of California at Berkeley at fifteen), who challenges Suse's intelligence as well as her traditionalist social codes. In turn, Helen Maria introduces Suse to Egon Krawitz, a young man who properly and firmly treats Suse as a delightful young comrade rather than as the romantic interest Suse would like to be. Each of these friends expands Suse's horizon, enlarges her world view, and moves beyond her—as she moves beyond each of them. Leffland uses the friendship motif to illustrate that maturation demands growth, change, and even sometimes abandonment of cherished relationships.

Closely allied to the pattern of friendship which must be let go in order that friends can mature properly is another: the friendship which circumstance dictates must be brief, even though it be profoundly affecting. Several authors, as examination of *Summer of My German Soldier*, *A Day Late*, and *I Never Promised You a Rose Garden* reveal, employ unlikely friendships as a mode of testing and strengthening their adolescent female characters. These friendships all occur while the young women are under great stress, and each intensifies that stress. Yet each alliance contributes a warmth and an acceptance, even in the face of potential disaster, which, though only briefly enacted, is forever felt.

A child who feels unloved by her parents, the only Jewish girl in her small circle, Patty Bergen of Bette Greene's *Summer of My German Soldier* (1973, YA) is alienated and friendless until she meets young Anton Reiker, a German prisoner of war. When Anton escapes, Patty offers him shelter, food, and compassion; for the first time, the lonely girl believes she has a friend. By these acts, Patty stands against her family and her community and in so doing takes a long step toward adulthood, for she also comes to love Anton. Wise beyond his years, Anton keeps her feelings and his own within the perspective of friendship: "Even if you forget everything else I want you always to remember that you are a person of value, and you have a friend who loved you enough to give you his most valued possession." Though this deep, brief friendship precipitates great trouble and further alienation for Patty, it also marks the beginning of her self-respect and of her maturation.

In Carolyn Doty's *A Day Late* (1980), Katy Daniels, seventeen, begins her journey home by hitching a ride from Sam Batinovich. Despite misadventure and misunderstanding, the pair become friends. Sam, the protagonist, is grieving over the recent death of his teenaged daughter, fretting over the apparent decay of his marriage. Katy is pregnant and unwed and dreads telling her parents about her situation. Both Katy and Sam are tempted and tested during their short time together, but Carolyn Doty suggests that both will survive and perhaps even be stronger as a result of their troubles. Their support for one another is symbolized by their very brief affair, their first positive step toward separate futures. By making love as loving friends rather than as lovers, Sam and Katy demonstrate, to themselves and to one another, the value each places upon their friendship, the healing it has effected.

Because Deborah Blau and her fellow inmates of a home for the insane, the setting of *I Never Promised You a Rose Garden* (1964) by Joanne Greenberg (pseudonym, Hannah Green), do not trust themselves, it is almost impossible for them to trust one another, even though they are thrown together in terrible intimacy. Her cautious acceptance of Carla, however, dramatizes Deborah's progress, and eventually, the girls become real friends.

> She had not seen Carla much lately, but when they were together there was a special closeness between them. They might have been friends anywhere, but because they had been sick together and had fought out of it at the same time, their comradeship was tinged with the aura of emergent life and struggle.

Greenberg contrasts this relationship with the wary—though loving —attitude of Deborah's family and the coldness and distrust of people "outside."

Friendships formed by adolescent females, then, are subject to the same pressures as are any friendships. Young women seem, however, to be particularly sensitive to the ways in which society evaluates these relationships, often wishing that their self-esteem be gratified not merely by the presence of a friend but by the presence of a socially desirable friend. In the selection of any friend, male or female, peer or elder, as in the multitude of other choices adolescents must make, there is a certain amount of peril, and some friendships are simply ill-considered and damaging. Surprisingly but gratifyingly, however, these authors suggest that occasionally the greatest risks—such as those taken by Patty Bergen (*Summer of My German Soldier*), Katy Daniels (*A Day Late*), and Deborah Blau (*I Never Promised You a Rose Garden*)—result in the greatest gain.

In friendship, as in almost every other relationship adolescent females undertake, the ultimate challenge is inescapable: young women must dare to change and to grow, and their comrades must allow them the freedom and scope to do so. Often, friends must chance the loss of their relationship in order to redefine it to suit newly emerging needs —or, sometimes, they must relinquish it and move on to new associations. As a hiding place, friendship is only temporarily useful; if young women maintain that refuge too long they fail their obligation to themselves and to their companions.

CHAPTER IV
Females in Crisis

A large number of novels of adolescence force their youthful protagonists or subordinate characters to confront various social problems—
crime, racism, drugs, alienation, etc.—in short, all the conflicts and tensions of contemporary society. For the teenager, such a confrontation
may be especially pivotal. Her life is just beginning, and the choices she
makes now will influence the course of her life. As we might expect,
some young women are victimized, even destroyed, by their moment of
crisis, while others find within themselves resources that enable them to
survive, even to be strengthened.

Additionally, it should be noted that the young person may play
many different roles, which sometimes shift as her adventure proceeds.
She may be primarily a victim, or she may be a victimizer. She may be
merely an observer, or she may be an active participant. She may begin
as potential victim and develop strength to become a solver of crime or
even an avenger. She may move toward or away from socially acceptable behavior.

The nature of the social evil that she confronts is also important. In
many novels of female adolescence, her sex or sexuality is central to her
experience. Thus we find a relatively large number of novels employing
themes of rape, prostitution, pornography, and the like. However—
and this might not have been expected, given assumptions about female
passivity and helplessness—the young women are not universally victims in these novels which consider the underworld of contemporary
sexuality. Occasionally, they are shown escaping from that world and
even acting to change—or destroy—it.

Nevertheless, the general pattern is one of female helplessness,
with the young women tending to be victims or, less often, observers.
And thus the novels in which they play more active, assertive roles form
an important counterbalance to those which tacitly accept or actively
support the conventional view of woman as passive accepter of her fate.

Three rather miscellaneous novels indicate the kinds of roles or
functions that writers of social criticism have tended to assign to their
important adolescent female characters in the period under study: as
primarily symbolic, as weak and passive, or as strong and assertive. In
Dagon (1968) by Fred Chappell, Mina Morgan, about sixteen, represents
the depths of degradation American culture can reach. So dense is the
imagery of this tale set in the contemporary South, that neither Mina nor

the protagonist, Peter Leland, can be grasped as a real person. When Leland, a minister, repairs to his decayed family farm to write a book about his theory that the ultraproductivity of modern America is a form of worship of Dagon, "symbol of both fertility and infertility," he falls prey first to his own weaknesses and then to Mina's debasing control. Mina is used as a motivating force in Leland's crisis of the soul depicted in this extended allegory, and she is thus a literary device, not a rounded character developed in her own right.

The other two authors, on the other hand, are interested in their characters *as* characters. In *Rumors of Peace* (1979), Ella Leffland uses an adolescent primarily as victim, buffeted by a variety of social currents and events. This novel vividly portrays the effects of fears of war and of wartime hatred and hysteria upon those not directly touched by the fighting. The teenager's lack of experience together with the woman's assumed passivity makes her especially appropriate to fill this role. Only eleven when World War II breaks out, Suse Hansen reacts sharply to it, and it haunts her adolescence. She is terrified that Mendoza, California, her home town, will be bombed; air-raid practices at school and on her block only increase her fright and offer no reassurance. An explosion in a nearby harbor sends her running seven miles to reach her parents so that they can die together, and when she finds that they are safe, she trudges all the way back to the home of friends, where she is staying the night. She worries about her brother, a serviceman overseas; every letter (and every gap between letters) increases her tension. She falls prey to extreme racism, hating the Japanese particularly and rejoicing in the "relocation camps" to which the Nisei have been banished. Through small events and epic moments, Leffland extends her use of the war as a symbol of the trials and pains of maturation, the key image in the novel.

The third of these novels makes of its adolescent female a more positive role model. In *The Amiable Meddlers* (1961) by Josephine Lawrence, in fact, it is the young woman who becomes the rescuer of older, but less competent adults. The title characters, Belle and Zinnia Bruell, are concerned about and distressed by the marginally legal but unethical exploitation of an elderly friend by a Snopes-like family of usurpers. Belle and Zinnia, however, can offer little more than sympathy and worry in behalf of their friend; in contrast, their quiet, sporadically efficient, law school–bound ward, Jenny Faler, fifteen, uses her network of studious friends to set potentially corrective legal aid into motion. Lawrence contrasts Jenny's quiet effectiveness with the Bruells' ineffectuality in a gentle study of the generation gap.

Dagon, Rumors of Peace, and *The Amiable Meddlers,* then, suggest something of the variety of attitudes toward and literary uses of young women to be found in novels of social criticism of our period. We will see these, and other, approaches to the adolescent female character as we look at a number of other books which illustrate the diversity of social conflicts and problems into which recent authors have plunged their youthful characters.

A major group of novels stresses sexuality. The central themes here are prostitution and rape, and the usual role for the young woman is that of victim, although some girls are shown profiting from their own apparent victimization or that of others. Joseph Hansen (*Skinflick*) and Joyce Carol Oates (*them*) feature characters who seek to use their sexuality to their own profit; for neither is the attempt successful.

As a teenager, Loretta Botsford, in *them* (1969), has a dreary, back-breaking job and keeps house for her unemployed, disoriented father and her sullen older brother. She lives for Saturday nights when romance and adventure may befall her. Unreasoning, vague, preoccupied with her looks and her femaleness, Loretta stumbles into a sexual relationship with a boy who excites but doesn't really interest her. When her lover is shot to death by Brock, her brother, Loretta protects herself by having intercourse with a young police officer who, in return, conceals the Botsford siblings' roles in the murder. Joyce Carol Oates recounts Loretta's adolescence and adulthood (which begins with marriage to the young policeman) and shows how Loretta's fate mangles the lives of her children. In a very real sense, the lives of all these characters are ordained by Loretta's brief affair, Brock's crime, and her subsequent "trade-off" marriage.

Charleen Sims, well into her teens but looking like a prepubescent child, is the major motivational force in Joseph Hansen's *Skinflick* (1979), and private detective Dave Brandstetter's search for the missing youngster is the organizational pattern for this crime novel. Determined to break into films, Charleen has been haunting Los Angeles' Sunset Strip, trading sex for "breaks," principally with men who deal in pornographic films. Charleen's characterization is slowly revealed as Brandstetter's search progresses, but the girl remains a shadowy, rather pitiful, incomplete character throughout; this device underscores her limited potential for developing into a fully matured, effective adult.

While both Loretta (*them*) and Charleen (*Skinflick*) use their sexuality in attempts to attain certain desired outcomes, neither truly becomes a prostitute. A number of other portraits, however, examine the experiences of young women who have actually entered that life. In fact, Oates' novel, *them*, includes another characterization, that of Loretta's daughter, who is affected by Loretta's own behavior in ways that are purely destructive; the daughter goes beyond her mother in overtly and consciously selling her sex.

According to the novel's introduction, Joyce Carol Oates based *them* on the history of one of her University of Detroit students. For protagonist Maureen Wendall, life is dream and nightmare. Growing up, Maureen studies the behavior of her mother and her mother's women friends, often puzzling over, even dreading, her own coming maturity.

Life becomes even more confusing when Loretta, the mother, pushes her daughter into a sort of surrogate wifehood toward Pat Furlong, Loretta's second husband. Because of tensions between husband and wife, Loretta often forces Maureen to care for Furlong when he is drunk, wait up for him, rub his "bad back." The hazily understood, unspoken, frightening sexual potential underlying this situation terrifies Maureen who wants to "get money" so that she can "get away." At sixteen, she earns a good bit of money as a prostitute, but when her hoard is discovered, Furlong beats her unmercifully, sending her into a kind of stasis for many months. Strangely untouched by her sexual activity, Maureen has enacted a kind of self-fulfilling prophecy, bringing truth and reality to her mother's earlier, unfounded accusations of "bad" behavior.

Equally grim pictures of helpless young women exploited and then, more often than not, discarded are given in several other novels. Interestingly, these youngsters are particularly vulnerable, for various reasons—because of membership in a minority group, because of extreme youth, or because they are runaways. For example, as a Chinese-American, Crystal Tam of *Hammett* (1975) by Joe Gores is considered fair game for procurers who believe that the law in 1920s San Francisco will take little interest.

Sandy Johnson's 1979 novel about child prostitution in New York City, *The CUPPI* (police jargon for "Circumstances Undetermined Pending Police Investigation"), follows the investigation of the death of twelve-year-old Frederica ("Freddie") Charles, who fell to her death from a hotel window. Freddie and Mary Ann ("Winter") Richards had run away from their New Jersey homes to New York City, where they became involved with pimps and pornographers. The protagonist is a free-lance photographer who becomes obsessed with the case because of Freddie's uncanny resemblance to his own daughter, Donna ("Donnie") Wood. All three girls are portrayed as still children, though Freddie was somewhat more knowing and experienced sexually than the others. Sometimes clumsy in style, the novel is an illuminating examination of a contemporary phenomenon.

The advice of an experienced prostitute, "Turn down any trick you have a funny feeling about; always get your money up front; go twice for no one; save your body," proves much harder to follow than to hear for sixteen-year-old Robin Ward, protagonist of *On the Stroll* (1981). Alix Kates Shulman uses Robin's experiences to explore the plight of teen-aged runaways, pimps' methods of luring these children into prostitution, the terrors and yearnings which bind the girls to their procurers, and some grim details of their encounters with their clients. For Robin, "Tricking was like Indian wrestling—seeing whose contempt was stronger." Because she meets no man who refrains from exploiting her, her contempt—and her panic—grow. Her abusive father, her pimp, a college-student lover, and a "straight" employer all see Robin as a commodity to be used in one way or another. Each man contributes to her sense of isolation, helpless anger, and self-contempt, emotions barely concealed beneath a veneer of toughness and confidence.

The fact of victimization and its impact upon the victim may lead to unexpected outcomes. Crystal Tam's Chinese-American heritage may have made her an easy target for those who wished to corrupt her to their own profit, but the process unleashed by her mistreatment takes unexpected directions. Evil begets evil, as this young woman responds to her experience in perhaps the only way open to her. *Hammett* (1975), by Joe Gores, portrays Crystal Tam, fifteen, as generator of homicide and corruption in a fictitious account of Dashiell Hammett's work as a private investigator. "He was looking at evil: sprightly, beautiful, and totally corrupt. . . . The face, framed in its gleaming mane of ebony hair, was a child's face. But it was made up as a woman's—and had a look of innocent depravity that was terrifying." Crystal acts to avenge the sexual abuse she has absorbed as the unwilling child-mistress of several older men and as a prostitute in Prohibition-era San Francisco. Her actions and motivations are described rather than dramatized, and the character never comes alive.

Characters in two other novels are in "the life" of their own free will and for their own reasons. These are assertive, angry young women who see prostitution as a way of expressing their bitter rejection of their society. Their method of expression may be self-destructive, but it is nevertheless the method they find possible and appropriate. Where Crystal (*Hammett*) sought to fight back against those who had forced her into prostitution, these girls use their profession as a weapon against others.

Neither her father's fury, her mother's tears, nor the best efforts of Spenser, a tough, Hemingwayesque private detective, can dissuade April Kyle from prostitution in *Ceremony* (1982) by Robert B. Parker. Though her school counselor sees this behavior as "extreme" rebellion against "a fixed parental expectation and an inflexible parental stance," in the eyes of Spenser and his creator, April's determination takes on even greater significance. Her behavior symbolizes the lives of many youths to whom modern American society has allowed no true childhoods, no true innocence. The best Spenser can achieve is a desperate compromise; he turns April over to a decent madam, thereby getting her out of Boston's "Combat Zone," and April's story stands as an indictment of contemporary morality and values.

Doreen, a major character in *McCaffrey* (1961), is a teenaged New York City prostitute under the protection of a smooth but dangerous pimp called the Tiger. The Tiger uses her in a successful effort to enlist the services of protagonist Vincent McCaffrey, another disillusioned teenager. For Doreen (as later for Vincent) prostitution is a means of retaliation against a vicious, disenchanting world; in her case, a world which discriminates against her for being partly black: "I'm ashamed of myself for being black and then I'm ashamed of being ashamed." Doreen is the means of Vincent's sexual initiation and also the only respite he can find from the prostitute's world, once he enters it, but in author Charles Gorham's view, the relief the two can offer one another can be, at best, only short-lived.

The veneer of cynical control and cheeky assurance attained by the successful prostitute enables her to ply her trade, but as Doreen illustrates, that veneer can cover anger, self-hatred, and fear. An equally deceptive appearance conceals the truth about Clemmie of *The Gaudy Place* (1973) by Fred Chappell. By the time she is nineteen, Clemmie has been a prostitute for three years and is about to be abandoned by her pimp. Though she appears to be street-wise and hard, Clemmie is really not self-confident, always worrying about her unruly hair and her lack of friends. In Clemmie, Fred Chappell creates a realistic and touching portrait of a girl whose limited dreams and ambitions are threatened.

Two novels by Robert Gover show a more genuinely confident young prostitute, one who seems to be at home in her world even while she seeks to use her success in it to move on to better things. To offset feelings of depression, loneliness, and immaturity ("No car, no girl, and that second half semester staring me in the face"), J.C. Holland, a college student in *One Hundred Dollar Misunderstanding* (1961), sets out to do a bit of "research" into the folklore that "the Negro is sexually superior to the Whiteman." He gets more than he bargains for when Kitten, a fourteen-year-old prostitute, assumes that he is rich and he assumes that she "likes" him. Mistakes and complications multiply during a hectic weekend; J.C. has lots of "experiences," but he doesn't learn much. J.C. and Kitten both narrate this story, he still trying to rationalize his behavior and his sexual and cultural ignorance, Kitten pursuing her own concept of upward mobility. Gover attempts to use his young protagonists to mock and debunk racist attitudes and misconceptions, but his efforts are not always successful. The characters' language is often blunt, explicit, and, in the case of Kitten, loaded with dialect.

In Robert Gover's *Here Goes Kitten* (1964), a sequel to *One Hundred Dollar Misunderstanding*, Kitten, now seventeen, is known as Gigi Abercrombie and is trying to break into a singing career in a shady nightclub. J.C. Holland reenters her life by introducing her to Herman Pennypacker, a political boss, who dies while in bed with Kitten (still also working as a prostitute). She proves to be as resourceful as she is street-wise during their efforts to conceal the disaster. These novels, however, lack depth both in their portrayal of the adolescent prostitute and in their examination of her life and milieu.

Prostitution presents at least the possibility of the young woman having chosen to use her sexuality for her own purposes; rape, however, is by definition the sexual violation of a woman by force—physical or psychological, actual or threatened. Only recently has it become widely understood that rape is not truly a sexual act; rather it is an act of violence, in which the victim's powerlessness is dramatically demonstrated as she is degraded in a particularly humiliating way. These statements apply also, we now realize, to homosexual rape of males, but their particular and usual application is to rape of women. These recent insights are not always present in fiction, even very recent fiction, and there is a long literary tradition of the "romantic rape" (the rape desired by the woman). Treatments of rape of very young women, however, universally stress the violence inherent in the act. The youth of the victim, perhaps, makes her rape particularly distasteful and makes her become, after the rape, a particularly pitiable personage.

In Evan Hunter's *Last Summer* (1968), two girls' developing sexuality leads to a violent crisis. Sandy, who is apparently sixteen, is vivacious, outgoing, open, and apparently kindhearted. She meets David and Peter at the beach on the Atlantic island where their families all spend the summers, and the three become inseparable. Sexual undertones are strong in their relationship. The boys are startled when she removes her bikini top in their presence, and then later they are pleased when she encourages them to "feel her up" simultaneously at a movie. In sharp contrast is Rhoda, who is, at fifteen, shy and insecure, if not prudish. The startling climax to the novel occurs when Sandy encourages the boys to rape Rhoda. The novel is a highly symbolic treatment of adolescent discovery of both sexuality and cruelty; the beach and water are suitable settings for childlike, innocent play, while acts of cruelty occur in a ruined forest which has been burned over as a result of human anger and thoughtlessness.

In Hunter's treatment, then, Sandy must bear most of the responsibility for Rhoda's violation, but Rhoda's weakness can also be seen as an invitation to the mistreatment which she receives. The connection of sex and violence here is surely not accidental. What happens to Susie Davis, one of a number of adolescents who play significant roles in Thomas Williams's *Whipple's Castle* (1968), is similar to what happens to Rhoda. With Susie, however, we see the impact upon the victim of the rape; and even though she is a subsidiary character, serving to motivate and explain the behavior of several other characters, her fate makes a strong statement about mistreatment of vulnerable women seen only as passive sexual beings. The shy, hero-worshipping daughter of a disreputable family, she is victimized by the son of a prominent family: he tricks her into believing she is to meet the young man she adores, and a gang rape ensues. Subsequently, she becomes promiscuous, apparently searching for companionship and esteem in the only way she knows—and never finding them except from clumsy young Horace Whipple, who comes to care about her. His rage at her repeated victimization and the slanders of her even after her pathetic and sordid death trigger the novel's violent and tragic climax. Her story reveals the evil in an apparently peaceful community.

The harshness of society toward the weak and helpless is clearly dramatized in *Orphan Jim* (1975) by Lonnie Coleman, when Trudy Maynard is brutally raped and beaten by a stranger who encounters Trudy and her little brother during their desperate search for a secure home. Trudy, practical and stern, accepts the violation as a fact of life—acknowledging only much later that it makes her hate and fear men.

Not surprisingly, little that is good, for either the developing young women or for their society, comes out of these tales of prostitution and rape. They are consistently stories of thwarted hopes, destroyed ambitions and talents, and embittered survival—for those who do survive. Novels treating other sorts of criminal activity show somewhat more varied patterns. In novels using murder as either an inciting event or as a climax, there are at least four possibilities for the role a girl might play: she might be victim, detective, perpetrator, or avenger, or, of course, some combination of these. If she is victim, the chances are that she will appear, in life, only very early in the novel, serving simply to get things going, and her character will be developed primarily to explain the motivations of others. Thus although use of adolescent females as murder victims might seem peculiarly appropriate, given the assumed double weakness and vulnerability of young women—because of their sex and their youth—such characterizations are not apt to be particularly rich or full.

The idea of the young woman as detective calls to mind images of Nancy Drew and her like. The genre of detective novels for girls continues to thrive, as any visit to a young people's section of a library or bookstore will make clear. Such books have the virtue of depicting assertive, vigorous young role models, but they lack distinction as novels and are not covered here. Margaret Echard's *I Met Murder on the Way* (1965), which does make interesting use of a pair of youngsters as detectives, however, is worth noting. Though both are only teenagers, Bryn Pomeroy and Betsy Foster are aunt and niece. When two of the girls' relatives die suddenly, each has good reason to suspect Dr. Phillip Grieg, with whom both are infatuated. Bryn's feelings are complicated by jealousy because Dr. Grieg is married to her sister, Kathie. Betsy's feelings are complicated by loyalty to Kathie and by frightening information only she knows. The steps Betsy and Bryn take to control the ensuing action are dictated by their widely differing personalities and by their often divergent goals. The resulting conflicts make this a satisfying mystery yarn.

Several interesting novels consider the adolescent female as actual murderer or as murder suspect. Interestingly, two of these novels are based on actual cases. Particularly vicious is Kate Bender of *The Bloody Benders* (1970) by Robert H. Adelman, based on the same events as Mari

Sandoz's 1937 novel, *Slogum House*. Known only through the perceptions of a young man she has exploited, Kate is not a fully realized character. Her activities as the driving force in a family who rob and murder
guests at their trail-side inn and as a seductress who persuades her lovers to sell off the family's booty are distilled and reported from historical
records, recollections, and gossip. The narrator suggests that her cruelty, greed, and cold pragmatism result from a childhood marked by
rape and incest; she is a symbol of corruption, her stark criminality contrasted with the violence of other frontier-dwellers whose motivation is
to civilize the area.

The inciting incident in *Where Love Has Gone* (1962) by Harold Rubin
(pseudonym, Harold Robbins) is the killing of Tony Riccio, lover of Nora
Hayden, by Dani Carey, Nora's daughter by her first marriage. According to Dani and Nora, the only two witnesses, a violent quarrel between
Nora and Tony had been in progress, and Dani had acted on impulse in
defense of her mother. The coroner's inquest brings in a verdict of "justifiable homicide," but Dani is placed in the hands of juvenile authorities
and her custody becomes an issue. However, gradually we learn that
the act itself and the relationships involved were not what they initially
seemed; the substance of the novel is the revelation of the characters
and relationships that led to the killing. Loosely based on an actual case,
the novel is more a sensational tale than a thoughtful examination of
motives and social forces.

In a far finer novel, a concealed accidental death, in effect though
not in intent a murder, shapes much of the later lives of the girls responsible. In *Sula* (1973) by Toni Morrison, Sula Peace and Nel Wright undergo an unusual and devastating initiation into maturity. The girls are
playing on a riverbank and are joined by a little boy, Chicken Little.

> Sula picked him up by his hands and swung him outward then
> around and around. His knickers ballooned and his shrieks of
> frightened joy startled the birds and the fat grasshoppers. When
> he slipped from her hands and sailed away out over the water
> they could still hear his bubbly laughter.
> The water darkened and closed quickly over the place where
> Chicken Little sank. The pressure of his hard and tight little fin-
> gers was still in Sula's palms as she stood looking at the closed
> place in the water. . . .
> The water was so peaceful now. There was nothing but the
> baking sun and something newly missing.

The girls tell no one about the incident, and when Chicken Little's body
is eventually found, no one connects them with his death. Nevertheless,
Sula and Nel are punished, for the accidental murder reveals that they
are unable to accept real responsibility and signifies that neither Sula nor
Nel will ever be able to establish an enduring relationship with any man.

And finally, a positive portrait of a strong, assertive young woman, who grows in strength as she learns about evil in herself and in others, emerges in Mattie Ross, an avenger. A youngster possessed of strong will and a sharp tongue, Mattie, fourteen, sets out to pursue and to punish the man who robbed and murdered her father. In *True Grit* (1968) by Charles Portis, Mattie recruits tough, "mean" Rooster Cogburn, a Federal Marshall, and LaBoef, a handsome Texas Ranger, to help her impose justice upon the killer and his gang. Her quest takes her into Indian Territory where she confronts evil in a number of guises. She learns a great deal about herself, her companions, and her enemies; and while she discovers that all human beings are sadly flawed, she also confirms her own principles and learns that strength, support, and tenderness are sometimes offered by seemingly calloused individuals. The avengers' uneasy alliance not only provides Mattie with an unusual extended family but also generates a useful subplot and contributes greatly to her maturation. The crime which triggers this plot can, then, fairly be said to be the most influential event in Mattie's life.

As complex in its thematic possibilities as the crime of murder is the crime of kidnapping, which may be taken also to include hijacking and criminal confinement of others. Again young female characters may be victims or victimizers or may be connected to victims or victimizers in varied ways. Added here is the potentiality for relationships between the captive and captors, relationships which may change over the course of the imprisonment.

A particularly interesting study in shifting relationships is found in Mendal W. Johnson's *Let's Go Play at the Adams'* (1974), in which five middle-class youngsters, including Dianne McVeigh, a girl of seventeen, and Cindy Adams, ten, imprison Barbara Miller, a twenty-year-old babysitter. They call themselves the Freedom Five and at first rejoice in the independence they will now have, with the Adams parents in Europe for two weeks and the babysitter under their control. What began as a game, continuing games played earlier by the youngsters in pure fun, gradually becomes deadly serious. With the controls represented by the parents absent, the young people discover the actual power that they now have and slowly begin to exercise that power in earnest, tormenting Barbara and living in hedonistic freedom. Their growing awareness of authority and their willingness to exploit their physical mastery of the situation accompany a chilling lack of empathy with the decent young woman, little older than they, who was intended to watch over them. Their lack of empathy for her doubtless develops from their adolescent lack of experience; testing out themselves and their willingness to risk, they descend into a maelstrom of amorality. The novel studies what happens to both captors and victim as the relationship between powerful and powerless, those positions ironically reversed, affects them all.

Contrasting with the captors of *Let's Go Play at the Adams'*, who are corrupted as a result of their actions, is Susan Crandall, in *The Under-*

ground Man (1971) by Kenneth Millar (pseudonym, Ross Macdonald), who becomes a kidnapper in a desperate attempt to evade evil. To find six-year-old Ronnie Broadhurst, detective Lew Archer must solve a crime buried in the past. Ronnie has been kidnapped by nineteen-year-old Susan Crandall, herself more victim than villain. As a very young child and again, recently, as a confused adolescent, Susan has been an innocent witness to murder. Irrational, frightened, often drugged, she believes that only by escape from her parents and their tainted, hidden relationships can she save herself and Ronnie. Her efforts, however, intensify their danger, terrorizing Ronnie, making Susan a criminal, and exposing them both to further exploitation. *The Underground Man* is one of several novels in which Millar explores the impact that the evil deeds of earlier generations have on their children and grandchildren.

For two victims of kidnappings, the experiences turn out to be ultimately undamaging or, surprisingly, even enriching. A first visit to a never previously met pen pal turns out to be a kidnapping in Doris Miles Disney's *The Hospitality of the House* (1964). Mandy O'Brien is eighteen, wealthy, experienced in some ways but naive in others. Her initial surprise at the crudeness and insensitivity of a young woman whom she had thought she knew well through their long correspondence grows to suspicions of the pen pal and her family as more and more details simply do not fit. She gradually realizes that it is no accident that she has been kept from any human contact outside of the pen pal and her family, and she finds the resources within herself to escape. Perhaps she does not really grow or mature, for she seems essentially unchanged by her experiences, but she is revealed as a thoroughly likable and believable young protagonist in an effectively plotted suspense novel.

Doris Mae Winter, in Nathaniel Benchley's *Welcome to Xanadu* (1968), is changed and matured by her experience as the victim of a crime. Kidnapped by a poetry-loving escapee from a mental hospital, she schemes to regain her freedom. An ignorant high-school dropout from a deprived background, she is practical and inventive. Her imaginative captor introduces her to Coleridge and Homer, teaching her that life and people are more complex than she has thought. She learns about

> the trouble of thinking things through; with two alternatives to choose from, you always had to worry if you were right. It was much simpler, say, to shoot a rattlesnake without thinking about it than to decide what to do about this man. But she had no choice right now, so all she could do was ride along and see what happened. She could decide later whether she'd been right or not.

Her wit and courage bring her through the experience unharmed physically, but the reader is led to believe she has been saddened and strengthened by her contact with the madman.

Another victim's experience is rather different because she is responsible not only for herself but also for a busload of children—she had been driving their bus when it was hijacked by terrorists in Robert Cormier's *After the First Death* (1979, YA). Young Kate Forrester feels responsible for managing escape for herself and her passengers. Her motivation is intensified by the realization that having seen the terrorists unmasked, she must surely be marked for death. As Kate copes with the children and her captors, much of her attention is also given to questioning her own bravery. Because there is no approving adult at hand, Kate remains largely unaware of the true courage and maturity she displays. Her struggle for control in a horrifying situation is an ironic, important subplot.

Prostitution, rape, murder, and kidnapping obviously present dramatic, often life-threatening challenges to immature young people involved in them, whether by choice or by accidents of situation. Physical survival is often at stake here. More ambiguous are the difficulties connected with other social problems such as drugs. Over the last several decades, complete social consensus about the dangers or values of drugs has been lacking, and the use of drugs has been particularly widespread among young people as well as among certain counter-culture groups largely made up of young people. Generally, however, our subject-novels stress the dangers of drugs, dramatizing their destructive effects.

Several authors examine the connection between drug use and membership in groups. These novels suggest that the adolescent need to belong, to feel part of some cohesive group beyond (perhaps replacing) the family is so strong that many girls are willing to adopt habits they believe to be harmful, such as drug use. Sometimes added to the power of the group is the attraction to a young male; the desire to be loved or needed can impel a girl to adopt the standards of her lover. Eventually, however, she may find those standards and behavior patterns destructive of other goals or of her own integrity, and so reject drugs and the group or person who led her to them. The relationship of drug use to group membership is dramatized by Alice Hoffman in *Property Of* and by Tony Hillerman in *Dance Hall of the Dead*; particularly clear descriptions of an eventual rejection of drugs occur in *Property Of* and in Kristin Hunter's *Lou in the Limelight*.

The nameless narrator of Alice Hoffman's *Property Of* (1977) lives with a gang leader and watches him destroy himself by drug-taking. When she recognizes that he is addicted, she tells us, "I knew McKay was a junkie. This was not an easy thing to know." She goes on to sum up her conclusions on drug addicts, gleaned from extensive observation:

> At first when he says he's holding the dope for someone, he is believed. I believed it, you would believe it, everyone believes it.

> Later when his eyes are heavy-lidded and dark it is most proba-
> bly a sty or the effect of too much gin and tonic. Surely. The nee-
> dle is a friend's; the works do not belong to him, they are a talis-
> man to ward off evil spirits or they belong to the diabetic who
> lives in the next apartment. He doesn't even know how the nee-
> dle got into his vein; it was a frame-up, someone implanted it
> there as he slept.
>
> This was not an easy thing to know; and I knew it. After all
> the tracks, after pawnshops began to display in their windows
> the electrical appliances that were once found in our apartment, I
> knew McKay had a habit.

Although she does sometimes take drugs with him, her stubborn sense
of self-worth and self-preservation enable her to keep from becoming
addicted herself, and she eventually frees herself from him. The novel is
oddly poetic, almost classically tragic.

Peripherally involved in drug-running because she is living with a
hippie-like gang of smugglers, Susanne, axis of a subplot in *Dance Hall of
the Dead* (1973) by Tony Hillerman, is alienated from the group because
she is not a party to the crimes, rejected by her boyfriend who values his
career above her, and unable to return to a loveless home. When she
must leave the commune, she is set adrift, searching for some sort of
stability, stability she has failed to find in the drug culture. Hillerman
compares and contrasts Susanne's painful situation with that of another
character, George Bowlegs, a Navajo lad, indicating failure on the part
of both Anglo and Indian parents to nurture their young successfully
and also signaling the potential failure of corrupt nontraditional "family" structures.

At first unwittingly, Louretta Hawkins becomes dependent to the
point of near brain damage upon psychotropic drugs, whose effects also
mar her performances as a singer. In *Lou in the Limelight* (1981, YA), the
sequel to *The Soul Brothers and Sister Lou*, Kristin Hunter fully exploits the
irony underlying Lou's addiction: she begins using alcohol and drugs in
order to foster her show-business career. Hunter also emphasizes the
suffering and changes in attitude and goals Lou must undergo before
she can say confidently, "I decided I wanted to use my brain—not lose
it." Though many challenges lie ahead, Lou believes that the temptation
to rely upon drugs is one maturation test safely behind her.

Hoffman (*Property Of*) and Hunter (*Lou in the Limelight*) center their
tales on youngsters from deprived backgrounds. Poverty and the need
for escape are crucial to the choices made by these young women. Patricia Welles, on the other hand, in *Babyhip* (1967), describes privileged
young people from the middle class, for whom drug use is primarily a
search for awareness, for experience, which they believe they can find
only through mood-altering drugs. Welles's subject is the effect on teenaged Sarah Green of drug experimentation and her brief involvement in
the counter-culture around Harvard in the 1960s. A dramatic revelation

that her "trip" on LSD had been caused by pure, unadulterated sugar is one of the factors causing her to leave her "fiancé" and head for New York with a more sensitive young man and with, perhaps, a greater awareness of herself and the responsibilities she owes to others. Throughout the novel, Sarah had been selfish and self-indulgent as well as extremely judgmental about others (she keeps Idiot Lists of those who fail to meet her very idiosyncratic standards). Drugs appeal, apparently, for physical sensation and for the sense of power they bring, and her forced recognition of the fake trip seems symbolic of other awakenings to the shallowness of her own life and attitudes.

A pervasive social ill of our period and country, less tangible and thus often less dramatic than the crimes and social problems discussed above, is racism. For young people, brought up to believe in the socially accepted ideals of the American system, a first confrontation with discrimination may be devastating. Conversely, for a young person reared in unthinking acceptance of the inferiority of some racial or ethnic group, a realization that members of that group are not after all very different from anyone else may be almost equally troublesome. In either event, the young person must acknowledge that her perception of reality does not match what she has been taught that reality is. For these adolescent females, the discovery of racism leads to knowledge of hypocrisy of the adult world and of society generally. That discovery is an important part of intellectual maturation; an emotional reaction to the discovery deeply influences other aspects of development.

Some novels stress the adolescent's awareness of what racism is. The girl may be shown in her first brush with prejudice, either as a victim or as an observer. Or, in novels of social protest concerned to depict the evils of discrimination, a long pattern of suffering may be established; in the latter case, the adolescent female, usually a victim, is less apt to be shown growing or learning from her experiences—she already understands and must simply be shown to suffer from the evil the author is dramatizing.

Two novels set in the past are particularly powerful in exemplifying the cruelty inflicted by racism. In *Jubilee* (1966), Margaret Walker examines the impact of slavery, the Civil War, and Reconstruction through the life story of Vyry, born a slave on a Georgia plantation. The fact that she is the daughter of her owner makes Vyry the object of a good deal of hatred from her mistress, and only her strong will, sound constitution, and courage enable her to survive. By the age of sixteen, Vyry has withstood personal abuse, watched others beaten and humiliated, observed the effects of the selling off of various fellow slaves, and become aware of the underground to the North. As the cook for the "main house," she is both capable and subject to considerable tension and pressure, for she is constantly under her mistress's eye, expected to exert a certain amount of authority without any acknowledged authorization for doing

so, and compelled to labor long and hard without the expectation of satisfaction or reward. Walker's matter-of-fact tone, her detailed portrait of
plantation life, and her depiction of Vyry as a determined, if often confused and suffering, survivor lend power to this indictment of slavery.

In *Orphan Jim* (1975) by Lonnie Coleman, set in the South of the Depression, Trudy Maynard and her little brother, Jim, are taken in by
kindly Hazel Fay. Formerly a prostitute, Hazel, who is black, is now the
cherished mistress of a white man, Mr. Harris. Like Harris, the children
are white, and this fact complicates Hazel's life. Quietly and matter-of-
factly, *Orphan Jim* comments upon the evils of racial discrimination, dramatizing them by the subterfuges Hazel undertakes to protect her new
family. Perhaps its most chilling indictment of racism is the children's
unspoken but clear understanding of the situation.

For some young American females, racial prejudice is an integral
part of the experience of growing up. The effects on the psyche of such a
girl can be devastating—whether she comes from the favored or the oppressed group. For example, Abigail Howland, the protagonist-narrator
of *The Keepers of the House* (1964) by Shirley Ann Grau, spends a fairly
isolated childhood, her primary companions the children of her white
grandfather, Will, and his white-Indian-Negro mistress, Margaret.

> Of course there were plenty of other children living on the place,
> Negro children from the tenant and the cropper cabins. . . . We
> didn't seem to play with them. I don't know why. Most times we
> didn't even see them; now and then we found them in the middle
> of a game, but they simply moved off. They wouldn't play—no
> matter we wanted to—they pulled away from us. . . . In town
> they played with white children. Maybe it was Margaret's chil-
> dren, the half-bloods, that they didn't want.

The situation causes Abigail to develop a passivity which marks much of
her life; throughout her adolescence and her early adulthood, she is consistently acted upon rather than acting. Only when the community calls
her to account for the liaison between Margaret and Will does Abigail
learn to make her own decisions, for she must strike back at the racial
bigotry that has simmered for years. Grau demonstrates how a person is
shaped by her personal and social backgrounds, for Abigail is clearly
pictured as the product of her area, the South, as well as of the storied,
violent, racist Howland clan.

Pecola Breedlove of *The Bluest Eye* (1970), Toni Morrison's powerful first novel, learns early that white people dismiss her as inconsequential.

> She looks at him and sees the vacuum where curiosity ought to
> lodge. And something more. The total absence of human recog-
> nition. . . . Yet this vacuum is not new to her. It has an edge;
> somewhere in the bottom lid is the distaste. She has seen it lurk-
> ing in the eyes of all white people. So. The distaste must be for

> her, her blackness. All things in her are flux and anticipation. But
> her blackness is static and dread. And it is the blackness that ac-
> counts for, that creates, the vacuum edged with distaste in white
> eyes.

She seeks solace in Mary Jane candies because she admires the pretty,
white, blue-eyed child depicted on the wrappers. To Pecola, eating the
candy is a kind of possession of blue eyes. Blue eyes, in fact, are her
symbol of beauty and acceptance, and she desperately sets about acquiring them for herself, praying persistently and passionately and even
consulting a sorcerer. Like everyone else in Pecola's life, the magician
exploits her, and she retreats into madness when the real world offers
no further hope.

While for obvious historical reasons, discrimination against blacks is
most familiar to American writers and readers, other group tensions exist and have been effectively employed in fiction. Anti-Semitism and
then, ironically, anti-German sentiments figure in a novel which uses
the special strains of the period of World War II. Patty Bergen of Bette
Greene's *Summer of My German Soldier* (1973, YA) is well aware of the racial bias of small-town Arkansas in the 1940s. She is also aware of religious discrimination: "my geography problem is in being a Jewish girl
where it's a really peculiar thing to be." But when it is revealed that she
aided an escaped German prisoner of war, she faces the full force of hatred; the town persecutes her parents; Patty is called a "Jew Nazi-lover"
and is ostracized even in the reform school to which she is sent.

Several novels use the special microcosms of school or neighborhood to represent the conflicts within and cruelties of the larger society.
In these works, vulnerable young people confront both overt racism and
the more subtle effects of careless cruelty.

The Friends (1973, YA) by Rosa Guy briefly but vividly dramatizes racial tension. Protagonist Phyllisia Cathy is taunted and despised by her
American-born black schoolmates because she comes from the West Indies. Her white teacher uses Phyllisia as a scapegoat.

> I knew it suddenly. Standing in front of the room, her blond hair
> pulled back to emphasize the determination of her face, her
> body girdled to emphasize the determination of her spine, her
> eyes holding determinedly to anger, *Miss Lass was afraid!!* She
> was afraid and she was using *me* to keep the hatred of the chil-
> dren away from *her*. I was the natural choice because I was a
> stranger and I was proud.

When Miss Lass's control snaps and she openly shows her hatred of
blacks, the students retaliate, and the class descends into screaming
chaos, all control gone. "When you want to get even with whitey, just
call them dirty cracker or Jew, and that gets 'em," is one of Phyllisia's
first lessons in American race relations, and it is set against her next major experience, a race riot in the Harlem streets. Rosa Guy clearly dem-

onstrates the pervasiveness of racism and shows how it damages the
children who are its victims.

In *Ruby* (1976, YA), the sequel to Rosa Guy's *The Friends*, Ruby
Cathy, also from the West Indies, is unprepared for the kind of racism
she encounters in her Harlem school as well as for the racial commitment of her lover, Daphne Duprey. Like the other students, Daphne
considers Ruby an Uncle Tom when she aids their crippled, white
teacher with unfailing courtesy in the face of Miss Gottlieb's open, unremitting hatred and scorn: "I can hardly wait until they leave my room
with their smell of eyetalian garlic and nigger sweat." Ruby believes that
her actions stem from her heritage of courtesy to the old and weak and
from her unwillingness to see anyone needlessly humiliated. While
Daphne recognizes a quality of heroism in Ruby's behavior, she also believes it arises from Ruby's profound need to be loved. These tensions
complicate and severely damage the girls' relationship, and this motif illustrates the pervasive damage racism inflicts.

The effect on two families, one black and one white, of a black family's moving into a previously all-white neighborhood is studied in
Christopher Davis's *First Family* (1961). Kate Charles, the thirteen-year-
old daughter of white liberals, befriends Scotty McKinley, the black son
of the new neighbors. Both are bright young people, and after some initial hesitations they become close. Kate is an outgoing girl, popular at
school, and trained by her parents to fairness and openness in her deal-
ings with others. Less precocious than Scotty, she lets him take the lead
in their relationship, which eventually founders because she is not able
to handle the strains put upon it by Scotty's intensity and his occasional
suspicions of her motives. The novel is intended to be "about people,
not about integration," but its sensitive characterization of people who
are both types and individuals as they face a pressing social problem
makes it both an implied plea for tolerance and a demonstration of
the real difficulties faced by well-intentioned people in such situations.
Kate, like the adults, tries to do her best but is ultimately defeated.

Two novels centering on youngsters' growing awareness contrast
interestingly with each other. *A Question of Harmony* shows what happens when an idealistic, unprejudiced young white suddenly is brought
to the realization of discrimination, and *My Sweet Charlie* studies a relationship, imposed by circumstance, which forces a bitterly prejudiced
white to overcome her socially ingrained assumptions.

Jeanne Blake, the protagonist of *A Question of Harmony* (1965, YA)
by Gretchen Sprague, is an almost startlingly naive high-school senior.
The product of an apparently all-white public school and neighborhood,
Jeanne has few prejudices and finds it easy to establish a warm friendship with Mel Johnson, who is black. Jeanne and Mel have much in
common; she is a good cellist; he is a fine violinist, and their work together in a string trio is very helpful to the musical development of both

youngsters. After a performance of the group, Mel, Jeanne, and their pianist, Dave Carpenter, are refused service in a local restaurant, and frightened and intimidated as they are, the three youngsters bravely engage in a mini–sit-in. While the resolution of the situation at the restaurant is satisfactory to no one, it does awaken Jeanne to the world around her—and for a time causes her to doubt the decency of a number of people, perhaps a bit self-righteously. Some of Jeanne's evaluations of her circle are correct (her best friend's mother, for instance, is clearly a racist and a proselyting one); others are wrong. Sprague's indictment of racism and her caution that bigotry can cut two ways are clearly well-meant social lessons, but they are a bit too pat to be wholly effective.

Two racists, one an ignorant poor-white Southerner and the other a highly educated Northern black, meet and learn to overcome their prejudices in David Westheimer's *My Sweet Charlie* (1965). Unmarried but pregnant at seventeen and fleeing an angry father, Marlene Chambers takes refuge in a deserted summer cottage, only to have her sanctuary invaded by Charlie Roberts, a young black attorney from the North who has come to the South partly out of curiosity and become himself a fugitive from the law. At first, they hate and fear each other, but gradually they begin to talk to each other, and their mutual mockery and contempt evaporate as they begin to see each other as individuals instead of representatives of hated races. Each is led to examine attitudes and to think about stereotypes previously accepted in thoughtless ignorance. And so they become companions and friends, Marlene even beginning to think of Charlie as her baby's father. But their idyllic existence cannot endure: Marlene's pregnancy and their need for food and fuel force them into contact with the outside world, with tragic consequences. Marlene, however, has learned to value people as individuals and to look behind assumptions and stereotypes. The novel's depiction of their gradually deepening relationship is sensitive and believable.

Common to these novels about racism is the obvious conclusion that it is destructive, emotionally and psychically if not physically. Both those discriminated against and those making easy assumptions of superiority may be damaged; the stunted emotional development of Pecola (*The Bluest Eye*) and Abigail (*The Keepers of the House*) remind readers that both black and white are harmed by an unjust social system. Their retreats—into madness for Pecola and into passivity for Abigail— are, from another point of view, symbolic of alienation from a society which has no real place for them or which warps their perceptions of reality.

Alienation from school and from the world of her middle-class parents leads Jean ("Dutch") Gillis, protagonist of Katherine Dunn's *Truck* (1971), to run away to join Heydorf, her only true friend (or so she usually considers him). Like a latter-day Huck Finn, she carefully plans her escape and lives cleverly by her wits, but she lacks Huck's sympathetic concern for others. Her great fear is that she may subside into the conventional life she hates:

> Go back home after my little fling and work at some hokey job. Marry a service station attendant and sit in a cozy fucking little house with a toaster bringing up sleazy brats and reading fancy books to forget I'm dead. . . . Could kill myself. That's the only real way out of a real hole. I can just see it, painting little pictures among the pots and pans. Writing dumb poems about the moon after the kids are asleep. Little pretend ways out. And always back to the same house and the same man and the waste. I couldn't stand it.

Told in Dutch's stream-of-consciousness, the novel dwells on mundane, even nasty, physical details, and little sympathy for Dutch is engendered. But her sense of desperate alienation, not atypical of her times, is well conveyed.

Unlike Dutch, who *chooses* withdrawal, is Hatter Fox, who is repeatedly rejected and who can only react, instead of making choices. Seventeen-year-old Hatter, a Navajo repudiated by Indians as well as whites, is totally alienated. "For her, it would always be 'too late,' or 'too soon,'" decides young Dr. Teague Summer, the narrator of Marilyn Harris's *Hatter Fox* (1973). In her brief life she has known little except abandonment and abuse; she responds by alternate violence and withdrawal. Strangely drawn to her, Dr. Summer soon is determined to save her, though the responsibility this entails is often more than he can easily accept. Their complex and often ambiguous relationship and the depth of Hatter's hurts are gradually revealed. This haunting novel raises many questions, some practical (about Indian-white relations, about our institutionalized methods of dealing with troubled young people) and some more universal (about guilt and our responsibility for each other). Poor doomed Hatter and well-intentioned young Summer, haunted in their different ways, tell us much about our society and ourselves.

Another extreme sort of alienation is apparent in the gang structure as depicted in Alice Hoffman's *Property Of* (1977). Because they have no place in society, these youngsters, mostly male, construct a strangely ordered structure for their own world. The female protagonist, rejecting society and never really a part of the gang, is doubly an outsider. The novel is set in New York City and told by a seventeen-year-old girl who is in love with a gang leader but who refuses to become a gang member herself. Thus she is able to describe the gang with an insider's knowledge and an outsider's objectivity. She conveys the ordered structure of the gangs with their standards of behavior and rules for succession, and her story covers a gang fight, a struggle for power within one gang, and that gang's ultimate falling into disarray. Murder, rape, and drugs are integral parts of this experience. The gang seems to serve for these young people the functions of all social institutions. None of the gang members seems to have a family; even the narrator never mentions a home or any life before her involvement with the gang. The only member with a job apparently becomes a policeman only to give the gang a spy inside the police department. Their world is the Avenue which is the gang's territory, and it is a sad and brutal world, conveyed powerfully in sometimes oddly poetic prose.

The female adolescents discussed in this chapter are among the most troubled—and troubling—in this study. Some of them learn and grow as a result of their confrontation with evil in the form of crime or social injustice. Some, who do not grow, are nevertheless revealed to have within them resources that enable them to survive terrible experiences. But many others are weakened, corrupted, or destroyed. Perhaps this is not surprising, for many of these novels are novels of social protest, their authors having intended primarily (or at least incidentally) to demonstrate the effects on character of certain evils in our society. To make this demonstration, then, the authors chose impressionable adolescent females, young women at just the pivotal moment when they are trying to define themselves, to free themselves from their families, and to shape their own characters and futures. Confronting crime, violence, or discrimination at a particularly vulnerable time, and lacking, as so many of these young women do, the protection of nurturing families, many easily succumb to the damaging impact of physical or psychic violence. Among the most vivid portraits of adolescent females in the finest novels, as discussed in this chapter, are Loretta Botsford and Maureen Wendall (*them*), Sula Peace and Nel Wright (*Sula*), Hoffman's narrator (*Property Of*), Vyry (*Jubilee*), Abigail Howland (*The Keepers of the House*), Pecola Breedlove (*The Bluest Eye*), and Hatter Fox (*Hatter Fox*)—and of these only Vyry (a character out of the past) and perhaps Hoffman's narrator survive their adolescent experiences with enough strength and integrity intact to enable them to build successful lives as mature adults.

CHAPTER V
Females and Social Institutions

In the preceding chapter, we were primarily concerned with youngsters who felt themselves to be—or were—outside of social norms. They faced crises so radical that they were in imminent danger of losing their place in the social structure. Here, although some similar situations and dilemmas will be examined and, indeed, a few of the same novels will even be studied, basically the intent is to look at adolescent females who are in connection with society or with some socially accepted norms of behavior or belief. This does not mean, of course, that they easily accept these behaviors or beliefs. Some girls reject principles inculcated by school or church or turn away from hypocritical social norms; some move from rejection of societal values to reacceptance of those values; some, through gradual growth, gain an awareness of the true meaning of moral principles or religious faith.

The term "social institutions" is used inclusively here; we touch on a variety of educational, economic, and religious forces as they impact upon the girls in the subject-novels. Thus, girls in schools or in preparation for future vocations (or, even, avocations) are included here; additionally girls specially influenced by the class background or degree of wealth or poverty of their families as well as girls in conflict over questions of religious faith or ethical values will be examined.

Our subject-novels do not take seriously the claims that social and class mobility are easy in the contemporary United States or that there are but few harmful social effects of a class structure which is pictured as relatively rigid. Some representative works, examining girls from varied classes, suggest that social improvement is not easy, and that wealth and power, no less than poverty, may be corrupting.

Julius Horwitz's starkly naturalistic *The Diary of A.N.: The Story of the House on West 104th Street* (1970) is an almost plotless study of the life of its narrator, a black high-school girl living under intolerable conditions in New York City. Horwitz stresses not only her appalling physical surroundings but also the effect of the welfare system upon those it purports to serve. With horror, A.N. sees her mother succumb to the system and give up all attempts to better their lives. Drugs, crime, delinquency are all around. The gloom of the novel is relieved only slightly by the presence of a good teacher and a kind librarian, whose efforts will enable A.N. to develop her abilities and escape to a better life.

Distinctions based on social class are at the heart of Patricia Gallagher's study of life in a small town in west Texas, *The Sons and the Daughters* (1961). Jill Turner, the protagonist, is the daughter of a hardworking woman who runs a diner. Because of unfounded rumors about her mother's chastity (and about the identity of Jill's father) as well as because of her lack of social status, Jill is an outsider with few friends. Caste lines are strongly drawn in Shady Bend, and Jill's desire to escape the town is partly caused by her perception of lack of opportunity there. A brief affair with the son of a wealthy family brings little joy, but Jill also observes despair and suffering caused by unfulfilling relationships among both wealthy and poor. At the end, Jill's experiences have led her to a mature sense of what is realistic for her and to a potentially rewarding relationship with a young journalist.

The life of a middle-class New Jersey family in the 1950s is depressingly but authentically described in Patricia Dizenzo's *An American Girl* (1971). The father, a lawyer in New York City, is not as successful as he had hoped to be, and the mother is alcoholic. They fight regularly, and the children accept these fights as just part of daily life. The eldest, Celia, goes off to college, glad to escape. The youngest, Johnnie, is too small to understand. But the unnamed narrator and protagonist is as aware of the emptiness of their lives as she is a creature of the materialistic ethos surrounding her. She tries to make the house attractive, she is preoccupied with clothes and makeup, and she records in detail how she spends the money she earns by babysitting. Through her careful little essays on her activities and observations, Dizenzo both evokes and criticizes the prevailing attitudes of the times.

A horrifying portrait of the daughter of a rich and powerful family is presented by Charlotte Armstrong in *The Turret Room* (1965), a novel of suspense. Wendy had married at sixteen, apparently only in hopes of gaining control of her wealth. When that failed, she allowed the marriage to be dissolved and her young husband to be unjustly institutionalized. She shows no interest in her baby, and when her young husband returns seeking the child, she victimizes him again. Spoiled and amoral, she has no conception of others' feelings or needs; Armstrong suggests that some of her actions stem from a desperate attempt to escape the environment that has dehumanized her.

Inherited money and power are also destructive forces in *Where Love Has Gone* (1962) by Harold Rubin (pseudonym, Harold Robbins). Nora Hayden, apparently corrupted by her privileged background, destroys her marriage and almost destroys her first husband. Their daughter, Dani Carey, at fourteen feels deserted by her father and unloved by her mother. The novel is built upon the events that precede (shown in flashback) and those that follow a scene, never directly presented, in which Dani has apparently killed her mother's current lover. After the event, Dani's maternal grandmother tries to use her power and wealth to shield Dani from some of the potential consequences of the act, while Nora simply tries to protect herself. Through much of the novel, Dani's character and behavior are somewhat ambiguous, and the reader only gradually comes to understand many of the effects upon her of her background.

From these novels, a depressing picture of the American social caste system and its destructive impact upon vulnerable adolescent girls emerges. The powerlessness of the poor, the thoughtless cruelties of the bureaucracy, and the constant terror of violence and crime make life for A.N. a constant battle (*The Diary of A.N.*), but lower-middle-class life for Jill (*The Sons and the Daughters*) and upper-middle-class life for Dizenzo's narrator (*An American Girl*), while physically easier, is only marginally more enriching. And Wendy (*The Turret Room*) has been made into a selfish monster, while Dani (*Where Love Has Gone*) has been totally victimized by a lack of any love or support or understanding, clearly illustrating the corrupting power of wealth and inherited position. A.N. and Jill manage to remain more decent young people than any of the others, and it is notable that they, especially A.N., are the least apparently favored by fortune of all these young women.

Education has historically been seen by Americans as a way of social advancement for members of minorities and for the poor. The function of the schools, in this view, is that of inculcating middle-class standards, of teaching "proper" English, and of preparing young people for the world of work. Recent authors have tended to take a rather more jaundiced view of our educational establishment and of the effects of the schools, especially the public schools, upon young women. A.N. (*The Diary of A.N.*) is an example of a youngster for whom a kindly, understanding teacher is crucial, and there are others. But many young women do not find the schools nurturing. Indeed, the schools may be just as cruel in their effects as the heartless welfare system that victimizes A.N.

In Harriet Arnow's *The Weedkiller's Daughter* (1970), fifteen-year-old Susan Schnitzer faces a crisis when she is subjected to long-term study by a school social worker. Because at six she was taken abruptly from the care of her grandmother who had reared her and because an accident early in her life left her scarred, she is expected to be a good subject for study. Susan fears lest her forbidden associations with her maternal relatives be revealed, but independent study of psychology texts, her own quick brain, and a flair for dissimulation preserve her privacy and point up the inadequacies of school and counselor. Susan's preparation for the final interview serves as a frame for the novel, and this sequence reinforces one of Arnow's major points—most adults, even highly trained educators, know very little about the young.

The sexual harassment of a naive high-school girl by a male teacher whom she innocently worships is studied by Ellen Douglas in *A Family's*

Affairs (1962). Anna, a bright girl who lacks confidence, becomes a disciple of her math teacher. When he begins making sexual overtures, she at first does not understand, then lets him kiss and fondle her because she desperately fears offending him.

> Anna was too much a product of Presbyterian moral rectitude to be seduced; and she was also enough a woman to avoid seduction without openly offending. But all the time she went through the motions of responding to and at the same time warding him off, she was so lonely and guilty and confused, it seemed as if her whole life had been pushed away, like a finished jigsaw puzzle with its pieces just out of line.

Finally she solves her problem by avoiding him, but Douglas makes it clear that she has been scarred by the experience.

In Lois Duncan's *Daughters of Eve* (1979, YA), the quite varied members of a high-school sorority experience or observe a number of kinds of sexism in their school, their families, and society; these range from wife abuse by the father of one to sexual exploitation to variations in standards used to judge their efforts against those of their male counterparts. Their new advisor, a teacher deeply hurt and embittered by her own experiences of sexual discrimination in her career, encourages their justifiable resentment, with disastrous results. The novel, by a prominent writer of books for young people, is an interesting and complex study of a good cause being subverted by the excessive rage and inappropriate tactics of its adherents. Two violent acts and the dissolution of the group climax the novel, and one of the students, a gifted and perceptive young woman, sums it all up as she withdraws from further participation: " 'It's gotten out of hand,' Fran said. 'It's gone too far. The basic premise is sound enough, but there's so much hate, we can't even look at it clearly any longer.' "

American secondary education is devastatingly satirized in Al Hine's *Lord Love a Duck* (1961). The Consolidated High School in Nichols Corners, Iowa, is brand new and suffused with a rather smug complacency. Its curriculum is made up of courses in Communications Skills, Safe Driving for the Citizen, Workshop of Dramatic Skills, Mankind's Problems Skills, and the like. Barbara Anne Greene, the central female character, becomes a leading student by dint of

> throwing herself into every activity of the new school, thrilling, bewildering kaleidoscope of color, fellowship, aptitude, integration, self-development, citizenship, communication, experientiality, audio-visual techniques, empiricism, dissemination, dramalogues, grammalogues, mock-ups, cutouts, breakdowns, think sheets, do charts, work graphs, play plans, tooth maps, posturepedics, Manicheism, fire worship, anthropophagy, God knows what all.

Like Barbara Anne, other young women internalize the false values, the fads and easy solutions, of their society as those values are reflected in the schools where they spend so much of their time and which are often far more significant to the girls as the center of social life than as places of learning. For the narrator of Patricia Dizenzo's *An American Girl* (1971), school is the best part of life. Lessons, extracurricular activities, and fashions worn by high-school girls in the 1950s are described realistically by Dizenzo. The novel is an apparently formless collection of largely chronological sketches, some set at the narrator's New Jersey high school and some dealing with homework and other topics related to school. Her family situation is so bad that school often seems an escape.

Some young women are able to grow beyond the superficialities of the social world as reflected in the customs and behaviors of the American school system. Henrietta Snow, in *The Cheerleader* (1973) by Ruth Doan MacDougall, is an example of a young woman who is first caught up in typical adolescent status-seeking, trying to find acceptance in the group, yearning to be popular. But she is intelligent and refuses to repress her love of learning and her ambitions. Although she is perfectly capable of playing the old "feminine" game of subordinating herself and her intelligence to eligible young men, she does not allow herself to become too caught up in the game. For Gunthwaite High School's female students, becoming a varsity cheerleader is a pinnacle of achievement, ranking right up there with being Prom Queen. MacDougall organizes her fine novel around protagonist Henrietta Snow's cheerleading career from junior varsity through varsity. The cheerleading and Prom Queen motifs reveal Snowy's development: cheerleading success indicates her social growth, and being omitted from the queen's court teaches her to deal with disappointment with poise and grace. Other school activities —holding class offices and eventually serving as editor of the school paper—mark Snowy's intellectual development, for talk of teachers and actual classes is largely missing, and it seems to be Snowy's skill not only at studies (which is noted but not detailed) but also at administrative work on the paper that develop her confidence in her mind: "This year Snowy was more an executive than a student. At first she was surprised that everyone seemed a little afraid of her . . . and then she got used to it." This pattern of development gives her courage to try for admission to several of the best women's colleges and to aim for a career different from teaching or housekeeping, the usual goals for Gunthwaite girls. Stressing social and extracurricular work and keeping the roles of most adults extremely minor lends a vivid sense of studenthood during the 1950s to this fine novel.

Two other novels, *Earth Angels* and *The Last of Eden*, depict less typical schools and educational experiences. Both are set in private schools,

Earth Angels in a parochial school and *The Last of Eden* in a competitive school for the wealthy. Thus they do not mirror society and its values as the public schools do; instead they offer their youthful protagonists special opportunities and challenges.

Bright and intellectual, Martha Girlinghausen, in *Earth Angels* (1976) by Susan Cahill, is proud of the scholastic demands of her Catholic education, even as she resists its methods and strictures. So wholehearted is her rebellion, that her vocation decision is startling—even to Martha: "My future was set, . . . and it was worthy. It was also radical, total, and insane. I was leaving everything behind on shore—interviews, job, the classifieds, Saturday nights, Waterford glass, bunny rabbits. With time's winged chariot rushing at my rear, I had decided to become a nun." *Earth Angels* also describes Martha's early months in the convent, and Cahill provides not only a clear characterization of her protagonist but also a fascinating analysis of female parochial education in the 1940s and 1950s.

An exclusive boarding school, Turnbull Hall, on the Michigan shore of Lake Huron, is the setting for Stephanie S. Tolan's *The Last of Eden* (1980, YA). The school is an Eden, a refuge from her arid home life, for fifteen-year-old Michelle ("Mike") Caine, for there she has good friends; she is a member of an informal club called the D.E.T.'s ("Daughters of Emily Turnbull"), who carry on a "modest [but good natured] guerrilla warfare . . . against Turnbull's carefully ordered system." Additionally, she has an English teacher who first showed her the joys of poetry and now reads critically but sympathetically her poems. During Mike's sophomore and junior years, a number of events and relationships demonstrate to her the evil that underlies even this Eden. But this is presented as a necessary part of her maturation and its results are ultimately good.

The American schools, according to these novels, are not particularly effective in preparing their young female charges for life—if anything girls tend to be trained primarily for certain social roles. Some, of course, like A.N. (*The Diary of A.N.*) and, at almost the other extreme, Snowy (*The Cheerleader*), are so talented and sensitive that they refuse to be destroyed or corrupted by the pervasive mediocrity around them. They maintain their characters and dreams despite rather than because of any institutional influences. Clearly, the ordinary school is not seen as being particularly helpful in the young person's choice of career or her preparation for it. These choices and preparations must come from somewhere else, and a number of writers have examined girls with special dreams for their lives.

Two particular sorts of dreams are especially frequent in the novels examined here: careers in entertainment, especially film acting, and in writing. Perhaps neither of these is particularly surprising. Writers tend to use what they know, and the aspiring poet or novelist may well be a reflection of the writer herself at a youthful age. And the career goals in entertainment mirror some assumptions of our society: lovely young girls are expected to use their bodies and faces rather than their minds, and acting is a profession in which, or so young people dream, overnight success can be attained.

A number of these novels belong to the genre of Hollywood novels, satiric studies of the film world which use star-struck adolescents to illustrate the false glamor, the seductive but dangerously illusory dream of wealth and fame, of an industry that most authors see as exploitative and ultimately dishonest, throwing aside the young woman when she is no longer useful, if she ever does achieve any success—and of course few do. For members of minority groups, especially blacks, music may seem to offer the longed-for happy ending. In either case, the yearning for an immediate and dramatic success, bringing with it fame and fortune, is perhaps a reflection of an adolescent need for instant gratification, a desire to have it all—and to have it all *now*. Females, of course, have not had the opportunities to make their fortunes in sports that males have had, so it is not surprising that this theme, significant in novels about males, is absent here.

Barbara Anne Greene and Cassandra Keen are two examples of shallow young women whose yearnings for Hollywood glamor are shown in satiric novels to be unrealistic. The dream of movie stardom is a driving motivation for young Barbara Anne Greene and generates an important subplot in Al Hine's *Lord Love a Duck* (1961). She is "discovered" by a drunken talent scout and works hard to prepare herself for her big chance. Ambitions for fame and fortune in Hollywood, first inculcated by her mother and then adopted as her own life goal, inspire Cassandra Keen in Sandra Berkley's *Coming Attractions* (1971). Little hope of her reaching these goals is suggested, though she is bright and grows up to be beautiful.

Similar in ambition and appearing in a novel named identically to Berkley's is Daisy Fay Harper, of Fannie Flagg's *Coming Attractions* (1981), who intends to become a movie star. Toward this end, she sees every film she can; endures membership in the zany Jr. Debutantes' Club (which meets in the back room of the live bait shop and sponsors activities designed to transform girls into "ladies"); participates in school plays; and, eventually, enters the 1959 Miss Mississippi Contest, which is depicted as a totally cynical, corrupt enterprise. For Daisy Fay, however, it represents a chance to escape from Mississippi, to move toward the big time; she wants to win a scholarship to the Academy of Dramatic Arts. And escape she does; though, true to the comic tone of Flagg's novel, the results of the competition are wildly ironic, a combination of happiness, triumph, and disappointment.

Unlike Barbara Anne Greene (Hine's *Lord Love a Duck*), Cassandra Keen (Berkley's *Coming Attractions*) and Daisy Fay Harper (Flagg's *Com-*

ing Attractions), who consciously although naively choose their ambitions, Patsy ("Pig") Higgins, of William Goldman's *Tinsel* (1979), allows inertia to carry her into the fringes of the acting world. Characterized as "just one of those California blondes," Pig considers herself "dumb" and unimportant. Even though she earns good grades in high school, Pig defines herself primarily through her fondness for her boyfriend and her brother, both baseball players of some ability. Consequently, when those relationships fade, she makes no career choice but drifts into acting, never actualizing her very real artistic potential. Instead, she becomes a "health nut," gets along by living with various men and doing bit parts in road companies, all the while taking intense, concentrated care of her spectacular body, in her eyes, her major asset, certainly the only asset she understands or trusts. *Tinsel* demonstrates that Pig's adolescence establishes her self-definition forever and that her world accepts it also: in Hollywood, she is simply one of many beautiful, talented, doomed women.

More successful than any of these young women, at least temporarily, are Rusty Engleberg (*Domestic Arrangements*) and Daisy Clover (*Inside Daisy Clover*). Their novels, however, like the others, stress the shallowness and corruption of Hollywood. Before she is fifteen, Tatiana "Rusty" Engleberg, the protagonist of Norma Klein's *Domestic Arrangements* (1981), has starred in a well-received film, managed personal appearances, dealt with sexual propositions, evaluated future roles, coped with jealousy and possessiveness—and chosen, she believes, a career. Though both her parents are show business folk and though acting may be "in her blood," Rusty decides against stardom: "Maybe I'll act a little in between, but that's all." More realistic than the other Hollywood hopefuls, she instead plans to become an obstetrician because babies "almost always survive and everybody is so happy. It must be a terrific feeling to make people happy that way." Possibly, in this fashion, Rusty is resolving an inner conflict between the standards of her actress mother who can readily compromise with "art" and appear in soap operas and television commercials and those of her director-producer father who insists on doing serious drama or filming socially important documentaries.

The indomitable protagonist and narrator of Gavin Lambert's *Inside Daisy Clover* (1963) becomes a child star at the age of thirteen. When we first meet her, she lives with her harmlessly crazy mother and spends much of her time wandering on the California beaches and making records of herself singing popular songs in a booth on the pier. She describes herself then as "adolescent—pushing fourteen, and two buds pushing up like pears on a tree—I am an extremely *happy, adjusted polite young lady*. It's true I'm quite sophisticated for my age, but that's only skin-deep, and underneath the veneer I'll bet my simple healthy instincts against yours any day" (italics in the original). When one of her recordings leads to her discovery and stardom in films, she enters a new world in which much of her freedom is lost and she must fight to retain control of her own destiny. Her sister and the executives at the studio try to manipulate her and succeed, despite her protests, in committing her mother. Brief and unsuccessful relationships with several men mark her private life but her motherhood, at seventeen, is more fulfilling. When she loses her feeling for her music, she leaves Hollywood with her daughter, and makes a new life for herself and little Myrna in New York. At twenty-four a has-been and almost forgotten, she suddenly recaptures her flair, and as the novel ends, she is making a comeback. Her irrepressible courage carries her through all her trials, and she finally likens life to coffee, with its "rich burnt-coffee aroma, something I've never been able to resist . . . I always fall for the wonderful smell even though I know the taste will be ghastly and bitter." Daisy is funny and likeable, and her comic and sardonic narration makes her come vibrantly alive. At the same time, the novel gives a sharply satiric picture of Hollywood and the system that manipulated stars, like Judy Garland, who lacked the gritty realism and spunk that characterize Daisy.

If film stardom seems to offer worldly success and power to attractive young white women, music holds out a similar promise to black youngsters who have been ineligible to become ingenues in films because of discrimination against their color. In two books, published at a wide interval but covering a relatively short span of time in the life of her central character, Kristin Hunter has given a somewhat more hopeful view of how hard work can lead to skill and ability—and ultimately success—than these other authors.

Toward the end of *The Soul Brothers and Sister Lou* (1968, YA), Kristin Hunter symbolizes the maturation of her protagonist, Louretta Hawkins, by the modest success of the singing group which gives the book its title. In discovering that her career lies in music, in learning to apply makeup, to dress maturely, and to handle herself during personal appearances, Louretta also learns how to strike a balance between her own ambition and her mother's strict, traditional standards of behavior. It is notable that in this novel Hunter leaves the group at the outset of their careers, indicating that while Louretta shows clear signs of being able to handle adulthood and success, other members may not, and that this new life does not separate Louretta from her family but rather seems to cement their relationship. These efforts at realism do not wholly balance the almost simplistic happy ending accorded to this young recording artist–songwriter.

As Kristin Hunter continues her story in *Lou in the Limelight* (1981), Louretta Hawkins might seem to many young readers to be living a dream as her singing group, The Soul Brothers and Sister Lou, work toward stardom. Actually, almost every aspect of their lives as young performers struggling toward the "top of the charts" is nightmare rather than dream. Working day and night, shaping their new "images," eating unfamiliar food, *smiling* all the time, losing their chances for decent educations, living luxuriously but always broke, all these debilitating factors generate personal trauma, group tension, fear, and jealousy. In the sequel, Hunter darkens the happy future implied for the group at the conclusion of *The Soul Brothers and Sister Lou* and reminds young people that untrained, misused talent is no sure passport to the good life. For Lou, the choice between her talents—her abilities as singer and song-writer and her intellectual abilities and interests—is a major step in her true maturation.

The career of an entertainer, then, is greatly attractive to many young women. They are trained to make themselves attractive, to play roles of various sorts (not least in pretending to be other than they are as they strive to be attractive to boys), and, if they are white, they may see in acting the opportunity to make practical use of their appearance and chameleon-like ability to conceal their true thoughts and feelings. Or, if they are black, they may hope to employ the music that is a part of their culture to bring them success. In both cases the goals are similar: wealth, fame, power, and perhaps above all else the admiration of the multitudes. These young women are dreamers, often unrealistic, stubbornly ignorant of the harsh competition they must survive and the compromises they will be forced to make. They are shallow, by and large, attracted to the *results* they hope to win, not to the work itself. The glitter of *being* a star appeals, not the self-expression or creativity.

Quite different are those girls for whom writing is either an avocation or a desired future vocation, who are committed to the act of writing, not to vague dreams of future fame and fortune. They actually write —because they must, for self-expression—instead of dreaming about what they will be and have after they have attained their pot of gold. In several novels, these literary ambitions and activities are developed in significant subplots.

Caddy Bartholomew, the focus of one subplot in *The Jumping Off Place* (1962) by Garet Rogers, thinks of herself as a poet and is prepared to take foolish risks in order to get her verses published. She undertakes to smuggle out the poems of an established minor poet now a patient at the mental hospital which Caddy's father supervises, and into each packet she inserts some of her own work. This ploy eventually triggers both an attack by the madman and a bizarre investigation of the hospital by a staff member of the magazine to which the material is submitted. The ultimate consequences of Caddy's behavior are far from what she anticipates.

The urge to write is also a subordinate theme in Margaret Gray Blanton's *The White Unicorn* (1961). Maidie Chapman begins writing on her own and then is persuaded to try for restraint and brevity by a young reporter. At his behest, she practices fifty-word sketches of things she has experienced or observed, some of which are published by his newspaper and are quite well received. Her literary ambitions, however, never become a major theme of the novel.

Writing as therapy is an important theme in another novel. Cordelia Miller, of *Chez Cordelia* (1980) by Kitty Burns Florey, unlike the aspiring actresses we have looked at earlier, is almost solely concerned with the creative act itself, rather than with writing as a potential profession. Despite a lifelong distrust of words, Cordelia Miller narrates her own story, an act she clearly perceives as the making of a book. This activity is anything but pleasant for her: "I'm writing this account of my life . . . because I need to make sense of it . . . this is a labor not of love or of faith but of pure anguish." In her realization that the peace resulting from "writing out" her life may well be temporary, Cordelia signifies her developing maturity, her growing ability to evaluate the past, cope with the present, and plan for the future within the bounds of realistic expectation. In painfully embracing her parents' profession—writing—as a healing, confessional avocation, Cordelia demonstrates her willingness to undertake the difficult and to expand her skills in ways she has heretofore disdained. Cordelia's painful avocation generates a gentle irony which author Florey sustains throughout *Chez Cordelia*.

Quite specifically dedicated to professional goals are another young writer and her artist friend, two gifted young women depicted in Stephanie S. Tolan's *The Last of Eden* (1980, YA). Michelle ("Mike") Caine discovers her desire to be a poet in Miss Engles's English class at a Michigan boarding school, while Martha ("Marty") Sheffield is already committed to art before she arrives there. In contrast to Mike, whose mother seems totally uninterested in Mike's feelings, Marty's choice of art has been bitterly opposed by her family, but for her no other vocation seems possible. Both devote themselves to their work, Marty even winning a competition on the professional level and Mike never being separated from her journal. Other forces intervene to distract both girls from their work, but at the end of the brief novel, each returns with renewed commitment. The novel depicts naturally gifted and materially privileged girls who overcome either opposition or indifference as they dedicate themselves to their future vocations.

Another young woman whose talents and ambitions are creative is a hard-working musician. By the summer of her sixteenth year, the protagonist of *A Question of Harmony* (1965) by Gretchen Sprague, Jeanne Blake, is aware that she loves music profoundly and that she is an exceptionally skilled young cellist. Weekly practice sessions with a string trio, some performances with that group, and very serious work toward a concert solo and a music scholarship competition help Jeanne to realize that she may well have the ability, the interest, and the "feeling" to become a professional cellist. Both pleased and alarmed by the demands that musicianship places—and will place—upon her, Jeanne ponders the question of career choice in many scenes, under many circumstances. Exploration of the joys and demands of skillful performance, of the seriousness of purpose necessary for such a commitment, and of a youngster's natural hesitation when confronting such a choice is the real strength of this somewhat oversimplified young adult novel.

Caddy (*The Jumping Off Place*), Maidie (*The White Unicorn*), Mike and Marty (*The Last of Eden*), and Jeanne (*A Question of Harmony*) are all talented young women who are strongly self-directed toward achievement in particular kinds of creative expression. Unlike many of the aspiring actresses, they have not internalized and blindly accepted societal directives about women's goals: to be decorative, to succeed by using their beauty and charm, to manipulate men in order to get what they want. These young artists know that to succeed they must work alone, in a lonely labor that is often painful and requires difficult self-knowledge as well as hard-won skill. They have the courage to buck the social assumptions that women can play only secondary roles or make minor contributions in the "serious" arts. Because of their dedication to their work, they seem relatively mature, and the awareness of self and perception of the world around them that their craft both requires and teaches enables them to continue to grow and mature in ways which seem hardly conceivable for some of the shallow future actresses.

Like the young writers, Catherine Marshall's protagonist in *Christy* (1967) seems relatively mature at the beginning of her story. A gently bred young city dweller, she has decided to become a teacher in an isolated mission school. However, her decision was an impulse, not a considered choice, and she did not have any very realistic conception of either the kind of place and people she was going to work with or the demands that the work itself would make upon her. Though Christy did not intentionally turn away from the social institutions which formed her, her "call" to be a mission teacher takes her to a very different, challenging social structure. The novel gives a balanced picture of life in the mountains of eastern Tennessee in the early years of this century. Narrated by its title character, a nineteen-year-old girl, it depicts the mountain people in all their superstition and ignorance, their pride and stubbornness, their family loyalties and deep enmities—all the love and violence of a long-isolated community—as seen by a perceptive, sympathetic, and often troubled, outsider. As she works with her pupils and their families, Christy grows to love some of these rugged folks, and her idealistic hopes of changing them are tempered by her growing admiration for all that is good in their culture. Thus for Christy, her period of living among and working with these mountain people is truly a time of maturation; she is more changed by them than they are by her. A fine and sensitive, if naive, girl at the beginning of her mountain experience, she is strengthened and grows in wisdom and in faith as a result of her experiences.

Other authors have chosen a wide variety of kinds of work experiences or vocational ambitions to symbolize their youthful characters' maturation or to serve as catalysts to growth or change. Some of these novels are set in the present time and some in the past, but all tend to stress two things: the hard work of which the young women are capable and the sense of accomplishment and independence their success gives them. The work ethic is alive and well in these novels!

Two novels by Mary Stetson Clarke present instructive examples. When Joanna Sprague's father dies during their voyage to the New World, in *The Iron Peacock* (1966, YA), Joanna is sold as a bond servant to pay the five pounds owing on their passage. According to her indenture,

> "The said master well and faithfully she shall serve, his secrets keep, his commandments lawful and honest shall gladly do." There followed a list of restrictions. She was not to waste her master's goods, nor lend them, nor to play at cards or dice . . . [the master] was to provide meat, drink, clothing, lodging, and all other necessities according to the custom of the land.

The girl's fortitude in the face of this forced employment earns her the nickname from which the book takes its title, *The Iron Peacock*. At first a kitchen drudge, Joanna learns about the dreary range of chores—from daily cooking to soap making and preserving—demanded of women in the Bay Colony. Later, the author uses Joanna's skillful needlework to dramatize the love of finery and color which existed within the limits of the theocratic code.

In *The Limner's Daughter* (1967, YA), also by Mary Stetson Clarke, Amity Lyte's father is unable to work because of an accident, and the family is destitute until Amity takes a job spinning thread in a sailcloth factory. When later financial reversals again force her to look for employment, Amity converts the old family home into an inn serving the passengers on the Middlesex Canal and proves that she is an able business manager as well as a willing worker. Clarke uses Amity's ventures into wage earning not only as means of characterization but also as devices for incorporating accurate details of early nineteenth-century New England life.

In Jessamyn West's *Leafy Rivers* (1967), her protagonist, a young wife, undertakes a dramatic and symbolically effective maturation journey. When an injury to her husband makes him unable to drive their herd of hogs to market, Leafy makes secret preparations and undertakes the job herself. The trip from southeastern Indiana to Cincinnati is arduous and tests Leafy physically and emotionally, but she takes courage from the fact that the Rivers' marginal financial security depends upon her success and from a brief affair with a young drover, Cashie Wade, who gives her both practical and emotional support. The ultimate results of the work, the journey, and the affair are positive, for by the conclusion of the novel, Leafy Rivers, the adolescent, has become Mary Pratt Converse Rivers, a woman capable of true emotional and economic partnership with her husband who has also matured.

In *Orphan Jim* (1975) by Lonnie Coleman, Trudy Maynard becomes a wage earner before her fourteenth birthday. She finds work she loves clerking in a general store. Sometimes, "I felt *I* was the man of the house, coming home from work to my friend Hazel and my brother Jim, and because I was the one that had worked long, they were obliging and generous to me." The job lends substance to Trudy's feeling of independence and provides her with a sense of identity and accomplishment, factors leading to her maturation.

For Cordelia Miller in Kitty Burns Florey's *Chez Cordelia* (1980), the choice of cooking as a profession is not only a symbol of maturity but also an act of self-definition; she is affirming herself by demonstrating that she need not become a writer (as is the pattern in her family) in order to be creative, useful, fulfilled, and admired. When a temporary job as kitchen helper in a small but excellent restaurant reveals her true vocation, Cordelia takes her choice very seriously; she intends to become a "real" chef, despite the difficulty of obtaining proper training. Her methods, during her late adolescence, of obtaining that training are extremely peculiar, even questionable, and reveal her lack of maturity. By the close of Florey's novel, however, Cordelia is supporting herself as a cook and laying plans for a restaurant of her own, "Chez Cordelia," and both these facts signify her movement into adulthood.

For some youngsters, a first (or an early) temporary job is an important step in growing up. It gives them a taste of mature responsibility and a sense of financial independence. It also allows them to observe facets of the adult world and its workings that had previously been closed to them. It may be, thus, both a ritual of initiation into social institutions and a time of personal testing of a girl's abilities and goals.

For Shannon Lightley, protagonist of *Greensleeves* (1968, YA) by Eloise Jarvis McGraw, the prospect of "A sort of three-month Nirvana" is very appealing, for she needs time and freedom to choose a career and a homeland—she is the child of aggressive, famous parents, the product of various European and American schools. During her summer "sorting out" period, Shannon works as a waitress in an Oregon neighborhood diner, and the job represents independence and self-discipline as well as the opportunity to meet new people and to define her own interests, aims, and desires.

These young women grow in strength through work that either symbolizes or motivates increasing maturity. Their authors seem to be reminding us that work is valuable either for its own sake—for the sake of the task that is accomplished, whether it be the making of something or the creation of beauty—or for the sake of the sense of worth it gives the worker, who gains knowledge of and increases her capabilities. Work for pay is important, for only it can give the financial independence so important, even necessary, to many of these young women, but avocational activities may also be rewarding, as in *Chez Cordelia*.

An unusual avocational activity, which ultimately fails to function as training for a future profession but which serves as a powerful foreshadowing device, is depicted in Evan Hunter's *Last Summer* (1968). Sandy finds an injured seagull on the beach of an Atlantic summer resort area just as she coincidentally meets Peter and David. She rescues, tames, and begins to train the bird, despite the boys' skepticism. Just when she seems to be succeeding with it, she commits an act of cruelty, which the boys afterward discover and to which they then become accomplices. This episode establishes their youthful callousness and presages the relationship the three will have with another girl.

A young woman working toward a career or devoting herself to some precious avocation is, in general, looking toward her future. For her, the act of practicing her craft is a strengthening rehearsal for the life she will lead as an adult. But before she can become a fully participating member of the adult world, she must also determine her value system. For many, this need for a system of values and ethics which will be right for them creates conflict with familiar values. Just as they must test out other aspects of their society, and just as they often discover hypocrisy and dishonesty in other institutions, so they also find flaws in the churches in which they are reared and in the beliefs urged upon them from childhood. A crisis of faith is thus not unusual in the later teen years; arguments of religious doctrine and belief are exceedingly common among young people of this age. At the end of this period of testing, either a reaffirmation of basic principles of belief or a break with the original faith may be used to indicate the maturation of the young woman.

A repressive and hollow faith is portrayed in one novel which uses the protagonist's rejection of her childhood faith to symbolize maturation. Devout Marcella Colby, in *Marcella* (1973) by Marilyn Coffey, spends her adolescence suffering from an almost total lack of communication with adults. She is terrified and ashamed because she masturbates and believes the act to be a sin. Her mother's counsel about sexual development is halting and obscure; her minister responds to Marcella's quest for guidance with the set sermonette he delivers to boys with the same problem. Big Jim Morgan, her hero because he saved her soul, replies to her pleas for help with cute, casual form letters, followed by sexual exploitation. Adults failing her, Marcella tries to achieve self-restraint through prayer, eventually facing a severe religious crisis. The climax of the novel records Marcella's break with the church.

A similarly unfavorable picture of one particular kind of organized religion is given by Cynthia Applewhite, but her central character does

not manage the escape achieved by Marcella. Technically, every character in *Sundays* (1979) is a Christian, but through the perceptions of her
teenaged protagonist, Cha'Lou Moonlight, Applewhite indicts the Bible
Belt faith practiced in Jaytree, Missouri, during the 1930s. In some ways
Cha'Lou is drawn toward the dramatic, flaunted faith of her mother's
sisters, and these women certainly strive to impress their beliefs upon
the girl—they talk religion constantly and warn Cha'Lou about the
wages of sin with almost sensual delight. Yet, Cha'Lou, a wise innocent,
perceives the lack of charity which lurks beneath her aunts' pious veneer and also dimly grasps the relish in sinning which seems to lie just
beneath the affirmation and reform salvation supposedly offers. During
the vividly rendered Glorioso Crusade, when the much touted revivalist
Orlando Dole offers platitudes to a desperately sick woman, Cha'Lou
feels like one of the "doomed souls"—and readers are given no real assurance that she ever really emerges from that torment.

A negative study of another sort of religious group, this one a special phenomenon of the recent past, is found in Kay Boyle's *The Underground Woman* (1975). Though this novel centers on the development
of middle-aged Athena Gregory, Athena's daughter is an important
character. Portrayed in brief flashbacks, Melanie consumes much of
her mother's energy as Athena ponders the Manson-like religious commune to which the girl is committed. Mother and daughter are totally
estranged; Melanie's "silence and her distance were saying to them that
they [non–cult members] should be judged because they looked with
judgment on the one way of life that had given her power. Her mission
was to convert them all." Athena's achievement of a true sense of herself depends heavily upon the resolution of this strained relationship,
and when the commune attempts to commandeer Athena's home, both
the main plot and the Melanie subplot come to a powerful climax.

Two other novels, both set in the past, present more positive depictions of the value of religious faith, even though for these young women
achievement or retention of faith is not easy. Nevertheless, for them, belief is possible, and religious faith and commitment do give them a useful support in facing the difficulties of their lives.

Jonreed Lauritzen examines the Church of Jesus Christ of the Latter
Day Saints in *The Everlasting Fire* (1962), demonstrating that deep faith
rather than their unusual marital or social practices sustains many Mormons depicted. Lauritzen uses two young women to present diverging
points of view: Milly Kettleby speaks persuasively for her faith, and
Myra Eyring challenges many of the Saints' tenets as both struggle to resolve conflicting allegiances, personal problems, romantic quandaries.
In the Midwest of 1844, it is not easy to be a Mormon, as Milly well
knows, and Myra learns that many of her assumptions must be
reevaluated. Both young women discover that genuine religious commitment and trust in decent, honorable men and women are the only re-

liable constants in lives complicated by religious bigotry and by personal crises of faith.

Comfortably middle class, Christy Huddleston, of Catherine Marshall's *Christy* (1967), is, in 1912, challenged at a church retreat to volunteer her services to a mission school in the eastern Tennessee mountains. With little real sense of what she is getting herself into, she goes —only to see superstition, ignorance, and unnecessary suffering and death among people whom she grows to love. Her faith is sorely tested, and she struggles painfully with her doubts, but the example and counsel of several experienced mission workers, as well as her observation of the strength and loving courage of the mountain people, enable her to reaffirm her faith. *Christy* is a fictionalized retelling from Christy's own point of view of eleven months in the life of the mother of its author, a well-known writer on religious themes.

For Milly and Myra (*The Everlasting Fire*) and Christy (*Christy*), a solid faith, taught them in childhood and still strong in the culture in which they are reared, survives the questioning to which they subject it in their times of doubt, and for them a successful maturation and capable adulthood seem assured. Marcella (*Marcella*) and Cha'Lou (*Sundays*), living nearer the present, find little comfort or nurturance in their faith, which seems primarily to inculcate guilt rather than love. Needing love and acceptance, as adolescents so desperately do, Marcella and Cha'Lou fail to find helpful values or support in these emotionally repressive beliefs.

It must be acknowledged that while some authors find institutionalized religion harmful, others, by implication, find it simply irrelevant. The choices facing young people may not change greatly over the years, but, according to our subject-authors, the ways of making these choices apparently do sometimes alter. If ours is an age of doubt, as has often been claimed, then it is not surprising that some youngsters confront moral and ethical dilemmas without reference to religious faith. Three novels give representative examples of young people plunged into very difficult situations, whether of their own making or not; these young women must make decisions about courses of action upon which a great deal hinges, and they make these choices largely on the basis of their feelings, not as a result of any religious or ethical system which they have been taught to follow. They seem to have fallen into a void where no previously learned creed or system of ethics clearly applies. Thus, these young people, all in their various ways closely integrated into their particular segments of society, find themselves forced in crucial moments to rely only upon their own impulses rather than depend on external help. In one case, the chosen course of action is presented as wise (*The Impermanence of Heroes*), in another as absolutely evil (*Let's Go Play at the Adams'*), but in the third no clear evaluation is indicated (*Ruby*).

In *The Impermanence of Heroes* (1965) by Eunice Cleland Fikso (pseudonym, C. F. Griffin) Jessica and Brock Brewer are initiated into adulthood by their friendship with Joe St. George, a Korean War veteran. The children's trials begin with their awareness that they are Joe's only friends in the small town, and that their defense of him complicates their lives. The climax of their initiation occurs when, hidden, they watch Joe murder a cruel and vicious intruder from his past. Though Jessica and Brock are too young to understand Joe's full motivation, they make their first adult choice when they decide to keep their knowledge secret. Fikso shows clearly that the children feel the importance of their decision: "In spite of wanting to protect Joe I had the most awful urge to speak up and tell the adults that I knew all about what had happened to the stranger, that I could answer all their questions." They accept the responsibility, however, and learn that ethics can sometimes run counter to law.

In Mendal W. Johnson's *Let's Go Play at the Adams'* (1974), five children first imprison, then torture, and finally kill the babysitter for two of them. Among the children are ten-year-old Cindy Adams, innocent and amoral, and Dianne McVeigh, at seventeen the oldest of the group. It all begins as a continuation of a game they had formerly played among themselves, when they had taken turns pretending to be the victim, but when they have a real victim, it turns serious and becomes a revelation of power relationships. Barbara Miller, the twenty-year-old prisoner, learns that her happily optimistic, almost Pollyannaish view of the world is false and discovers, tragically, a great deal about her own inner self, while Dianne, the strongest of the youngsters, is implacable in her view of life as a game in which being killed is simply the penalty for losing. " 'People kill people,' she said. 'Losers lose. . . . Everybody's always been doing it, and we're doing it, I guess. It's nothing all that new.' " Finally Dianne sees the murder as a work of art; because she likes the victim, "it's got to be pretty, as pretty as I can make it." The novel is a gripping and horrifyingly believable study of a descent into darkness by seemingly ordinary and pampered middle-class youngsters.

Daphne Duprey, a major character in *Ruby* (1976, YA) by Rosa Guy, is the lover of the protagonist and seeks to dominate Ruby politically as well as emotionally. Proud of her dead father's sense of black pride, Daphne defines herself by her dedication to her race and her self-control: "I pride myself in always being cool, calm, collected, cultured, poised, refined and . . . intelligent." Daphne's determination to make her life count is seen as admirable, but her equally strong determination "to work within the structure" for black rights—beginning by matriculating at Brandeis—is denounced by Ruby's sister, Phyllisia, and questioned by Ruby who believes that Daphne is compromising too much. Though Daphne has heretofore been strangely adult for her sixteen years, her new dependence on her mother may indicate a weakening of her political goals. Author Rosa Guy vividly depicts all three girls' positions on civil rights, indicates how their personal desires affect those positions, and shows that Daphne undergoes a real crisis of decision. She wisely leaves the reader to determine the correctness of Daphne's choice.

Family background, especially class origins and wealth, early help to shape a girl's ways of looking at herself and her world. The schools, largely middle-class institutions to whose tutelage all youngsters are compelled to submit themselves, continue the process of giving the young person the materials she must examine and select from or reject as she makes herself. Religious faith or socially approved ethical systems add still another layer of ready-made beliefs and assumptions. The church, once an institution of greater power than the schools but now in decline, no longer has the influence of former times, although its impact is still strong on some individuals, and this impact may be either damaging or strengthening. A young woman must come to understand these phenomena and their power over her, at least as they impinge upon her sense of who she is and who she wishes to be, if her maturation process is to be a successful one. Particularly fortunate, some of our authors suggest, are those girls who have special talents and know from an early age what they wish to do with themselves and their lives, especially if their ambitions carry them into creative or productive work. Also happy are those who, without regard to professional or creative ambitions, nevertheless find worthwhile labor which gives them a sense of achievement and allows them to find independence. The key, however, is that they ultimately free themselves from blind adherence to standards and ideas of others and determine what is right for them, as individuals. This may mean accepting, with a wise and full understanding, what they have been taught. Or it may mean rejecting familiar, formerly accepted values. But the point, as many of these subject-novels illustrate, is that they must come to their own conclusions, independently and thoughtfully.

CHAPTER VI
Female Response to Settings

In all fiction, a setting may be either a simple backdrop to the action or may be crucial in itself, depending on whether the author was interested in examining the impact of time and place on character or simply wished to give a personage "a local habitation and a name." Thus some novels of adolescence emphasize the interaction with and influence of a particular kind of background (city, small town, rural area), a particular region of the country, or a particular time. Others may be equally vivid in their descriptions of their times and places, and yet those settings may be simply decorative, not truly functional to plot or character development. For the most part, the novels discussed here are those in which the setting serves some important function in determining an aspect of the adolescent female characters' growth or lack of growth.

Since adolescence is, by definition, a time of change, these novels tend to connect customs or assumptions peculiar to their chosen times and places with the problems faced by their youthful characters. The more realistic and believable the settings, the more effectively motivated the dilemmas or choices of the characters, and the more clear and logical the connections of settings and dilemmas, the more successful these novels generally become.

It is difficult to generalize about the sorts of problems depicted in these novels; they range as widely as do the problems faced by young women in all the rest of this study. What distinguishes them is primarily the special stress on external conditions or forces that informs these novels. Nevertheless, certain patterns do emerge. Maturation in the city is more difficult than in the small town or in a rural area. Recollections of urban adolescence often seem embittered, while memories of rural girlhood may show nostalgia for a simpler past now lost (although small-town life may also be remembered as stultifying). Some treatments of the small town and particular regions are satiric, and these tend to show their youthful women as either shallow, lacking the potential for growth, or as being warped or otherwise damaged by their surroundings. Nature may serve as a harsh crucible, testing the young woman's very will to survive, and historical forces or events may force her to confront danger or to make crucial ethical or moral choices.

In the years covered by this study, large cities have tended to be portrayed unfavorably. Poverty and racial prejudice and discrimination, along with narrow views of life and what it may hold for young women, are emphasized. One important novel which gives a particularly grim picture of city life and what it means for a working-class family is Joyce Carol Oates's *them* (1969). The urban desert that is Detroit, Michigan, during the middle third of the twentieth century serves as a symbol for the frustrating, tormented, impoverished lives of Jules and Maureen Wendall and their mother, Loretta. *them* depicts the family—essentially rootless, *in* but not *of* the city—living marginal, turbulent, violent lives that reflect life on the streets around them. Essentially deprived of childhoods, suffering the absence of any positive nurture, the Wendalls, like their city, are prime examples of Joyce Carol Oates's social commentary: always uneasy, often afraid, they yet cannot perceive real danger and thus stumble into violence and tragedy.

Other novels of city life depict the special world of the ghetto. While these novels may be rich in portrayals of black culture, they also stress the horrible impact of poverty, crime, and surrounding degradation on impressionable young female characters. One example is the grim picture of life in Harlem during the Depression given by Louise Meriwether in *Daddy Was a Number Runner* (1970). Francie Coffin, the narrator and protagonist, is bright, observant, and realistic; she adores her vital father and loves her devoted, hard-working mother. All her mother's efforts, however, are not enough to hold the family together, and her father's pride harms their well-being. Francie moves among prostitutes and pimps, gang members, petty crooks, white shopkeepers and other exploiters of her people, sex perverts who wish to expose themselves to her or fondle her, and other assorted misfits and victims. She maintains her objectivity, but by the end of the novel she seems to be accepting the hopelessness of her situation. A sensitive depiction of the deprived early adolescence of a lively and likable young woman, the novel effectively recreates its troubled world.

More optimistic is another sensitive depiction of growing up in a black slum, surrounded by crime and poverty, given by Alice Childress in *Rainbow Jordan* (1981). Told through a variety of points of view, it shows fourteen-year-old Rainbow in relationships with her sexually assertive boyfriend and a number of women, all black but Rachel, an elderly and loving Quaker. Her twenty-nine-year-old mother is untrustworthy, but Josephine Lamont, her foster mother, despite real problems of her own, is ultimately able to form a warm and mutually supportive relationship with her. The reader is thus able to feel much more hopeful about Rainbow's future than about that of the protagonist of Meriwether's *Daddy Was a Number Runner*, despite the similarities of the two novels in basic setting and situation.

Two smaller cities, cleverly rendered, serve important motivational and symbolic functions in *Lessons* (1981), by Lee Zacharias. Hammond, Indiana, protagonist Janie Hurdle's home town, stands for aridity and frustration. A gifted musician, Janie believes that Hammond can offer her only public school teaching jobs and a life divorced from major orchestral performances, good talk about music and books, rich relationships. For refuge, she flees to Bloomington, Indiana, where she expects to find a golden future through her studies in the Music School of Indiana University and among the professionals and students she intends to meet there. Instead, Janie discovers that people carry their problems and disabilities with them wherever they go and that cultural centers can harbor exploitative human beings as well as steel towns can. Only when, as an adult, she learns to seek answers from her personal strength can Janie begin to find the fulfillment that both Hammond and Bloomington deny her.

Another novel examines both city and country life, though neither is shown to be truly nurturing to its youthful inhabitants. Newland, Tennessee, the setting for Lisa Alther's *Original Sins* (1981), attempts to mold Sally and Emily into perfect ladies, Jed and Raymond into "good old boys," and their childhood best friend, Donny, into a subservient black who "knows his place." Alther contrasts urban Newland with rural Tatro Cove, Kentucky, where life is slower but equally frustrating for Raymond, who, like Emily and Donny, rebels against the Newland code even while hating northern liberals' blind, uninformed scorn for the South. As refugees in New York City, these three protagonists find little happiness. But though Sally and Jed subscribe to Newland mores, they, too, are unhappy. Alther depicts both the pleasant and the grim aspects of Newland and Tatro Cove, both the advantages and disadvantages of New York, poses many questions about the viability of all three places as life-enhancing homes, and suggests few answers.

If the world of the urban center is often shown to be frightening, frustrating, or dangerous, small towns sometimes seem only a little better. Instead of warping the young character because of material deprivation, the small town is more apt to be shown as emotionally or psychologically damaging. Social pressures to conform to habits of behavior or ways of thinking that are unrealistic or hypocritical can be just as stressful, although in different ways, as those elements of the physical environment so often emphasized in depictions of city life. The reactions of the young women to their towns, however, are crucial, and a number of them are shown, like Childress's protagonist in *Rainbow Jordan*, as finally being able to survive the potentially harmful effects of their backgrounds.

Leah, New Hampshire, the setting for Thomas Williams's *Whipple's Castle* (1968), is presented during the years from 1942 to 1948, with a brief concluding section set in 1958. The portrayal of the town is blunt. The three major youthful female characters all suffer troubled maturation processes partly as a result of social pressures exerted by the small-town mentality. Kate Whipple, fortunately placed in the community's hierarchy and talented as well as pretty, has difficulty forming relationships of any depth and in trusting people, for she fears they may try to use her. Susie David, from a poor, broken, uncaring family, is used sexually and then traduced by the young men of the town, and Peggy Mudd, deserted by a worthless mother, is pathetically grateful for any crumb of notice given her. Although scorned by the community, Peggy finds a home with the title family; ultimately her adulthood is the most fulfilled of the three, perhaps because she has used her talents unselfishly and has learned to form deep relationships with people who are worthy of them.

More restricted in time, Edwin Lanham's *Speak Not Evil* (1964) covers one summer in the life of a Connecticut small town, beginning with the high-school graduation, carrying through the planning for the town's tercentenary celebration, and climaxing with that celebration, which is overshadowed by a hurricane. In the meantime, many of the secrets of the small town are revealed to us, including the pregnancy of Faithful Zybioski, high-school valedictorian, and the existence of sex orgies in which Vera Blaine, another recent graduate, participates. Though the appearance and reality of small-town life are shown to be very different, the novel has a basically affirmative tone, and at its end both young women are shown seizing opportunities to remake their lives.

A still more positive picture is given in yet another novel set in New England. May Sarton's *Kinds of Love* (1970) gives considerable attention to Willard, New Hampshire, a now tiny, once vigorous town. The various efforts of local citizens to prepare for Willard's bicentennial celebration uncover multitudes of facts about local history including a steady loss of population and a failing economy. Also well handled is the sometimes hidden but almost constant tension between "winter" people (permanent inhabitants) and "summer" people (who also regard the town as theirs). An important subplot focuses on the loving relationship which develops between Cathy, fifteen, and Joel Smith, a college dropout, both temporary residents, who see Willard as a refuge from the troubled urban worlds they are escaping. Both Cathy and Joel find surrogate parents in Willard; both regard it as symbolic of some of the most sustaining features of American life. The youngsters' affectionate response to the town and their fruitful growth while residing there symbolize the fact that Willard, diminished and impoverished though it now may be, is still a vital, useful factor in American culture and that both part-time and permanent residents are key factors in its future.

Even more nostalgic and positive is the sensitive evocation, central to Babs H. Deal's *The Reason for Roses* (1974), of a small Alabama town— which might have been any small town anywhere, despite the effectiveness of its local coloration—just before World War II.

Unlike city life, country life sometimes is idealized, usually when a warm view of the farm is combined with nostalgia for the past. Perhaps the advent of huge farms and "agribusiness" and the concurrent decline of small, single-family farms has made less easy the depiction of a free, happy adolescence on a small farm in the present. In any event, novels idealizing farm life tend to be set in the past or to be backward looking. For example, the maturation of Sheila, an important secondary character in Curtis Harnack's *Limits of the Land* (1979), symbolizes the end of an era. Though, like her father, the protagonist, Sheila loves the land, she plans to live in town, desiring not only the financial and emotional sustenance of agrarian life but also the companionship and convenience of town life. Her father, who narrates the story, perceives Sheila's decision as symptomatic of young Americans' attitudes during the Korean War period, and her final choice is one of many factors which teach him that the healing, peace, and balance he had hoped to find in rural life are as limited here as elsewhere.

Janet Majerus, in *Grandpa and Frank* (1976), turns to a slightly earlier period, the late 1940s, for her evocation of rural Illinois. The protagonist, Sarah MacDermott, is very much the product of Williard County, and she enlivens her account of a crisis in her life with details of farm management, descriptions of the county fair, and accounts of local habits.

> I had not seen so much excitement since Ellie Morrison got a long-distance call from California. That time there were so many people listening on the party line that the operator threatened to send a man out to cut the lines if they did not hang up. Of course, no one did, but Ellie's young man said he would just write. He did, too—at least that's what the mailman said.

These comments enrich the story, clarify Sarah's motivations, and validate her reliability as narrator, for she clearly perceives the good intent as well as the potential destructiveness of the community's keen interest in the MacDermotts' affairs.

Adolescence is a time of testing and being tested. The wilderness, the harshest possible background for a brutal testing of the ability to survive, is used by several authors, as they dramatize the maturation of young women who come through extremely desperate experiences. These wilderness settings are widely separated in time and space as well as being quite different in type: one is an eastern world of woods, water, and snow in this century, while the other is a land of sun, heat, and aridity more than a century earlier.

The winter wilderness of the Adirondacks in 1921 is the setting for William Judson's *Cold River* (1974). Taken on a camping trip by her father, fourteen-year-old Lizzie Allison and her step-brother, thirteen-year-old Tim Hood, are stranded through a series of mishaps climaxed by the death of Mr. Allison. Their survival, through desperate adventures, is made possible by the hunter's skills Mr. Allison has carefully taught them, by their native intelligence and ingenuity, and by their close and cooperative relationship. Lizzie, the elder, is the stronger and wiser at first, but both youngsters mature as they are toughened by their experiences and find themselves accomplishing feats they know their schoolmates would find totally unbelievable. The novel is narrated many years later by an elderly Lizzie; her comments on the experience give the reader a double perspective and direct attention to the "how" (not the "whether") of their survival.

A striking evocation of survival against great odds, some created by people and others by the harsh southwest climate, occurs in R. G. Vliet's *Rockspring* (1974). Jensie, daughter of a westering frontier family in the Texas of 1830, is kidnapped by Mexican bandits. Repeatedly raped, she at first tries to die, but her vitality is too strong, and she survives. An attempted escape fails because she is unable to find her way home alone, and she soon realizes that the strong sun and arid land are even crueler enemies than her captors. Jensie is a survivor, however, and the novel, effectively told from her point of view, sometimes her stream-of-consciousness, ends with her return to her family, a much changed young woman who feels herself a stranger to the relatives she had longed for.

Lizzie (*Cold River*) and Jensie (*Rockspring*) are hardened and strengthened by the experiences which pit them against both humanity and nature. Lizzie we know has achieved perspective on her adventures, but Jensie's story ends just at the point of her return to "civilization," a return that ironically, as she observes a violent and gratuitous act, demonstrates to her that her own civilization is corrupt and unthinkingly cruel. How she will adapt herself again to her people, however, is left unexplored. These two novels create sensitive and stimulating portraits of strong young women; the depth of these portraits and the clarity with which their growth is motivated are striking. "Woman against nature" serves just as well as a maturation device as the more conventional "man against nature."

The region of the country in which a city, town, or rural area is situated may, of course, have as much to do with its manners and mores as the density of population or the relative wealth of its inhabitants. And the customs as well as the landscape may be stressed for their interconnections with the characters; they may also been seen either favorably or unfavorably. Regional novels, loving or critical, tend to be quite detailed in their description of scene, and the relationship of the adolescent young woman to her surroundings is often analyzed or dramatized quite fully.

Description of a particular place as it is being experienced by a youngster may either reveal the character's emotions, her confusions in this time of change in her life, or it may symbolize her maturation or failure to mature. Thus the author may create a firm sense of a particular time and place even while also developing character. One example of a novel with such functional regionalism is *The Impermanence of Heroes* (1965) by Eunice Cleland Fikso (pseudonym, C. F. Griffin), which details the flora and fauna of the New England seacoast setting. The descriptive passages and the pleasure Jessica and Brock Brewer take in their surroundings dramatize the innocence of the Brewers' childhoods and contrast with the grimness of their initiation into adulthood.

A contrast between widely different parts of the country may also be used symbolically. In an oversimplified but effective device, Norma Klein uses the love affair between Jody Epstein and her new boyfriend, Lyle, major characters in *It's OK If You Don't Love Me* (1977, YA), to dramatize the "geography gap" commonly assumed to exist between social standards in the Midwest and those in New York City. Jody, the protagonist-narrator, symbolizes New York, her home town, and she believes that a premarital sexual relationship is worthwhile and fulfilling even if the partners are very young and are not in love with one another. Lyle represents the more restrictive code Klein identifies with the Midwest, and it takes him a while to accept Jody's standards and become her lover. Though he enjoys their affair, Lyle cannot initially accept the fact that to Jody, sexual freedom is complete. Consequently, he is hurt and angry when she sleeps with an old boyfriend, and tells him about it. Both youngsters learn much about the value of constancy and truth in this comic, poignant study of contemporary sexual values.

A number of novels comment negatively about varied regions of the country using small towns as their foci. They satirize or dramatize the flaws of their areas, while at the same time they reveal the struggles of young women attempting to come of age and to create themselves in hostile or restricting surroundings.

Shady Bend, a bleak small town in west Texas, depicted by Patricia Gallagher in *The Sons and the Daughters* (1961), seethes with racism, sexuality, and hypocrisy. At seventeen, Jill Turner, whose mother runs a diner and is thought to have been the mistress of its former Jewish owner, is bright and eager for education and romance. But her mother cannot afford the education, and the town can offer only disillusionment: all around she sees thwarted lives and hopes. Observation of lust, madness, and death all play important parts in Jill's maturation, so that at the end of the novel she turns from the rich, shallow young man she had idolized to the solid young newspaperman she had long undervalued. Though not particularly original, the novel is an engrossing study of young adults facing life in a constricting environment.

Cynthia Applewhite uses the heat and tension of a Missouri summer during the worst days of the Depression to symbolize the tormented development of Charlotte Louella Moonlight from child to young woman in the course of *Sundays* (1979). The surface Christianity of Jaytree, Missouri, is symbolized by the outward lives of Cha'Lou's aunts, active in local church affairs, dedicated attenders of revivals, denouncers of Mrs. Moonlight's values and former life in St. Louis. At the same time, however, the hypocrisy of life in Jaytree is depicted in the aunts' willingness to gossip, to dwell on the violence beneath the surface of the seemingly placid community, and their brutalization of their "hired help," another teenager, the duplicitous, sensual Irma Renner. Mysterious talk about a local sex murder, the secret life of Cha'Lou's adored uncle, and the town's lionization of gangsters like Pretty Boy Floyd all help to confuse Cha'Lou's developing sense of values, and the novel's conclusion, deliberately double-edged, gives little hope for the youngster's fruitful maturation.

A satiric portrait of an Iowa small town, largely as seen by an ambitious, manipulative, but somehow likable high-school girl, Barbara Anne Greene, is given in Al Hine's *Lord Love a Duck* (1961). Though the setting is believable and recognizable, the author states that he has "possibly played fast and loose with the laws and mores of [the] actual state, not out of any disrespect for the area normally known as Iowa," that state having been chosen "to suggest a centralness in the American scene." Particularly stressed in the satire are the complacency of the small town, its provincial morality and smugness, and the intellectual dishonesty of its high school.

Life in Mississippi during the 1950s provides an enormous amount of local color in *Coming Attractions* (1981). According to author Fannie Flagg, Bible Belt piety and conventionalism can be a cover for the duplicity, violence, religious exploitation, and gangsterism which also define the area. Flagg uses these elements as an important part of the initiation of her protagonist, Daisy Fay Harper, who observes more than she understands and records it all in her diary, the narrative device of the novel. Though double-dealing is a constant factor in her life—her father employs suspect practices in his "malt shop"; a criminal terrorizes the child; and she and her father join the Reverend Billy Bundy (who once "got in trouble" selling autographed pictures of the Last Supper) in a religious hoax—Daisy Fay remains curiously decent and innocent, even when her "big break" is the direct result of manipulation and deceit. Daisy Fay's ability to cope with and surmount (or at least ignore) evil and her determination to leave Mississippi, symbolically associated with evil, are the key symbols for the fact that she is a survivor.

Worthy of note is another satire, a representative of the subgenre of Hollywood stories in which the film capital is depicted as both place and state of mind. Sandra Berkley's 1971 study of Hollywood is also called *Coming Attractions*. Though its protagonist, Cassie Keen, never gets into the movies but lives on their fringes, the Hollywood scene of the 1930s and 1940s is evoked well. The chapter headings ("Child Star," "The Awkward Age," "Ingenue," "Starlet," and "Leading Lady") indicate how Cassie sees the stages in her life, and cinematic techniques used in the narration further enhance the sense of real life as only a disappointing imitation of screen life. Though she is beautiful and intelligent, Cassie, it seems clear, will never really get a chance at stardom. Unlike many Hollywood novels, this one never takes us inside the studios and the world of those who have succeeded. Its sardonic attack is strengthened by the fact that it shows us only the outsiders and the failures.

Location of plot and character in time may be made to serve many of the same functions as location in place. Some authors are primarily interested in studying an era from the past and thus use characters and events to illustrate the life or political and social world of that time, while others use the past as an incidental backdrop to their depiction of more universal human traits. Since attitudes towards sexuality and sexual roles have changed markedly throughout American history, fictional studies of adolescent females in the past often remind us how we have changed from what we once were.

Set in an almost mythic Old West, Clyde Ware's *The Innocents* (1969) centers around a young white girl, orphaned by Indians and carried off by them but not accepted into the tribe. Left to fend for herself, she survives by following after the tribe, scavenging with the dogs for the few scraps of food thrown their way and thus earning the name "Dog-Girl." Pitying her, an old prospector takes her and renames her "Doe"; they build a strangely beautiful and loving life together, until outsiders, both white and Indian, affected by Doe's beauty as she matures, intrude into their world. The novel stresses the harshness of its southwestern scene and Doe's stubborn will to live as well as the gentleness, courage, and ability to love which make her an appealing character.

Four novels set in the nineteenth century, *Rockspring*, *The Massacre at Fall Creek*, *The Glass Dove*, and *The Everlasting Fire*, are solidly based on their particular times and places. The adolescent women in these novels face challenges and trials peculiar to their particular environments, and thus their experiences, while they may be parallel to experiences of adolescents living in other times and places, are also very special and serve to form the young women in very special ways.

Landscape, climate, and brigandage (connected to the clash of native Mexican and newly invading Anglo-Saxon settlers who are changing the course of history of the Southwest) set the stage for the first of these novels. Texas in 1830, the setting of R. G. Vliet's *Rockspring* (1974), is shown as an unsettled, harsh, and hostile land, inhabited only by a few American frontier and farming families, represented by fourteen-year-old Jensie and her family, and by some wandering Mexican bandits, represented by the three men (one of them a mere boy) who kidnap her. The short novel movingly depicts Jensie's struggles to survive and her slowly growing, tender relationship with the boy, himself an earlier victim of kidnapping by soldiers.

A somewhat gentler nature but an equally violent clash between cultures is studied in another novel. The growing pains of the Indiana frontier in 1824, a year in which the Fall Creek community opts for civilization over the bloody, violent freedom of wilderness territory, are the focus of Jessamyn West's *The Massacre at Fall Creek* (1975). While the story of the first trial of American white men accused of murdering Indians is the center of this novel, West strengthens and dramatizes it by using the maturation of Hannah Cape, seventeen, as a parallel pattern. Both community and young woman make moral and ethical choices which will determine their private and public stances forever. The device is a strong one; both stories are compelling, and they are welded together with skill and artistry.

While land, climate, and a historical clash of cultures make Jensie's maturation particularly painful in *Rockspring*, and dilemmas of cultural relationships and human worth torment Hannah's community in *The Massacre at Fall Creek*, it is primarily psychological pressures, related to her family's abolitionist activities in the period before the Civil War, that make Sylvia MacIntosh's growing up difficult. In *The Glass Dove* (1961) by Sally Carrighar, even Sylvia's love story is overshadowed—and complicated—by the demands of the underground railway station the family runs. The situation is especially difficult for Sylvia because the commitment to the abolitionists' cause is more her father's than her own. Through Sylvia's reactions, Carrighar vividly dramatizes the extreme danger and tension of the family's situation, their sense of isolation when friendships must be severed to preserve the necessary secrecy, and the hard work of maintaining the family farm and caring for the fugitives at the same time.

The political, economic, ethical, and moral implications of the westward migration of members of the Church of Jesus Christ of the Latter Day Saints are central to *The Everlasting Fire* (1962) by Jonreed Lauritzen. Early scenes set in Nauvoo, Illinois, in the 1840s demonstrate the impact Mormon settlers make on the social fabric of the community and also illustrate the threat that the townspeople's bigotry and preconceptions pose toward the Mormons. Personal choices and individual problems are described through the events complicating the lives of the Eyring family, including the father, a prominent citizen, his son Rafael, and his daughter Myra. Local mores and faiths conflict with those of the Mormons, entangling the Eyrings, testing Judge Nathan Eyring's principles, shadowing the romances of Nathan and Myra, measuring the faith and steadfastness of all three who represent the traditional non-Mormon Nauvoo folk. Lauritzen's panoramic account of the Saints' westward movement and of the trials of his major characters (both Mormon and non-Mormon) again raises questions about the viability of Americans' belief in freedom of religion. Nauvoo and other settings become microcosms of the United States, and the Eyrings and their associates become symbols for typical Americans' habits and beliefs. Thus this novel, while being deeply rooted in the historical past, also generalizes beyond its specific subject.

Closer to our own times in setting, Ruth Doan MacDougall's *The Cheerleader* (1973) studies the manners and mores of a recent period of conformity. Though *The Cheerleader* gives a clear sense of its locale, a small New Hampshire town, author MacDougall's finest achievement in the neatly rendered setting is her evocation of the 1950s. Protagonist Henrietta Snow's preoccupation with dress codes, the highly structured rules for exactly which degree of sexual activity is appropriate to each "level" of dating, and the importance of high-school extracurricular activities is set against a background of the popular music, the headlines, and the artifacts of the period. The final result is a marvelous evocation of the times which steadily illuminates Snowy's character.

Other novelists, using the past but less interested in studying it for its own sake, stress universals and in so doing remind us that the need of a young person to discover who she is and to create for herself a clear, livable niche in her world, wherever and whenever it may be, are unchanging. One novel joins present and past, as its protagonist, attempting to find her own identity, enters the world of her exiled ancestress and imaginatively relives the experiences of flight and bigotry of some colonial American refugees. Connecticut and Louisiana, in both the eighteenth and twentieth centuries, as well as Nova Scotia in the eighteenth, form the backdrop for Anya Seton's *Smouldering Fires* (1975). Amy Delatour, a shy and unpopular high-school senior, is descended from Acadians and "dreams true" about the life and horrible death of an Acadian ancestress. A sympathetic teacher of Louisiana Creole background recognizes her intelligence and potential attractiveness (in obviously symbolic fashion, he gets her to remove her thick reading glasses and let her hair out of its bun). Through hypnosis and travel from her Connecticut home to Louisiana, he enables her to relive the experiences of her ancestress. Thus she both learns the truth about the past and is freed in the present to become a normal young woman.

A competent, likable, assertive young woman who would surely have succeeded in almost any time and place is Hetty Downing. Set in 1629 in Massachusetts, Barbara Dodge Borland's *The Greater Hunger* (1962) is both a love story and the story of a brave and independent girl who makes her own way in a man's world. Hetty has been reared by her horticulturist father as his companion and co-worker. When he dies on the voyage to the New World, she takes over his work and, against great odds but very quickly, makes a place for herself among the leaders of the colony. The love theme makes the novel a latter-day version of *The Scarlet Letter*, and Hetty, an eighteen-year-old in a day when girls marry at twelve, has almost from the beginning Hester Prynne's strength and courage. She stands consistently for religious tolerance, seeking desperately to rescue Nat Trumbull from the bigotry and sense of sin that destroy Hawthorne's Dimmesdale. The novel does not always succeed in making its seventeenth-century background seem authentic, the central characters having some attitudes and ideas more typical of our own times, but Hetty's portrayal is a reminder of the early maturing of young people, of the absence of a real period of adolescence during this time.

Shirley Barker's *Strange Wives* (1963) is set in Revolutionary War times among the Sephardic Jews of Newport, Rhode Island (the subject also of Longfellow's poem, "The Jewish Cemetery at Newport"). Its central character, Jenny Tupper, the poor daughter of a bigoted Christian father, falls in love with and marries a Jew. Approximately the first half of the novel carries her from the age of seven to her marriage at twenty-one and shows how she gradually overcomes her fear of the Jews and her sense of their strangeness. But her adolescent growth is not enough, and the latter half of the novel details the problems of the marriage, caused by their foreignness to each other, and Jenny's final understanding. In its effect, the novel is both a plea for tolerance that does not seek to soften the difficulties of understanding between cultures and a sympathetic treatment of a small group of often forgotten Americans. The use of young Jenny's point of view is central to both these aspects of the book.

Doris Betts's story of troubled adolescence, *The Scarlet Thread* (1964), is set in North Carolina in the latter nineteenth and early twentieth centuries. Esther Allen, the oldest of three children, is assertive and imaginative; her reaction to menstruation is disbelief and then anger at all men. Some of her experiences appear to be strengthening, but several misunderstandings (that her brother hates her, that her lover has rejected her) cause her to run away. The epilogue, set in 1922, seems to indicate, however, that she has overcome the traumas of her girlhood. The novel begins as a comic study of the middle-class Southern life of its period, but gradually the serious results of apparently funny events are made clear.

In a period when young women barely out of high school frequently became country teachers the nineteen-year-old protagonist of *Christy* (1967) by Catherine Marshall has experiences in the eastern Tennessee mountains of 1912 that might parallel those of later—older and presumably more mature—Peace Corps volunteers. Marshall's fictionalized reconstruction of a brief period in her mother's life is a moving depiction of the coming of age of a gently reared young woman who idealistically, and against the wishes of her parents, volunteers to teach in a backwoods mission school. The title character of *Christy* (1967) is a warmhearted, loving, impulsive, and imaginative young woman who is appalled by the conditions she finds among the ignorant but proud mountain people. A gifted teacher who quickly grows to love her pupils, she makes a place for herself and finds fulfillment in her work.

In evaluating these novels, crucial questions often are how well the authors have depicted the special settings chosen and how effective and functional is the interplay between character, plot, and setting. Thus the occasional jarring note in *The Greater Hunger*, making the characters seem more like twentieth- than seventeenth-century people, weakens the portrait of Hetty and lessens our ability to believe in her struggles and success. And the somewhat awkward mixture of occultism, psychology, and trite symbolism of *Smouldering Fires* makes Amy's transformation seem almost as much a cliché as a persuasive depiction of the maturation process.

Other novels, however, in which the setting and its connection to character are well realized become particularly rich because of the complexity of thematic development which this dual concern helps to create. Major novels like *them* by Joyce Carol Oates and *The Massacre at Fall Creek* by Jessamyn West are especially good examples of novels that clearly re-create a special place and time, contain well-realized adolescent female characters who undergo crucial experiences, and demonstrate the essential relationship of setting and character in the growth or failure of growth of these girls.

CHAPTER VII
Females and Fate

One of the hardest lessons for any person—of either sex and any age—
to learn is that some things are simply beyond human control. Illness,
pain, suffering, physical handicaps, are part of the human condition,
and the best any individual can do is learn to accept their existence and
cope with them when they fall to her lot. For most young people, adolescence is a time of glowing health and vigor, reinforcing their sense of
invulnerability, their inability to believe that they will ever grow old or
die. The illnesses most of them contract are apt to be minor in nature
and brief in duration. Not without reason do we think of "childhood
diseases" as relatively insignificant—unless suffered by adults. When
serious illnesses occur, the young people suffering them often do not
recognize their life-threatening nature, simply because they cannot yet
believe in their own mortality.

In the chapter "Females within Families," we have commented at
length upon the shattering consequences that a family death may have
upon both the cohesiveness of the family and the equilibrium of the girls
within it. Here we will approach a similar theme, but our concern now
is to suggest how a number of physical limiters, including death, may
demonstrate irrevocably the helplessness of the individual human being
against what might be thought of as fate or as acts of God because they
are outside human control.

Most youngsters feel themselves powerless and believe that adults
have power or control. For the young, reaching toward the independence of adulthood is also striving for the control over their own lives
and fates that they believe they will have, magically, when they are
freed from the constraints of family and school, have their own money,
and can make their own rules. When they are small, their parents seem
to them omnipotent and one aspect of living through the adolescent
years is that of gradually discovering that the parents are *not* all-power-
ful or all-wise. Beginning to take issue with parents starts the adolescents' process of freeing themselves from their control.

Such lessons must be learned by all human beings, and the adolescent years are pivotal in the process. For young female adolescents,
other special lessons are added. These are the lessons of puberty, the
natural, universal, if disconcerting, bodily changes that prepare the
girl's body for childbearing and thus for what has historically been considered her most important adult role, that of motherhood. Responses
to the changes in her body vary with the individual, of course: one may
fear them and see them as hated reminders of the limitations placed

upon women in contemporary Western culture, and another may welcome them as signs of approaching maturity. But for all, these changes, appearing suddenly and mysteriously, all too often without proper preparation, must indicate to the young woman that she does not completely control her body, that strange and complicated processes are taking place within her, whether she approves or not. Thus she must feel a new awareness of her inability to control not only her world but also what she is.

Strangely, our subject-authors pay far less attention to these physical changes of puberty (though their presence is often an underlying theme, at least by implication) than they do to the additional existence of complicating physical conditions—illness, disability, or the danger or death, all of which teach profoundly difficult lessons about the fragility of life, about the vulnerability of the individual. These lessons may be taught in many ways: through the youngster's own disability or illness, either physical or mental, or through the serious illness or death of someone dear to her. Mental or emotional disabilities may seem, at first glance, less clear evidence of human helplessness than are physical ailments, but, according to our subject-authors, the difference is not as absolute than one might at first suppose. Mental disability may be less visible to others, and clear organic, scientific causes may seem lacking, thus making it easy for the insensitive to make light of mental or emotional problems. But the girl suffering the illness feels herself no less incapable of controlling her world or herself or the relationships between the two. In fact, she may feel even more helpless, for her mental disability may cut her off from perceiving her world as it is in a way that a physical impairment never will.

Of the uncontrollable limiting characteristics with which an adolescent may be afflicted, among the most difficult for her to deal with are physical disabilities which cause her to differ obviously from others and which yet leave her in full awareness of how others perceive her. To be different and not to be able to make oneself like others is to be reminded constantly of one's helplessness in a world that is often indifferent, sometimes cruel. Painful as such recognitions must be to any human being, they are particularly excruciating for an adolescent, who has not yet had much time to accustom herself to her world and who is, as we have seen repeatedly in other connections, at a time in her life when "fitting in" is especially important to her sense of worth. And for a young woman, socialized from infancy to believe that her appearance is central to what she is, such recognitions must be even more difficult than for a young man. Perhaps because of the very intractability of the problem, because the only possible solution is acceptance of the situation, few authors have used such physical impairment as the central theme of novels.

One who has is Iris Dornfeld. The title character and narrator of Dornfeld's moving *Jeeney Ray* (1962) is a spastic in her early teens, whose older brother, in his ignorance, has always considered her a half-wit; only the grandmother, who dies as the novel opens, has seen intelligence in her eye, has encouraged her to walk, and has read to her from the Bible. Her treatment by the country people among whom she lives is brutal, but in her innocence she somehow escapes being totally destroyed by their cruelty and by the violence which often touches her. Her intelligence, revealed by her closeness to nature, her ability to mimic bird calls, and her memorized knowledge of many long Biblical passages, is finally recognized, and she receives the answer to the question she has repeatedly asked: "What am I?" Knowing that there are others like her gives her a sense of identity, and she explains her sense of new hope:

> "I been all the names of half-wit, idiot, and whore and spy and blackmailer and murderer. I been all them in shame and feeling. Every one I been and felt and was. . . . But I never been the thing I am till now!" I look at my legs and arms; I feel good knowing; I am the mystery of a wounded brain, and there are others and there is no shame in it—there are others.

Jeeney Ray's physical condition has left her mind and soul whole. Thus her suffering awareness of her difference from others is profound, but thus also her eventual accommodation to her situation and her belief in her own worth are wise and moving. A contrasting theme is used by Fred Chappell in *The Inkling* (1965), in which we meet a girl whose physical development is more or less normal but whose mental handicap makes her incapable of relating to her world in any productive way. Jeeney Ray has a sound mind in an unhealthy body, but Timmie Anderson is cursed by an unhealthy mind in a sound body. In *The Inkling*, Timmie absorbs all the attention of her brother, Jan. Though Jan is believed to be a person of extraordinary will, it becomes clear that Timmie manipulates him, using her handicap and her eventual madness as tools. For Timmie, Jan *is* the whole world; she counts on him for protection from the details of daily life which terrify her, and she imagines him as her lover as she masturbates. When she discovers him having intercourse with another girl, she resorts to violence. Denied any hope of independence, Timmie cannot love wisely, cannot grow by letting go.

Jeeney Ray (*Jeeney Ray*) and Timmie (*The Inkling*) are both the innocent victims of congenital defects, the one physical and the other mental. For these unfortunates, few options are available; Jeeney Ray makes a wise adjustment to her situation, and Timmie cannot be really blamed for the damage she wreaks. Lacking the awareness and ability to choose, lacking even the ability to understand her fated difference from others, Timmie also lacks responsibility for her actions. Adolescents also suffer other sorts of mental incapacity. Sometimes these mental or emotional disabilities are shown as unhealthy responses to intolerable situations, and sometimes they are studied as causes of damage to the young women or to others. William Goldman (*Tinsel*) and Rebecca Josephs (*Early Disorder*) demonstrate how some young women succumb to *anorexia nervosa* because of their need for an unattainable perfection which to them symbolizes maturity and control as well as the ability to win full social approval.

William Goldman, in *Tinsel* (1979), introduces a major character by saying, "Ginger, from the beginning, had it all." But actually, Ginger Abraham, like most of the characters in this "Hollywood novel," has considerable potential but almost no satisfaction or happiness. As a teenager, Ginger loses her emotional balance when her parents insist that she change to a "better" school, a school where Ginger fears she will be ostracized and will lose her excellent academic average. Though she succeeds at Brearley, the cost is high, for in proving herself to be "perfect," Ginger falls prey to *anorexia nervosa* and barely survives the attack. During much of her adulthood, she carefully avoids situations which would trigger the obsessiveness she sees as the underlying cause of the *anorexia*. *Tinsel* describes not only Ginger's adolescent illness but also later periods when her control slips and her desires (or fears) dominate her life.

Toward the opening of *Early Disorder* (1980) by Rebecca Josephs, protagonist Willa Rahv comments, "I bet I could do some pretty crazy things if I let myself loose," and this remark is a clear signal that Willa's need for control is one motivation for her attack of *anorexia nervosa*, an episode which threatens her life. Also important is the fifteen-year-old's great dissatisfaction with herself (she thinks, of course, that she's too fat, that she isn't "good" enough), with her family (they seem "perfect," but Willa sees dozens of faults beneath the surface) and her circle (she doesn't deal with boys easily and is dissatisfied with her friendships). She feels very alienated from the loving, if sometimes preoccupied, people who surround her. All these details of motivation are woven smoothly into the narrative, and Willa, actually a bright, competent youngster, is an appealing, saddening victim, effectively drawn by author Rebecca Josephs. (The publishers note that Josephs publishes fiction under another name also, but further indication of her identity is unavailable.)

Similar conflicts between the need for achievement, if not for perfection, and a sense of unworthiness afflict Susannah Ellison, narrator and protagonist of Harriet Hahn's *The Plantain Season* (1976, YA), but her psychological mode of coping is somewhat different; again, however, physical and psychological effects are intertwined. Seventeen-year-old Susannah is presented as bright and independent on the one hand, but insecure and neurotic on the other. She has psychologically induced asthma attacks, has not menstruated for a year, and develops hearing difficulties. Her mother, by her beauty and her competence as well as by the overt pressures she puts on Susannah, makes her feel inferior, although from the beginning of the novel Susannah reveals a realistic acceptance of things as they are. Observing a rat pick up peanuts that she has thrown for a bird, she tells us, "I would rather a bird had got the peanuts, but the rat didn't bother me. . . . I don't mind rats. I wouldn't want them in my home, but I know they're in the sewage pipes that run under my neighborhood—every neighborhood. There are always going to be some rats around, so you might as well not mind them." She goes her own way, leaving home, achieving the loss of her virginity, and forming new relationships. By the end of the novel, which is suitable for young adults, she has gained confidence and her psychosomatic symptoms have lessened. Susannah and other characters are likable and come to seem very real. Her matter-of-fact appraisal of herself and her experiences conveys this crucial year of her development very well.

More self-destructive, either potentially or actually, are characters in three other novels of adolescence. Harris Downey (*The Key to My Prison*), John Neufeld (*Lisa, Bright and Dark*), and Joanne Greenberg (*I Never Promised You a Rose Garden*) depict troubled girls whose mental instability poises them on the brink of insanity or death.

The central subjects of Harris Downey's *The Key to My Prison* (1964) are time and suicide. Delia Wright feels compelled toward self-destruction; her other compulsion leads her to chronicle the events and experiences that lead her toward death. She tells of a romantic first love at age seventeen, a friendship with an older woman who took the orphaned nineteen-year-old Delia into her home, and a sexual relationship with a laborer when Delia was twenty-two. The first and third episodes end in Delia's being rejected, while the second ends because of her resentment at her loss of freedom. All three point her toward isolation (which she often seems to see as independence) and even insanity. The novel belongs in the large category of fiction portraying southern female gentility and decadence, and Delia is never convincingly depicted as an adolescent.

John Neufeld's short novel, *Lisa, Bright and Dark* (1969), is a sensitive study of both Lisa, a talented sixteen-year-old who feels herself sliding into insanity, and the three girlfriends who try to help her (her parents refuse to believe that anything is wrong). As the tale is narrated by one of the friends, Betsy Goodman, a likable, sympathetic, and practical girl, we see Lisa only from the outside and never come fully to comprehend the nature of her illness. The title sums up her paradoxical appearance: "bright," she is outgoing, alert, talented, apparently well-adjusted; "dark," she is withdrawn, somberly dressed, hostile, and sometimes self-destructive. Lisa's friends offer support as best they can and try to understand her, but the novel's happy ending comes when she and they are finally able to demonstrate to her parents that she does indeed need professional treatment.

Deborah Blau, in *I Never Promised You a Rose Garden* (1964) by Joanne Greenberg (pseudonym, Hannah Green), has created a fantasy world. Once a refuge, it is now, like the real world, often a place of torture. Her mental illness is deeply rooted and complex: "A secret language concealing a still more secret one; a world veiling a hidden world; and symptoms guarding still deeper symptoms to which it was not yet time to go, and those in turn concealing a still, still deeper burning wish to live." Greenberg effectively conveys Deborah's slow, painful recovery. As Deborah learns to understand and value herself, the reader also comes to know her and to rejoice at each bit of progress. From childhood, the girl has believed herself the carrier of a poisonous aura, capable of destroying her and anyone else it touches. When repressed memories of the happiness of her very early years become acceptable to Deborah as proof "that she was not damned genetically—damned bone and fiber," both protagonist and reader feel genuine hope. Greenberg successfully weds two styles—stark realism for the real world, dark lyricism for Yr, the imaginary world—clearly demonstrating the lure of both places.

Neufeld and Greenberg both suggest optimistically that a return from madness is possible for even their very disturbed adolescents. It is to be noted, however, that both Lisa (*Lisa, Bright and Dark*) and Deborah (*I Never Promised You a Rose Garden*) are fortunate in having the help of sympathetic and loving people as well as financial resources which make possible the very special care that they need. Less fortunate is Pecola (*The Bluest Eye*), who has the burdens of poverty and a racist society to contend with and no advantages to set against those burdens.

Madness is the ultimate—and the only—refuge of Pecola Breedlove, the protagonist of *The Bluest Eye* (1970) by Toni Morrison. Because her parents are poor, ugly, and totally unable to cope with the world. the Breedloves are scorned by their black neighbors and Pecola is taunted by other black children. Because she has been raped by her father, Pecola is ostracized by the black community, becoming its scapegoat. Because she is black, white society counts her as valueless, offering her no valid role. The result of these various factors is Pecola's total isolation, and insanity becomes her sole option. But even that alternative is ironic, for Pecola's final, pitiful delusion not only symbolizes her complete alienation but also intensifies it.

The final lesson in human helplessness—even beyond madness —is taught by death, the death of a loved person or one's own threatened death. In *I Am in Urgent Need of Advice* (1962), Josephine Lawrence depicts an initially rather petulant young woman whose maturation comes about in part because of the traumatic experience of the loss of a close friend and her own concomitant sense of guilt. Amanda Carpenter, daughter of a prosperous lawyer and a loving mother, at fourteen feels that her parents do not understand her. They disapprove of her closest friend, Tully, considering Tully too mature and worldly-wise, and they refuse to let her have a telephone of her own. When Tully dies as the result of an automobile accident, Amanda feels guilty for having lied to protect Tully (she had told Tully's parents that Tully was with her when actually Tully was on a date). But she comes through the experience well. At the beginning of the novel, she had been terrified by the prospect of giving a party, but at the end of the novel she behaves with dignity and courage. Taken by a nineteen-year-old boy to a New Year's Eve party, she remains sober while her date and the couple accompanying them drink too much; though inexperienced behind the wheel, she takes charge. The policeman who picks them up says of her, "The kid has guts." Amanda is only one of several characters of approximately equal importance in the novel, all of whom must learn to rely on themselves rather than on others, but her portrait is perhaps the most believable and appealing.

More sensitive in its depiction of the guilt of those left behind after a death and more complex in its study of mental instability is Caroline Leavitt's *Meeting Rozzy Halfway* (1980). This novel touches on a theme examined at greater length elsewhere (see "Females within Families"), but it is also relevant here. From childhood to their college years, the relationship between sisters Rozzy and Bess Nelson is close, loving, and very difficult. Rozzy, bright, beautiful, and impetuous, is also emotionally unstable, a problem which becomes more serious with the passage of time. Bess, younger, also attractive, also very intelligent, protects her sister as best she can, even though her preoccupation with Rozzy threatens all other friendships and even disrupts her love affairs. In Bess's view, she was once disloyal to Rozzy, rebelling against the family's centering all activity, all their modes of living, around Rozzy's needs, and on some level—conscious or unconscious—Rozzy is aware of her ability to manipulate Bess. Guilt over that "lapse," her strong love for her sister, and her determination to make up to Rozzy for the void the older girl feels when her parents finally seem to despair of helping her, are the cords which bind Bess forever in thrall—even, perhaps, after Rozzy has sought relief from confusion and suffering in suicide. *Meeting Rozzy Halfway* is a powerful novel which offers remarkably fair portraits of both young women and a compelling examination of mental illness and suicide.

Suicide, as Leavitt suggests, is doubtless the most difficult kind of death for those left behind to come to terms with. A sense of guilt and failure almost necessarily torments the survivors. This fact gives Gina Berriault the basic premise for her novel, *Conference of Victims* (1962), which studies the impact of a suicide on a number of those left behind, one of whom is a female adolescent. The suicide of a young congressional candidate shortly after he had been seen with Dolores Lenci, his seventeen-year-old mistress, is a pivotal event in the lives of a number of characters, not the least Dolores herself. From that time on, she is obsessed with being an "enchantress who enthralled men forever," and she tells her lovers, older married men, that he had killed himself for love of her. But each new affair ends, and six years later she is still desperately searching, fighting the knowledge that she has little to offer men besides her sexual favors. While the novel studies members of the politician's family equally closely, young Dolores's portrait is particularly striking.

Disability, illness, and death, like other sorts of challenges, can be ultimately strengthening or destructive, depending on the innate toughness of the young woman facing them and upon the kind of support she receives from others. Despite the apparent hopelessness of her situation, the protagonist of *Jeeney Ray* has both intelligence and sweetness; although nothing can be done to better her physical condition, the quality of her life and of her sense of self can be profoundly improved. Young women suffering from psychosomatic illnesses can be helped to understand themselves and thus to arrive at more workable relationships with imperfect selves and an imperfect world (Josephs's *Early Disorder*, for example, and Hahn's *The Plaintain Season*). Proper care and support are crucial, as suggested by Neufeld (*Lisa, Bright and Dark*). The same point is also implicit in Morrison's *The Bluest Eye*; for Pecola, the absolute lack of people who care about her makes her situation hopeless. Particularly fortunate is Deborah (*I Never Promised You a Rose Garden*), because her family cares deeply for her and is able to procure needed and competent care and therapy—and because she has within her the native gifts and strength which enable her, with help, to travel the long journey from illness back to health. That road, difficult to travel by the experienced adult, is especially fraught with impediment and danger for the vulnerable adolescent; those who are confronted with these especially difficult challenges need especially great help to come through them to a full maturity. But for those that do come through, the lessons learned may well be profound, for these youngsters have been forced to examine not only the usual adolescent questions of life in this world but problems relating to their very nature as human beings. They know much about what it means to be an insecure being in a universe with no rules guaranteeing them any success or happiness. Knowing that they do not control their own physical and emotional or mental well-being, they know how fragile life and sanity are; and, if they come through their ordeals with any degree of acceptance and understanding, they are certain to be wise, loving adults, able to cope with their own future trials and to empathize with others in their hours of despair.

Part Two

CHAPTER VIII
Male Love and Sexuality

Adolescents are beset by two extraordinarily pressing questions: "Who am I?" and "How can I prove that I control my own life?" As old as humankind, these riddles are nevertheless ever new, freshly and uniquely posed to each of us by ourselves. Almost every male adolescent figuring in the novels discussed here perceives sexual intercourse as a major factor in his initiation experience; sexual activity, he believes, is clear proof of masculinity, of adult power.

Furthermore, some adolescent male characters equate their first experiences of intercourse almost completely with initiation, whereas among the female characters included in this survey, only one, the protagonist of Merrill Joan Gerber's *Now Molly Knows* (1974), considers intercourse to be full initiation. Like Molly, many single-minded male initiates believe that through intercourse they will arrive at true, powerful answers to the eternal questions which will grant them adulthood, will endow them with a sense of their own maturity, and will reward them with recognition of their maturity by others. Though Molly's inner declaration that now she "knows" all echoes a bit hollowly, overtones of triumphant confidence may inform adolescent males' assessments. Ironically, one vivid statement of this attitude is expressed by a young rapist who feels that because of his experience, he has come of age.

In Mendal W. Johnson's *Let's Go Play at the Adams'* (1974), five children imprison and then take turns tormenting Barbara, the twenty-year-old babysitter for two of them. Each, through his or her own relationship with Barbara, learns about his or her own feelings and desires as well as about evil within. For sixteen-year-old John Randall, eldest of the three boys, the relationship is largely, but not wholly, sexual; he rapes her twice. The first time he is clumsy, out of his great ignorance; the second time he is both more knowing and oddly tender. He discovers that, despite the cruelty he is wreaking upon her, part of him also loves her; still he is content to continue to torture her. He considers the experience his coming of age.

> He had broken out of the prison of childhood; he was no longer someone just to be ordered around, he had solved what he too considered the "mystery." He could *do it* from here on as well as any grown-up—and he had done it. With a defiant, self-immolatory glee, he was absolutely delighted with himself. He had exe-

cuted a real, fundamental, human act: he had entered life in spite of them all. (*Them* he defined as adults—those tedious, living pains-in-the-ass who held you down so long and took such pleasure in doing it.) And he had sampled something of love as well, not simply the physical side, but the spiritual and revelatory side, too. He saw now—at last—the possibility of falling in love himself someday.

John Randall is both an anomaly (he is a rapist) and a prototype (he represents exactly the attitudes many young males hold toward adolescent sexual activity), but readers wonder what the future holds for single-minded youths such as John and Molly (*Now Molly Knows*) who define themselves so narrowly, relying primarily upon their sexuality to grant them adult power. Because they are still too inexperienced to know (let alone to accept) that redefinition of one's self-image is demanded again and again at various stages of life, young people attempt to devise answers which will suffice throughout their lifetimes; authors and mature readers understand that quick acceptance of any one answer to any of life's crucial questions often leads to unhappiness and perpetual immaturity.

Nevertheless, unaware that they are undertaking an all but impossible task; feeling positive that self-assertion will somehow help them to discover wonderful, liberating answers; and enchanted, alarmed, or enchanted *and* alarmed by their sexual awakening, most male adolescents set about finding and, very often, *possessing* a lover, assuming that sexual activity (of almost any level of intensity) will define their identities and confer—or confirm—maturity. To be desired, they feel, affirms that there is a viable personality inside each suddenly exciting, perplexing young body; to achieve consummation, they feel, means escape from adolescence. They want what fiction, poetry, folklore, advertising all promise—everything—physical, emotional, and psychological gratification which will ratify the sense of self. On another level, of course, this search for sexual maturity also connotes emancipation from parental rule, progress toward alliances intended to sustain them through adulthood.

These expectations, however, are almost never wholly met. According to the novels read for this study, youngsters of both sexes often discover instead that sexual alliances, ranging from crushes through marriage, pose more questions than they answer. Their first experience of sexual intercourse does, of course, teach most of them the basic, physical facts about sex, heretofore usually the object of much speculation and discussion among both males and females. For many adolescents, the experience also confirms their heterosexuality or their homosexuality. But sexual activity also raises questions of responsibility and responsiveness that, to many of these fictional adolescents, seem endlessly perplexing. For heterosexual adolescent males as for heterosexual adolescent females, much of that perplexity stems directly from society's expectation that traditionally passive females must control the level of intimacy a couple enjoy despite the importunities of traditionally assertive males.

As a rule, society requires young men to be more aggressive than young women, an expectation which endangers their emerging self-confidence even as it flatters them. The burden of initiating a simple date or a long-term affair or marriage is, society assumes, primarily the male's responsibility. For male adolescents who may be uncertain of their looks or their sexual appeal—or even of the very nature of their sexuality—making overtures at each step of courtship requires considerable courage. Though heterosexual young men can expect both overt and covert encouragement from women, they don't know until the invitation has been issued whether acceptance, acquiescence, or rejection will ensue, and rejection—harsh, coy, or gentle—is as devastating to them as it is to young women. Rejection suggests the absence of a viable, attractive personality and the absence of control; the boys in these novels frequently assume that they alone or they especially suffer from unattractiveness, uncertainty, or ineptness. Their suffering in these instances is much like that of adolescent females, with one major difference: in the love affairs depicted in our subject-novels, adolescent males do not define themselves according to the acceptance of others so wholly as do adolescent females.

Instead, they usually measure their worth according to the degree of success achieved by aggressive behavior, rather a different matter. The distinction is a fine one, but it is crucial. For the young men depicted in these novels, possession of a lover is often more important than being possessed. That is, being loved (and thus valued) does not so much define their characters as does loving a partner or even simply engaging in sexual intercourse. The act of persuading a partner to comply seems very important to their self-images.

The possession of a lover who is very attractive, who is won in open competition with another male, or who is generally thought by one's peers to be very desirable obviously enhances a lad's immediate social status, exciting envy among his male associates and enriching his feeling of traditional manliness. To win a great prize is, they assume, to win everything. Hence, the temptation to see very desirable partners not only as sex-objects but also as status-objects is always present, demeaning the female partner, burnishing the young male partner's public image, but quite possibly limiting his inner growth. The success of conquest can blind one to the need to nurture a relationship, and the acquisition of an enviable love-object can intensify the impulse to press for ever greater sexual intimacy as physical desire exacerbates the continuing need to prove one's masculinity. Quite often, the need to prove one's masculinity also prompts young males to talk about their conquests. More frequently than the females (only a few of whom speak quite frankly to close friends about their sexual experimentations), adolescent males describe, boast, or even lie about their experiences, thus insisting to themselves and to their male peers that they are "really men."

Because they have been taught that to be male is to be aggressive, it seems far more necessary for these fictional males to act (and to advertise their actions) than to be receptive. Because they have been taught to be aggressive, they tend to demand gratification rather than to recognize their need for love. In a way, then, they must deny one important need to serve another. One way of serving both the need to assert oneself and the need to feel loved is, of course, to press for more and more intimate sexual contact with one's partner and thus to complicate the young female's responsibility for regulating the degree of allowed intimacy. Escalation of intimacy is difficult for young females (who are expected to say "no" but still retain their lovers), and demands for ever greater proofs of love can seem hazardous to young males also because they multiply the possibilities for rejection.

Moreover, if an adolescent male impregnates his partner, he must then confront his responsibility toward her and their child. Though few of the novels studied here treat young males' reaction to abortion, several do discuss the consequences of marriages undertaken because of pregnancy, and only infrequently do the authors depict such unions as positive or even wise. The sudden assumption of the traditional role of provider and decision-maker is apparently too burdensome for these youngsters, who bend or break or rebel against it.

In many ways, combining assertiveness with the need to feel loved can be, of course, at least as hard for young heterosexuals who desire older lovers as for those who desire peers, for then, rejection can be taken to mean rejection by the adult establishment which their sexual experiments are supposedly preparing them to join. Similarly, young homosexuals, well aware of the predominant social attitudes toward homosexuality, also know that to approach the "wrong" potential lover could mean public disdain as well as personal rejection. For both heterosexual and homosexual adolescent males, the risk is very great.

Authors' emphasis on possession, pride, ego, and status does not, however, obviate the intensity or seriousness with which many fictional youths approach their affairs, as even John Randall's assessment of his initiation (*Let's Go Play at the Adams'*) indicates. Like their female counterparts, many love deeply and are genuinely committed to their partners. Also, like many girls, many boys are willing to brave parental disapproval, social disapprobation, and, unwittingly, the corrosive effect of time. Because they are very young and because one object of their affairs is initiation into manhood, another object of their alliances is personal development and maturation. With change often comes stress, the dissolution of the relationship, and genuine suffering.

The pain of relinquishment poses yet another trial for young lovers, teaching them an important lesson. Despite the supposition of many young men (such as John Randall of *Let's Go Play at the Adams'*), acquiring a love-object, being loved, and sustaining love are really but three of the *many* tests which occur on successful maturation journeys. Adolescent males who fail to grasp this concept do not truly mature.

Elliott Baker, John Weston, and other authors stress the point that sexual curiosity and development function as only two among many factors in young men's initiatory experiences. In the summer of 1939, sixteen-year-old Tyler A. Bishop, in Elliott Baker's *The Penny Wars* (1968), loses his father and sees his mother become involved with an arrogant German refugee dentist. Fascinated by sex, more bookish than the other boys in his ethnically mixed neighborhood, Tyler experiences and observes much of the pathos and suffering of life. The novel, a complex depiction of the confusions of growing up, begins comically but turns serious before its violent ending.

Apparently autobiographical, Elliott Baker's *Unrequited Loves* (1974), a collection of episodes narrated by "Elliott," dramatizes five stages in a boy's maturation. At nine he observes the mental breakdown of a favorite aunt, at twelve he becomes a peeping tom, at sixteen he begins sexual experimentation and is drawn into the question of what art is, at seventeen he plays baseball for a small Hoosier college, and at twenty-two he participates in the end of World War II. A central theme is the adolescent preoccupation with sex, and a subsidiary motif is that of the nature of art.

Jolly Osment, a typical teenager and the protagonist of John Weston's *Jolly* (1965), is preoccupied with sex but naive about it. During the week covered by the novel, he meets a young woman who seems to represent his ideal, takes her out but loses her to his best friend (a much more knowing and crude young man), and visits a brothel just across the Mexican border. His curiosity and idealism mixed with rough lust are effectively conveyed, although the novel is relatively plotless, and the use of multiple points of view seems irrelevant to the central issue of Jolly's search for identity.

Other novels focus much more directly upon sexual initiation as a prime factor in male development. A major concern of Harry Craft, one of the many characters followed in Harvey Jacobs's *Summer on a Mountain of Spices* (1975), for instance, is attaining his first sexual experience. Still other books in which the theme of sexual initiation predominates link sexuality with violence as in Mendal W. Johnson's *Let's Go Play at the Adams'*. Also, like Johnson, Evan Hunter and Robert H. Adelman depict young females' propensity for cruelty as vividly as they reveal males'.

In Evan Hunter's *Last Summer* (1968), Peter (the narrator) and David observe and then participate in innocent and then brutal sexual activity as a result of their involvement with Sandy, a girl who is paradoxically both kind-hearted and cruel. The boys are titillated by Sandy's willingness to show them and then allow them to caress her body, and, hoping she will allow them to have intercourse with her, they supply themselves with condoms. But Rhoda, slightly younger, less sexually frank, and never really a part of their group, intrudes, and, with Sandy's encouragement, the boys rape her. Their thoughtless cruelty had been summed up when, in another connection, Peter had rationalized to Rhoda, "We didn't mean any harm last night. . . . We were only trying to have a little fun. . . . We didn't know the night was going to turn out the way it did. Rhoda, we *couldn't* have known." The dark side of adolescent sensation-seeking and sexual fumbling is hauntingly revealed in this sensitive and restrained novel.

In *The Bloody Benders* (1970), based on fact, Robert H. Adelman analyzes law-supporting and law-breaking violence on the Kansas frontier through the voice of Bradley Fisher. Of particular interest is Bradley's concept of maturity. He first believes himself to have achieved manhood by becoming the lover of young Kate Bender, a thief and a murderer. But his maturation is not really complete until he and a posse of Kate's other lovers "purge" themselves and the community by killing Kate and her family. Awkwardly written, the disturbing novel is a startling commentary about one connection between sex, violence, and corruption.

Let's Go Play at the Adams' and *Last Summer* illustrate the social proposition that weak or helpless females are meant to be possessed and used (a disturbing belief shared by some of the female characters). *The Bloody Benders* reflects the frontier tradition that taking the law into one's own hands is somehow redemptive and cleansing for the community and rather grimly echoes the hunters' tradition of ritually "blooding" the young hunter after his first kill as an obvious initiation rite.

Significantly, Robert H. Adelman also addresses the question of guilt in *The Bloody Benders*. Expected to engage in sexual experimentation even though many of them have been taught that sex is dirty or wrong, many youngsters suffer considerably, torn between conflicting desires and confused by contradictory signals from adults. Another novel treating the guilts of adolescent sexuality, this time in relationship to Roman Catholicism, is Rocco Fumento's *Tree of Dark Reflection* (1962). In most of our subject-novels, however, the theme of guilt is less dominant, and young male characters' ability to control or to withstand guiltiness is considered as a collateral test on the road to maturity, their developing capacity to distinguish between right and wrong, to know when to accept or reject society's preachments being an important sign of growth.

William Goldman, however, in *Tinsel* (1979), depicts a character perpetually unable to accept responsibility for his actions, perpetually guiltless in his own eyes, perpetually destructive and immature. As a very young adolescent, Noel Garvey has time on his hands, plenty of money, few friends, and little positive attention from his parents. When his preoccupation with comic books is jeered into oblivion by his family, Noel feeds his imagination on television, particularly a program called *Dogpatch*, whose female lead, Dixie Crowder, becomes the object of his adolescent fantasies. Years later, those fantasies motivate Noel to seduce and exploit Dixie, who badly wants a role in a film he is "producing" under the tutelage of his father, a powerful Hollywood figure. *Tinsel* demonstrates, through Noel's characterization, that in Tinsel Town some adults never outgrow their adolescent fantasies; they merely learn to exploit others in order to satisfy them.

As William Goldman uses Noel Garvey's sexual exploitativeness to comment upon the Hollywood mentality (*Tinsel*), so do other authors illustrate social problems and destructive adult attitudes by showing their infringement upon young men's love affairs. One powerful example is *them* (1969) by Joyce Carol Oates. Although he is clearly "the favorite" of both his mother and his grandmother, the authority figures of his childhood and adolescence, Jules Wendall yearns for yet more love: "The affection of other people was like a fishhook in Jules." Thus, when he becomes instantly infatuated with Nadeen, another uneasy adolescent, the two run off together in a crazy, frustrating junket which ends amid the heat, dirt, and aridity of a cheap Texas motel. Nadeen fears intercourse (does Jules have "a disease"?) and steadily demands various supplies even though the pair have no money. But because he does love her and because "Nadeen fed his idle dreams of becoming rich," Jules is willing to steal in order to satisfy her desires. When Jules falls ill, Nadeen deserts him, stealing his car and heading home toward economic security. Her abandonment marks the end of his adolescence. Nevertheless, the fishhook is firmly embedded, and *them* also records the adult Jules's loyalty to Nadeen, his chosen, dangerous love-object; for him, she represents the American Dream—and the unlikelihood of his ever attaining it.

The young lovers of *Danger Song* (1967) by Bryant Rollins are doomed from the start. The protagonist, Martin Williams, a young black, is slow to mature because of conflicting signals and pressures from his family, from peers, from white society. Eventually, however, Martin does grow up: "It was the strange kind of growth a Negro boy passes through as he attempts to move out of his small world and into the greater world, but cannot and is repeatedly rebuffed and forced back into himself. It is the frustrating attempt to burst out of a cocoon of negritude and the repeated failures." The chief symbol of his new maturity is Martin's developing love for Arla McMahon, a young white girl who works with him at a Roxbury teen center. Clearly, a successful, nurturing relationship between Martin and Arla would signify hope for the racial torment of Boston, their home, and for the United States, their larger home. Instead, for Martin and Arla, maturation and love, movement toward independence and free choice can lead only to tragedy. Neither their immediate nor their larger environment is ready to permit them to live lives fulfilled by one another.

Two examples illustrate happier, more strengthening results of young males' confrontation with corruption, with the overt and the covert rules by which adult society operates. This device is very common in novels treating males' sexual development, appearing in almost every subject-novel. But in *A Family Gathering* and *The Reivers*, it is a point of major emphasis. In T. Alan Broughton's *A Family Gathering* (1977), young Lawson Wright's awareness of new and puzzling physical sensations is associated with his adoration of his older cousin, Bonnie. He is twelve, a shy and inarticulate boy, and she is nineteen and about to be married. Briefly they turn to each other for understanding (there are no others in the family of their generation for them to turn to), and Lawson then feels destroyed by her marriage. His glimpses of her naked body when they are skinny-dipping is an innocent preparation for the shock that comes later when he sees his father and another woman naked, thus learning of his father's adultery. Though the father is the true central figure of the novel, Lawson's viewpoint is important and sensitively rendered, and his sexual awakening is poignantly conveyed.

Though Lucius Priest, of William Faulkner's *The Reivers* (1962), is only eleven when he takes a trip to a Memphis boardinghouse, his experiences are clearly his initiation into manhood. Instincts tell him that one of the "boarders," Everbe Corinthia (last name unknown) is a good person because she is pretty, gentle, and kind. Lucius loves her, and she loves him; he is caught up in a sort of worshipful crush; she is maternal and supportive. Actually, Lucius's instincts are correct even though the boardinghouse is really a brothel and Everbe is really a prostitute. When Lucius, a true knight, fights to protect his lady's reputation, she promises him to quit her job, and later, when circumstances force her to have intercourse with an unsavory lawman in order to protect Lucius and his rogue companions, the boy is disappointed and hurt. Everbe's behavior, however, is one of Lucius's most important maturation lessons, for he learns that adults must often compromise and that evil—and good—takes many shapes. Everbe has discharged human responsibility as she perceives it, and in *The Reivers* human responsibility is Faulkner's most important theme.

Generally, treatment of an adolescent as a sex-object is confined to female characters, just as society tends to see only females in this light. But Ruth Doan MacDougall's *The Cheerleader* (1973) depicts one male adolescent's first serious love affair simply as a means of revealing her female protagonist's development. Attractive, popular, and athletic, Tom Forbes is a desirable steady boyfriend, and "Snowy" Snow's efforts to attract and hold him as her "steady" are a major focus of the novel. Because Tom is revealed primarily through Snowy's thoughts about him, her discussions of him with other girls, and the couple's brief snatches of dialogue (which don't reveal many of Tom's real thoughts), we see him primarily through the girl's point of view. He serves as Snowy's partner in the sexual experimentation which reveals her maturation, as her support in some times of stress, as a source of pain when he breaks off the relationship, and as the motivation for one of Snowy's most important decisions, a decision which will help determine the shape of her future. Primarily a sex object, Tom is, nevertheless, an appealing figure, and his own development, though shadowy, is a deepening factor in the novel.

Both Don Bredes and John Bowers reflect the more common treatment of young women as sex-objects, but both also inform their characterizations with adolescent males' awareness (however dim) that physicality is only one element in a healthy relationship. The world of high-school boys and their adolescent obsession with their sexuality is realistically evoked in Don Bredes's *Hard Feelings* (1977). At sixteen, Bernie Hergruter, a member of the tennis team and a bright student, loves Barbara but also becomes involved with several other girls. He and his friends think of little but sex, and Bernie is proud to become somewhat more experienced than his closest friend. The dialogue reflects their fascination, for it is full of sexual and scatological references. Bernie wonders privately about the relation between sex and love, and he does see Barbara and one other girl, a black who lives in a different world from his, as friends and human beings, not just as sexual vessels. But his (and the book's) main interest is in sex as a physiological phenomenon.

Adolescent obsession with sexuality is also a central theme in John Bowers's *No More Reunions* (1973), a treatment of high-school days in Tennessee that is partly comic and partly nostalgic but always realistic. Boney, the protagonist and narrator, and his friends are taken from naive fascination through fumbled gropings to clumsy consummation. Their language is crude and their attitudes are vulgar, but Boney's half-articulated desire for something beyond the simple and physical, especially with the one particular girl, is hinted at.

For other adolescent male lovers, sexual initiation symbolizes healing or security in addition to approaching manhood. Though the symbolism is conventional, it is cast in a rather unusual mode in Frank Herbert's *Soul Catcher* (1972), in which the male character is more acted upon than acting. David Marshall's initiation into sex by a young American Indian woman is only one small, but symbolic, aspect of the maturation he undergoes when kidnapped by an insane Indian. The kidnapper has selected him as an Innocent, suitable for sacrifice, and the young woman seeks to destroy David's innocence, thus saving him. The event itself is touchingly handled, as David's apprehension is erased by her skill and his discovery of his own prowess.

Ordinary People (1976) by Judith Guest shows conventionally, but nevertheless effectively, the protagonist's reawakened ability to give succor. Con Jarrett, who has been mentally ill, fears responsibility because he thinks he is weak and unstable. For this reason, he avoids friendships among his peers. When he begins to date Jeannine Pratt, the relationship signals an important step in his recovery. Eventually, he discovers that Jeannine, too, has problems, and she turns to him for comfort. "He stands there holding her; tests the feeling of someone leaning on him, looking to him for support. He feels as if he could stand here holding her forever. . . . He has never felt so strong, so needed." Con's newly discovered ability to help Jeannine rather than to be helped indicates genuine progress toward mental health and foreshadows his recovery.

For the most part, the examples we have discussed to this point depict relationships between male and female peers that teach the male partners important lessons about themselves, life, society, and the relative importance of their sexuality. Just as John Randall's triumphant evaluation of his shocking initiation (*Let's Go Play at the Adams'*) expresses the attitudes of young males who see sexual initiation as full initiation, so Colin Wynn's experiences summarize the milder, more positive experiences of hosts of fictional male adolescents. Colin, the protagonist of *The Year the Lights Came On* (1976) by Terry Kay, is smitten with Megan Priest.

> Megan Priest was my girl.
> At least, I suspected she was my girl. I did not know for certain how those experiences developed. Megan was kind and gentle and there was a warmth about her that only I seemed to feel. She smiled each time I looked at her and her smile would lodge in my breathing and suffocate me for an eye-blink of time. When we played softball, I could sense her eyes following me and if I stole a glance to the place where I thought she would be, she was always there, watching.

Though Megan belongs to a rival crowd, she and Colin pursue their innocent courtship which forces Colin to test and redefine his loyalties. The relationship is portrayed gently, with insight and humor. Though Colin Wynn's sexual initiation is a positive experience, it is also a test of his mettle and his developing maturity. Peer pressure threatens to disrupt Colin and Megan's relationship, and they must evaluate their importance to one another in the light of their friends' attitudes as well as their own desires.

Other authors depict protagonists who must suffer the loss of their partners before their initiations can be complete. Handsome Alan Bennett, the protagonist, narrates *If I Love You, Am I Trapped Forever?* (1973, YA) by Marijane Meaker (pseudonym, M. E. Kerr). During his senior year in high school, Alan, the most popular boy in school, deeply loves Leah Pennington, a charming, attractive girl. The two seem to be an ideal couple until Leah becomes attracted to another boy. Alan is puzzled and hurt.

> I'd meant what I said when I'd told Leah . . . . that I didn't know what the word 'love' meant. Maybe I still don't, but that Sunday night it seemed to me that there was absolutely no safety in that word. I associated it with warning signs like 'Thin Ice' and 'Narrow Passage' and 'Dangerous Crossing.' The only thing . . . that made any sense was that love was just too hard.

The end of their affair is Alan's initiation experience; it leaves him sadder but wiser and more understanding, certainly more mature than he was at the beginning of the school term.

Zebulon Whalley of *Entering Ephesus* (1971) by Daphne Athas feels betrayed when Urania Bishop, his friend of long standing, undertakes an affair with Edmund Bostwick, a much older man and Zebul's hero. He turns to Urie's younger sister, Loco Poco, and their romance is marked by genuinely innocent sexual abandon. When Bostwick, a naval officer, is ordered away, both affairs stop. Though it is Loco who first withdraws from Zebul, he recognizes the correctness of her decision: "If he had learned sex with Loco, he was now changing from boy to man by giving up sex with her." In his new status, Zebul is able to enjoy a renewal of friendship with Urie. As Bostwick has betrayed Zebul, Loco has betrayed Urie, and Zebul understands that innocence and betrayal are both factors in human life.

Zebul Whalley (*Entering Ephesus*), Alan Bennett (*If I Love You, Am I Trapped Forever?*), and Colin Wynn (*The Year the Lights Came On*), major characters in these novels, are introspective youths who examine their lives and their personal development and come to understand that challenge and loss, while painful, are important determinants of their mature personalities.

An important secondary character in Thomas Berger's *Sneaky People* (1975), fifteen-year-old Ralph Sandifer, though still lacking in experience, is almost as preoccupied with sex as his womanizing father. Not particularly thoughtful or introspective, Ralph is, nevertheless, a basically decent and honest boy, though almost no one else in the novel turns out to be what he—or she—seems. Ralph, however, full of his own affairs, realizes little of this and finds joy in adoration of the woman who, unknown to him, is his father's mistress. He is a wholly believable boy and perhaps the most likable character in this sardonically comic novel.

As a rule, affairs between adolescent males and more mature women are subject to the same pressures as affairs between adolescent couples. Though the women may be aware of social disapproval (since older-female–young-male alliances have not been the norm in American culture), these pressures are not seriously addressed in these novels. Some few of these relationships damage or fail the male partners.

The real center of consciousness in Rosalyn Drexler's comic, erratic, and surrealistic *One or Another* (1970) is Melissa Johnson, a thirty-year-old housewife having an affair with J, her husband's seventeen-year-old student. Reality and fantasy merge and J's consciousness is never revealed, but his attempts to end the affair and his descent into madness are believably presented.

Another example of a destructive affair between an adolescent male and an older woman treats the subject of incest. In Pete Hamill's *Flesh & Blood* (1977), young Bobby Fallon feels a fascinated hatred of the father who deserted him long ago and a desperate love for his attractive but shallow young mother. Eventually a brief affair between mother and son, in which she is the seducer, takes place. The emotional violence which she inflicts upon him is only one aspect of the sordid life which he must learn to cope with in this plain-spoken novel which has been variously described as "sensitive," "lyrical," "lifeless," and "recycled pulp."

Another taboo, American society's belief that a black male and a white female should not engage in intercourse, is exploited by Erskine Caldwell in *The Weather Shelter* (1969) to motivate a father's tardy acknowledgment of his illegitimate son. Jeff Bazemore is the mulatto natural son of white Grover Danford, a Tennessee pony rancher. Jeff is seduced by a white woman, and when the resulting baby is born, local whites plot to lynch him. This grim sexual initiation is partially redeemed by Jeff's discovery of his paternity during Grover's efforts to spirit him to safety. Despite the vicious racial bias depicted in *The Weather Shelter*, Caldwell seems to foreshadow a better future through Grover's promise that Jeff will inherit the family business.

By far the majority of subject-novels depicting sexual attraction between May-September male-female couples, however, use the relationships (which range from unconsummated crushes to extended affairs) very positively, as the following examples demonstrate. In each, the adolescent male learns something of his own capacity for tenderness, often giving as much support as he receives. In these cases, parting—even the irrevocable loss of the loved one through terminal illness—is presented as a useful, instructive element in the boy's maturation process.

While Alan Bennett, the narrator of *If I Love You, Am I Trapped Forever?* (1973) by Marijane Meaker (pseudonym, M. E. Kerr), is trying to cope with his troubled courtship of a fellow student, he is also experiencing a serious crush on Catherine Stein, the mother of one of his acquaintances. Despite the fact that he suspects Catherine of having an affair with the high-school football coach, Alan idolizes her, cherishing the impact and the memories of their few meetings. When Catherine reveals that she is not perfect but only human, Alan is deeply shaken. Marijane Meaker depicts this relationship with clear understanding, neither sentimentalizing nor trivializing it.

When John Hand, protagonist of Jane Langton's *Natural Enemy* (1982), takes a summer job as man of all work for the Heron family, he gets more excitement than he bargained for. Mr. Heron is murdered early in the plot, and the killer competes with young John for the attentions of the younger Heron daughter, Virginia. John's growing love for Virginia is further complicated by the fact that she is an "older woman" (she is about twenty-three), and he fears that he will seem "like a kid" to her. Virginia is both more sensible and more sensitive than she first seems, however, and she responds to the lad's affection with propriety and grace. This old twist on the even older story of young love is handled skillfully and lends a deepening dimension to a mystery tale.

A brief affair with an older woman (she is twenty-five to his eighteen) is one of the few good moments in Paul Adamic's life in Robert Baylor's *To Sting the Child* (1964). By treating her gently and with respect, he gives her back the passion and sense of womanliness she has lost, and she gives him his first truly successful relationship with a woman.

In Gerald Warner Brace's sensitive depiction of a boy's maturation, *The Wind's Will* (1964), David Wayne becomes briefly involved with two older women during the pivotal summer between his graduation from high school and setting off for college. The first is a twenty-five-year-old teacher, who tactfully rejects his sexual advances, trying not to embarrass or hurt him. The second is a mature woman, a lonely refugee, who seduces him out of her own desperate need. This affair is broken off when her concomitant affair with David's father is revealed. The impact on David is shattering. If the affair itself made David a man sexually, the fact that he comes through its messy aftermath shows that he has also matured emotionally and has gained the courage he had lacked at the book's opening.

A crucial but troubled affair between eighteen-year-old Steve Harper and a mature woman, a successful poet whose work he had adored, is at the center of Barbara Wersba's *The Country of the Heart* (1975, YA). Dying of cancer, she resists his clumsy attempts at friendship but finally their relationship ripens into physical passion. It is cut short, however, by her worsening condition. The novel is both his tribute to her and his attempt to understand her and himself. Tender, puzzled, tormented, it conveys his youthful intensity and passion, and at the end it seems clear that his memory of the affair will enrich his life and work.

As we have observed earlier, teenagers often believe that a lengthy affair is by definition a nurturing relationship or that it is good preparation for marriage. The authors of these subject-novels, however, use extended relationships, long courtship, cohabitation, and marriage both positively and negatively, in exactly the same ways they use affairs of shorter duration. In some novels, long alliances foreshadow or symbolize failure or inability to mature, sometimes because of outside interference, sometimes because of personal inadequacy. Roderick Chapin, for instance, grows up in a camp for white prisoners of the Comanches on the Texas frontier, escaping only for a brief period of service in the Confederate Army and returning sick and lame. The central action of John H. Culp's *A Whistle in the Wind* (1968) depicts Roderick's dangerous courtship of Cesre, a fellow captive, who is also desired by a powerful Indian chief and by a Comanchero. Roderick's struggle to establish a herd of sheep parallels his courtship, the two actions symbolizing his difficult and doomed maturation.

A brief youthful marriage, entered idealistically by the boy and calculatingly by the girl, sets up the situation for Charlotte Armstrong's suspense novel *The Turret Room* (1965). At eighteen, Harold Page, a simple and good young man, had married a spoiled rich girl. Her people not only had the marriage dissolved but got him committed to a mental hospital. When the novel opens, he has just been released and comes in search of his little son, for whom he feels both love and responsibility, partly because the child has inherited a congenital deafness from Harold. The girl, however, still single-mindedly working for her own selfish ends, victimizes Harold again, and only the intervention of a young woman, a social worker distantly connected with the family, gives him any chance of escape. He is clearly and unsentimentally characterized as "an ordinary nice kid, a little naive. One without defenses, who had suffered in a way that the tougher kind of young male animal . . . might not."

One of the five main characters of *Original Sins* (1981) by Lisa Alther, Donny is a star athlete in his all-black high school and shares dreams of college and a profession with Rochelle, his equally capable, ambitious "steady." The couple enjoy a happy, stable relationship until Rochelle must drop out of school to care for and support her mother and her several siblings. Because Donny truly loves Rochelle and her little brothers and sisters, he, too, leaves school; they marry; and both take menial jobs to support their extended family. Locked into the limited future open to young blacks in Newland, Tennessee, in the late 1950s and 1960s, Donny and Rochelle turn their anger against one another, and even their ultimate escape from the South offers only limited hope that they can achieve happiness and security.

The shockingly unexpected suicide of the girl with whom he has been living helps persuade young Arthur Skelton, protagonist of B. H. Friedman's *Yarborough* (1964), that life is meaningless. She had been one of the very few stabilizing influences in his life, and his discovery of her apparently unmotivated self-destruction is a shattering experience.

A strange but long-lasting heterosexual relationship is followed in

Al Hine's *Lord Love a Duck* (1961). When Alan ("Gooney Bird") Musgrave meets high-school classmate Barbara Anne Greene, he is a mathematical genius but physically unprepossessing while she is both beautiful and popular. Because he sees her as a representative of the world of ordinary people which he both hates and fears, he successfully seeks to control her through hypnotism. While there is an important erotic element to their relationship, this remains secondary to his secret satisfaction in being able to manipulate her actions with no one, including Barbara Anne, being aware of it. A satire of the middle-America world, the novel is sharply critical and extremely funny.

Though "he hasn't forgotten why he wanted to get married, how good it feels to wake up in the morning curled around her," Mark, in *Baby Love* (1981) by Joyce Maynard, feels trapped in his marriage to Sandy, the high-school sweetheart he has known since childhood; their marriage is the result of an unplanned pregnancy. Mark is restless because Sandy makes him feel childish, he feels no strong bond to his son, and the remainder of his life now seems like a gaping void. Anger, sexual fantasies, and an extramarital affair are Mark's means of coping with his uneasiness, and the problems inherent in his marriage form one of several plots in *Baby Love*.

There are also novels that use extended sexual relationships as essentially happy plot complications, allowing alienated young artist-protagonists to find peace and an integrated sense of self by means of their affairs and thus to gain enough confidence and poise to face the outside world with augmented self-esteem. James Baldwin's Leo Proud-hammer, in *Tell Me How Long the Train's Been Gone* (1968), identifies himself as bisexual and describes an important relationship with a young man, but his deepest and most lasting affair, beginning when they are both aspiring young actors, is with Barbara King. He is black and poor and she is white and a Kentucky heiress, but they become friends as well as lovers. Though their friendship is only one of a number of continuing motifs in this large, complex novel, it is crucial for Leo in that it gives him the stability he needs.

Despite some homosexual fantasies and initial failures at heterosexual activity, fifteen-year-old Richard Goodman, the protagonist of Rafael Yglesias's *The Work Is Innocent* (1976), eventually finds a sexual outlet with Joan, a young woman who understands his precocity (he has just finished his first novel, which is published during their liaison). Their lovemaking and his feelings about it are fully and specifically described; with her help he progresses from a bumbler to a reasonably sensitive lover. And for him, his sexual success, long despaired of, is a symbol of his maturation; it gives him the confidence to behave as an equal of the other members of his talented family.

David Marks, narrator of Barbara Wersba's *Run Softly, Go Fast* (1970, YA), finds his salvation in his love for Maggie, the young woman with whom he lives in New York's East Village. Bitterly estranged from his father and trying to find himself as an artist, he has become deeply involved with hard drugs. By her love and strength, Maggie is able to help him leave behind the destructive elements of his life and become rather surprisingly successful. Although his father is horrified that they live together without marriage, it is clear that Maggie, whom we meet only in flashbacks, gives David the stability and security he has needed. Thus their strong and nurturing relationship is presented as crucial in his attempt to find himself both as a man and as an artist.

Bizarre though his situation and his personality may seem to many readers, Mig, another alienated young man, finds the motivation to redefine his long-term affair during a period of crisis. In B. J. Chute's *The Story of a Small Life* (1971), Mig, "small king of his streets," has abandoned his family because "he was not going to run with them, scraping for food, scratching for rent, whining for welfare services, praying to saints who gave no relief," and taken up with Anna, who relies totally upon him. Seeing himself as tough and absolute, Mig fights her dependence and refuses to face the fact of her pregnancy. He scorns her weakness and wants no brake upon his mobility. When Anna is rendered completely helpless by a botched abortion, however, his affection and sense of responsibility are awakened, and he makes a confused but sincere commitment to her, assuming familial ties though he is ill equipped to handle them. Anna's need has accomplished what social agencies and church have failed to do, and Mig chooses permanent alliance and responsible action as signs of his intended maturation.

Ike Bender's marriage is in one sense imposed upon him by his mate's determination, but in another sense is freely chosen by him, and the Benders' relationship is all that teenagers hope adolescent marriage will be. In 1859, young Ike, narrator-protagonist of David Wagoner's *The Road to Many a Wonder* (1974), flees his Nebraska home to follow his brother west to the Colorado gold fields. When his fifteen-year-old sweetheart, Milly Slaughter, follows him, they are married, and the experience of marriage is a constant surprise to him. She manages him quite capably, and he soon learns to express his love for her. They meet many adventures, and Milly is always as brave, cool, and competent as Ike. Ike narrates their story good-naturedly, frequently expressing his awe at what they see and experience. But he is a thoroughly sensible young man, and he always knows that Milly and their love for each other are far more important than the gold he discovers. The novel is warm and funny, a charming depiction of two likable young people beginning a new life together.

While plots frankly depicting male homosexuality appear only infrequently in the novels read for this study, several do deal with the extreme pressure even the perception of being homosexuals can exert on boys' friendships, even on their lives (see also Chapter X, "Male Friendships"). John Hough, Jr., writes about the problem of homosexual practices forced upon adolescent prisoners. He studies the occurrence of homosexuality in penal institutions, in this case a reformatory, in *A Two-Car Funeral* (1973). The novel tells of three fifteen-year-old boys incarcerated in a "Center for Juvenile Guidance." One of them, Stewart Browne, attempts a coldly premeditated homosexual act with a younger boy who is himself essentially a male prostitute, while another, "Kentucky" Danovic, is brutally raped by a teacher. Homosexual exploitation is presented as only one of the degrading aspects of the boys' experiences in this institution, whose administrators seem more concerned about politics than about the boys they are supposed to help.

The themes of homosexuality and violence are again combined in James Kirkwood's *Good Times/Bad Times* (1968). The protagonist, Peter Kilburn, is deviously pursued by the headmaster of his school, Mr. Hoyt. In the guise of professional interest in a pupil, Hoyt seeks Peter's company and twice makes overtly sexual overtures. The first occurs while Peter feigns sleep; the second happens during a fistfight between teacher and student. Neither Peter nor Hoyt fully understands the headmaster's sexual nature, but Hoyt's desire for the boy leads him to misinterpret—and to sully—Peter's friendship with Jordan Legier, another student. Hoyt's violence contributes to Jordan's death as well as to the final attack on Peter—who kills the headmaster in the struggle.

Though Jeff Lynn's history is less overtly horrific, his creator, Laura Z. Hobson, author of *Consenting Adult* (1975), like John Hough and James Kirkwood, emphasizes the extreme pressure a homophobic society imposes upon its homosexual members. In 1960, seventeen-year-old Jeff Lynn realizes that he is homosexual. Consumed by shame and guilt, he seeks help from his mother, the central character of *Consenting Adult*. She agrees to pay for psychoanalytical treatment in hopes that he may be "cured." He almost immediately realizes the need to lie and dissemble in order to conceal his awful secret:

> There were lots of things he must remember; he was learning them every day. If he slipped he would be found out. That one thing he would never be able to stand. Having everybody know would kill him. He had heard them all laugh and snicker at just about any joke with the word "fag" in it, or "queer" or "fairy" or "queen," and if ever any guy said, "Guess what, Jeff Lynn's a fag," he would kill him.

The first and longest of three sections of the novel covers the year of his discovery of his sexual nature, stressing his revulsion at what he is, his attempts to change, his horror after his first overt sexual activity at realizing he enjoyed it, and his alienation from his appalled father. The most hopeful moments come, first, when he learns, after some chance comments by his brother-in-law, that there are some people who believe that homosexuals are like other people and that what they do in private is their own business, and, second, when that brother-in-law and Jeff's sister matter-of-factly accept his revelation of his sexual nature. But satisfactory resolution of his problems must wait until he is much older. This "problem novel" sensitively and authentically portrays troubled characters and also effectively conveys a good deal of information on its subject. Though Jeff Lynn, like James Baldwin's bisexual Leo Proudhammer (*Tell Me How Long the Train's Been Gone*), does resolve his sexual identity, the effort is great, the struggle extended, even more taxing apparently than the efforts of heterosexual adolescent males.

The novels under consideration here, then, clearly demonstrate adolescent males' preoccupation with their sexuality and with their intense desire to become sexually active. Some authors acknowledge the fact that initial experiences of intercourse are often perceived as the whole of the initiation experience by fictional young men, but most also suggest that a far healthier, more useful perception recognizes that a variety of learning experiences, of which sexual activity is but one (though a very important one), usually leads to fuller maturation. Often, failure in a sexual alliance symbolizes a young man's inability to achieve maturation, and it is of almost no consequence whether his limitations arise within the boy's own personality or are imposed by others or by social attitudes; the negative results are almost always the same.

According to the subject-novels, rather fewer young males than young females use sexual activity as a means of rebellion against their parents or guardians. Also, fewer adolescent males than adolescent females, as portrayed in the subject-novels, use their attractiveness or their sexuality to buy or curry favor or for professional or financial gain. Rather, young men tend to use their attractiveness and their socially recognized "strong sexual needs" to press their partners for greater and greater degrees of sexual intimacy. In a society dominated by heterosexual males, male adolescents apparently feel great pressure to practice the exercise of power by sexual activity and dominance. In this fashion, they seek initiation into the male power structure, the goal toward which they restlessly and sometimes relentlessly press.

CHAPTER IX
Males within Families

Adolescent American males understand, consciously or unconsciously, that as adults they can dominate their culture, and unquestionably they are eager to exercise adult male powers. Less eager, perhaps, to undergo the chastening that preparation for adulthood traditionally requires, they must perforce undergo it, learning to understand the social code as adults manipulate it.

Too often their required social lessons seem to be contradictions in terms: prepare to head a new family; seek approbation, but assert your individuality; obey your elders, but develop your own initiative. Constantly enjoined to be decent, honest, even noble, young men look to their elders for role models even as they cope with pressure to conform to their peers' often hectic, sometimes destructive life styles. They assume that they will discover exemplary lives, attitudes, behaviors in older men which will be useful to imitate or to emulate.

Without positive role models, boys all too often plunge into ever greater confusion, often into suffering, anger, and rebellion. When attempts to evade parents' or guardians' strictures are met with demands for submission, even for blind obedience, boys eager to seize the power awaiting them sometimes rebel. If rebels substitute defiance for self-definition, learning and maturation do not take place, and they remain angry, usually destructive "lost boys" forever. Other frustrated youths surrender to outside control or break under testing, and they, too, are perpetual boys, if they survive at all. According to the novels surveyed here, unwillingness or inability to locate or to follow role models can be disastrous. But numerous tests occur during the maturation journey, and even sincere efforts to find and emulate a good role model do not guarantee success.

Traditionally, male adolescents look first to family members, particularly parents, most especially, perhaps, to fathers, for role models. When the family has been disrupted by death or divorce, of course, such exemplars may be unavailable. But even when positive role models seem evident, available, even willing, a boy's study of his hero can lead to the most painful reassessment he must make on the pathway to manhood. Because they are inexperienced, because, as children and very young adolescents, most believe that everyone tries hard to be decent, honest, even noble, youngsters assume that their heroes are thoroughly good, but many discover that their honored models are corrupt, and almost every boy discovers that his hero is flawed and, at best, only human.

One of our protagonists makes such a discovery and learns a useful lesson. In Lester Atwell's *Life with Its Sorrow, Life with Its Tear* (1971), Paul Forrest's guardian, Uncle Reggie Carmody, not only introduces him to some of the simpler joys of youth—biking, swimming, skating —but also helps him to develop a love of books and a yearning for education. Though Paul recognizes some of his uncle's minor faults, he believes him to be a wholly good and genial man, easy to know and understand. The discovery that loving and lovable Reggie is also an embezzler is a major turning point in Paul's maturation, suddenly forcing upon him the first of many adult insights: "I realized, making the discovery for the first time, there would still be many facets to his personality unknown to us that others would have to attest to—and the same probably could be said of every human being in the world." Paul's attempt to grasp the essential mysteriousness of human nature and to understand but not to excuse his uncle is precisely the mature response society wants from the male apprentice to life. Other youngsters, though, are not able to balance glowing assumptions against disillusioning realities.

Rejection of a chosen model stemming from repugnance or disappointment (or both) frequently incites much the same sort of anger and rebellion that repression triggers; or a youth may, once again, choose passivity and continuing immaturity, concluding that no one can be an honorable male adult if his model cannot manage it. Equally disastrous, a lad can become priggish and superior, assuming that only he and his standards are decent, and actually, this response is simply another, perhaps more arrogant, form of passivity. Each of these reactions is unproductive, however, for each rules out the possibility of understanding and compromise. For the young male initiate, learning to compromise is the chief lesson to be mastered; failure at that task usually signifies failure to become a man.

Because boys are expected to become men of action, society expects even disillusioned boys to act and to act wisely. Most manage to do so, overcoming their disappointment in their role models, absorbing the lesson that ordinary human beings can but *try* to be truly good people, accepting the realization that they, too, cannot attain perfection.

The corollary to these important observations generally goes unspoken but not unobserved by fictive adolescent males. They learn that the ironic old saw "Do what I say, not what I do," is even greater evidence of hypocrisy than first they realized. A thoughtful adolescent must conclude that in his initiation tests he is expected to adhere to standards *known* by adults to be impossible to maintain. He is being asked to undergo trials no one can endure unscathed. Not fully aware that the ability to proceed though wounded is one of the qualities society demands of adults, unaware that compromise is the major lesson, introspective youngsters often feel put upon, cheated, belittled, used. They feel that their struggles to behave manfully are being ridiculed by adults who know how impossible such behavior is to achieve. If they protest, they may well be considered self-centered, disruptive, or sullen, and indeed, some embrace these very attitudes from panic or defensiveness. Youngsters who can settle great value on behaving gracefully under pressure are, according to the authors studied here, the ones who learn to compromise decently, to maintain their honor and their self-worth in the face of certain failure, accepting humiliation and adult males' knowing smiles as one price of initiation. The Hemingway code is alive and well among the novels we surveyed.

The motif of disenchanted, disillusioned youth runs through the majority of our subject-novels as central topic or subtheme, and certainly female adolescents as well as males must contend with disappointing role models. But the theme seems particularly important in novels which discuss adolescent males in relationship with their families, disillusionment often inciting or exacerbating the necessary but painful dissolution of family ties and parental authority. In the best of all possible worlds, male adolescents would learn these hard lessons cushioned by the support of loving families. In the fictional worlds pictured here, however, most must learn them while also withdrawing from parents' support or in broken, misguided, or inept families. At best, these boys must understand that loving familial protectiveness cannot save them from the pains of initiation; at worst, they must accept the fact that their families contribute to the pain and confusion they suffer.

Even in the midst of a boy's battle for independence from parental control, the sense that the family is stable, secure, and permanent is vitally important to him. The realization that nothing is permanent often arises for subject-characters when a family member dies. Several authors, as exemplified by Winston M. Estes, Robert Baylor, and T. Alan Broughton, use the theme of loss coupled with shame or guilt as a means of examining family relationships. In Estes's *Another Part of the House* (1970), Larry Morrison takes a long step toward adulthood in the year between his tenth and eleventh birthdays. The death of his brother, Tad, fifteen, saddles Larry with guilt because he feels responsible for Tad's contracting pneumonia. Unwilling to trouble his parents, already deeply grieved, Larry consults the family doctor who gently and wisely helps the boy to grasp three difficult lessons: that the genesis of some events is never really known, that guilt for guilt's sake is fruitless, and that sometimes responsibility must be borne silently. Though Larry is not artificially thrust into premature adulthood—his interests are still those of a child entering his teens—Estes does make clear that Larry has become a man in some very important ways.

Even serious illness or the threat of death can have devastating effects upon adolescents, driving home the mutability of family structure.

In Robert Baylor's *To Sting the Child* (1964), the temporary commitment of the young protagonist's mother to a mental hospital is only one of the painful experiences that warp and embitter him.

The father's loss of his job in T. Alan Broughton's *A Family Gathering* (1977) is the event that touches off much of what happens, all observed by Lawson Wright, a quiet and sensitive boy of twelve. Themes of isolation, alienation, and guilt permeate the novel. Father and son evade each other; the father commits adultery and then attempts suicide. Lawson is unable to understand much of what he observes, but he is nevertheless deeply affected by it, his withdrawal into himself being symbolized by his frequently locking himself into his room. The near break-up of the family, coming just when Lawson is particularly vulnerable as he enters the uncertainties of adolescence, is especially traumatic for the boy, but Broughton suggests, at the end of this perceptive study of a troubled family, that both boy and family will survive.

Use of the death motif to emphasize other feelings of alienation and loss is a strong and very frequent device among our subject-authors, ranging from the use of a family member's death to exacerbate the commonly recognized conventional tensions between generations (*The Dove Tree*) to its use as the most irrevocable, most awful expression of a youngster's disenchantment with his elders (*My Main Mother, McCaffrey*). Rarely striking readers as melodramatic (surprising though that fact may seem), the death motif is the most powerful mode of dramatizing the loneliness and isolation felt by most adolescents.

In the heavily symbolic *The Dove Tree* (1961) by L. D. Clark, Haley Blair and his son, Duncan, strive to find meaning and structure in their lives after the death of Lissie, Haley's wife and Duncan's mother. Over the barrier erected by their differing reactions to Lissie's death, Haley watches and attempts to understand his son's development. Clark's novel is a sensitive exploration of the generation gap from the father's point of view.

The maturation of Benjamin Kahn, in *About Us* (1967) by Chester Aaron, is marked by loss and isolation. Benny's first awareness of life's difficulties occurs when he is eight and loses a Christmas poster contest; his family contend that he loses because he is a Jew. Much more serious tragedies—the estrangement of a brother, the disappearance of a friend, and the deaths of sister, cousin, another brother, and his mother —follow in rapid succession during the next twelve years. Certainly these events exacerbate a sense of isolation born of belonging to the only Jewish family in Sundown, Pennsylvania, and enlarged by being the only son exempted from World War II. His parents' sense of betrayal by God undermines their once profound faith and once high standards of behavior and leaves Benny with nothing to cling to. This episodic *Bildungsroman*, told in the present tense, portrays an adolescent buffeted and chastened by disaster beyond understanding—and perhaps beyond acceptance.

In *I Am the Cheese* (1977, YA) by Robert Cormier, Adam Farmer suffers a mental breakdown when mysterious criminal forces attempt to assassinate the boy and his parents. Adam has seen his mother die but is unsure of his father's fate. The shock obliterates his memory, and the novel traces his painful efforts to reclaim it.

Family relationships, especially those of a boy and his mother and uncle, are the core of Barry Beckham's *My Main Mother* (1969). At the novel's opening, Mitchell Mibbs tells us he has killed his mother; the novel, which follows him from age seven to college, is Mitchell's manuscript, his explanation of the reasons:

> A young black genius, sitting comfortably in an abandoned auto on the outskirts of town, announced today that he had killed his mother for the best of all concerned. His testimony is a novel, profound manuscript of some eighty-thousand words, listing various and sundry acts alleged to have prompted the macabre slaying. The acts have been arranged in narrative form, and the manuscript has been cited by leading literary authorities as extremely accomplished.

He had both loved and hated his mother; her sexuality and her drinking particularly troubled him, but the murder is precipitated by his horror of her callous behavior after the death of his uncle, the one person who had brought stability to his life.

In *McCaffrey* (1961) by Charles Gorham, the death of Vincent McCaffrey's mother exacerbates the boy's already established antagonism toward his father, for Vincent has idolized his mother and resented "the old bull's" sexual demands upon her. When, not very long after Mrs. McCaffrey's death, Vincent interrupts his father and his mother's pallid, extremely religious sister in the midst of intercourse, the boy's disenchantment with the world and his hatred of old McCaffrey escalate into frenzy; he first attempts to kill them and then leaves home to become a male prostitute. Ultimately, *McCaffrey* reaches a bloody, murderous climax, for which Vincent's tormented family relationships are one major motivation.

As *The Outsiders*, *The Car Thief*, *Run Softly, Go Fast*, and *Gone Away* illustrate, however, other male characters who feel their losses no less keenly than Duncan Blair (*The Dove Tree*), Benny Kahn (*About Us*), Adam Farmer (*I Am the Cheese*), Mitchell Mibbs (*My Main Mother*), and Vincent McCaffrey (*McCaffrey*) are able to recoup their inner resources and to view their experiences as exacting but necessary steps in the maturation process. For instance, S. E. Hinton's *The Outsiders* (1967, YA) centers on Ponyboy Curtis, youngest of three brothers left alone by the deaths of their parents. The eldest, Darrel, at twenty has quit school, though he was a promising student-athlete, to support his brothers and keep the family together. The second, Sodapop, not good at school, has happily dropped out, while Ponyboy, the narrator, is still in school and like Darrel is academically and athletically talented. The novel depicts the boys' involvement in gang activities and Ponyboy's growing maturity as he observes the waste of human potential resulting from delinquency and violence.

A climactic event in the story of sixteen-year-old Alex Housman, told in Theodore Weesner's *The Car Thief* (1972), is the suicide of young Alex's father. This episode follows a succession of failures and misadjustments on Alex's part; the father, though alcoholic and far from sensitive to Alex's needs, had been the only stabilizing influence in his son's futile life. Alex reveals little emotion, but joining the army (as he had already planned) appears to give him a new chance to make a place for himself. The novel is a sensitive depiction of disturbed youth, and its portrayal of a young punk is credible and never sentimentalized.

The death of Leo Marks is the inciting action of Barbara Wersba's *Run Softly, Go Fast* (1970, YA). His nineteen-year-old son, David, on the day of the funeral, remembers their troubled relationship, trying to understand how his early love for his father had turned into bitterness and angry estrangement. As he remembers, he becomes aware of the complexities of his father's character, and he is able to close with words of loving reconciliation. He has come to understand that his father truly did love him, that his materialism and shady business practices were explained by his memories of the desperate poverty of his own youth, that his mother's forgiveness of repeated adulteries was motivated by her recognition of his true love for her and for David, and that his intolerance of David's chosen life and friends resulted from his real, if shortsighted, concern for David's welfare. The novel is a complex double character study, for both Leo and David, as well as their tangled relationship, are clearly portrayed.

Gone Away (1975) by David H. Brooks is the story of the near destruction and then rebuilding of a family. A key event is the death from cancer of the grandmother of the two boys on whose experiences the novel is based. Since she had always seemed young and vital, her sickness and physical decay are deeply disturbing to them. The younger brother (the narrator) visits her in the hospital shortly before she dies.

> In a way [he says] I'm sorry I went to see her. I'll never feel the same about anybody again—or anything either. A lot of things that I used to think were important seemed unimportant after that. I began to think I ought to stop fooling around so much. Maybe be a minister or join the Peace Corps or something like that.

But he must soon react to still other upsetting events: the separation of his parents and the running away of his older brother. Fortunately, however, the break-up of the family is not irretrievable, and the grand-mother's death, like the other traumatic experiences the boys undergo, is ultimately a cause of their growth in maturity.

As in *Gone Away*, parents' divorce or separation, like death, some-times forces male adolescents to accept change and loss as factors in their lives, severs relationships with important models, or motivates youngsters to revise their evaluations of one or both parents. Earl Ham-ner, Jr., in *You Can't Get There from Here* (1965), combines patterns of temporary and permanent loss to suggest the confusion many teenagers feel about relationships with their parents. The disappearance of Wes Scott's father after he was fired sends sixteen-year-old Wes on a day-long quest through New York City. Always just a few moments behind his father, Wes goes from adventure to adventure, repeatedly finding himself in the uncomfortable role of the Good Samaritan rebuffed by his beneficiaries. He rescues a lost child and a lost dog and befriends a shoplifting bag lady; his travels take him to bars, the Plaza Hotel, Span-ish Harlem, and the United Nations. Flashbacks to his earlier life with his father, Joe, and stepmother as well as with his father's large family in Virginia show him to be a loving, self-reliant, but sometimes insecure boy. Near the novel's comically dramatic climax, he begins to under-stand that his search is not just a matter of finding his father this particu-lar day, but a quest to understand his father and thus his own origins:

> It was something I had spent sixteen years trying to find out. What had happened to my mother? How had she died? Why had I been shipped off to Virginia to be raised by my grandparents, but I guess what it all boiled down to was the one question: Did Joe *really* love me? Why hadn't he kept me with him if he did? Was something buried way back there in my mind that had hap-pened when I was still only hours old? Did he really love me? I had to close my eyes because hot tears were pressing against my eyelids.

The restrained emotion and usually gentle, though sometimes slapstick, comedy make this novel an effective treatment of a crucial day in the life of a very likable boy.

Imposed by forces outside his family, a father's separation from wife and child pushes his son into early manhood in both *Sounder* and *Red Sky at Morning*. In William H. Armstrong's *Sounder* (1969, YA), the nameless narrator's father, impelled by poverty, steals some food, is quickly arrested, and sentenced to a chain gang term which stretches over six years. "The boy" becomes his mother's mainstay, helping to support the family through this severe crisis by field work. In the course of long journeys to discover his father's whereabouts, "the boy" learns a great deal about the society in which he lives. Despite the grimness of his lessons, he and his mother sustain life, hope, and family solidarity through inner strength and faith. Armstrong also clearly conveys this black family's almost wordless but abiding love for one another.

His father's enlistment in the navy during World War II causes seventeen-year-old Joshua and his frivolous mother, characters in Richard Bradford's *Red Sky at Morning* (1968), to move from their native Alabama to New Mexico. As a result, Joshua is forced to take on new familial responsibilities as well as to adjust himself to surroundings where customs and the social caste system are strange to him. He quickly makes friends among both Anglos and Spanish-speaking inhabitants; less easily resolved are problems caused by his shallow mother and a parasitic "friend" who follows her to New Mexico. His increasing ability to deal sensitively and wisely with his situation reveals his growing maturity. The novel is at once a comic treatment of the pains of adolescence, narrated by its youthful protagonist, and a perceptive depiction of a pivotal year in the experience of a fine young man.

Clearly, the fathers depicted in both *Sounder* and *Red Sky at Morning* continue to serve their sons as models despite their absences. Both William H. Armstrong and Richard Bradford suggest that firmly laid foundations of paternal love, trust, and respect support their protagonists during times of separation and testing. Other distanced fictional fathers, however, have to work harder to regain or retain fruitful relationships with their sons. *If I Love You, Am I Trapped Forever?* and *Second Heaven* provide representative examples of this situation.

Alan Bennett's senior year of high school, depicted in *If I Love You, Am I Trapped Forever?* (1973, YA) by Marijane Meaker (pseudonym, M. E. Kerr), is crowded with problems. One of the most serious is his father's awkward attempt to bridge the years-long gap created by his early desertion of Alan and Alan's mother. The reconciliation does not go smoothly—both father and son are ill at ease; neither really understands how to give or accept love, and Alan leaves abruptly. Though the relationship is still unresolved at the book's conclusion, Alan has learned from it, has expanded his horizons. Most importantly, he is coming to terms with a very serious and important question, "How do people who love each other get to be so understanding?"

Though attorney Michael Atwood, a major character, has two children, his son, Daniel, is a shade more important to *Second Heaven* (1982) because Judith Guest uses him to contrast with Gale Murray, around whom a major plot complication centers. Daniel and his father strive to maintain a solid relationship even though his parents are divorced, his mother remarried and relocated, and visits between father and son occur only after long intervals. For Daniel and Michael Atwood, both decent people, the visits mean not only adjusting to the new situation (including Daniel's relationship with his stepfather), but also acclimating to Daniel's evolving maturity and independence and his father's natural inability to "keep up" fully with the boy's development. The Atwoods' story indicates that even in the best of families, parents and children must accept some failures, will achieve some successes; this lesson is impossible for Gale Murray's father to grasp, a fact Guest indicates by the implications in the Atwood situation as well as by overt analysis of the Murrays' home life.

Unlike characters such as Daniel Atwood (*Second Heaven*), other adolescent male characters simply cannot achieve the acceptance or goodwill necessary to move ahead toward maturity though wounded by a parent's absence. Though few are subjected to the multiplicity of abusiveness and abandonment inflicted upon Ben of *Like a Lion's Tooth*, many, like Bobby Fallon (*Flesh & Blood*) and the unnamed son in *Memoir of an Aged Child*, nevertheless seem irreparably damaged by their losses. In Pete Hamill's *Flesh & Blood* (1977), the long-past desertion by his father, when Bobby Fallon was six, triggered deep resentment in Bobby as well as a kind of hero worship for the father, an almost legendary gambler. The father's reappearance, when Bobby has become a boxer, teaches Bobby a final and bitter lesson about human perversity and betrayal.

The divorces, remarriages, and affairs of the parents of the unnamed narrator of Alfred Duhrssen's *Memoir of an Aged Child* (1967) form a constant background to this story of the childhood, adolescence, and young manhood of a healthy, sensitive, but detached boy. Fragmentary and often cryptic in presentation, the novel suggests more about youth than it actually tells, but the boy's uncertain and unsettling family life seems at the base of his restlessness and lack of purpose.

The protagonist of *Like the Lion's Tooth* (1972) by Marjorie Kellogg is Ben, a resident of a school for abandoned or abused children. Ben's adored mother has placed him in the school because the child has been repeatedly raped and beaten by his father, and she fears for the boy's life. Ben does not adjust.

> And Ben thought of home. In the classroom, as the teacher's voice droned on and on, he thought of his mother, wondered what she had made for breakfast. . . . Instead of the longing growing less in him as the time passed, it became more intense, until he could feel it in the pit of his stomach from the time he woke up in the morning until he went to bed. Homesick and growing sicker. Then, in order to tolerate it, he made a plan. He would leave the School on the Fourth of July weekend.

When he does leave on July fourth, he discovers that his mother and sisters have disappeared, perhaps to avoid his father, perhaps to force Ben to accept the school. The school, a miserable place at best, then becomes his only refuge. Abandonment has been his initiation experience, and the future seems irredeemably blank.

Like Ben, Benjy Johnson of *A Hero Ain't Nothin' But a Sandwich* (1973, YA) by Alice Childress needs his mother desperately, but guilt, alienation, and jealousy prevent him from acknowledging—or meeting—his need. Benjy makes a great point of being from a broken home, despite the efforts of his mother and her lover, Butler Craig, who try to create a stable environment for the family. Very aware of the strong bond of affection Rose and Butler share, Benjy feels abandoned because of it.

> But all of a sudden I'm wondering in my mind, what they need with me? . . . What they need with anybody? I feel like a accident that happen to people. My blood father cut out on Mama. Musta gone cause he didn't dig me. Mama look at me lotta times and say, "My God, you look just like Big Benny, just like him." Her eyes be sad when she say it. Other times she studyin my face lookin like bout to say somethin, she almost say it, then wave her hand and say, "Never mind." She sayin never mind cause it's me. She don't say that to Butler.

This loneliness is partially responsible for Benjy's addiction to heroin. Childress clearly dramatizes the strain between mother and son as Rose and Benjy Johnson try to understand one another better.

The Concrete Wilderness (1967) by Jack Couffer depicts another strained mother-son relationship, that between Archie Larsen and his mother, Pat. The boy idolizes the memory of his father who has been killed on duty in the Forest Service, and, like his father, the boy has come to prefer animals to people. Fearing this trait in her son and unable to communicate with him, Pat has moved to New York City in the hope that urban life will change Archie's attitudes, will force him to rely on human relationships. Her plan fails, and the tension between the two reaches a crisis when Archie befriends a dog believed to be rabid.

Most commonly a lesser shock than the death of a loved one or the loss of a parent through divorce or separation, his family's relocation is also an unsettling event in a boy's life. As in *Red Sky at Morning*, forced relocation is the inciting action for Borden Deal's *The Least One* (1967). Lee Sword, father of the small family, is a poor southern white who loses what little he has had in the early days of the Depression and is forced to settle his family in the marvelously named hamlet of Bugscuffle Bottoms. Young Boy Sword, narrator of the novel, describes the move and his family's reactions to it as he begins the story of his own coming of age.

In *I Am the Cheese* and *False Entry*, relocation becomes the central symbol of protagonists' desperate search for identity and self-definition. Living, until the age of ten, in his native England, the unnamed protagonist of Hortense Calisher's *False Entry* (1961) is a satellite of the Goodman family, to whom his mother is seamstress. When he and his mother emigrate to Alabama, the boy feels twice exiled and never becomes part of the town's life. His one young friend, Johnny Fortuna, disappears on the night of a Klan raid, leaving him lonelier than before. At eighteen, he rejects the attempt of his mother and stepfather to draw him into the family circle and changes his name to "Pierre Goodman." As a man, he recalls his early history, interweaving passages from his memories with commentary about his adult life—all of it a search for identity and self-understanding.

Adam Farmer, of Robert Cormier's *I Am the Cheese* (1977, YA), lives a strangely alienated life, recognizing that his sense of "loneness" goes beyond shyness and includes an awareness that his parents also remain aloof from their Massachusetts community. At fourteen, Adam begins to question his family's mysterious behavior and discovers that the Farmers are fugitives, relocated by a government agency because of his father's testimony, years before, in a criminal case. *I Am the Cheese* depicts Adam's struggle to come to terms with his terrifying background. Adam's relocation is both the symbol for the extreme disjointedness of his life and, when he finally learns the reason for it, an explanation for his sense of alienation. Harsh though the facts of Alan's life are, they can be understood; some of them can even be seen as conducive to growth.

As we have already noted, young men seem to depend far less on the esteem of their elders than do young women, though both adolescent males and females wish equally to be liked and accepted. A youth's search for a model is often not only for someone he will admire but for someone who will approve of him. Even in the heat of the struggle to win emancipation from parental rule, male children, like females, almost always warmly desire the approval of their parents, although they may openly reject their parents' attitudes and standards. Disapproval means rejection, and no human being, child or adult, male or female, relishes feeling unwanted, rejected, or disliked. Sensitive, prickly, usually unsure of who they are (or will become), adolescents are quick to interpret any disparity between their points of view and their parents' as rejection. In the lives of the young men who are the objects of this study, rejection runs the full gamut from outright child abuse to temporary but painful differences in opinions, social standards, and life-choices. To the young male characters, self-absorbed and self-inventing, almost any of these crises can seem monumental; for some, crises *are* monumental, even life-threatening, not only in their eyes but in the eyes of older, already tempered authors and readers alike.

The term "child abuse" appears very infrequently on the pages of our subject-novels; nonetheless, physical, emotional, and mental abusiveness toward adolescent males is *not* infrequent therein. Judith Guest treats all the forms of abuse imposed on Gale Murray (*Second Heaven*) very directly; Terence Fugate (*Drum and Bugle*) and George Cuomo (*Bright Day, Dark Runner*) dramatize situations fraught with emotional and mental abusiveness; all three authors clearly trace many, if not all, their young protagonists' difficulties with the maturation and socialization processes to their family situations.

In Judith Guest's *Second Heaven* (1982), her second novel, she again, as in *Ordinary People*, takes up the topic of the troubled teenaged boy with a desperate "secret." Gale Murray, sixteen, maintains a façade of "cool and private arrogance" which masks his terror and dread. The object of severe abuse by his father (to which his timid mother tacitly acquiesces), he runs away repeatedly, dreaming of achieving total escape from his terrible life, hoping to emulate his older brother who has already fled. Eventually, Gale seeks refuge in the home of Cat Holzman, a divorced woman, and his father uses this move as an excuse for having the courts declare Gale incorrigible. This crisis forces Gale to confront his past and cope with his memories, even while striving to put them behind him: "All those times he hurt me and I just let him do it!" Fearful of all adults, tormented by hidden guilt, and hesitating to face or reveal the full truth about his family life, Gale is reserved, sometimes surly, always defensive, ashamed without actually understanding the sources of his shame. Taut and unsentimental, his portrait is a useful examination of the abused child.

In *Drum and Bugle* (1961) Terence Fugate depicts a desperately bad relationship between a father and his son, Carl Roundtree, the protagonist. Antagonistic, diminishing, sometimes violent, the situation can offer no positive value to parent or child.

The protagonist of George Cuomo's *Bright Day, Dark Runner* (1964) is named Judas Iscariot Holtzmann because his mother died in childbirth: "Since his father's love for his wife had been complete and nearly perfect, so had the hatred it inspired been perfect. . . . the father did not initiate it to torment his son. Created out of its own independent force, it existed purely, smothering them both impartially." The father and son live in a cold, affectionless world until "J.I." abandons his parent and his name in his fifteenth year. The poison generated by this unnatural relationship affects the boy's entire life.

Despite his overt cruelty in naming Judas Iscariot Holtzmann as he has, the senior Holtzmann might be taken by his neighbors as a man so racked with pain that he simply hasn't the emotional vigor to love his child (*Bright Day, Dark Runner*); a similar situation appears in *Yates Paul, His Grand Flights, His Tootings*, which portrays a youth without guidance or parental support. Other fictional parents are so preoccupied with daily routine, the demands of family life, or their own interests that they, too, fail their sons. When essentially unparented boys also fail to acquire useful models from outside their families, there is little hope for fruitful maturation, according to many subject-authors, as the following examples illustrate. Dreadful as these boys' circumstances are, however, they go largely unnoticed by the community, their families appearing adequate enough to outsiders.

An unsatisfactory relationship with his father, his sole parent, makes life difficult for the protagonist and title character of James Baker Hall's *Yates Paul, His Grand Flights, His Tootings* (1963). Yates is thirteen and afraid of life; his father, a mediocre professional photographer, has given up on life and offers Yates little help or guidance. Yates thus spends much of his time in his father's darkroom, developing photographic images of the world as he evades its reality. Outside the darkroom he lives a rich and varied fantasy life. The discovery of many series of photographs of nude women, secretly shot by his father after hours, is a shock to Yates.

> He did not want to think of his father as some kind of pervert. He did not want to be afraid of him or to hate him. That scared him more than anything. While there was something queer and unsettling about all those nudes there was also something childlike and pathetic about it. He kept seeing his father, an unattractive and lonesome man, sitting at the kitchen table late at night staring at his reflection in the window, and lying on the couch in the outer office asleep like a child . . . and he did not want to begrudge his father whatever kind of companionship he could find. . . . Yates did not know how to feel about his father.

With the encouragement of Jane, his father's secretary and the closest thing to a surrogate mother Yates has, he learns some self-confidence. Though at the end of the novel his relationship with his father remains ambiguous, and Yates still relies heavily on his fantasies, his courage is strengthening, and the reader feels he is learning to cope with his fears and uncertainties. The novel has little plot, consisting largely of a series of loosely related events, but it is a sensitive evocation of the life, both external and internal, of a bright, troubled, and appealing boy.

Though Anne Nash, mother of Tom, the protagonist of *Such Nice People* (1980) by Sandra Scoppettone, is troubled by changes in the personality and habits of her son, she is too preoccupied with her own difficulties (a weak marriage, an affair) and too distrustful of her husband, Cole (who believes his children to be well if they are physically healthy), to take the steps necessary to avert tragedy. Scoppettone uses the Nash family's seeming normalcy and balance as well as their genuine attractiveness to contrast with the pain Tom and, to a lesser degree, his siblings are suffering. Because both his parents are distracted by their own lives (Cole plans to abandon his family) and because they tend to oversimplify or excuse the problems of their children, Tom slips unnoticed ever more deeply into religious mania. Disappointment with his parents, his siblings, and, especially, with himself exacerbates the boy's state of mind. Scoppettone's blunt novel warns modern parents to give heed and direction to their children before, as in the case of the Nashes, it is far too late for redemptive action.

In Lois Gould's *Necessary Objects* (1972), the only male child produced by the wealthy, self-centered, life-wrecking Lowen sisters of New York City is Jason, who has enormous potential but little hope of fulfilling it. Musically gifted, Jason spends most of his time rebelling against his mother, his absent father, and his clumsy stepfather. Elly, Jason's mother, substitutes private schools and camps for home life, is unable to carry on even the shortest conversation with her son, closes her mind to his probable homosexuality, and simply ignores a suicide attempt undertaken when the latest camp becomes unbearable. More an object lesson than a fully developed character, Jason and his feeble efforts to assert himself generate a subplot in *Necessary Objects*.

At sixteen, Jan Anderson, of Fred Chappel's *The Inkling* (1965), has survived the climactic experiences of his adolescence: he has been discovered having intercourse with his teenaged aunt and he has shed blood. For years, Jan has been virtually a prisoner of his need to care for his retarded sister, Timmie, and the affair with "Aunt Lora" marks his first overt act to gain something for himself. Jan has, however, a secret history of violence which foreshadows the tragic act by which he cuts his family ties. In *The Inkling*, a Southern Gothic novel, Chappel suggests the grim fate which threatens children who have no adult on whom to rely. Jan's father has been killed at Pearl Harbor; his mother invests her strength in her job which supports the family, and his uncle is a drunk. Forced to rely solely on his own will, Jan's choices are often destructive.

His father's preoccupation and inability to cope with his own life propel David Wayne, of *The Wind's Will* (1964) by Gerald Warner Brace, out of boyhood; unlike the majority of boys unparented by their living parents, however, this protagonist not only survives, he survives intact. The discovery of his father's adultery with a woman who had also seduced David is one of a series of events occurring during one summer. It is followed by the guilt-ridden father's elopement with his mistress and then his return and suicide. For David, these events are traumatic, but their effect is ultimately strengthening, and by the novel's end, David has grown in maturity.

Like David Wayne, Adam Blessing, more assertive and self-directed than David, is a survivor. In *The Son of Someone Famous* (1974,YA), Marijane Meaker (pseudonym, M. E. Kerr) returns to her frequent theme, the negative impact preoccupied, successful parents sometimes have upon their children. Doubting his ability to create an identity of his own in the shade of his famous father, Adam Blessing changes his name and retreats to his grandfather's home. Using a device that is no less effective because it is traditional, Meaker dramatizes Adam's growing ability to cope through his turbulent, but generally sustaining, relationships with Brenda Bell, a schoolmate, and with his grandfather. Adam learns that self-confidence and self-understanding can lead to the acceptance and understanding of others.

If lack of parental attention can be destructive, intense parental attention should, perhaps, be beneficial. According to these subject-novels, however, indulgence that passes for nurture (*Someone Great*) and unremitting attempts to undermine a son's beliefs that pass for counsel (*I'm Really Dragged But Nothing Gets Me Down*) are forms of attention which do more harm than good. Neither the Schectmans nor Sam Wolf intend anything but the best for their child; still, these families are families in crisis, the Schectmans failing to grant their son emancipation, Wolf equating Jeremy's maturity with acceptance of his own standards.

In *Someone Great* (1971) by Robert Grossbach, Stuie Schectmans's parents cushion his boyhood with dreams of his future success, excusing his shortcomings, never really exploring his interests, allowing him to manipulate them. As a result, Stuie is pleasantly spoiled and aimless, drifting in school and in life. He remains childish and wishful, rarely coping with reality, surrendering rather than assuming any real responsibility. *Someone Great* depicts Stuie's failure to live up to his potential.

By alternating the point of view between Jeremy Wolf and his father, Nat Hentoff dramatizes the much-discussed generation gap of the 1960s in *I'm Really Dragged But Nothing Gets Me Down* (1968, YA). The draft and the war in Vietnam are the subjects of disagreement between seventeen-year-old Jeremy and his father, a liberal Jewish advertising salesman. Sam, the father, resents Jeremy's loud rock music and long hair; he partially understands Jeremy's position, but finds it idealistic and doomed to failure. Jeremy considers his father a sell-out to the establishment. The series of brief chapters in their shifting perspectives makes clear Sam's desperate frustration with the son whom he does, after all, love deeply, and Jeremy's alienation from the father who seems to him both immoral and irrelevant. The brief novel, suitable for young adult readers, now seems dated but depicts well some of the controversies of the late 1960s.

As in *I'm Really Dragged But Nothing Gets Me Down*, discrepancies between a son's value system and that of his parents are the chief subject of *Before My Time* and *The Redneck Poacher's Son*. In all three novels, sons' ethical and moral values are rejected by their parents; in all three, the youngsters' difficult, necessary process of evaluating their parents' codes are exacerbated by anger. Both Maureen Howard and Luke Wallin ratify their young male characters' choices with plot developments which demonstrate the youths' strength and the parents' failures. Jim Cogan must behave more maturely than his folks (*Before My Time*), and Jesse Watersmith must confront both past and present violence to assert his adulthood (*The Redneck Poacher's Son*).

In Maureen Howard's *Before My Time* (1974), Laura Quinn's memories of her own youth are reawakened by a visit from Jim Cogan, a young relative in trouble with the law. Flashbacks reveal that Jim's difficulties with his parents arise from the same misunderstandings and disappointments that once generated tension between Laura's brother, Robert, and their parents. Robert's preoccupation with poetry and drama and Jim's with a strange religious sect are both incomprehensible to their parents, and though Robert's family are affluent, successful people and Jim's are only marginally solvent and respectable (his father is a gambler, his mother a drinker), neither set of parents understands anything about its son. By spanning the two social classes and two generations in her studies of difficult parental relationships, Howard suggests a continuing weakness in American family life, a statement underscored by the ironic fact that Jim's ties to his family are the stronger. He will return to them whereas Robert fled into military service and death.

The family of Jesse Watersmith, the sixteen-year-old protagonist of Luke Wallin's *The Redneck Poacher's Son* (1981), consists of his father, two older brothers, and aunt. Their only home is a camp in the Alabama swamps, and their livelihood comes from illegal hunting, trapping, and moonshining. Jesse's father is a violent, hate-filled man who has turned his two elder sons into younger versions of himself. Jesse and Aunt May hate and live in fear of the other three. When Aunt May helps Jesse escape to a job in town and a room in the home of an old friend, the conflict within the family is joined. Jesse is, despite his origins, a sensitive boy who deeply loves nature, including the wild animals his father wantonly and joyfully kills, and his suspicions that his father had killed his mother lead to a climactic confrontation. The novel shows a boy of great potential but equally great moral and psychological handicaps finding strength and courage to overcome the bigotry, hatred, and ignorance of his beginnings.

When young men cannot or cannot yet bring themselves to reject their parents' exacting expectations but still seek parental approval and useful adult models, their suffering is just as extreme as that depicted in *The Redneck Poacher's Son* or *Before My Time*, as the family situations of *Ordinary People* and *After the First Death* suggest. Caught in the crux between the wish to win approval and the uncertainty of their ability to live according to imposed standards, youngsters must learn to trust themselves, a difficult task for all, impossible for some.

In *After the First Death* (1979, YA) by Robert Cormier, Ben Marchand's courage is put to a terrible test. Used as a messenger in negotiations between terrorist hijackers and the authorities, Ben is tortured for information. Further pressure is exerted because it is Ben's father, General Marchand, who chooses him for the mission. The general is a man with exacting standards whose own successes and high expectations have already contributed to tensions between father and son. Ben measures his performance in this crucial mission solely according to his concept of his father's values. Cormier's psychological study of Ben's self-image after the hijacking frames the central action of the novel.

Recently released from a hospital, Con Jarrett of *Ordinary People* (1976) by Judith Guest is progressing toward mental health, but his relationship with his mother remains cool and strained. His feelings of guilt toward her are blocking progress.

> Once I tried to kill myself. . . . Listen. . . . I am never going to be
> forgiven for that, *never*! You can't get it out, you know! All that
> blood on her rug and her goddamn towels—everything had to
> be pitched! Even the goddam *tile* in the bathroom had to be re-
> grouted. Christ, she fired a *goddamn maid* because she couldn't
> dust the living room right, and if you think she's ever going to
> forgive me. . . .

Beth Jarrett's perfectionism and her enormous concern about the opinions of her social circle are clearly identified as partial causes for Con's
attempted suicide and breakdown, events which precede the action of
the novel. Judith Guest avoids the simplistic, however, and she depicts
the Con-Beth relationship as damaging and painful to both mother and
son, revealing the goodwill and anger, the strengths and weaknesses of
both characters. The result is a remarkably well-balanced portrait of a
family under stress.

Characters like Paul Christopher (*A Lost King*) and Reuven and
Danny (*The Chosen*) discover that seemingly undramatic victories in the
struggle between parent and child are, nevertheless, important victories. Less flamboyant than the maturation contests of will engaged in by
other boys, their tests of strength, determination, or tenacity are equally
taxing. Their creators suggest that in the struggle to gain maturity and
understanding, all successes matter because all require evaluation of
models, reassessment of parental behavior, and development of self-
determination.

Paul Christopher, the son of an Italian immigrant father in Raymond
DeCapite's *A Lost King* (1961), loves his domineering father and seeks
earnestly for his approval. But Paul is a chronic loser and fails at almost
everything—in his courtship and at all the jobs he tries (except as a
seller on a watermelon wagon, a job which brings ridicule instead of respect). Only playing the harmonica gives him any real satisfaction, but
this too wins him no recognition from the father. His failures and losses
do, however, teach him to sympathize and to care about humanity, and
thus his experience (like the novel) is ultimately life affirming.

In *The Chosen* (1967), Chaim Potok characterizes two boys who are
immersed in their Jewish heritage and deeply influenced by strong fathers. Danny, the son of a Hasidic leader and his presumed successor, is
being reared in "silence"; that is, his father speaks to him only when
teaching him, thus creating in him a sense of isolation and alienation.
Reuven, the son of an Orthodox scholar and teacher, has a warm and
loving relationship with his father. Both boys eventually choose careers
not anticipated by their fathers—Danny to become a psychologist and
Reuven a rabbi. Both have matured beyond their years by the end of the
book and are able to understand and respect (while not necessarily
agree with) Danny's father's apparently heartless treatment of him. Like
Potok's other novels, *The Chosen* is an effective examination of some as-

pects of American Judaism and its reactions to the stresses placed upon it by the contemporary world. The boys have the difficult task of adjusting both to their strict religion and to the secular world, and the novel affirms the possibility of meeting this double challenge.

Traditionally, the resolution of a boy's conflict with his parents or his reassessment of them occurs at the end of his adolescence and signals his maturation. Frequently, as we have seen, factors outside the family—such as war and politics, in *Red Sky at Morning* and *I'm Really Dragged But Nothing Gets Me Down*, or religion, in *Before My Time* and *The Chosen*—complicate the process, in part because parents fear other adults' reactions to their children's attitudes. When parents share the general social disapprobation of homosexuality, dreading the public disdain which may be reflected upon them, the discovery of a son's homosexuality may delay acceptance and reconciliation for years.

In Laura Z. Hobson's *Consenting Adult* (1975), a long-lasting family crisis is created by the revelation that the youngest child of a well-to-do New York publishing family is homosexual. Jeff Lynn, from his private school in Connecticut, writes his mother with his confession and asks for her help. She reacts lovingly and tries to be supportive, but she tries too hard, and Jeff finds her concern "obtrusive." His father is so horrified that he avoids being with his son, even constructing an elaborate excuse to miss Jeff's graduation. But fortunately his sister Margie and her husband Nate are able to accept Jeff and his homosexuality naturally, and he finds love, security, and a home with them. The novel is divided into three sections: the first and longest, "1960–1961," covers the period of Jeff's greatest anguish and the most severe family tensions. Later sections, "1965–1966" and "1968–1973," bring both Jeff and his family to reconciliation with each other and with Jeff's nature. Indeed, the change in the family is paralleled with the society's change in these years of the beginning struggles for gay rights.

Like their female counterparts, other adolescent males are tested by parenting their parents. For them rather more than for female adolescents, the emphasis is upon economic support as well as emotional support. The title of *The Caretaker* (1980, YA) by Arthur Roth has several levels of meaning, and one important implication is protagonist-narrator Mark Cooper's relationship with his parents. At seventeen, Mark is really his parents' parent, a responsibility he feels keenly and discusses at some length. The central problem for the family is Mr. Cooper's drinking; he is an alcoholic who refuses to admit his illness, and his binges throw much of the responsibility for the family business (they oversee summer homes in East Hampton, Long Island) upon the son. As Mark makes clear, juggling school, work, and caring for his father add up to a heavy load. In addition, Mr. Cooper's inability to stay sober has forced his wife to consider a permanent separation, and she turns to Mark for aid and advice in this matter. To the boy, the threatened dissolution of the family means separation from his much loved (though also sometimes despised) father and the formalization of his own role as chief family provider, a prospect which dismays him. Mark's frankness about his conflicting emotions toward his parents is a strong point in a fairly simplistic young adult novel.

Another youthful "caretaker," young Martin Brent, of Richard Lockridge's *The Empty Day* (1965), had been forced to go to work early to help his family because of his father's financial irresponsibility. Beginning as a newspaper carrier with full rights to his earnings, he is compelled, as repeated reverses are suffered by his father, first to contribute a large share of his earnings to the family and then to go to work full time for the newspaper. As his sisters and parents grow more and more to depend upon him, he gives more and more of himself to their needs. The novel shows elderly Martin Brent remembering his boyhood, youth, young adulthood, and his rise to success. He concludes that somehow his early acceptance of responsibility and of living for others had caused him to miss much, and the result is a sense of emptiness:

> Somewhere along the way (he thought) I lost myself, if I ever was myself. The others had themselves, for whatever came of it. My father was a man of cloud, but himself. When he was dying he spoke his name into the darkness. What name will I speak when darkness comes? I started this day trying to remember, to find, a boy named Marty. I did not really find him, and now, as this day draws into the afternoon, I think that was because I cannot find myself; because I feel, dully, that no one named Martin Brent exists. The name of Martin Brent was a label put on a caretaker. . . . A caretaker lives only in what he takes care of. . . . When he no longer has anything to take care of, he no longer is.

One of the most striking facts that emerge from a study of fictional adolescent males is the preponderance of extremely troubled family relationships. Certainly female adolescents, according to these subject-authors, experience uneasiness, anger, and rebellion while redefining relationships with their mothers and fathers, but fewer of those tensions stretch to the breaking point, as happens frequently in stories of male adolescents.

In *Cages* (1971), Paul Covert contrasts two family situations that reflect the American literary myth that the all-male society is the tension-free society and exploit the even older myth that females are disruptors of society. Eric Mathews, the narrator, loves and respects his father:

> I couldn't remember my mother, nor did I know how or when she had died. I knew that there always had been an Old Man, and that we had always lived in the grey farmhouse. . . . This was our domain and we ruled it with an understanding that could be experienced only between men. A woman would not have understood it. . . . A woman would have disliked the priorities

> which ruled our lives—the first day of trout season, the running
> of the deer. . . . I would not have changed a thing about it.

The Mathews' relationship contrasts with that between Bob Ward, Eric's best friend, and his parents, for Bob believes that he fails them constantly. True to the pattern of the novel, the problem is associated primarily with the woman involved, for Mrs. Ward seems to favor Bob's younger brother. These pressures cause Bob to be happier and more comfortable in the wholly masculine Mathews household and eventually contribute to Bob's death.

In contrast to the rather negative views of fictional boys' relationships with their birth-parents, adolescent males' relationship with foster or substitute parents are generally depicted as positive in our subject-novels. Tippy Blaney is an important exception, illustrating that concealment, late revelation of important facts, and mistakes (his own and others') are equally foolish in untraditional as well as in traditional families. A striking study of a seventeen-year-old boy who touches off an unusual family crisis is presented in George Baxt's *A Parade of Cockeyed Creatures; or, Did Someone Murder Our Wandering Boy?* (1967). Tippy Blaney has learned some disturbing facts about his birth and his relationships with the people he has believed to be his parents and aunt. Illegitimacy, past familial connections with organized crime, drugs, the anti-war movement, Tippy's history of theft, and his girlfriend's pregnancy are all involved in the investigation of his disappearance that makes up the novel. He had been an aspiring poet, and samples of his verse (skillfully composed doggerel) serve as clues to his feelings and problems. He never appears directly in the novel, but his presence is always felt, and he gradually becomes a clearly etched portrait of a troubled but essentially likable boy.

Relatively few of our subject-novels depict the traditional conflict between boys and their stepmothers or stepfathers; among those that do, Tom E. Clarke's *The Big Road* (1964) is a useful example in which the protagonist decides that departure is his best defense. Vic Martin's strained relationship with his stepfather is the primary motivation for his leaving home and spending some months riding the rails. Vic's disapproval of his stepfather's gambling is exacerbated by the man's inability to provide for the family as well as by Vic's anger that his mother never "takes his side." Several grim experiences on the road convince the boy that he might be able to adjust to his family's demands.

Vic Martin's pragmatic decision to accept a flawed home life is, of course, an important compromise, symbolizing his maturation. Other characters who feel more warmly toward their surrogate parents must similarly accept their foster parents' eccentricities or faults. Both George Cuomo and Lester Atwell suggest that their characters' best evidence of maturation will be their realization that they can hate (or reject) the sin (or flaw) and yet love the sinner.

At fifteen, Judas Iscariot Holtzmann, protagonist of George Cuomo's *Bright Day, Dark Runner* (1964), finds his first job—as an apprentice to a painter, Stanton Paladler. In contrast to the totally arid life he has lived with his father, his time with Paladler is a period of great emotional and intellectual richness: "He shocked me into an awareness of what I had never realized before, that life was various and complex and funny and confusing and capable of infinite surprises. . . . to live with him . . . was to be born again." As an employer and foster father, Paladler is eccentric but determined, and his ability to care for others and to enjoy life deeply affect J.I.'s values.

Paul Forrest's family, the jolly, profligate Carmodys, dominate and enliven his adolescence in Lester Atwell's *Life with Its Sorrow, Life with Its Tear* (1971). Aunt Dottie and Uncle Reg are delighted to rear their sister's orphaned son, who soon becomes devoted to them despite a continuing awareness that his stern, thrifty father distrusted the Carmodys' value system and regarded them as careless and parasitic. Paul early learns to cope with the tension this awareness induces by closing his mind to any criticism of his beloved guardians: "we believe what we want to believe, what in our weakness and need we find most comforting and sustaining."

Like Paul Forrest, though far less consciously, both Brad Nichols (*Home Is the North*) and Billy Vogelin Starr (*Fire on the Mountain*) begin by believing what they want to believe. In their cases, they not only believe in the worth of their surrogate parents but also in the ways of life their foster families represent. In fighting circumstance, the boys are not only resisting yet another restructuring of already restructured families, they are also resisting the fact of social change and the necessity for growing up. Both learn that those battles cannot be won; both, like hosts of other adolescent male protagonists, learn accommodation and compromise, discovering that loving reevaluation of parent figures and models need not mean rejection.

Walt Morey's *Home Is the North* (1967, YA) centers on Brad Nichols's fight to remain under the care of Captain Ed Bishop and his wife, "Stampede Annie," who have informally adopted the boy after his grandmother's death. Brad comes to love his new family, valuing their efforts to foster his developing maturity, and he resorts to lies and trickery to avoid going to live with his Aunt Clara, whom he has never met. When Clara invokes her legal rights, even Captain Ed's promise that "We'll all be right here waiting" for Brad's ultimate return is not enough reassurance to give Brad the courage to face a strange city and potential loneliness—so he makes a last brave, but foolish and dangerous, effort to stay. Ultimately, Brad learns new definitions for "home" and "family" which motivate his final choice. The portraits of the four major characters are drawn sparely but vividly so as to make the story's conclusion just and convincing.

Billy Vogelin Starr, twelve, takes a long step toward maturity, in Edward Abbey's *Fire on the Mountain* (1962), as he tries to help his grandfather fend off the appropriation of the Box V Ranch by the White Sands Missile Base. John Vogelin represents the Old West: "I am the land. . . . I've been eating its dust for seventy years. . . . They'll have to plow me under." Similarly, his friend and Billy's hero, Lee Mackie, represents the New West, and Billy feels totally betrayed when Lee aids in the eviction. The strong love the three feel for one another, their mutual reverence for the harshly beautiful New Mexican desert, and the trouble they face alter all three. Billy changes from child to very young man who has seen love and friendship rendered helpless in the face of change. When he and Lee unite in one final act affirming their love for John, Abbey makes his final point: times may change, but human values need not be surrendered.

The intrusion of warped social attitudes can perhaps threaten a surrogate family even more than a conventional family. When racism endangers another foster parent–foster child relationship, both Hubby and his unnamed foster brother learn, as do Brad Nichols (*Home Is the North*) and Billy Vogelin Starr (*Fire on the Mountain*), that there is no wholly safe refuge from society or time. In *King* (1967) by Lonnie Coleman, the unnamed narrator tells a fairly gentle story set in the South of the 1920s. Like the narrator, Hubby is taken in by the narrator's aunt and uncle, a childless white couple. Though the runaway Hubby is black, he is generally well accepted by the tiny community and serves as mentor and protector for the narrator and his friends. Aided by a white racist, Hubby's father traces him, and the family face the first serious loss of their life together.

Novels depicting reverse situations to those in *Home Is the North*, *Fire on the Mountain*, and *King* take the evolution of surrogate parent–foster child relationships as the means of generating action. In these plots, one partner—either child or adult—hesitates to undertake the relationship, sometimes for rational, sometimes for irrational reasons. As the following novels illustrate, however, a youngster's need and an adult's capacity to meet that need can override even the pronounced reluctance of either partner.

Butler Craig and Benjy Johnson's mother live together, and the man wishes to be a true father to the boy, though Rose is unable to marry him because she is not yet divorced from Big Benny Johnson. In *A Hero Ain't Nothin' But a Sandwich* (1973, YA) by Alice Childress, some of the strongest passages are devoted to Butler's efforts to "connect" with Benjy, to establish a firm relationship in order to help the boy break his heroin habit. When Benjy is finally able to voice his admiration for Butler, he acknowledges his pride in his stepfather as man and parent:

> Butler is cool. I dig how he walks down the street like he ain't to be meddled with, dig? . . . I also dig him talkin straight to a social worker, a doctor, or even police. Like when the social worker ast him, "Are you the child's father?" Butler look him in the eye and say, "Let's put it this-a-way. I am who he has *got* for a father, that is sufficient to make him mine and me his."

Benjy's hard-won responsiveness to Butler is Childress's strongest symbol of hope for Benjy's recovery.

Because she feels somewhat unable to cope with her own present life, Cat Holzman, of Judith Guest's *Second Heaven* (1982), is puzzled, worried, and unconfident when she finds herself acting as surrogate parent and supportive, older friend to Gale Murray, an abused teenager. Gale, too, is fearful, and seeks Cat's help because he literally doesn't know what else to do. In a sense, his escape to Cat's home is one of several practice "runs," rehearsals for his ultimate escape from their Michigan town and his life as the terrorized son of an overdemanding father and an intimidated mother, but until the crisis precipitated by his stay with Cat, Gale is not quite ready to renounce his "real" family. Tentatively, Cat and Gale learn to understand and trust one another, learn that though relationships may not be perfect, they may yet be viable and nurturing. Both feeling that they are failures (because they have accepted others' evaluations of themselves), they find new, if imperfect, self-images, and both gain from the relationship; both mature considerably, and their parallel development is central to *Second Heaven*.

David Stokes, one of the two main characters in Joseph Caldwell's *In Such Dark Places* (1978), exists primarily as a means of redemption for the protagonist, Eugene McNiven. Barred from his mother's apartment, David dwells in a burned-out building, living by his wits, a victim of homosexual rape and other abuse. At first David's fascination with Eugene is an annoyance, keeping Eugene from successful pursuit of Raimundo, to whom he is attracted. But eventually, Eugene recognizes David's need and offers him a home. The Christian imagery informing this urban allegory indicates hope for both young men—Eugene may regain his faith and his self-respect; David has an opportunity for a more regulated, ordinary life.

No boy could expect to find more worthy, more willing models than does Lucius Priest, protagonist of *The Reivers* (1962), William Faulkner's "Golden Book." His grandfather, "Boss" Priest, rules the entire family lovingly but firmly, and ultimately, it is he who points out to Lucius that a gentleman assumes "the burden of the consequences" of his actions, thus affirming the boy's initiation. This lesson stems from Lucius's cross-country trip with a pair of scalawags who get him into considerable, sometimes serious, trouble. Comfort and support from "Uncle" Parsham ("Possum") Hood, the black leader of a small rural community, teach the boy that honor and decency do not recognize the color bar. Both "Boss" and "Uncle Possum" influence Lucius's move toward adulthood, away from childish irresponsibility. Lucius, a paradigmatic *Bildungsroman* hero, is wholly successful in his quest. He suffers, awakens to some very unpalatable realities, realizes his limitations, and yet grasps the importance of living gracefully under pressure. Aware that perfection is unattainable, he will settle for behaving honorably, bending the code when he must (especially when it is wrong or injurious), upholding it when—and as best—he can. Apparently the child of fairly ineffectual parents, Lucius Priest is blessed with elderly substitute parent–models who guide him through his hilarious, dangerous, exacting rites of passage. He discovers that to be adult is to be, essentially, alone, but he avoids bitterness and alienation.

Male adolescents often turn to their siblings for models, sometimes as replacements for inadequate or failed parents, sometimes for the benefit of peer support, sometimes simply because they are there. But other factors also influence the relationships between male adolescents and their siblings, just as they do relationships between female adolescents and their brothers and sisters. Jealousy, competition for parents' attention, and differing abilities and values sometimes generate strain and ill will. Anger and rejection may result when one sibling tries to impose his or her standards or image upon another, usually younger, brother; these reactions are similar to those that adolescents feel toward parents or other models who are—or are perceived to be—too directive. Sibling relationships, like all other forms of kinship, almost always must be assessed and redefined during adolescence, and for males, as for their female peers, the process is more often arduous than comfortable.

Some authors depict rather large nuclear families as microcosms of the world which adolescents are expected to face as adults. In these instances, as *Whipple's Castle* and *Lion on the Hearth* illustrate, competition and strain within the family parallel situations in the outside world. Frequently, in novels of this type, some of the children succeed more fully than others, and some subplots centering on various siblings are traditionally comic, others traditionally tragic, and these novels are almost always realistic in tone.

In Thomas Williams's *Whipple's Castle* (1968), the four children, including three sons, of the Whipple family of Leah, New Hampshire, are followed for six crucial years during their growing up. The family life is strained and difficult (the father is a cripple, embittered by injuries he suffered in an automobile accident some years earlier). Each son faces special problems of his own: Wood ("the good") enters the army at eighteen (the novel covers World War II and the years immediately succeeding), has some troubling relationships during his military service, is severely wounded physically and scarred emotionally by his experiences. David, the middle son, is athletic and competent; he has a less traumatic military experience, but faces some dark truths in the painful scene in which he attempts to render euthanasia to a pet cat. And Horace, the youngest, called "Horse," is clumsy, insecure, frightened of all sorts of "monsters." The young people do try to help each other cope with their varied problems, and ultimately, despite a tragic climax, the family's cohesion is preserved. Two of the three sons survive and are at least apparently happy, successful, and productive in the lives they choose.

The third surviving son of a contentious mercantile family, Kin King, of John Ehle's *Lion on the Hearth* (1961), grows up amid violent competition for dominance among his father and older brothers. Harsh Paul plots to control the family business. Sullen Mathew vacillates between drunken self-indulgence and his own desire for control of the store. Only gregarious Collins, the wanderer-brother; Beth, a cousin; and Cal, Kin's father, offer the boy any sort of supportive love. Tempted to leave home to search for happiness, Kin leaves that option to his cosseted younger brother, Johnny, and becomes his own man, finding his own identity and abjuring his brothers as models. Aware that the North Carolina hill country is changing and conscious of his own skills as a merchant, Kin sees better times coming. As "heir to his father's spirit and his loyalties and friends," he intends to preserve the best of the old times and exploit the best of the new.

Like female adolescents who share the same burden, males who must behave as substitute parents toward siblings face a frightening, almost overwhelming responsibility. Usually motivated by profound love as well as by accountability, these boys, like Jan Anderson of *The Inkling*, are nevertheless more apt to fail than to succeed, according to the novels studied here. Commonly, pairs of parenting-parented siblings feel themselves alone against the world, an attitude which augments the pressure on the parenting lad. Indeed, the burdens are too great; the young substitute parents are too inexperienced and too powerless, and the cost to both siblings is high.

The loss of his beloved little brother, Philip, marks the end of childhood and the utter dissolution of family for Ben, the protagonist of *Like the Lion's Tooth* (1972) by Marjorie Kellogg. Because their father is a child abuser and their mother a well-intentioned, loving person who is totally incapable of coping with the poverty and the violence of their life, the boys cling to one another. Ben is affectionate, patient, and protective of his brother, sustaining his worst beating while defending Philip from the sexual exploitation of their father. Philip is slow, silent, and almost totally dependent on Ben. When the boys are separated, Philip takes action that results in his own death, leaving Ben with nothing.

In Al Hine's *Lord Love a Duck* (1961), Gooney Bird Musgrave, a high-school student, realizes he has exceptional abilities when he discovers he is able to control his sister's epileptic seizures through hypnosis, although physicians are helpless. This discovery combines with his realization that his concern for his sister, Coralou or Coley, is both more sympathetically real and unconventional than that of his parents:

> *All by himself, when the bleeding hearts and the swanky quacks were still fumbling along in the dark, he'd found that he could bring old Coley out of her fits himself, that when he took her off alone with him and away from the darn folks she could almost pass for normal. . . .*
> *. . . . The one doctor he'd tried to tell had nodded without listening, and Gooney learned his lesson, that big lesson that the world was run their way, so you might as well learn to play inside their rules.*
> *Part of their rules being total respect for nothing but strength, whether it was muscles or money or other manipulation. As easy to learn as the rest of their infantile laws.*

As a result, Gooney Bird becomes both alienated from and fascinated by the society of ordinary people, and he shows his contempt for it by consciously manipulating for his own purposes those who are most conventionally successful in ordinary society.

The denouements of novels depicting sibling behavior models, usually elders who dominate their younger brothers to greater or lesser degrees, are far less unilaterally tragic than those treating adolescent substitute fathers. Some, of course, discuss relationships in which unrealistic expectations are imposed by an older brother or sister; others reflect realistic tensions as younger siblings seek independence. *Danger Song* employs both these patterns. Still other, sunnier novels depict sibling relationships as everyone would like to believe they really are. In novels such as *I Tell a Lie Every So Often* and *The Year the Lights Came On*, though one youth is clearly the leader (and often the model) for the other, the spirit of shared adventure is the dominant, enlivening tone, and very often the follower influences his leader almost as much as he is influenced.

For Martin Williams, protagonist of Bryant Rollins's *Danger Song* (1967), the relationship with his older sister, Martha, is complex, frightening, and often frustrating. His sister is ten years older than her brother and has been able to combine the power that street survival in Boston's Roxbury district and college training have given her. Martha is determined that Martin will follow in her path, and she tries, through dominance, to assure herself that Martin will develop the same strength and toughness which make her able to cope with a society controlled by whites. Though eventually the brother and sister become close, the novel teaches one of life's most bitter lessons: in a destructive society, one can never protect a loved one quite well enough. Martin goes his own way, finds his own fate.

Bruce Clements depicts a warm and amusing relationship between two brothers in *I Tell a Lie Every So Often* (1974, YA), a frontier story. At fourteen, Henry Desant, innocent, practical, generous, and likable, is very much aware that he owes obedience as well as loyalty to Clayton, who is in his late teens. Clayton is in love with love and entranced with two ambitions. He yearns to be a hero, and so concocts a plan to free a long-lost cousin from the Indians who supposedly stole her, and he eagerly and sincerely anticipates a call to the ministry. The boys' maturation journey—the rescue mission—precipitates mild adventures which reveal their personalities and their influence over one another.

Colin Wynn, the protagonist of *The Year the Lights Came On* (1976) by Terry Kay, is a member of a large, loving, supportive family. But to Colin, his brother Wesley, slightly older, is a very special person:

> He was my brother, and I was prejudiced, but in those years when it was easy to trust unreservedly in the magic of people, I regarded Wesley as the most gifted person I knew, or would ever know. He was an Always There person. Once—I was eleven, I think—I was certain I saw a cosmic blessing descend on Wesley. He had walked out of the sunlight into the shade, and the sun twisted and bent to follow him. Wesley had presence, and that presence filled the emptiness of many moments and many lives.

Terry Kay portrays the boys' loving comradeship simply and without sentimentality, showing Wesley's steady and steadying influence over Colin's maturation.

Like female adolescent characters, then, the male adolescents who populate our subject-novels discover that their families are not always buffering support against the trials and dangers of their initiation years; indeed, for many, family crises are major tests of their mettle and developing maturity. For males, the search for a useful role model (usually within the family, outside it if extended search becomes necessary) is a more important step in the maturation process than for females, according to these novels. And authors are as unsparing in their assessments of the damage ineffectual or inept parents and siblings can inflict upon young men as they are in depicting similar situations involving young women.

Though some novels, such as *Sounder*, *The Reivers*, *I Tell a Lie Every So Often*, and *The Year the Lights Came On*, celebrate the joyousness of successful familial relationships and the redemptive aspects of adolescent males' alliances with sound role models—even as they describe the stringency of the tests to which their young protagonists are subjected—by far the great majority of novels studied here stress the harsher, more destructive elements of familial relationships. Perhaps in the eyes of these authors, the necessary process of reevaluation, dissolution, and reestablishment of family bonds is even more trying for males, who are expected to be aggressive, assertive, dominant adults, than for females, who are expected to be passive. Perhaps, until only very recently, American society as exemplified by the authors and readers of these novels tended to take more seriously the problems of male adolescents than those of female adolescents. Whatever the explanation may be, however, loss, destruction, despair, and violence (*McCaffrey, About Us, Such Nice People, Second Heaven, Like the Lion's Tooth, Danger Song*, to cite only a very few examples) are dominant elements in numerous stories of adolescent males and their families.

CHAPTER X
Male Friendships

Like young females, male adolescents also seek companionship on the journey toward adulthood, and, as we have observed, the young share, with all people of all ages, the need for supportive friendship. Young men, again like young women, sometimes perceive their friendships as buffers against powerful adults whose society they intend to penetrate. The fictional boys portrayed in the novels studied here seem to depart, however, from some patterns fictional girls follow. Their friendships seem to be directed more toward exploration than self-ratification; that is, friendships are a means of actively examining the world about them and testing their ability to enter it.

This slightly different attitude toward the preparatory function of adolescence most probably stems from society's traditional belief that males are more assertive, more aggressive than females. It may well be that young men are *allowed* —overtly or covertly—vigorous experiments with the elasticity (or inelasticity) of many rules and codes by which adults operate. In most of these novels, male friends seem to be aware that society grants them permission to sow the proverbial wild oats. As they are being tried and tested, then, male adolescents are also testing and evaluating the power structure— they may not intend to change it (though some, usually the more idealistic, do hope to effect social betterment), but they certainly intend, according to their creators, to *use* it rather than simply to fit into it.

The dual motifs of testing and being tested create difficult problems for young men, largely because they are expected to understand the rules without being given clear explanations (if, indeed, rational explanation is possible for some social patterns) or to gain understanding by straining the boundaries of propriety without actually breaking them. Being expected to grasp for power, to take chances, to break rules—but to do none of these things too much or too obviously—is both immensely appealing and very menacing. For young males, then, as for young females, the adult world is mysterious and attractive, but also dangerous in only vaguely understood ways.

One of the most puzzling facts about adults' tacit permissiveness for (even approval of) boys' wild oat period is the equally powerful expectation that though they are expected to learn rules by violating some of them, they are also expected to accommodate to society. The tests of adolescence will, it is generally understood, chasten them to one degree or another. Though the intent of this attitude is to allow youths to learn how to use the society they will one day control, the consequence is often painful confusion. If they are covertly expected to prove their male strength and power, why then, should disapprobation and retribution constantly threaten them? Why must they be chastened? For youngsters, the realization that chastening may be a part of the human condition is no more comfort than for anyone else—but it is a lesson male adolescents are expected to learn and to learn, as the old saw says, the hard way, sometimes suffering punishment for their experiments, always being tempered. They are expected to learn to be active, powerful, assertive beings; they are expected to learn to use the social structure for their own ends; and happily most are expected to learn to understand and assume responsibility.

Hidden in these expectations seems to be yet another message similar to the dual signals which guide their adolescent experiments: that breaking and bending the rules is, in fact, an important factor in adult male activity; that men of action and power are, indeed, expected to break them—just enough to demonstrate their power, just enough to exert control, and just enough to discharge responsibility. This lesson is difficult and burdensome in the extreme, and it is not surprising, therefore, that male adolescents seek the comfort and support of fellow initiates, friends who can experiment and sow and learn with them. For them, the bond of friendship reassures even as it tests; to adult observers, it implies the beginnings of a power-base, a network which will sustain the friends socially and professionally in the future; for lucky adolescents, it will continue to support them personally as well.

A very traditional, folkloric treatment of male adolescent friendships is presented in David Wagoner's *Where Is My Wandering Boy Tonight?* (1970), as even its title indicates. Here, boys' high jinks and trickery both reflect and test the flawed adult society the youngsters confront, and the high social status of the professions marked out for them by their elders indicates that the boys will become power-wielding adults. This 1970 novel is paradigmatic of one common fictional approach to male adolescent friendships, and its humor both undercuts and underscores the seriousness of the boys' accommodation to the unsavory aspects of adult society. Andrew Jackson Holcomb, Jr., and Fred Haskell are depicted as close friends, although the fact of their friendship is not overtly stressed as a theme. Jackson, the narrator and protagonist, is the son of a judge and is intended by his father to go to Harvard Law School. Fred, a minister's son, is intended by his father for the ministry. Both boys, true sons of the Old West which they inhabit, resist these choices made for them, and their lives, at age seventeen, consist primarily of pranks such as stealing freshly cooked pies, deceiving their ignorant tutors by making up impressive-sounding nonsensical answers, and sneaking into the town brothel. Jackson, the braver and more inventive of the two, is generally the ringleader in their exploits, which become progressively wilder and more potentially serious. But the boys are indomitable, and their comradeship clearly helps them survive and cope with the comically corrupt West of the 1890s.

In contrast, B. H. Friedman's *Yarborough* (1964) is a good example of another frequently used pattern in novels of male friendship: the supportive, effective bonding between two boys of varying degrees of sensitivity, one of whom accommodates, the other of whom rejects society. Arthur Skelton and Henry Rosen meet as prep-school classmates and form the intimate friendship which is to endure for the rest of Arthur's short life. Even after Henry's early marriage, they continue to be inseparable. Alienated from life and society, Arthur finds meaning in this friendship and in little else. The intimacy and strength of the relationship as it grows and changes over a period of years, from preadolescence to young adulthood, is believably developed. They confide to each other their deepest thoughts about their families, their first sexual gropings, their scorn for those less brilliant than they. Although Arthur largely withdraws from conventional life and society and Henry follows a more conventional course, their close dependence on each other endures.

A third pattern common in portrayals of male adolescent friendships depicts the interrelationships and interactions of a group of friends whose diversity allows for varied means of comparing and contrasting the youngsters. Kenneth H. Brown's *The Narrows* (1970) has no single protagonist, though Howie Smith comes close to filling that role. Instead, the novel deals with a large number of boys and girls, particularly the boys. Their friendships—rivalries, loyalties, and comradeship— and their shifting relationships over their high-school years, in various public and parochial schools in Brooklyn, are authentically depicted. We see them grow in sophistication and daring from the first party the boys self-consciously give, through such other group activities as fighting and stealing, to enlistment for some in the Marine Corps, their badge of manhood.

The Narrows, Yarborough, and *Where Is My Wandering Boy Tonight?* all treat, in diverse ways and with various degrees of prominence, young males' first sexual experimentation. This theme, of course, is important in almost every novel discussed here as it is in many depicting female adolescent friendships. The difference in these treatments lies in the boys' shared activities—exploring brothels, for instance—and in the fact that these young fictional males seem to talk (and sometimes lie) about their experiences a bit more openly with one another than do most of the fictional female friends who appear in novels read for this study. While for many of these young males, sexual initiation means pleasure, freedom, and ratification of their manliness, for others, such as William Faulkner's Lucius Priest of *The Reivers* (1962), for example, the developing awareness of sexuality in others is one of many disquieting revelations he must assimilate. When others' attitudes about sexuality are used to attack young men, however, assimilation may become impossible, and some friendships are disrupted or destroyed.

One such example is the friendship, in *Cages* (1971) by Paul Covert, between Bob Ward and Eric Mathews, which is of primary importance in the boys' lives. Bob's preoccupation with words, his curiosity about people's motives, and his introspection contrast with and complement Eric's bluff, blunt, open personality. Left alone, the boys are happy in their comradeship, but the outside world, represented by Bob's mother and the boys' first girlfriends, intrudes, suggesting that their friendship is really a homosexual affair. Bob is especially threatened by the accusation and by the isolation that is bound to follow, and his reactions are violent and tragic. *Cages* illustrates the evanescence of youthful idyls.

Cages falls into the pattern represented by *Yarborough*, centering upon the alliance between two boys who have different interests, differing abilities to withstand the harsher social lessons imposed during adolescence. It also, however, introduces another motif which appears in a number of novels depicting male adolescent friendships. Though social disapprobation is generally held at bay while the boys discover and test the limits of permissiveness, there is one area in which society, as depicted in these novels, is utterly unpermissive; any hint of homosexual activity between male friends is cause for severe disapprobation, disdain, even punishment. Like Paul Covert's *Cages, Good Times/Bad Times* by James Kirkwood and *Run Softly, Go Fast* by Barbara Wersba depict friendships invaded by others' suspicions that the friends might be homosexuals.

Early in *Good Times/Bad Times* (1968) by James Kirkwood, the protagonist, Peter Kilburn, declares,

> If I'm a fanatic about one thing, it's having one particular best friend that I can really connect with. Although I can make friends easily . . . I've never really wanted, nor had, a large circle of just plain friends. . . . Give me one good close friend any day. I suppose I'm what you'd call monogamous when it comes to friends. So that was what I was really looking forward to.

Peter's expectations are fulfilled when Jordan Legier also matriculates at Guilford Academy: "By the end of Jordan's first day at Guilford, we were locked in total friendship." At first, Jordan's fragile health is the only shadow over the relationship, and the boys flourish and grow in one another's company. Their friendship withstands even the headmaster's accusations that Peter and Jordan are having an affair, charges springing largely from the man's own attraction to Peter. Though Hoyt, the headmaster, cannot destroy the friendship, he does irreparable damage to the friends—he contributes to Jordan's death from a fatal heart attack and ultimately goads Peter into murder. The novel is told in a long flashback which concludes on a slim note of hope. Peter, awaiting trial for his crime, confides to his attorney that his memory of the friendship and the lessons Jordan has taught him about dealing with trouble not only sustain him but also lead him to believe that better times are ahead.

One important motif among several in Barbara Wersba's *Run Softly, Go Fast* (1970, YA), a study of the complex relationship between Leo and David Marks, an estranged father and son, is that of the friendship between Davy and Richard Heaton, "the third." Davy comes from a Jewish immigrant background while Rick's background seems impeccably WASP. But both are bright, artistic, and sensitive. Two crucial events help to explain Davy's rejection of his father: Leo's attempt to destroy their friendship when he discovers them wrestling playfully (he apparently suspects homosexual activity) and Rick's death in Vietnam (despite his pacifism, he is led there by an ironic chain of events in which his own father's stiff-necked pride and insensitivity play a central role). Davy sees parallels between the actions and attitudes of the two fathers; bitterly blaming Rick's father for Rick's death, he equally bitterly blames his own father for all that goes wrong in his own life. The novel finally, however, depicts Davy coming to terms with his own father, whose actions, even if misguided, did come from love. The friendship between Davy and Rick, thus, functions in two ways in the novel: as an enriching experience during an important part of Davy's adolescence and as a motivating factor in the break with his father that is the novel's central subject.

Perhaps because they have traditionally been expected to take more physical risks than young women, and certainly because they have been expected to fight the nation's wars, young men, according to these authors, more often lose friends through accidents or on the battlefield, as in *Run Softly, Go Fast*. Certainly more violence occurs in novels focusing on pairs or groups of boys or, sometimes, on groups of both sexes that are dominated by a male member (*Blade of Light*). This fact is surely linked with young men's need (imposed by society or perceived by them as imposed by society) to prove their courage, endurance, and hence their manhood. This need, coupled with an extreme threat to a youth's developing selfhood and his sense of social acceptance, contributes to the violent reactions of Bob Ward (*Cages*) and Peter Kilburn (*Good Times/Bad Times*). Paul Covert and James Kirkwood suggest that in a society which defines itself as homophobic, some young men cannot endure even the suspicion of homosexual activity.

Among the novels studied here, this propensity for violence is shown much more commonly as a male than as a female reaction. Sandra Scoppettone's *Happy Endings Are All Alike*, for instance, directly addresses young lesbians' felt need for secrecy. The couple ensure a tormentor's silence by placating her over and over again. Nevertheless, when one lover is raped, she entertains no thought of exacting vengeance personally, but prosecutes her attacker, knowing he will make her affair public. These dissimilar responses, however, are far more likely to reflect the passivity traditionally taught females and the aggression traditionally taught males than to suggest that male homosexuals suffer more from social disapprobation. No author considered here understates the problems society imposes upon young homosexuals of either sex.

The disruption of a male friendship by sudden, accidental death works on several levels for author Judith Guest, who shows that loss and the consequent guilt and notoriety can separate surviving friends at the very time when they most need one another. The protagonist of *Ordinary People* (1976), Con Jarrett, has been isolated from his friends by his brother's death and his own subsequent suicide attempt. Joe Lazenby, who has been a good friend to both brothers, makes repeated attempts to bridge the gap between him and Con, only to be rebuffed: "It hurts too much to be around you." When Con finally initiates reassociation with Joe, the gesture signifies his own recovery and his ability to cope with memories of his brother.

Other, seemingly lesser, disruptions of male friendships can also result in severe consequences, even in death. In pairs or groups of males or mixed groups dominated by males, all of whom are expected to be assertive, all of whom are expected to be aggressive, some competition for leadership ensues. The desire for status supplants the equality which friendship among peers promises to youngsters.

Sometimes, even though a group of friends has chosen a leader, all the boys share adventure and danger, and all believe that the act of sharing is itself one measure of their worth. Freeman Boyd plays an important role in *The Year the Lights Came On* (1976) by Terry Kay. Freeman is the leader of the Big Gully Crime-Busters, the crowd to which protagonist Colin Wynn belongs. When Freeman is accused of theft, he takes refuge in Black Pool Swamp, an area he knows better than anyone else in the county. His adventures in the swamp test his developing manhood. Freeman's maturation experience is shared by all the other gang members, especially Colin and his brother, whose responses foreshadow the kind of men they will become.

Other young male leaders or would-be leaders exploit their influence in self-seeking, devastating ways. Harold Hunt, in *Blade of Light* (1968) by Don Carpenter, is a boy marked by total self-interest, a quality which causes him to abuse all his young associates. Harold's utter destructiveness is symbolized by his treatment of his car, rebuilt with loving skill by his closest companion, Rattner, and demolished in one of Harold's angry outbursts. Harold coldly forces plain, lonely Marjorie Butts, who loves him, to share out her sexual favors among his gang. His intense but frustrating sexual relationship with Carole Weigandt and his exploitative "friendship" with handicapped Irwin Semple climax together and result in Carole's death and Irwin's institutionalization. *Blade of Light* examines young males' use and abuse of power over their peers; another novel, *Founder's Praise* by Joanne Greenberg, examines a young leader's freedom to abandon his position and consequently to threaten the security and privileges it has won for his friends. Harold Hunt is selfish, totally absorbed in his own cruel aims; Edgar Kornarens, in *Founder's Praise*, is perceived to be selfish by his friends. In both cases, violence and suffering result; both also involve sexual desire and jealousy, and both authors raise questions about guilt, innocence, and responsibility.

Edgar Kornarens, Mike Anton, and Glover Castle are the closest of friends in *Founder's Praise* (1976) by Joanne Greenberg. One of the many forces drawing the boys together is their mutual belief and participation in the Praise Dances of a religious sect founded by Edgar's family. Because of his heritage, Edgar is treated "specially" by the small community, and this treatment extends to Mike and Glover. Beginning in innocence and continuing in unrecognized cynicism, the boys undertake a four-year scheme to inspire the town to offer the three of them college scholarships, sustaining an incredible effort of organization, hard work, and manipulation. When success is within their grasp, Edgar bitterly offends Mike and Glover (already jealous of Edgar's love for Martha Wyer) when he decides to use his scholarship at a different school, temporarily leaving the threesome, which the others anticipate will be lifelong. The boys have become so used to power that Mike and Glover turn the graduation Praise Dance against Edgar and Martha:

> What if the will isn't good and the ends aren't good? What happens if the thought or the wish is sick and jealous? Then the magic goes bad, doesn't it? Mike and Glover and all our friends in that Praise—they were doing black magic against us . . . against Martha and me. They were calling down a power against us, not with voodoo and demon books, but in an ordinary Praise with all the ordinary and well-meant words. For our own good, they said. All in our own best interests.

The results are terrible and ironic, leaving the three forever disrupted after all.

Like Edgar Kornarens, other fictional male adolescents must assess their responsibility toward their friends. These youngsters, like many female adolescent characters, sometimes find such assessments extremely difficult because of their limited experience. Too young to realize, perhaps, that all human beings are flawed, too young to know that one must behave responsibly toward others but that they, too, must be responsible, many of these young men suffer considerably. The "burden" of the consequences of one's actions is the central theme of *The Reivers* (1962) by William Faulkner. In order to lend a vague aura of legitimacy to their "borrowing" of an employer's car, Boon Hogganbeck and Ned McCaslin persuade the auto-owner's grandson, Lucius Priest, to accompany them on a wild, funny, dangerous ride from Jefferson, Mississippi, to Memphis, Tennessee. For Lucius, the trip is an initiation journey, and not the least of the lessons he learns are those taught by his companions. Because Lucius is white, has full possession of his wits, and, in effect, employs his friends, he is expected to be responsible *for* them and *to* his grandfather. Boon is a "natural," clever with automobiles but inept at personal, social, and economic relationships. Ned is black, and though he is strong, wily, and clever, society denies him full maturity. Thus, Lucius is putative leader of the trio, but actually the pawn of the older men, who are themselves pawns of a society which will not grant them full adulthood. Though he is only eleven, Lucius must maintain some sort of balance between his older friends, exercising control (if and when he can) without seeming to do so. In this, his happiest novel, Faulkner continues his indictment of the enervating, destructive "white man's burden" which a racist, bigoted society imposes upon itself.

Jimmy-Lee Powell, like Lucius Priest, feels the burden of the consequences of his actions keenly. His attempts to redeem the situation are, however, further complicated by his friend's desire for autonomy. In *A Hero Ain't Nothin' But a Sandwich* (1973, YA), Alice Childress portrays the troubled friendship between Benjy Johnson, a thirteen-year-old heroin addict, and Jimmy-Lee Powell, his "boon," who feels guilty because he introduced Benjy to pot. Jimmy-Lee believes that the pot smoking cemented Benjy's casual friendships with the drug crowd and led directly to Benjy's addiction, but his efforts to talk his buddy out of heroin dependence backfire, because Benjy resents Jimmy-Lee's refusal to try the drug, feeling that sharing kicks would symbolize their friendship. Also, Benjy drifts further from Jimmy-Lee's influence because he identifies his friend's pleas with the straight world:

> It bugged me hard when Jimmy-Lee start layin them jive-ass heart-to-heart raps on me. Talking like he already a social worker. "Man," he say, "straighten up cause you gonna kill yourself." Answer me this, if Jimmy-Lee is my friend and I'm his, then that make us equal, right? Then how come he talking like he got it made and I'm lost? That ain't no way to be equal and reach somebody. He don't reach me a-tall!

The boys' friendship not only augments the main plot of the novel but also serves as a subplot, the relationship between the boys lending drama and poignancy to Benjy's story.

The protagonist of *Like the Lion's Tooth* (1972) by Marjorie Kellogg also, like Benjy Johnson, resents his friend's demonstrations of concern and loyalty. Ben has only one friend at the school for destitute children to which he has been remanded. He and Madeline are drawn together because both were repeatedly raped by their fathers. Bigger and slightly older than Ben, Madeline makes him uncomfortable by handling, patting, and preening him like, Ben thinks, "a monkey mother." Further, Ben believes that his maleness (already, in his view, attacked by another) should be reason enough for him to dictate the lines of their relationship; and he almost deliberately ruptures their friendship. But when he is stripped of all family ties, Ben becomes desperate enough to accept her again: "Monkey mother, he thought, but her hands were soothing and the pain in his head seemed to be getting less." Neither Ben nor the reader, however, is really comforted by this alliance born of despair.

Though the tests and trials imposed upon—and by—many friendships between adolescent males are severe, as the novels examined here indicate, other authors portray friendships—between males and females, between males and males, peers and peers, peers and elders—as supportive, positive, and useful. The treatments of these boys' stories range from realistic to allegorical, and in them, as in some grimmer stories, the authors' and readers' ability to smile or even laugh at the vicissitudes of youth helps to reassure us that adolescence is generally not only survivable but bearable.

Richard Bradford's *Red Sky at Morning* (1968), the story of the coming of age of Joshua Arnold in New Mexico during World War II, realistically depicts the fumblings of young people as they try to learn about and relate to the world around them. Joshua and his friends Steenie (William Stenopolous, Jr., son of a Greek-American physician) and Marcia Davidson (daughter of an Episcopal rector) satisfy their curiosity about sex, venereal disease, and other physical mysteries by reading Steenie's father's medical books. Steenie and Marcia help to interpret the strange New Mexico society to Joshua, a newcomer to the area. They are all likable young people, seeing their own gropings and confusions with detachment and sometimes even humor. Through various troubles they support and help each other, and their comradeship becomes very important to all three.

Because Joey Martin is a true friend to Sarah MacDermott, protagonist of Janet Majerus's *Grandpa and Frank* (1976)—and because he's fascinated with the prospect of repairing and driving the MacDermotts' old Model-A Ford truck—he agrees to help Sarah spirit her grandfather to Chicago in an effort to protect the sick old man's interests. Joey, practical, deliberate, and deft with his hands, offsets Sarah's imaginativeness and intensity, acting as both follower and leader as the occasion demands. In many ways, Joey represents the admirable qualities and the sounder values of the rural life which has shaped both children.

Archie Larsen is an exile from the natural wilderness he loves, living in New York City, "The Concrete Wilderness," in the 1967 novel of that title by Jack Couffer. Preferring animals to people, Archie avoids school for a year, roaming the city and observing its wildlife, disdaining to have any human friend. Couffer describes the boy's slowly growing trust in Martin Hanley, a photographer doing a picture essay on urban animal life. Their developing affection is tested severely when Martin's adult attitudes clash with the boy's youthful passion for a dog he has befriended.

The friendship of two boys of almost fourteen is poetically and movingly dramatized in Ray Bradbury's suspenseful and allegorical fantasy *Something Wicked This Way Comes* (1962). Jim Nightshade and Will Halloway have the joy and capacity of wonder of an idealized youth, and their friendship is almost idyllically presented.

> Like all boys, they never walked anywhere, but named a goal and lit for it, scissors and elbows. Nobody won. Nobody wanted to win. It was in their friendship they just wanted to run forever, shadow and shadow. Their hands slapped library door handles together, their chests broke track tapes together, their tennis shoes beat parallel pony tracks over lawns, trimmed bushes, squirreled trees, no one losing, both winning, thus saving their friendship for other times of loss.

Idyllic though the friendship between Jim Nightshade and Will Halloway may be insofar as the boys' sense of equal comradeship goes, nevertheless, they must, like all adolescents, confront evil. They must also, Ray Bradbury reminds us, face the possibility of loss.

For most fictional adolescent male friends, the difficult lessons of evil and loss are exacerbated by the necessity to learn to balance responsible behavior against desire for those prizes that might be won by secretly and cleverly abandoning the rules by which society claims to operate. Expected to be both mischievous and good, both assertive and forbearing, both active and accommodating, young males look to their friends for support and comfort, hoping that together they can solve the mystery of acceptable adult male behavior.

CHAPTER XI
Males in Crisis

For male adolescents, a main goal is that of learning to channel aggression in socially acceptable or personally rewarding ways. Simultaneously, the boy searches for freedom from constraints imposed by childhood helplessness and feels a need to prove his manhood, often according to some outside definition of what manhood is. Paradoxically, while the young male is trying to discover and assert his adult manliness, he is also particularly concerned to fit into some group, to achieve social approval. Thus his attempts at asserting himself as an individual are often inseparable from his participation in group activity; depending on the nature of the group, that activity may involve antisocial behavior.

Contemporary novelists have seen especially great challenges to our youth in such phenomena as urban gangs, crime and delinquency, institutionalized racism and ghetto life, and drug abuse. As the young male, still trying to define himself, confronts these aspects of the darker side of American society, his socially conditioned need to be assertive, if not aggressive, may lead him into participation in brutal, violent acts. Or, at the other extreme, he may react negatively, by withdrawal into alienation from the society that produces all these evils.

Many cultures have clear rites of passage into adulthood for young males—initiation rites that may involve ordeals of some sort. Lacking such rituals, our society has imposed upon young people the need to invent their own symbolic acts. This is no easy task, and it has proved extremely difficult for many of the boys in the novels of social criticism analyzed in this chapter. Many boys examined here are greatly in need of rituals, of constructive ways of validating their entry into adulthood, for they are mostly from backgrounds that make especially difficult their definition of self and their discovery of purpose for their lives.

A novel that illustrates particularly well the necessity, even for privileged youths, of a symbolic entry into manhood and the consequences of its absence is John Knowles's *Peace Breaks Out* (1981). The cautionary theme of this novel is that, in many respects, World War II will never end. Members of the Devon School Class of 1946 feel lost and at loose ends; though they are, of course, relieved and grateful that they will not have to face combat, destruction, and death, they also feel that there will be no special test of manhood for them, no glorious initiation into adulthood. The fund drive for installation and dedication of a memorial window to Devon servicemen seems, at first, one means of assuaging the postwar generation's unease, but when a student smashes the memorial, violence is unleashed among these supposedly civil, biddable boys. One of the students is "an incipient monster," and Pete Hallam—Old Boy, veteran, and now Devon faculty member—realizes that such destructive leaders could be developing anywhere and that "people will have to . . . risk everything in . . . defeating them once again, for a time."

The emptiness of these boys' lives and the violence that results from their lack of a sense of purpose as well as of necessary rituals are echoed in other books of male adolescence. Most such novels deal with young men far less materially fortunate than Knowles's youths. For many, poverty, familial problems, or some experience of evil leads to attempts to define themselves and prove their manhood in violent, often criminal ways, frequently (as with Knowles's privileged students) through mob or gang action. One particularly effective depiction of gang activity is found in a novel by S. E. Hinton; she takes us into the world of troubled, violent youths and helps us feel the depth of their alienation. Gangs in an unnamed Oklahoma city, drawn largely along class lines, are the subject of Hinton's *The Outsiders* (1967, YA). The two major groupings are the "Socs" ("Socials," boys from the "right" side of town) and the "Greasers" (poor youths who wear their hair long and greasy), though there are also smaller, tightly-knit groups within each main grouping. The hostility between the two groups causes three deaths and finally leads the protagonist-narrator, Ponyboy Curtis, to turn against gang violence.

Perhaps rather surprisingly, another novelist finds some positive strengths in a gang. The gang members are at least vigorously *alive*, and this energy is the better side of their more obvious failings. The gang members, from twelve to sixteen years in age, are crucial secondary characters in Herbert Wilner's *All the Little Heroes* (1966). The protagonist, in failing health and much concerned with mortality, becomes involved with these Brooklyn juvenile delinquents, and their crudeness and vigor revitalize his life and his search for identity. The novel uses shifting points of view, so we see the boys' responses to him and to their own lives and situations as well as his to them. Long and sprawling, the novel also includes extensive flashbacks, as the boys teach life to a man set toward death, though he remains an enigma to them.

Cynicism and a lack of regard for the lives and feelings of others mark these gangs. Their members live for the moment, often primarily for the sensation of the moment. Social status and manliness are extremely important and are achieved by particularly daring acts of physical courage. While there may be rudimentary ethical systems at work (one doesn't rat on another gang member, and territorial lines between gangs are scrupulously observed, for example), these have little application to the outside world. Outsiders exist to be exploited for personal gain or ignored, insofar as is possible. Terrorists, by contrast, at least claim idealistic goals for their violent acts, but the power of the group's received opinions is equally strong and may be equally troubling for a youngster who begins to question his cause.

Miro Shantas, sixteen, is an experienced, highly trained terrorist who participates in a hijacking. In *After the First Death* (1979, YA), Robert Cormier focuses attention on Miro's reactions to the pressures of the situation, on his awe and admiration for the leader of the hijackers, and on his tense and confusing relationship with young Kate Forrester, driver of the captured bus. Miro's chief assignment is to kill the driver, and he has looked forward to that act as his ultimate initiation into full comradeship with the "freedom fighters" and into manhood. Miro is well aware of the risks of his job: "He knew that he would be dead before he reached twenty or twenty-one. His brother had died at seventeen, in the Detroit confrontation." Thus he is anxious for his first kill. When the terrorists' plans change, postponing the murder, and Miro's new instructions include gaining Kate's sympathies, he is torn between his desire to be blooded and obedience to his masters. His resolution of that tension is typical of Cormier's grim realism in his books for young adults.

Novels characterizing groups of youths who are outside the law emphasize the power of attitudes accepted by the groups; while an individual youth may be able to break free, he does so only with difficulty, for the social pressures to conform are great, and it is all too easy to follow the crowd. The insidious temptation to engage in violence may override family and social training, almost anywhere, anytime. Previously well-behaved, apparently quite normal and ordinary middle-class young people may, when social constraints are removed, descend into an abyss of group amorality.

Imprisonment, then rape and torture, and finally a horrible death are inflicted upon an innocent babysitter by five youngsters, including three boys, in Mendal W. Johnson's *Let's Go Play at the Adams'* (1974). Bobby Adams (thirteen), Paul McVeigh (also thirteen), and John Randall (sixteen) find themselves caught up in the inescapable logic of the situation, once it has begun. Though they are in most ways ordinary middle-class young people, the loss of inhibitions leads to acts of unspeakable cruelty in which they all participate. Even Bobby, who opposes murdering the girl, finally takes part in the act. The novel is a horrifying study in the awful potential for violence which is part of the human condition, though perhaps especially dangerous in the adolescent who does not yet understand adult responsibility or fully empathize with others.

A number of novels study individual young criminals, following them through a process of involvement in violent acts of varied sorts. Often a series of illegal activities occurs, and, as in *Let's Go Play at the Adams'*, the brutal acts are further corrupting to the young people who engage in them. Violence is an important theme in Don Bredes's *Hard Feelings* (1977). The protagonist, Bernie Hergruter, fears another boy, a dull, handicapped, and sadistic schoolmate. While the novel's main theme is sexuality, throughout it, Bernie's concern about Richard is present. It is one motive for his running away, it causes him to acquire a gun, and it leads to a violent climax. Paired with a bloody fight is an example of meaningless suffering caused by teenaged recklessness: because of a risky game, a girl may be paralyzed for life. The world of the adolescent, at least in this novel, is frightening.

Partly from boredom, partly to gain money, partly as an act of rebellion against family and church, Vincent McCaffrey, a restless, sexually frustrated seventeen-year-old in *McCaffrey* (1961) by Charles Gorham, takes to "jackrolling" male homosexuals in Central Park. Vincent acts as the bait; his buddy, Conny, then attacks the victim. For Conny, the crimes are simply a means to an end, money; for Vincent, however, the attacks are a revelation. He discovers a streak of extreme cruelty in himself and finds that he likes not only the danger and the excitement of the thefts but also violence itself. These youthful crimes lead the protagonist into a life of prostitution, then into the ultimate violence, murder.

Though readers briefly enter the consciousness of Mid Summers, in *Happy Endings Are All Alike* (1978, YA) by Sandra Scoppettone, his characterization is more flat than round. Mid is jealous of his older brother, resentful of his mother's attention to his brother, perpetually angry, violent, and sadistic; and before he is well into his high-school career, Mid has become a voyeur, a blackmailer, and a rapist. He rapes protagonist Jaret Tyler, incorrectly thinking he can bar her from identifying him by threatening to reveal that she is a lesbian. Mid's characterization serves to demonstrate that rape is a crime of violence rather than of passion and to contrast with the feminist beliefs of his older brother. While Mid's fate is uncertain (the story ends before the trial, and only a suggestion is made that his sentence will be light), Scoppettone does make clear the devastation that his act has imposed upon others.

When we first meet Alex Housman, the sixteen-year-old protagonist of Theodore Weesner's *The Car Thief* (1972), he is driving the fourteenth car he has stolen; in addition, he has stolen money from some of his schoolmates. His crimes seem little more motivated than anything else in his life. He is an intelligent young man, but alienated and easily discouraged by failure, and he seems not to care deeply about much of anything. The headings of the novel's sections indicate the process he goes through: "The Arrest," "Detention," "The Beating," "Withdrawal," and "Summer Death." The death in the last section is his father's. Alex's subsequent enlistment in the army may bring hope for his future, but we leave his story there, too soon to learn whether he will simply repeat his old patterns of delinquency.

These novels, then, in emphasizing the bleak desperation of young criminals' lives, suggest little hope that the boys will be able to—or even want to—adopt more socially acceptable patterns of behavior. A much

more hopeful novel, rather surprisingly so, deals with the prison experience of eighteen-year-old Bobby Fallon. Pete Hamill's *Flesh & Blood*
(1977) gives a graphic description of that experience, which might have
been expected to be extremely damaging. Gangs and their rivalries, violent racism, homosexual exploitation and threats of rape, ever-present
fear—all are made oppressively clear. That Bobby comes through whole
is partly a matter of luck and partly a result of his own strength. The
prison experience is pivotal for him, for it is there that he begins to learn
to box and thus starts the journey that ultimately makes him a contender
for the title.

Gang membership, violent behavior, and criminal activity, then,
are generally shown to be as harmful to the young man engaged in them
as to the society against which they are directed. They either lack moral
or ethical awareness, are so embittered against society that they feel the
need to strike back violently against it, or are so deeply involved in the
subsociety of an antisocial group that they do not want, or are not able,
to participate in society in a more wholesome way. One crime or violent
act leads to another, each making them more intimately members of a
violent underclass or more radically alienated from society.

These are boys who act, and the majority of authors treating juvenile males in contact with crime do stress violent, or at least aggressive,
behavior in their young male characters. This is not surprising, given
our social expectations of assertive behavior from males. Unlike females,
who are expected to be passive, even to be victims, young men are expected to interact actively with their environment—to use it for self-
aggrandizement or, if that be impossible, to attempt to change it. Nevertheless, there are some examples of young males shown as either
victims or observers, and thus passive to a degree.

Thirteen-year-old David Marshall is the victim of the crime of kidnapping in Frank Herbert's *Soul Catcher* (1972). He is kidnapped by
Katshuk, an embittered American Indian who wishes to avenge the rape
and death of his sister by sacrificing a white Innocent. Although he
clearly states his purpose, the crime is not rightly understood by the
boy's parents or the law enforcement agencies and is assumed to be kidnapping for ransom. During the thirteen-day period that David and
Katshuk are together, their relationship grows and deepens; each protects the other at some crucial moment. Though David is very boyish in
some ways, he is also resourceful and grows rapidly in strength and maturity. Like his captor, he fears loss of his own identity as they grow together. Katshuk understands part of what happens with the boy:

> There would come a moment when the boy was tied so firmly to
> this wilderness that he could not escape it. If the link were forged
> in the right way, innocence maintained, there would be a power
> in it to challenge any spirit.
> *I was marked by his world; now he is marked by mine.*

> This had become a contest on two levels—the straightfor-
> ward capture of a victim and the victim's desire to escape, but be-
> neath that a wrestling of spirits.

But the understanding between the two never becomes complete, and a double failure to understand causes a final catastrophe. The novel, by an author best known for such science fiction novels as *Dune,* is a skillful contrasting of cultures in conflict, effectively clarifying the differences between western and Indian attitudes and assumptions.

The fact of his great youth (only thirteen years old) makes David (*Soul Catcher*) an easy victim; likewise, Rusty-James's subordination to his elder brother helps explain why his role as observer is so important to his development. In S. E. Hinton's *Rumble Fish* (1975, YA), Rusty-James painfully remembers his old adoration of his elder brother, the Motorcycle Boy, who was the toughest, coolest boy around. It was a time when the gangs were not operating, and the Motorcycle Boy, by his amoral courage and strength, had won a great reputation; Rusty-James wanted desperately to be like him and felt his own inferiority deeply. The Motorcycle Boy's warped view of the world is symbolically paralleled by his color blindness and partial deafness, but it is the boy's father, a drunken former lawyer, who finally characterizes the Motorcycle Boy: "He is merely miscast in a play. He would have made a perfect knight, in a different century, or a very good pagan prince in a time of heroes. He was born in the wrong era, on the wrong side of the river, with the ability to do anything and finding nothing he wants to do." Two final acts of violence find the Motorcycle Boy dead and Rusty-James seriously injured and then sent to the reformatory. In the passages with the older, perhaps wiser Rusty-James that frame his memories, we see the effects on him: he has become a drifter and has turned away from the violence by which he had lived earlier, but now he has, ironically, come to resemble the Motorcycle Boy as he had not done earlier. This short novel, suitable for young people, is a sensitive and believable portrayal of troubled youth.

Hinton's protagonists, Rusty-James in *Rumble-Fish* and Pony-Boy in *The Outsiders*, attain some objectivity about the amorality which they observe: despite his worship of the Motorcycle Boy, Rusty-James is finally able to free himself from the violence his older brother represents. Her novels suggest that the adolescent male, despite his deep need to prove himself in some physical way and the equally deep need for belonging that often impels him to accept the standards of a youthful mob or role model, can declare his own independence, can break away from the destructive milieu to which he is accustomed.

In an even more positive vein, in *Another Part of the House* (1970) by Winston M. Estes, Larry Morrison's initially demoralizing observations of evil are ultimately strengthening. When Larry, ten, first becomes aware of dishonesty, he is confused about its source: "Everytime something happens, Mama and Papa blame it on the Depression and hard times. . . . It looks like the Depression is making everybody a thief." But when a member of his own family steals from Larry's father, the boy gradually comes to understand that such simple explanations are invalid. His growing awareness of evil is one factor which contributes to Larry's very early maturation.

Similarly, in *The Watchman* (1961) by Davis Grubb, Jason Hunnicutt's abrupt, painful maturation is also imposed by crimes that affect him by association rather than directly. The murder of his close friend, Cole Blake, draws him closer to Cole's sweetheart, Jill Alt, and precipitates an attack upon Jason himself. As Jill's history, particularly the story of her rape at age four, is revealed, Jason is forced to reevaluate not only Jill, whom he is coming to love, but his entire concept of "good" and "evil" human behavior. Shocked, disillusioned, but far more realistic, Jason eventually begins a quest to find Jill's sister, Cristi, his first love, a youngster who never pretends to be a "good girl," but who is capable of loving people as they are rather than as they seem to be. The various crimes which have informed Jason's awareness teach him to value Cristi's acceptance of flawed human beings and are central symbols of human behavior.

Other young observers are less fortunate, and the knowledge of evil which comes to them vicariously may be so damaging that they eventually engage in acts as violent or as evil as those they initially have reacted against. In these cases, the result of a growing awareness of evil is the corruption of the impressionable adolescent who has been unable to find a nondestructive way to channel his valid anger. For example, the drinking of young Mitchell Mibbs's mother, in Barry Beckham's *My Main Mother* (1969), is a major cause of his ambivalent feelings about her, feelings that ultimately lead to his killing her.

As a boy of fourteen, Horace ("Horse") Whipple, the character who comes closest to being the protagonist of Thomas Williams's many-charactered *Whipple's Castle* (1968), is aware of the brutal gang rape of a defenseless and pathetic older girl, Susie Davis. Awkward and troubled himself, Horace steals money from the rapists and then throws it away in a futile attempt at vengeance. He manages slowly to overcome many of his insecurities and fears and eventually enters a liaison with Susie. Her death and the continued cruel insensitivity of the young man primarily responsible for the rape so enrage gentle Horace that he commits a violent act, leading to the novel's dramatic and painful climax. The rape, then, is most important for its effect on a sensitive character not directly concerned—it motivates his behavior. Because he cared for Susie, a natural victim, his own fate is sealed.

For these young men, a difficult balancing act seems required. They must learn who they are and what they wish to make of their lives; they must establish their independence; they must learn how to fit into groups, including society at large; they must establish moral and ethical standards that are appropriate to them as individuals and that also are compatible with those of the society in which they must live. And beyond all these tasks, they must also establish their manhood—in the senses of both masculine potency and adulthood. The nature of the society surrounding them can make these multifarious tasks painful as well as difficult. If that society is violent, if criminal activity seems the norm, then their maturation is likely to be endangered or even thwarted. Masculinity may come to be equated with brutality or with criminal behavior. Alienation may come to seem the only possible response to an evil or hypocritical world. Yet a number of authors show youngsters struggling through to a rejection of crime and violence, most often as a result of their own native intelligence and strength, though sometimes luck seems very important.

Many youngsters are faced with the challenges of racism. Depictions of ghettos and ghetto life are frequently similar to studies of crime and violence, and, indeed, often they are inseparable. A number of authors, however, set out to demonstrate the pervasive nature of racism in American society by setting their novels in middle-class neighborhoods or private schools, by dealing with other than black-white tensions, or by choosing some special, atypical time and place for their settings.

Through Scotty McKinley, the twelve-year-old central figure in *First Family* (1961), Christopher Davis illustrates the difficulties American society faces in achieving real integration in housing. Scotty and his family, however, are far from typical of black families "integrating" previously all-white neighborhoods: Mr. McKinley is a professor of classics, Mrs. McKinley is highly educated and has inherited wealth, and Scotty's intelligence places him in the genius class. In addition, Scotty has serious health problems: an enlarged heart and epilepsy. He is perfectly aware of racial prejudices and the difficulties of his family's new situation, and his anger leads him to strike out against those who oppose his family and also, sometimes, against Kate Charles, his new white friend. The injustice of his and his family's troubles is made the more apparent because in almost every way they are superior to their new neighbors. In some respects, the novel is simplistic and perhaps dated, but the characterization of Scotty as a brilliant, likable, though troubled young adolescent facing tremendous difficulties is moving.

Early in David J. Michael's *A Blow to the Head* (1970), Anthony "Pooch" Pansella comments about his classmates, "For the rest of our lives we'll hear that great catch-all phrase Racial Problem like stomach flu or juvenile delinquency . . . [But] this really wasn't. It was a thing with the kids at Bernard's." In some ways, Pooch is correct; the St. Bernard School students' preoccupation with the differences between themselves and a new student, J. Roger Gaffrey (who may or may not be a mulatto and whose attitudes, appearance, and wardrobe diverge from the school norms), is largely a matter of the student body's self-image, which J. Roger seems to threaten. Nevertheless, author Michael makes clear that racial and cultural biases—particularly fear and hatred of blacks and "hillbillys"—permeate the thinking at St. Bernard's and of the urban neighborhood in which the school is located. The solid, upwardly mobile, Roman Catholic middle-class character of the area is changing: blacks and Southerners are moving in, economic forces are shifting, and the values and ambitions of the established families are under assault. The novel not only portrays tensions between young people incapable of extending their imaginations to meet a new, puzzling situation but also offers a striking, valuable portrait of pre–Rust Bowl upper-Midwest urban life.

An unusual kind of discrimination is depicted in *The Year the Lights Came On* (1976) by Terry Kay. The rural Georgia community is divided between those who do and those who do not have electricity. Among the children, the split is reflected in two rival gangs. The Highway 17 Gang's members have electricity and hence modern kitchens and indoor plumbing; the Big Gully Crime-Busters' families have none of these amenities. The social distinctions between the two groups are clearly drawn, as are the resultant childish cruelties. The Crime-Busters take heart when the REA (Rural Electrification Administration) moves into the area, thinking that all problems will be solved. The children learn, however, that there are no easy answers. The family farm of the Crime-Busters' leader, Freeman Boyd, lies too far away from the lines, so the Boyds become a tiny, still isolated minority, despite the good intentions of many of their neighbors. Never fully assimilated into the community as it is newly defined, Freeman comes to symbolize to the protagonist-narrator the spirit and the attitudes of pre-electrification times.

In Erskine Caldwell's *Summertime Island* (1968), Steve Henderson, his uncle Guthrie, Troy Pickett, an overt racist, and Duke Hopkins, a black teacher, take a fishing trip to a Mississippi River island. Guthrie tells Steve, you should have this chance to "put a man's feet in your shoes." Steve learns that some whites seek to lose their sense of worthlessness by abusing blacks, and he observes that the forced and awkward equality maintained on the island disappears ashore. Erskine Caldwell bluntly illustrates society's tacit endorsement of racism.

When Henry and Clayton Desant, of *I Tell a Lie Every So Often* (1974, YA), set out to rescue a long-missing cousin who is vaguely supposed to have been stolen by Indians, they take for granted that whites have the right—perhaps even the obligation—to dominate Indian lives; equality is never considered, for it "rents up" Clayton's heart to see "Americans" and Indians mix. Author Bruce Clements is gentle in his portrayal of most of the boys' follies, but he is uncompromising as he effectively dramatizes the arrogant and careless attitudes of many whites toward their Native American neighbors in the Midwest of the late 1840s.

The male protagonists of *First Family, A Blow to the Head, The Year the Lights Came On, Summertime Island,* and *I Tell a Lie Every So Often* are all decent enough youngsters; they are trying to do the best they can to grow up and get along in an often confusing world. Their creators are primarily concerned to indicate the contradictions and cruelties of their society, and the male adolescents are useful figures in that depiction. Since the boys are still, in most cases, coming to understand what their society is, preparatory to making their own place in it, the authors can use their puzzlement, their awareness or lack of awareness, to reveal hypocrisy and conscious or unthinking racism. Some of these characters grow in awareness (Steve in *Summertime Island,* for example), but most remain relatively static.

Other novels, featuring growing and developing characters, demonstrate the harmful effects of racism, and ways that (in some cases) strong young men may escape from its oppression. Octavia E. Butler, Bryant Rollins, and Ronald Fair all exhibit characters and situations which clearly reveal the damage done by racism. Butler relates present and past to each other as she stresses the horrors of slavery—here, unusually, the greater emphasis is on the psychological hurt done to the oppressors, than to the oppressed.

Child of an ineffectual mother and a self-indulgent, violent, sexually exploitative father, Rufe Weylin, of Octavia E. Butler's *Kindred* (1979), is, above all, the child of slave-owners and the product of a society which teaches him that it is correct and proper for him to exercise absolute control over the destinies of other human beings. Rufe is so damaged by family and society that he is a frighteningly dangerous adolescent, a person with no center, little capacity for introspection, wholly governed by his desires. Through Rufe and his extended, episodic relationship with Dana, his modern black descendent who is mysteriously forced back in time to serve as Rufe's protector and mentor, Butler dramatizes the vicious effects slave-holding has on those who presumably benefit from the system.

Bryant Rollins and Ronald Fair dramatize, in novels set in our own times, the damage done by racism to oppressed youngsters. In the Boston of the 1960s, Martin Williams, protagonist of Bryant Rollins's *Danger Song* (1967), confronts racial discrimination at every turn. Some of his difficulties stem from his relationships with his fellow blacks: reluctance to participate in a gang war and encroachment onto other gangs' territories, his transfer to a largely white high school, and even his refusal to drop out of high school are taken as signs of disaffection from his peers. But Martin's most serious problems, of course, stem from the steady pressure of discrimination by the dominant white society, a pressure which slowly, steadily incites fierce, violent anger in the youngster. Initially gentle and passive, Martin one day realizes that "in another instant he would have swung at one of them, out of the fury. Any one of them. Out of the anger and the frustration and the impotence and the vulnerability and the turmoil that were in his mind." Rollins's careful portrayal of this building anger and violence is one of the most effective features of his novel and lays sound groundwork for Martin's final, dreadful fate.

Ronald Fair's *We Can't Breathe* (1972) is the story of Ernie Johnson's maturation in a Chicago black ghetto, from the 1930s through World War II. At nine, when the novel opens, he has learned to hate all whites, has been lamed as a result of playing in vacant lots with broken bottles, and sees rats as both a permanent enemy and the prey of boyish hunting expeditions. The poverty and filth of the ghetto, the corrupt cruelty of police and courts, and the tantalizing but illusory appearance of better times during World War II are all dramatically depicted. But always stressed are the frustrated anger and desperation of Ernie and his friends and their deep awareness that white society neither understands how they feel nor cares and that it has always lied about them and to them. His forays into petty theft are motivated by his hatred:

> It was our custom to hit one of the three dime stores at least once a week for sun glasses, knives, compasses, candy, pencils, and sometimes even a spool or two of thread. It wasn't always important that we take something we really wanted. It was only important that we were stealing from the white man. And stealing from the white man was justified because he had stolen everything he had from someone else. Stealing from the white man was rebelling against white authority. Stealing from the white man was beating the white man, was conquering him, was letting him know that we had nothing but contempt for him and that we had won.

Some other novels suggest that the effects of racism can be counterbalanced, at least partly, by youngsters of good will who reject the hypocrisy of their elders and by talented young people willing to work hard to escape the poverty and institutionalized racism of their ghetto backgrounds.

The learning of race hatred is a crucial part of Leo Proudhammer's experience in James Baldwin's *Tell Me How Long the Train's Been Gone* (1968). By the time he is ten he fears whites and is aware of the dangers of venturing outside Harlem. But when his adored older brother, just released from prison, tells of sadistic treatment he has received, fourteen-year-old Leo's hatred becomes sharply focused: "Because I could love, I realized I could hate. And I realized that I would feed my hatred, feed it every day and every hour. I would keep it healthy, I would make it strong, and I would find a use for it one day." Leo, however, is able to control his hatred and does not hate indiscriminately. Later, in fact, a young white woman becomes the single person closest to him.

Set in a Georgia ghetto in the 1950s, *A Cry of Angels* (1974) by Jeff Fields shows the maturation of a white, Earl Whitaker, who has white, black, and Indian friends. Resentment of the Supreme Court decision outlawing segregated schools, which occurs during the time span of the novel, dramatizes the enmity of whites for blacks. A violent climax to the novel is caused by economic and social tensions between the two races. Against this background of racial mistrust, Earl and his friends maintain their close relationships, and Earl learns much about the hypocrisy and cruelty of the world he must inhabit.

Kristin Hunter and Al Young center their youthful characters' efforts around the traditional dream of repressed black Americans of escaping the ghetto through their music. In Kristin Hunter's *The Soul Brothers and Sister Lou* (1968, YA), Philip Satterthwaite, called "Fess," is first introduced as a very young black militant whose mission is to infiltrate, influence, and eventually take over the "gang" of boys who are friendly with protagonist Louretta Hawkins. His efforts to achieve this goal bring him into direct confrontation with Lou, whom he accuses of placating the white establishment. Though Fess fails to convert Lou to his point of view (she is scorned for her light skin at a militants' meeting), the two do come to a good working relationship, for they collaborate as a song-writing team, and Fess becomes the manager of the Soul Brothers and Sister Lou, a singing group. Author Hunter uses Fess as an object lesson, for "it was just that a little success had been enough to turn Fess completely around. From an ardent revolutionary, he had become an enthusiastic booster of business, free enterprise and capitalism." In this way, Hunter dramatizes two major themes: that many social and racial problems could be solved by decent economic opportunities and that the racism of both Fess and the neighborhood's vicious white police officers is wrong. The fact that few youngsters can escape the ghetto by becoming recording artists, song writers, or managers is, however, not really addressed.

Al Young's *Snakes* (1970) is similar in subject but less overt in its thematic presentation of racism and oppression. This tale of growing up black in the Detroit ghetto of the 1960s creates a vivid portrait of a survivor. MC Moore, "going on 17," experiments with sex and drugs, gets into various scrapes, and experiences the poverty and hopelessness that have destroyed others. But through his friendship with other boys, his love for the grandmother who has reared him, and, especially, his music, he not only survives but seems destined for success. He and several friends form a group; their long hours of hard, dedicated practice and their new sound, a blending of jazz and rhythm and blues, lead to a surprising early success. A record of MC's composition, "Snakes," becomes a hit, giving MC confidence that through his music he can make a life for himself. The novella's ending shows us MC, having graduated from high school, as he sets off for New York City, hopeful of creating a musical career. MC's narration of his story and experiences is realistic in depicting the pains and joys of a ghetto adolescence and warmly affirmative in revealing the talent, optimism, and dedication that enable MC to overcome his disadvantages.

Like the social phenomena of gangs and racism, drugs and drug use have been problems particularly prominent in the consciousness of the most recent generation. Like gangs, drugs have sometimes seemed a problem peculiarly associated with young people. Connected with a seemingly laudable desire to "expand consciousness," and attractive precisely because condemned by the hypocritical adult world so many youths wished to rebel against, they attracted adolescents both for what they offered in themselves and for what they symbolized. One novel which joyfully adopts this iconoclastic view shows an adolescent converting an elderly man to their use, thus reversing the expected teacher-pupil relationship and making the youth the symbolically mature and knowing one.

Drugs are treated positively in Ralph Blum's *Old Glory and the Real-Time Freaks: A Children's Story and Patriotic Goodtime Book with Maps* (1972). Quintus Ells, who describes himself as "a rich, happy, intelligent freak who runs on real-time and a smoke-filled head," decides to fill in the thirty-nine days before his eighteenth birthday, when he will become legally adult and eligible for the draft, in writing for his imagined grandson a "map" of his own life. This map turns out to be a journal in which he discusses his friends, his beloved grandfather's terminal cancer, and above all his happy involvement with drugs. He promises his grandfather, in fact, that he will write only after smoking pot, and he introduces his grandfather to its joys. Quintus is a loving and honest young man at peace with himself and his world, and the drugs are presented as an integral and useful part of his life.

More typical in attacking drug use and showing its potential for harm are several other novels. B. H. Friedman (*Yarborough*), William Goldman (*Tinsel*), and Alice Childress (*A Hero Ain't Nothin' But a Sandwich*) all stress the debilitating effects of drug-taking; only Childress even suggests escape from the drug habit as a realistic possibility.

Along with sex and (especially) playing bridge, Arthur Skelton and his friend Henry Rosen, in B. H. Friedman's *Yarborough* (1964), make heavy use of a wide variety of drugs. For Arthur, who has a brilliant but detached intellect, drug use is an escape from life, which he sees as only a pathway to death. The novel includes several scenes which attempt to convey drug experiences, and Arthur's and Henry's attitudes seem to anticipate what was to happen later on a much wider scale (the novel closes in 1950).

In the opening chapters of William Goldman's *Tinsel* (1979), Noel

Garvey is a burnt-out drug case whose powerful, corrupt parents are determined to salvage the young man by involving him in one of his father's projects, *Tinsel*, a major film. Goldman uses an extended flashback to document Noel's adolescent preoccupation with drugs in the California drug culture, suggesting that the seeds of Noel's mature personality and value structure were sown during his adolescence: drugs have demoralized him, made him permanently dependent upon others, permanently self-indulgent. The only one of his circle, the Flab Four, to survive with even the slightest chance for a seemingly normal life, Noel has not learned from the deaths of two friends or the permanent disability of another. Instead, as an emotional adolescent but a chronological adult, he embraces his parents' tainted values and becomes an embryonic Hollywood mogul, exploitative and crass.

At thirteen, Benjy Johnson of *A Hero Ain't Nothin' But a Sandwich* (1973, YA), by Alice Childress, is a heroin addict. Several factors motivate the boy's dependence, but one of the most important is his desire to be thought a man; he feels like a hero when he first "shoots up," and he is aware that his ghetto neighborhood is a dangerous place for children.

> My block ain't no place to be a chile in peace. Somebody gonna cop your money and might even knock you down cause you walkin with short bread and didn't even make it worth their while to stop and frisk you over. Ain't no letrit light bulb in my hallway for two three floors and we livin up next to the top floor. You best get over bein seven or eight, right soon, cause seven and eight is too big for relatives to be holdin your hand like when you was three, four, and five. No, Jack, you on your own and they got they thing to do, like workin, or going to court, or seein after they gas and letrit bills, and they dispossess — or final notice, bout on-time payments — and like that, you dig?

Childress traces Benjy's uncertain progress toward true maturity, a state she equates with the breaking of his habit. Benjy's maturation journey is difficult and dangerous, dramatizing life in the New York ghetto with insight, skill, and controlled compassion.

Drug abuse is, of course, one method of escape from an intolerable environment or life. It thus is a symptom of and a reaction against some of the tensions of our contemporary urban society with its harshly drawn race and class structure. Like membership in a gang, drug use may give a sense of beauty and meaning to an otherwise ugly and chaotic world. Membership in gangs and obsessive work at music as a passport out of an insupportable existence are other ways of coping. Some of the most pathetic adolescents are those who are able to adopt none of these methods, not even the negative and destructive ones. They become portraits of pure alienation. One example is Ernest Jenkins, a seventeen-year-old dropout in Paula Fox's *Poor George* (1967), who sets the novel's action in motion when he intrudes into the home and life of

George Mecklin, the protagonist. A subsidiary character seen always from the outside, Ernest remains enigmatic to the end; his importance is in the obsession he inspires in George, who hopes to rescue him from his ignorance and alienation.

Also seen only from the outside, by the often puzzled elderly narrator of Herbert Lieberman's *Crawlspace* (1971), Richard Atlee never can be completely understood by the reader. Apparently about eighteen, he simply appears and takes up residence in Albert and Alice Graves's crawlspace. They pity him and take him into their lives, but the relationship becomes unhealthy as well as loving. Though Richard is victimized first by an unsympathetic community, he becomes a danger because of his only imperfectly controlled violence and his warped sense of responsibility. A predictably tragic ending occurs. The novel is suspenseful, though Richard's torment seems used more for dramatic effect than for psychological insight.

A thirteen-year-old truant, William Noone, is the protagonist and narrator of Neal Faasen's *The Toyfair* (1963). He is convinced he will end up in prison and describes himself as a "bitter selfish punk," "a big-mouth troublemaker without a brain in his head." With two girls, nick-named Ace and Worm, he sets out from Michigan for Chicago to find his father, who long before had deserted the family. The father, a drunk and little more than a derelict, sends them home—after lecturing them on their superiority to the middle-class culture they all have fled:

> Don't give up your sneakiness or your cunning. Those are the only weapons you have and they know that, and they are going to disarm you if they can. They will try to disarm you with a horrible collection of unworkable clichés, they are not above trying kindness or even love, but those words are flip-flop in their minds and they don't have the same meaning that you have for them. They will try to make you ashamed because you are different and maybe stronger and maybe even wiser.

The novel's support of the rebellion of its central characters is not totally convincing, because they all seem merely angry, bitter, and irresponsible, with no apparent positive values.

Robert Probish, an eighteen-year-old schlemiel in L. J. Davis's *Whence All But He Had Fled* (1968), has left his home and parents to live in a New York City slum and be an artist. He is a chronic loser for whom nothing ever goes right, and his search for identity is no more successful than any of his other endeavors in this sardonically comic picture of an aimless life. His sense of being lost is most pathetically revealed as he repeats to himself a talismanic formula from his childhood: " 'My name is Robert Probish and I'm seven years old and I live at 143 Tuckerton Street in Jamaica and I'm lost, please take me home.' But no matter how often he repeated it to himself, it didn't do him a bit of good."

Johnny Fortune, of *False Entry* (1961) by Hortense Calisher, has only one friend, protagonist Pierre Goodman. Socially scorned by a small Southern town because his mother is its white prostitute, Johnny attempts to establish roots by serving as chore boy for the Ku Klux Klan, but he comes to despise the local Klan leader, seeing him as the source of all the town's faults—"He was only a less than fatherless boy who had placed all evil in one man. . . . He had no knowledge of where to ascribe evil except singly." When the Klan conducts a raid, the boys observe it together. That same night, Johnny, still rootless and feeling betrayed by his friend, disappears, there being no real place for him in either the overt or the clandestine social orders of the community. Johnny's sense of alienation parallels Pierre's and casts serious doubt on the supposed classlessness of American society.

If Ernest Jenkins (*Poor George*) and Richard Atlee (*Crawlspace*) are flat characters whom we never come to understand very well, they, along with Johnny Fortune (*False Entry*), are still merely extreme examples of some accommodations to the strains of contemporary male adolescence exemplified in many of the novels discussed in this chapter. For most of these boys, however, the tacit assumption that they will act is always present. Unlike female adolescents, who may be seen as passive, as accepting what comes to them, as appropriately being primarily acted upon, the male adolescents are expected to assert themselves and their masculinity. For them, masculinity implies generally assertive if not aggressive behavior. The crucial choice is not that of whether but rather *how* to use their aggressiveness. That so many youngsters use it in violent, destructive ways is not surprising, given the backgrounds and choices posited for them in the novels discussed here. What is perhaps somewhat surprising is that so many manage to see beyond their present and shape more positive, constructive futures for themselves.

CHAPTER XII

Males and Social Institutions

Like some young women, some young men are so radically in conflict with their society that they are basically outside it (such characters are the focus of the preceding chapter, "Males in Crisis"), while others remain basically within the social structure. A youth's awareness of injustice is often keen and may lead to withdrawal from or rejection of a hypocritical or cruel society. But not all males are presented with such extreme challenges or react to their challenges in such extreme ways. For some, class, school, preparation for a career, avocation, religion, and selection of value systems present quite sufficient maturation lessons and tests, and these are the kinds of experiences we will be looking at in this chapter.

The term "social institutions" is an elastic one, here primarily referring to educational, economic, and religious forces as they impinge upon the experiences and outlooks of adolescent males. Some distinctions between depictions of girls and of boys emerge. Negative economic factors—poverty, lower-class status—seem of more interest to authors depicting adolescent boys than do wealth and power; treatments of girls tend to be more varied in this regard. Schools are often seen as places of initiation into power structures for boys; for girls they tend to be presented as largely irrelevant, only sometimes serving initiatory purposes —but for girls, the initiation is into social roles. The variety of future vocations is no less for males than for young women, but a larger number of authors study avocational interests, especially pets or other animals and sports. Religious or moral dilemmas are certainly no less significant and no less varied for boys than for girls.

In all these connections, boys, like girls, have the need to define their relationships to the predominant institutions and assumptions of their society. For some, our authors suggest, this may be a relatively easy process—that of accepting the principles taught them by family, school, or church and emerging into maturity as they gradually grow in awareness of the true meanings and importance of what they have been taught. More typically, however, moments of conflict or dissent occur; as the youth seeks to establish his independence and to develop his autonomous adult persona, he must decide what is right for him, what suits his needs, his abilities, his dreams of life.

Such a process is not always easy, although it may seem much simpler than the situations we have examined in "Males in Crisis." Those were dramatic issues, boys placed in conflict with or outside of their social order, and the results were, all too often, violence, crime, or alienation. The youths we will be looking at in this chapter, often less radically tested, nevertheless face some similar lessons. They must learn, as many of the boys studied in "Males in Crisis" knew all along, that society has great power over us all, that none of us, no matter how favored, can completely control his own path or experience in life. Whether one is basically inside or fundamentally outside of social norms, those norms nevertheless affect one's behavior—as one follows what is expected or reacts against social expectations.

There is often a thin line between those youths we have considered under the rubric "in crisis" and those within "social institutions." In fact, a few novels, because of the complexities of their presentations, appear in both chapters. One novel, portraying a group of youngsters —both male and female—and their only slightly older eventual victim, can illustrate the narrowness of that distinction. These are fortunate young people, whom no one, least of all themselves, would have expected to be anything but ordinary, respectable members of society. Yet, given special combinations of circumstances, they discover within themselves a horrible capacity for evil—a potentiality which becomes actual as they reject all norms of civilized behavior. Youthful games turn serious—and violent—in Mendal W. Johnson's *Let's Go Play at the Adams'* (1974), in which five youngsters imprison, torture, and eventually kill a twenty-year-old girl. These pampered youngsters destroy slowly a girl they actually rather like even though she does represent to them the hated adult world of authority and responsibility. Only Bobby Adams, at thirteen still naive and basically goodhearted, is sympathetic and argues against killing the girl. But even he, when outvoted, considers the "rules" previously agreed to more important than her life, and he acquiesces. John Randall, sixteen, twice rapes her, and Paul McVeigh, thirteen, the only one who had previously shown signs of being psychologically disturbed, tortures her with a knife and takes the lead in inflicting the horrors that immediately precede her death. Shortly before her death, the girl realizes what has happened to them all: "For every step, there had been another step. Bobby had been right: it began because it could. The sheer possibility was irresistibly compulsive, addictive. Was that all anybody needed to become torturer, rapist, killer, just the possibility and then the power and then a way out-free?" The novel demonstrates how some rather ordinary young people are led into committing unspeakable acts, step by step.

One of the most horrifying aspects of this novel is the ability of the youthful torturers to maintain their appearance of respectability through the period in which they are living also a secret life of cruelty. In fact, for them, a private social order governed by its own rules has taken the place of the civilized world into which their families, indeed all their previous experience, have tried to introduce them. The strong pull of the peer group, the adolescent need for belonging, the desire for experience and sensation, and the accident of freedom from social controls enable these youngsters to plumb the depths of evil within them. Their odyssey is from apparently normal participation in society to a rejection of all that makes that society civilized. Mentally and emotionally, they have removed themselves from their society, while apparently remaining members in good standing. Had not a group of accidents occurred together, however, setting up the precise set of circumstances that made possible their "games," most of these young people (all except perhaps Paul McVeigh) would have led perfectly ordinary, law-abiding lives, with no hint of the brutality they actually discover within themselves. They remind us how fragile is the veneer of civilization and of civilizing institutions so crucial in the socializing process of most ordinary young people.

Nevertheless, few of our subject-characters follow the almost atavistic reversion to barbarism of the youngsters in *Let's Go Play at the Adams'*. Others may criticize aspects of school or church or may come in conflict with values inculcated by parents or society, but they nevertheless mostly remain within that society. Their challenges are less extreme than those examined in "Males in Crisis," but they are no less real, no less crucial to the boys concerned.

Class and economic background may be very basic limiters to a young person trying to define himself and his place in the world. While some of our authors suggest that wealth and power may be especially corrupting to girls (see "Females and Social Institutions"), the greater interest among authors studying male adolescents is in poverty and social powerlessness as influences upon vulnerable youths. Borden Deal, using a poor Southern white family, and especially its younger son, as his subject in *The Least One* (1967), points out that such families may have strong social values; a youngster may gain much, despite his obvious material disadvantages, from such a beginning. The father of this family is a farmer, and the mother, the real power in the family, is a proud, stubborn helpmeet to him. They are shamed by the need to accept what they consider charity, and prosperity is a small inheritance which enables the mother to begin a small dairy herd and thus have a little regular cash income. Boy, the protagonist, is deeply loved by his parents, but they are unable to pamper him, and he learns early to look out for himself.

Like Borden Deal, Mary Stetson Clarke reminds her readers in *The Iron Peacock* (1966, YA) of the strength and courage to be found in apparently underprivileged members of society. When the fortunes of war send young Ross McCrae to the New World as a bond servant, he is infuriated and rebellious. Sold to the master of a Bay Colony ironworks, Ross dislikes his first job as a woodcutter and collier and plans to escape, despite the dangers of the journey and the severe penalties meted out to captured runaways. A chance to work inside the foundry and to learn the trade changes his mind and ensures his upward mobility when his bond is paid. Through Ross and his sweetheart, protagonist Joanna Sprague, Clarke makes the point that many of the early bond servants became skillful, valued free persons in colonial America. Ross's sturdy independence is not unlike Boy's in *The Least One*; both, despite unprepossessing beginnings, illustrate the worth of hard work and personal pride. Both clearly have the potential and the desire to become contributing members of society.

David J. Michael, in *A Blow to the Head* (1970), is less sanguine in his study of a blue-collar family that has lost its basic integrity as materialistic upward-striving has replaced more basic values. More prosperous than Deal's and Clarke's characters, Michael's characters have moved from one social framework to another, and the result is disjunction. The blue-collar ethic is the organizational motif in the Pansella household. Having moved into a factory town from a relatively rural area, all the Pansellas, led by Mrs. Pansella, their driving force, set about working hard and constantly strive to make their home one of the "best" in the neighborhood, to earn enough money to keep up appearances and to achieve success (in the form of household goods), and to force their way into prominence in their local church. Though their material goals are achieved, the family pays a high price: death from overwork and unattended illness for Mr. Pansella; utter alienation of their daughter; and tragic, almost total, withdrawal of their son, Anthony, the narrator of the novel. As exhaustion separates Mr. Pansella from his son, as Mrs. Pansella's nagging bitterness victimizes her daughter, dissent rules the family: "All our holidays were pretty disastrous. I guess maybe because holidays should be love and the hate really shows then. Like heat hitting cold. *Steam*." Michael's powerful novel illustrates the dark underside of the American Dream, as Anthony tries to understand how and why such popular and seemingly desirable goals should have destroyed his family.

Three other novels, all set in the South among poor folks, study the impact upon adolescent males of caste systems as well as of ignorance and, often, contempt for or fear of the established law. In these books, readers are shown subcultures in conflict with the dominant culture. The subcultures are what the boys had known best as children, but when they begin to become more familiar with the wider world and to see the subculture in its relationships with the outside world, they confront new challenges that go to the heart of what they had previously assumed.

Earl Edge and Coley Simms, central characters of William Price Fox's *Moonshine Light, Moonshine Bright* (1967), are poor white boys growing up in South Carolina. Money is scarce for adults as well as for boys, and most characters' energies are directed largely into concocting schemes to get cash—by fair means or foul. Earl and Coley are already well indoctrinated into the contempt for authority that pervades these people; an early scene shows Earl in court for spitting from the balcony of the moving picture theater (his father takes his act little more seriously than does Earl himself), and the novel follows the boys in various escapades, mostly illegal, and all comic, as they live through one summer vacation.

The hope suggested by the title of James Lee Burke's *To the Bright and Shining Sun* (1970) is illusory for the Kentucky coal miners among whom it is set. The action occurs during a prolonged and bitter strike and details the efforts of sixteen-year-old Perry James to support himself, his incapacitated father, his mother, and brothers and sisters. Illiterate, in the mines since the age of fifteen, proud, and stubborn, Perry does the best he can against great odds. Descended from the Hatfields (of feuding fame), he exemplifies a determined self-reliance, and his two loyalties are to his family and to the union. But all his efforts lead only to failure and frustrations. His one chance to break free, through learning to operate heavy machinery and getting a basic education in the Job Corps, is lost, for he is called home when his father is mortally injured in an explosion related to the strike. The novel indicts the companies for ruthless exploitation of the miners and their families, but the union and government relief agencies are also shown to be insensitive to the real needs and feelings of people like Perry and his family. The hopelessness of the situation is the more pathetic because of Perry's real courage and dignity: he seems a man who has never been a child or an adolescent and whose manhood has been achieved at great cost.

The life of an Alabama swamp family is graphically shown in Luke Wallin's *The Redneck Poacher's Son* (1981). A violent father, a fearful, subservient aunt, and two crude brothers are all the family sixteen-year-old Jesse Watersmith knows. Their home is a camp, and their survival depends on hunting, trapping, and moonshining. Alone among these men, Jesse feels emotions other than hatred, resentment, and envy, and with the help of his aunt, he succeeds in escaping to a new life. A job in town and education are his means of escape, and when the novel ends, the reader feels sure that Jesse has not only escaped economic and physical hardship and deprivation but has come through morally and psychologically whole—unlike his father and brothers, for whose depravity there is no cure.

These books depicting social caste are largely negative; like many of the works we have examined in "Males in Crisis," they are intended as novels of social criticism, which use their adolescent characters to demonstrate inherent flaws in society. Nevertheless, some of these authors remind us that many youngsters do survive bleak beginnings to become men of strength and courage, that from their flawed backgrounds some learn independence and love. The converse is the damage done to those unable to find anything beyond destructive social values—the boys in *Moonshine Light, Moonshine Bright*, for example, whose people live purely selfishly, and Anthony Pansella of *A Blow to the Head*, from a family that has sold out to the materialism of American society.

The greed which motivates characters in some of these novels about the negative underside of American society is also seen by many of our subject-authors to infect American education. The secondary schools are almost always seen as anti-intellectual, insensitive, and largely irrelevant to the real lives led by youngsters and to their dreams for their futures. Little real learning seems to go on in the schools; few treatments of schools or school life have much, if anything, to say about books, and those that do stress their male adolescents' desire for education generally do not include many scenes showing that education actually in progress in the classroom. One partial exception is *Entering Ephesus* (1971) by Daphne Athas, though even here the school is not very effective. Zebulon Whalley is a major character in this novel. Early in his life, Zebul abandons the standards of his poor white parents, looking to them only for food. His whole being becomes focused on gaining an education, and to that end, he steals books and supplies. Though he attends school and studies voraciously, Zebul's main education comes from independent study and his deep friendship with the Bishop family, unconventional newcomers. The Bishop parents are well educated and believe in the life of the mind. Zebul's best friend, Urie Bishop, shares his passion for learning, and the two stimulate one another to exploit every educational opportunity. Athas conveys the excitement of learning and celebrates the positive force of good minds working together to discover and master new ideas.

A true exception to the rule that few recent novels about male adolescents have much good to say about what goes on in American schools is Burke Davis's *The Summer Land* (1965); sadly, this novel is set in the past—in 1916, in a one-room school in North Carolina—suggesting that only through nostalgia for what no longer exists is a positive treatment of American education possible. Fax Starling, at fifteen the one book lover of his large family, has always loved school, somewhat to his embarrassment. When a new, young teacher comes, he quickly gives her his heart, and she is instrumental in his growth in courage as well as in knowledge. The school itself and Miss Cassie's problems and wisdom in dealing with her oddly assorted and high-spirited pupils are effectively depicted in this comic novel.

And finally there is *Sounder* (1969, YA) by William H. Armstrong, whose unnamed black hero yearns for an education, despite his family's extreme poverty. A schoolmaster's offer to teach "the boy" in exchange for his doing chores is taken by his religious mother as a good "sign." Mother and son opt for education even though it causes "the boy" to be absent from home for long periods during a time when he is the family's main support. The boy's struggle for learning is a symbol of his own strength and of hope for the family.

Most other depictions of American schools, however, portray boys less motivated, less hungry for learning than Zebul (*Entering Ephesus*), Fax (*The Summer Land*), and the protagonist of *Sounder*. These youngsters are so intelligent and so eager that they would learn wherever they are, given the most minimal of opportunities. Other boys, less brilliant, less avid for education, are depicted in a number of novels that show the public schools as grim, unstimulating places to be. Particularly negative pictures are given by Neal Faasen in *The Toyfair* and Theodore Weesner in *The Car Thief*. For the protagonists of both books, school is irrelevant and meaningless, and the result is alienation from it and from the society which it represents and expresses.

Bitter hatred of school and the world ordered by adults is characteristic of young William Noone in Neal Faasen's *The Toyfair* (1963).

> Why don't we want to learn [he writes], why do we skip school? Because it simply doesn't interest us. Because you tell us that it is the most important thing in the world, and if it's important to you, then it's you that want more out of it than we, and we start distrusting you again. Go and sit in one of our English classes and listen to those thin and fat smiling teachers shoot us a lot of names of people we don't know. So some dear man in England wrote a lot of words that rhyme, what are we supposed to do, bump ourselves off because we don't understand it, whose fault is it.

School is a place where the "principal hates the teachers and teachers hate us students and we students hate each other and the teachers and the principal, and if we thought about it long enough we would hate the janitor, Mr. Love, too." But since William hates himself and almost everyone else as well, his indictment of the educational system is not very convincing—though some young readers might be tempted to find it so!

The failures of an urban high school to aid antisocial or troubled adolescents are clearly shown in Theodore Weesner's *The Car Thief* (1972). Alex Housman, at sixteen, is a skilled car thief and frequent truant. Though he reads well and sometimes is able to lose himself in fiction, school is totally unrewarding for him, and extracurricular activities, notably basketball, seem to have little more meaning for him. He lacks discipline and persistence, and as a result, one failure follows another, while the few adults to take any interest in him lack depth of concern and soon become discouraged and discard him. His dropping out seems inevitable.

William Noone (*The Toyfair*) and Alex Housman (*The Car Thief*) reject their society, as symbolized by their schools, but Jerry Renault, in

The Chocolate War (1974, YA) by Robert Cormier, involuntarily becomes involved in a struggle carried on within the school, although outside the classroom. Cormier demonstrates that the school, as a microcosm, is subject to all the stresses of the larger society which it mirrors, and pupils in the schools must suffer tensions much like those imposed upon adults in the outside world. And meanwhile, he suggests, the true purpose of the schools, education of young people, becomes lost.

An important part of Jerry Renault's education takes place outside the classroom, when he suddenly finds himself the focus of attention during a school-wide chocolate sale designed to raise money for Trinity High. At the command of a school gang, the Vigils, Jerry refuses to sell the chocolates, the only student to do so. When the decree is remanded, some impulse of independence, some will to be free, forces the boy to continue to refuse. The results are dire, and not the least of the punishment Jerry must absorb is the "silent treatment": "Suddenly, he was invisible, without body, without structure, a ghost passing transparently through the hours. . . . It was as if he were the carrier of a terrible disease and nobody wanted to be contaminated. And so they rendered him invisible, eliminating him from their presence."

Jerry's chief antagonist is Archie Costello. Archie is the driving force behind the Vigils, the source of the gang's amazing power, for he makes the "assignments" to the students, tasks created to humiliate the assignee and to demonstrate both the might of the Vigils and the brilliance of Archie's grasp of human psychology. As Jerry is the symbol of the individual, Archie is the symbol of triumphant evil: "I can con anybody. I am Archie." The conflict ultimately infects the faculty as well as the entire student body, making Cormier's *The Chocolate War* a serious and commanding study of the struggle for control over one boy's fate.

Faasen (*The Toyfair*), Weesner (*The Car Thief*), and Cormier (*The Chocolate War*) place their portraits of the schools in the context of larger social environments and relate them to a variety of contemporary social concerns. Jesse Stuart, however, in *Mr. Gallion's School* (1967), quite specifically sets out to demonstrate what has, in his view, gone wrong with American education. His method is to invent a school which has fallen prey to every evil that Stuart finds in the schools—lack of discipline and intellectual standards, primarily—and then to show how that school is set right, rather surprisingly quickly. *Mr. Gallion's School* is a portrait of a troubled high school and of the principal who saves it by insisting on high standards of behavior as well as of academic work, by strongly supporting such activities as band and football, and by encouraging and helping his pupils personally as much as he can. A number of boys—some borderline juvenile delinquents, some hardworking but impoverished farm boys, some tough hot-rodders—are briefly depicted, and in almost every case Mr. Gallion's blend of sternness and affection is sufficient to help them toward productive citizenship. The boys, however, are individually less important to the novel than is the school as a whole. Mr. Gallion's success in saving the school results from his dedication and toughness, qualities which he seems also to be instilling in his pupils.

Two other novels examine educational institutions with special missions and goals, one a reformatory and one a summer camp. Both are, in some respects, microcosms, and both reflect the values of the society that has created them.

A Two-Car Funeral (1973) by John Hough, Jr., is a study, both external and internal, of a reformatory for boys. The father of an inmate persistently raises questions about conditions within the institution, with the result that a political scandal and a good deal of unsavory infighting and maneuvering among politicians ensue. Meanwhile, inside the reformatory, the boys brutalize each other and are victimized by guards and teachers. Three fifteen-year-olds, Stewart Browne, Raymond Karras, and Ernest ("Kentucky") Danovic, are central to events inside the institution, and we soon see that their experience there will necessarily be damaging to them rather than rehabilitating. Ironically, many of those involved, both inside and outside, actually mean well, but their overriding concerns are personal and selfish, and as a result little is done to help the boys or to change conditions. The novel effectively and compassionately describes a complex and difficult social problem.

In Burt Blechman's *The War of Camp Omongo* (1963), a story of a Jewish summer camp for boys, Randy Levine and the other boys, mostly from wealthy families, are taught sports and crafts as well as the value of competition. Early on, the camp owner expresses the camp philosophy:

> To train boys to fight for the love of fighting, to win for the love of winning. On the baseball field, we will bat our way to victory. At the rifle range, we will shoot our way to victory! Because that's what our country is—a victorious nation, a nation of men imbued with the will-to-win, in sports, in business, in war. . . . Learn to compete, to excel, to become worth-while citizens of our brave land. . . . Because—fellow tribesmen—America and Omongo are one and the same!

The wild and obstreperous boys learn this lesson well; by the end of the novel, Randy unscrupulously cheats to win a contest that is actually meaningless to him. The novel is comic, but its satire of our society is biting.

Blechman's summer camp inculcates its competitive ethic into privileged boys, youngsters expected to become future leaders; their indoctrination is supposed to help them to take their places in the society's power structure. Such camps, then, perform very specific functions in passing on certain principles that a young man must learn if he is to exercise power and achieve wealth beyond that accruing to him by birth. Several other novels demonstrate how private schools perform that same function in an even more important way—for they reach larger numbers of youngsters and work with them for a much longer period of time.

The Devon School, of John Knowles's *Peace Breaks Out* (1981), represents much of the best of American culture; its male students are clearly destined to become leaders, and these preparatory-school boys are remarkably responsive to the Devon concept of civilization—that there are no rules until one is broken. Beneath this Edenic veneer, however, lurks incipient violence, and one of these young leaders, corrupted by pride and arrogance, manipulates others to commit murder. John Knowles uses an ironic twist in identifying the real evil in *Peace Breaks Out*, a sequel of sorts to *A Separate Peace* (1959), in order to point out that constant vigilance against the corruption of democracy is essential.The parallels in conception to Stephanie Tolan's novel of a girl's private school, *The Last of Eden*, are remarkable; both use their school settings as microcosms and remind readers of the universal tension between appearance and reality.

The goal of MacFarland Military Academy, setting for *Drum and Bugle* (1961), Terence Fugate's first novel, is developing and testing the "manhood" of its students. The rules and traditions of the academy are meant to instill fortitude and courage in the cadets, and the boys' training at MacFarland is presumably intended as a rigorous but enriching initiation into adulthood. However, violence, hatred, and bitterness lie close beneath the surface at this Georgia school, and for protagonist Carl Roundtree, cadet life is far from an ennobling experience. Indeed, the only satisfaction Carl can derive from his truncated career at MacFarland is merely the grim awareness that he survived it—more or less intact.

Several other authors, less concerned to portray private schools as bastions of a powerful ruling class and that caste's tool for perpetuating its values, examine other aspects of the boarding school experience; for Peter Kilburn (*Good Times/Bad Times*) the years at school are totally disastrous, while for Bill Grove (*A Good School*), some good balances against the bad.

Guilford Academy, the setting for James Kirkwood's *Good Times/Bad Times* (1968), "was a sick school, crippled and limping along with the shadow of death hanging over it. And Mr. Hoyt [the headmaster] was the doctor." Hoyt's intensity about rehabilitating Guilford's reputation (damaged by a homosexual student's suicide) leads him to bully Peter Kilburn, the protagonist, into taking an unwilling part in Guilford's long-term competition with other schools. Author Kirkwood portrays Peter's painful and tragic boarding school experience against a background composed of the skillfully evoked atmosphere of the campus and vivid portraits of the pupils.

Though Bill Grove, of Richard Yates's *A Good School* (1978), soon realizes that Dorset Academy "had a wide reputation for accepting boys who, for any number of reasons, no other school would touch" and that his mother has enrolled him there through a typical mixture of carelessness and good intent, he nevertheless determines to do well at Dorset. In an extended, highly episodic flashback, the adult Bill depicts Dorset on the eve of World War II, a period which coincides with the school's dissolution. Gang "jerk offs" (ritualized "pranks" which come perilously close to rape), other hazing, the serious personal and emotional problems of some members of the student body and faculty, serve to initiate Bill in the harsher aspects of life. Lessons about friendship, extensive experience on the school paper, and occasional academic successes teach him about his capabilities and goals, and these moments are fruitful. Ultimately, he concludes that "in ways still important to me it *was* a good school. It saw me through the worst of my adolescence, as few other schools would have done, and it taught me the rudiments of my trade." In *A Good School*, Yates contrasts the development of his protagonist with the disintegration of the prep school that forms him.

Little more favorable are the depictions of two nonresidential private schools. One, a Catholic parochial institution, educates lower-middle-class boys, thus drawing its pupils from a very different social stratum than the elite boarding schools we have just been examining. These boys, and their families, are by no stretch of the imagination from a leadership caste, although the same emphasis on competition, on winning at all costs, as training for later life is present.

The tragic climax in David J. Michael's *A Blow to the Head* (1970) centers around two isolated teenagers. Narrator-protagonist Anthony ("Pooch") Pansella, student athletic manager, is set apart in appearance and limited in athletic ability by "bone marrow anemia," which he is quick to explain is *not* cancer but which nevertheless influences every aspect of his life. J. Roger Gaffrey, a newcomer to the school, St. Bernard's, is also different; his marked reserve, sharp clothes, and social eccentricity make him an object of suspicion to the other students who have been classmates for years. "That was the problem," Pooch observes, "we couldn't see him as a person." Instead, the students see him as an alien, as a potential savior, and, finally, as a threat. J. Roger's refusal to play on the school's faltering football team arouses fury among the students, whose pride and identity are seriously damaged by St. Bernard's dismal record in athletic competition, for they believe that J. Roger could change their luck. Even when the team somehow manages to win a game, their anger does not dissipate because at the victory celebration, the coeds pay far more attention to J. Roger's marvelous dancing than to the winning athletes. The girls' attentions, however, do nothing to draw J. Roger into the school's inner circle. Instead, his reserve off the dance floor makes them feel rejected: "J. Roger was a threat to both sides—the guys couldn't match him and the girls couldn't make him." Ultimately, the student body closes ranks against the stranger and seeks vengeance. Pooch, who "didn't want to graduate from Bernard's without one goddam friend," joins the attack, and it is he who, alone among the students, recognizes the horror of their action. In this way, he finds himself more isolated than ever, as much a victim of mob rule as J. Roger Gaffrey, the students' mysterious antagonist.

The other nonresidential private school is a New York institution which claims a special intellectual rigor. In an apparently autobiographical novel written, according to his publisher, when he was fifteen, Rafael Yglesias portrays Raul Sabas, fourteen-year-old protagonist of *Hide Fox, and All After* (1972), as an actor and writer of great ability who is in conflict with his parents and finds his private school unchallenging, although its reputation places it among the very finest institutions. But only his work in its theater is of interest and value to him, although he also has hopes for a course in creative writing he will be able to take the following year. He cuts classes frequently and purposefully, spending his time with a few friends, with whom he carries on long, intellectual, cynical conversations. At the end of the novel, a confrontation with his parents seems instrumental in causing him to forfeit, almost joyously, a last chance to remain in the school. An unusually talented adolescent, Raul is sympathetically depicted throughout, and although an omniscient narrative method is used, he is the only character we come to know very well. A few others, notably one school friend and the school's headmaster, are also sympathetically portrayed, for their concern for Raul is deep and genuine.

The general picture given by these novels is grim. Few boys emerge from their institutionalized educational experiences with any great love of learning or, indeed, with many skills that will fit them for productive adulthood. Some, including the brightest, find school largely irrelevant to their lives, their most important learning going on elsewhere—anywhere but in the classroom. Some learn lessons which seem basically destructive, and others simply reject school, either suffering in silence through the required hours and years or dropping out.

More varied treatments are given of boys working toward special vocations. Just as writing is a popular calling felt by many girls in subject-novels (see "Females and Social Institutions"), so many boys dream of careers as poets or novelists or journalists. And like the girls, they actually *write*. One novel, *If I Love You, Am I Trapped Forever?* (1973, YA) by Marijane Meaker (pseudonym, M.E. Kerr), is presented as the first production of its protagonist-narrator, Alan Bennett, who plans to be a writer. It is an account of his tempestuous senior year of high school. Meaker does a splendid job of sustaining Alan's point of view, allowing him just enough insight into himself and others to make the novel convincing.

Richard Goodman, a subsidiary character in Rafael Yglesias's *Hide Fox, and All After*, becomes the protagonist of the same author's *The Work*

Is Innocent (1976). A gifted fifteen-year-old from a talented, intellectual, and politically committed family, Richard has already dropped out of high school and is working on his first novel when the book opens. During the course of the book, he finishes his novel, shows it to his parents (who are stunned by its quality), and has it published. The reviews are favorable, and for a heady month Richard is ecstatic over his early success. But a letdown comes, and he begins to fear an inability to live up to this early promise: it has all come too fast, and he sees it as a "deadening progression of success." However, Richard soon realizes that he has already changed, has grown beyond the boy he depicted in the novel, even beyond the boy he was when he wrote the novel. Although he "couldn't face what was weak and ridiculous in people," he has nevertheless "had to face it in himself." With this recognition, the novel ends, and Richard's literary achievement becomes a promise for his future as well as a symbol of his maturation.

Another gifted writer, though from the opposite end of the social scale, is young Ernie Johnson, protagonist and narrator of Ronald Fair's *We Can't Breathe* (1972), a talented black youth growing up in a Chicago ghetto. With his friends, he is involved in early sexual experimentation and petty crime, and his hatred of whites is searing (and the novel clearly demonstrates that it is justified). A wise black teacher introduces him to a biography of Toussaint L'Ouverture, however, and thus awakes in him the desire to be a writer and tell the truth about black life and experience. Made uncomfortable by the obscene language in one of Ernie's stories, she gives him "the one truth that I would carry through the rest of my life":

> Never lie. You must always tell the whole truth. If that's the way some of us talk, then that's the way we talk and there's nothing you can do about it except have people talk that way. But you could explain why they talk that way. That you could do for our people and for yourself, so that when you become a writer people who read your writing will know that even though your characters talk in a—well, I guess you'd have to say in a nasty way, it's not because they have lost their dignity. That's what you can do; you can write about your people with love.

With much difficulty Ernie hides his new preoccupation with books and writing from his friends, for he fears becoming the butt of their jokes, but he perseveres, reading and writing almost obsessively. And it seems clear that this new goal will be the means of enabling him, unlike many of his friends, to survive.

Barbara Wersba's *The Country of the Heart* (1975, YA) centers around the struggles of Steven Harper, aged eighteen, to become a poet. He attends a community college, writes constantly, and sends his poems off regularly to magazines, which just as regularly reject them. Then into his middle-class and, to him, drab life comes a famous poet, a mature woman, whose work he has long admired. A harsh, even brutal critic of his work, she helps him learn to move beyond the derivative work he had been doing and find his own voice. Their relationship is troubled—obsessive and filled with both passion and bitter quarrels. He learns only later that she had been dying of cancer. The novel, narrated by Steve five years later, is his tribute to her and his attempt to understand their relationship. Her influence on him, it seems clear, has been crucial in the making of a poet.

Journalism is the career of Martin Brent, protagonist of Richard Lockridge's *The Empty Day* (1965). Young Marty begins in the early years of this century as a newspaper carrier, then while still in his teens becomes a reporter, and finally rises to a position of great power and prominence. His choice of career is natural; coming from a bookish family with a father (himself a small-time editor) who constantly quoted Shakespeare, he never really considers anything else. When family circumstances require that he make significant financial contributions, he quits school to become a full-time newspaperman. From that point on, his rise is rapid, for to natural ability he adds hard work and, occasionally, the courage to take risks. But all along, his personal relationships suffer. The title, which refers to a day in which the elderly Martin recalls the experiences of his youth, could also refer to the quality of the life that has resulted from his early dedication of himself to his profession and to a family that took his self-sacrifice for granted.

We observed earlier the frequency with which careers in entertainment, especially in films and music, are shown as goals for female adolescent characters (see "Females and Social Institutions"). Similarly, many boys are depicted working toward careers in what might be called the performing arts. But there are important differences: Hollywood is not a goal, and appearance is not a prime qualification for any of the young males. Instead, like the male writers, these boys are mostly shown as dedicated to their art for its own sake, and they too work at their craft. Once again, a difference in social expectations—that girls will be decorative, subsidiary, making their contribution by *being* rather than by anything they *do*, that boys will participate, will make some contribution of substance to their society—seems to underlie the sorts of goals and dreams our subject-authors tend to give their young characters.

Nat Hentoff, William Melvin Kelley, and Iris Dornfeld depict young men who are gifted and thoroughly dedicated to music. For each of them there is no choice about what he will do with his life; he simply knows, and he directs his life toward fulfillment through his music.

Tom Curtis, the sixteen-year-old white middle-class protagonist of Nat Hentoff's *Jazz Country* (1965, YA), is almost obsessed by his love of jazz and his desire to become a great jazz trumpeter. Though his mother fails to understand, his father is sympathetic and encourages Tom to work at his music and find his own path, even when it seems Tom may decide to forgo college for an immediate attempt at a career in music. The novel, suitable for young people, makes believable Tom's growth in musicianship and his slow acceptance into the largely black jazz world.

Because he is a fine musician, Ludlow Washington is discharged early from the "home" for blind black boys. A lengthy section of *A Drop of Patience* (1965) by William Melvin Kelley describes the period between Ludlow's sixteenth and eighteenth years as one of sexual and social initiation —he learns how "to be a man" and how to handle the social roles forced upon blacks. Most importantly, however, he learns that his remarkable musicianship is potentially the key to fulfillment, a goal he seeks throughout the novel.

A musical genius from a totally nonacademic background is the title character and protagonist of Iris Dornfeld's *Boy Gravely* (1965). He finds school completely unrewarding, despite the interest he arouses in an incompetent teacher. His great gift for concentration is directed only to his music (and later to ping-pong!). He drops out of school and wanders the country, teaching himself what he requires and finding mentors as he needs them. The novel is a striking portrait of a self-contained and self-directed prodigy, ignorant about most areas of life but totally assured and in control of his music.

Similarly, Leo Proudhammer is dedicated to a career in the theater, and he undergoes a stage apprenticeship in James Baldwin's *Tell Me How Long the Train's Been Gone* (1968). Leo, the protagonist, and his closest friend, Barbara King, participate in a theatrical workshop. Though he has the obstacle of his race to overcome (he is black) and the director considers him lacking in talent, we know he will succeed, for the novel consists largely of flashbacks touched off by a heart attack suffered on stage by Leo, a hard-driving, prominent actor of thirty-nine. The workshop is crucial to him: not only does it give him his first actual experience as an actor, but it also establishes certain important elements in his personal life.

For these boys, fortunate because of their native ability and their certitude of how they wish to use their gift, hard work and single-minded dedication to professional goals lead to maturity. Others with different sorts of creative gifts demonstrate similar dedication and achieve—or show promise of—similar successes.

David Marks, of Barbara Wersba's *Run Softly, Go Fast* (1970, YA), is a sensitive young man, a lover of poetry and an aspiring artist. His father, whose death inspires David to think back over their troubled relationship, was the son of immigrants and had risen from abject poverty to become a wealthy businessman. The father's total failure to understand or sympathize with his son's yearning leads to a total break between them. Through his art, as well as through a wise and loving young woman, David builds a satisfying life, and at nineteen he has already had a successful one-man show. His and his father's values had been completely different, but after the father's death, David is at last able to understand the sources of his father's attitudes; his father, however, apparently never achieved any such understanding of him.

Photography as a future (and present) occupation figures prominently in *Yates Paul, His Grand Flights, His Tootings* (1963) by James Baker Hall. Yates's father is a second-rate professional photographer, but thirteen-year-old Yates is already the better of the two in the darkroom and confident he will be better as a photographer when given the chance. Among his fantasies (the "Flights" and "Tootings" of the title), the most recurrent is of himself as a great photographer, world-renowned for his art.

In the passages depicting the adolescence of Arley Minor, protagonist of Zane Kotker's *A Certain Man* (1976), the boy rejects joining the family business—undertaking—and elects to train himself for the ministry. Interested in and curious about religion all his life, Arley begins with childish commitment.

> God had loved the world after all, He had sent it his son. Some gift! And sent him as a baby. Now, that was really taking a chance! They could have killed him right there in the straw. He could have got German measles. Appendicitis. Spanish influenza. But God had chosen to take that chance, had trusted him, Arley Minor, to receive that gift! Pride came swelling up from his knees. . . . He would take that baby into his heart, where it would grow inside him, reaching all the way to his fingers and toes, to replace the gray sack of shadow that acted out his dreams. He would be safe then, the baby would grow into the Lord Jesus Christ!

His perceptions of faith grow as he matures, however, and Kotker clearly conveys Arley's theological as well as his personal development.

Arley's motivations for entering the ministry are his faith and his desire to serve. A sharply contrasting character is Nin Rabun, to whose story Christian ministry is also central. Crucial to Vinnie Williams's *Greenbones* (1967) is the relationship between the protagonist, Nin Rabun, and his mother, Doesticks. At twelve the boy, deeply desirous of achieving an education, discovers a gift for public speech, and his driving, vital mother tricks him into becoming an itinerant preacher. Her motive, however, is purely mercenary, and she is willing to force him to use his gift in a way likely to extract cash from the rural Georgians of the period around World War I. Nin deeply resents his mother and struggles, through a variety of adventures and misadventures, to win his literal and psychological freedom from her. Injured and made speechless just when he does escape her, he is convicted of larceny and sent to a convict camp. Later, free, he makes a home with an eccentric Quaker, only to be reunited with his mother, but this time, finally, they reach an accommodation. Nin has become his own person.

Another lad for whom performing is a method of getting by in the world, as well as a means of self-expression, is depicted by David Wagoner in *The Escape Artist* (1965). A career as a magician is the goal of Danny Masters, the protagonist. A country boy in the city, he seeks his uncle and aunt, who perform various sorts of magic and mind-reading acts in seedy nightclubs. Danny is gifted at his art as well as at quick thinking, and despite the fact that he gets in trouble with a powerful man, he regularly bests the adult world. His magic and trickery seem almost as much a way of life (or of survival) as a vocation during the three frantic days covered by this modern picaresque novel.

Physical strength and skill figure prominently in two other novels. In both these books, boys are shown achieving their manhood through professional activity which is potentially dangerous and through which brute courage can be manifested. Cowboy, the high-school-dropout protagonist of *The Night Crew* (1970) by J. R. Goddard, has taken a job with the state firecrew, a force greatly depleted by World War II. Despite his assignment to the disreputable night crew, the boy takes pride in caring for and driving the truck, the Indiana, finding a manly identity in "the badge which set him apart from other eighteen-year-olds." Ironically, the book's central action—the huge and dangerous San Patricio fire— requires him to work on foot, and his true initiation occurs not through flamboyant action, but huddled among a crowd of prone men, trying to survive an updraft.

> There was no more human sound. A brittle great cracking came every direction. Rushed in cracking loud enveloping them inside it. After four days keeping their distance, they were now full inside the rushing force. More trees went somewhere, seemed to happen in seconds, whomp, sharp crack of branches falling. Frantically Cowboy pulled his jacket over his head. Pressed hard as he could into dirt, wanted to burrow like a mole on down under thinness of jacket.

Nevertheless, Cowboy is aware that he has passed a major symbolic test and has emerged, traditionally, a man.

The journalistic skills and sporting interests of author Pete Hamill are evident in *Flesh & Blood* (1977). The protagonist, eighteen-year-old Bobby Fallon, who tells the story in a shifting first- and second-person narrative, is a slum youth, product of a father who has long ago deserted him and an irresponsible, lovely, cruel young mother. Boxing, which he begins to learn in prison, becomes both his means of harnessing and directing his sometimes murderous angers and his hope of achieving fame and fortune. When he begins to become known, promoters seize on him as a "white hope," but betrayals of various sorts follow him as he gropes his way to manhood. The dignity with which he behaves after the novel's climactic fight suggests he has begun to achieve maturity.

In many cases it is difficult to draw a line between a vocation and an avocation, between that which one does to support oneself and that which one does because one loves it. A number of our authors depict boys for whom present or future job and hobby are almost indistinguishable, for whom the job is done for love or the hobby will become a lifework. Donna Hill's *Catch a Brass Canary* (1965, YA), for example, shows how the world of books opens up to a sixteen-year-old Puerto Rican boy, Miguel Campos, when he gets a job as a page in a branch of the New York Public Library.

Mathematics is the special gift and presumably the future vocation of a boy presented by Al Hine in *Lord Love a Duck* (1961). Alan Byrd ("Gooney Bird") Musgrave is contemptuous of those less brilliant than he and he soon learns how to manipulate them to his will. His special type of intelligence manifests itself both in his intellectual abilities and in his method of relating to other people.

More wholesome and humane is another youth with scientific interests and abilities, described in Jane Langton's *Natural Enemy* (1982). During the summer before his freshman year in college, John Hand works at odd jobs for the Heron family, distant neighbors. In addition to falling in love and to helping solve a murder mystery, John pursues his avocation, soon to be his profession. He plans to become an entomologist, with a specialization in spiders. Toward this end, he maintains a small spider collection and devotes a good deal of his leisure time to a documented study of a barn door spider whose webs are near his room. In John's observation journal, recorded in *Natural Enemy*, and in the story of the spider's own adventuresome summer, Langton weaves a clever subplot to John's own growth and development. Further, John's commitment to his future profession lends persuasiveness to his characterization and interest to the plot.

For other protagonists, pursuits that seem more typically boyish —airplanes and cars—serve as symbols of maturation: for Rich Newman (*The Fledgling*), flight brings true maturity, while for Earl Edge and Coley Simms (*Moonshine Light, Moonshine Bright*), cars represent the adulthood and freedom they yearn for but have not yet attained.

Flying a small airplane becomes Rich Newman's obsession in John Tomerlin's *The Fledgling* (1968, YA). Rich had been severely injured in an automobile accident in which his brother was killed (and for which, we eventually learn, he feels a deep sense of guilt). His mother, still grieving for her lost son, strongly resists Rich's taking any risks, but Rich's discovery of flight and his growing competence at flying help him to overcome his guilt and even to become more confident and open in his relationships with others. Finally, in a climactic scene, he proves that he can behave with courage under stress, and the novel closes with Rich's having found a new maturity and with his family both closer and more relaxed than it had been since the accident.

Earl Edge and Coley Simms, two fourteen-year-old South Carolina boys, protagonists of William Price Fox's *Moonshine Light, Moonshine Bright* (1967), have learner's permits and a passionate desire for a car of their own. The novel follows them through one summer as they search for a cheap but good used car and for the money to buy it. Even their attempts at working to earn the needed money are illegal, for they are underage—and other money-making schemes are both more seriously illegal and more comic. They set up a still, but the sour mash oozes out and its smell announces their activity to the world. When they do buy a car, they use it to transport huge blocks of butter stolen from a dairy, but after a farcical chase scene they helplessly watch car and melted butter sink deep into a river. Their boyish obsession with cars, their high spirits, and their generally amoral attitudes are effectively portrayed.

If a love of cars is typical of boys in their early teens, so is a love of sports. The "game of life" is a popular cliché in our culture, and sports are often held up as worthy because they "build character" and "teach competition." Competitiveness is a characteristic much desired in American men, and it is popularly thought that sports are a particularly effective way for young men to learn to measure themselves against others, and to judge themselves by their success in besting others. If only one can win, then one must be defeated, and sports can, or so it is thought, teach a boy both how to avoid being the one to lose and how to accept defeat with grace when he must. These are the lessons of the camp in Burt Blechman's *The War of Camp Omongo* (1963), a summer camp in which sports are specifically stressed for their competitive value and in which the camp is explicitly made an image for America: a country great because of its "will-to-win, in sports, in business, in war." The campers learn their lesson, and Blechman shows how disastrous to the boys' character an excessive stress on competitiveness can actually—and ironically—be.

A more lighthearted look at sports and games becomes a subsidiary theme in *No More Reunions* (1973), John Bowers's story of growing up in Tennessee. Pool, and the forbidden delights of the pool hall with its aura of adult machismo, is a frequent diversion. A striking episode occurs the night Pancho, the protagonist's best friend, has a hot streak and defeats the town's best players. He follows that with success at poker. But his mother takes the money, and Pancho never again has such luck. That night turns out to be the high point of his life, and from this point on he and the protagonist begin to grow apart. Also important to these young men, especially Boney, the protagonist, are football and basketball. Boney's fervent attempts to excel and his failures are comically and poignantly depicted.

Bridge, another competitive activity often valued (or denigrated) for that very competitiveness, is used as a similar metaphor for life in B. H. Friedman's *Yarborough* (1964). For protagonist Arthur Skelton, bridge is both a metaphor for and an escape from life. A child prodigy at bridge, he always insists it is just a game, as meaningless as everything else. He delights in its mathematical beauty and lack of cruelty: "It's clean at the bridge table. Nobody really gets hurt." Introduced to the game at an early age by his bridge-playing father, he soon becomes far better than the adults with whom he plays. His one deep and lasting friendship, with Henry Rosen, is based on bridge; the boys meet at a private prep school and form a partnership that leads to, among other things, a national championship when they are only fifteen and sixteen respectively and to their invention of a particularly accurate but complex method of point counting. Drugs and sex also serve as escapes from the randomness of experience and bring moments of joy, but they remain avocations while bridge is an obsession. Ultimately Arthur believes that bridge is

> like life, if life were more like life *should be.* It's life with all the shit filtered out of it. Life without any obligation to play. Life played only where and when you want. Life without the need to produce something someone else wants. Life in which everyone is playing according to the same rules.

The novel's title underlines Arthur's view of things: a Yarborough is a bridge hand with no honors. As Arthur says, "You can never beat the game itself. The choice is between losing and not playing." A deeply pessimistic book, the novel nevertheless is full of humor, and Arthur's character and his relationship with Henry are as fully effectively portrayed as is his adolescent growth into a nihilistic philosophy.

Most of these subject-novels take issue with the popular American assumptions that sports, precisely because of the competitiveness they instill, are both a valid symbol of American life and a valuable training for young men in the virtues they must learn in order to participate fully and productively in that life. The novelists suggest that competitiveness can be dangerous, especially when carried to extremes, that sports teach selfishness and inculcate a lack of empathy, which are the opposite side of the will to win.

Similar points are made by Alan S. Foster, who also finds in popular films and male idols another metaphor for the excessive stress on competition that mars, in his view, the contemporary world. *Goodbye, Bobby Thomson! Goodbye, John Wayne!* (1973) criticizes the American ideals of manly valor epitomized by sports and film heroes. Pete Murray, the protagonist, is seen at the ages of eighteen, twenty-three, and thirty, as he faces crucial moments of his life; in each the world of competitive sports is set against a reality of twentieth-century history: the Korean War, the Hungarian Revolution of 1956, and the assassination of President Kennedy. In only the first section of the novel is he an adolescent, of course, but that first section (with the World Series as metaphor for his anguish over the death of his brother in Korea and his struggle to decide whether to quit playing football and join the army) sets the tone and poses the questions that the remainder of this short novel will consider.

Alan Foster, then, suggests that both sports and films are dangerous avocations, that when seen as metaphors for successful adult life, they are misleading, teaching ideals that are ultimately harmful. A somewhat more favorable view of the celluloid world as a training school for adult reality appears in David Madden's *Bijou* (1974). Films—their stars, plots, and settings—are as vitally important to Lucius Hutchfield as are the actual events and relationships in his chaotic family life: a soldier's death in World War II, his brother's imprisonments, tensions and countertensions between adult relatives. His job as an usher in a movie house is an obvious symbol of the strong connection between dream and fact. For him, then, films become an aid to understanding life as well as a means of escaping trouble or pressure, and Lucius grows toward adulthood informed not only by parents, siblings, girlfriends, peers but also by his perceptions of such movie stars as Hedy Lamarr, Sabu, Bambi, Alan Ladd, and the Marx Brothers. Like most *Bildungsroman* heroes, Lucius discovers that some of his mentors are wise and helpful, others foolish and useless.

Such avocations as cars, airplanes, sports, and films are all important in these subject-novels as activities loved by boys who see in them some sort of representation of what adulthood means or will bring to them—either a symbol of adulthood attained (cars, flying) or a metaphor for society or a representation of true maturity (sports, films). But they are also activities in themselves, and the *doing* of the activities is also a learning experience, a kind of training, for good or ill.

Other avocations also act as training devices for various sorts of character traits or skills. Appearing with rather great frequency in treatments of boys (though almost entirely lacking in studies of girls) are pets and animals. Care for or companionship with an animal, most often a dog, enriches the lives of lonely boys, and usually the pet or the boy's relationship with it is presented as valuable in and of itself and also as worthy training in responsibility and empathy, valued adult traits. For example, Mickie, the Malamute owned by orphaned Brad Nichols, protagonist of *Home Is the North* (1967, YA) by Walt Morey, represents stability and responsibility as the boy makes a new life in a new family. Morey's treatment of the relationship is unsentimental and effective. In Barry Beckham's *My Main Mother* (1969), a story of a complex mother-son relationship leading to murder, Mitchell Mibbs's boxer Jeff and his uncle are the only beings he can love simply and directly. Bernie Hergruter's pet Damaltian Zeke, in *Hard Feelings* (1977) by Don Bredes, serves a different function: his poisoning is one example of the cruel violence of the adolescent world in that book, and it also sets off much of the action which follows.

In *Sounder* (1969, YA) by William H. Armstrong, the protagonist (called only "the boy") loves his father's hound, Sounder, as a symbol of his father's manly skills and of his own approaching manhood. The dog's survival of a brutal attack gives "the boy" hope that his father will survive a long prison term. Armstrong's spare, powerful treatment of this symbol structure is almost mythic in its impact.

In *The Concrete Wilderness* (1967) by Jack Couffer, Archie Larsen, a boy who hates urban life, spends months cautiously trying to make friends with Wolf, a wild dog who ranges New York City's shoreline. The boy is patient, but the dog is wary. Nevertheless, Archie's success is evident when Wolf twice saves him from peril—once from the hands of a child molester, once from a deadly juvenile gang. To Archie, Wolf symbolizes his own wild spirit and his determination to resist civilization, and when Wolf becomes the object of a concentrated hunt by the civil authorities, Archie faces a terrible decision. He must defend Wolf and his own instincts or surrender the dog and accept the responsibilities of city life.

In Will Bryant's *The Big Lonesome* (1971), a bear cub becomes much more than a pet to Tobin Shattuck. Mauled and almost killed by a female grizzly, after his long recuperation, Tobin adopts her cub, called Gabriel. Several times Gabriel, well-trained by Tobin, saves Tobin's life or the lives of others, and he plays a role equal to that of Tobin's father in Tobin's maturation.

These youngsters learn to love and be responsible through their relationships with their pets; alone among the kinds of maturation experiences treated in this chapter, this one is always presented as enriching and rewarding. Why this theme should be so much more prominent in books about boys than in novels on girls is not easy to understand. Perhaps because girls are expected and trained to be nurturing, they are not thought to need the special training in loving and caring for others that boys can gain through relationships with animals. At any rate, these subject-novelists see in love for an animal companion a way for lonely youngsters to form ties with something outside themselves and thus to maintain a connection with a world that is often unfriendly.

Just as our subject-authors found only slight worth in the training given young men by our schools and little validity in the assumption of social value in athletics, so they also view organized religions as often more hindrance than help to youngsters seeking answers to religious and ethical questions. Often, the problem is a rigid orthodoxy, out of touch with the world as it is now, or a gulf between the practice of the religious group and the faith that it preaches. Young men reared in such rigid or hypocritical religious bodies often go through periods of questioning which then end in rejection of the faith. In so rejecting their childhood faith, they may either win through to a better, deeper, truer belief, or they may reject all religious belief, and cynicism is one possible end result of the process. Here the particular church under study may, like sports in other novels, be seen as a metaphor for American society.

Though Pooch Pansella, of David J. Michael's *A Blow to the Head* (1970), is proud of being a Roman Catholic (seeing his church as the true church which traces its history directly to Christ through St. Peter) and though his parents are very active in their parish, Pooch himself (like his fellow students at St. Bernard's parish school) is fearful of absolute devotion or even deep commitment to his religious beliefs: "Christ was a great guy and I give him credit but this Christianity thing is like artists. You end up off your nut. . . . you'd go screwy trying to live by it like a whole lot of the older Catholics." Michael uses shifting attitudes toward the church to illustrate the social changes taking place among the blue-collar, Catholic characters who dominate his story and to symbolize the decay of values that occurs when social mobility replaces faith and honor as the center of family life. The confusion Pooch feels about formulaic Christianity as practiced by his friends, parents, and fellow parishioners reflects his confusion about all the standards adults attempt to impose upon him. Though he cannot fully define his feelings, Pooch rejects hypocrisy—but is unable to discover any useful, honorable creed. Left without a moral center, he drifts into tragedy and then stasis.

A mature Daniele Faustino, trying to resolve the conflict between his sexuality and the Roman Catholic Church in which he had been reared by his pious mother, remembers his childhood, youth, and young adulthood in Rocco Fumento's *Tree of Dark Reflection* (1962). Danny's torments are reflected in the enigma of his father, who is alternately cruel and loving, an atheist who once aspired to the priesthood only to succumb to the lure of the flesh, as the son finally learns. Providing still further complexities is his relationship with Miriam and Mark Stern, Jewish sister and brother; their activities center on a secret lovely place symbolically named Canaan—it is both beautiful and dangerous of access. He and Mark hate each other, but Danny is always strongly attracted to Miriam. While Mark is almost obsessively Jewish, she professes atheism. And yet Danny's final reconciliation with the Church is tantalizingly presaged by the title and first sentence of the novel's opening passage: it is "Dedicated to a Nun" and begins, "This is for you, Miriam—no, I must call you Sister Grace now, I suppose—because it was you who initiated this journey into the past." Introspective, realistic, and symbolic, the novel re-creates well its time and place, Massachusetts in the 1930s.

In Mel Ellis's *This Mysterious River* (1972, YA), Hammond Drumm suffers a genuine crisis of faith during his twelfth summer. A child of the Depression, the boy is astounded when a stranger drops a ten-dollar bill into the church collection plate. Ham steals the ten dollars and uses it to buy a long-coveted bicycle. The subsequent theft of the bike is only the first of a long series of adventures which initiate the boy into adulthood by forcing him to face danger, death, and the chicanery of the adult world. The motivation for Ham's adventures is his desire to repay the money, a gesture demanded not only by his own fierce conscience but also because he cannot take communion with his sin unconfessed, and confession is unthinkable because the priest will recognize the voice of the confessor and reveal his theft. Father Zamanski's concept of hellfire and his own experiences of pain and sin are confusing to Ham, as he becomes increasingly aware that authority is not always just and that established religion can mean different things to different people. The Rock River, the central symbol of *This Mysterious River*, is the center of Ham's activity and represents the stream of the boy's life and the river of faith.

An important theme in Gerald Warner Brace's *The Wind's Will* (1964) is David Wayne's reaction against the harshly Calvinistic religion which his father, a small-town minister, preaches. Obsessed with sin and seeing it everywhere, the father has already driven his elder son out of the home, and from the beginning of the novel David simply does not listen to his father's tirades. When the father then commits adultery, his sense of guilt leads inevitably to his destruction, but David seems strengthened in both courage and tolerance as a result of observing his father's suffering.

In Joanne Greenberg's *Founder's Praise* (1976), Edgar Bisset Kornarens's early life is one of joy and security. Much of his happiness arises from his "special" place among the Praise Dancers, a sect his grandfather helped found around the memory of Edgar Bisset, young Edgar's great-uncle. A few people doubt the validity of a faith that doesn't recognize evil: "It's all high noon at Praise—no shadows, no difficult questions, nothing that looks like something else, no one that isn't what he is announced to be, no fears, no hopes turning downward." Edgar, however, finds no fault with his belief until he discovers his ability to corrupt the faith by using his popularity among the Dancers to achieve his own ends. He learns that believers who ignore evil cannot recognize it when it arises, thus allowing it to function unopposed. His initiation experience is costly, but it transforms him into a seeker after greater truths, and ironically, it transforms him into the reflection of his uncle that the Praise Dancers have always imagined they've seen: "You put me so in mind of Edgar. He was always talkin' like that, askin' questions, turnin' things inside out. He did it believin' and sometimes half believin' and you do it half doubtin', but some way it's like I hear him now."

In *Before My Time* (1974) by Maureen Howard, a bizarre religious cult intrigues Jim Cogan by its promise of a deeper awareness: "It was peaceful there, so peaceful. I thought there might be another way—and the way I knew didn't work." However, he becomes involved with the sect primarily because he is obsessed with Shelley Waltz, one of its most devoted followers. The mixture of sex and religion Jim finds through

Shelley and her Creative Love cult is heady, perplexing, and ultimately dangerous, for he is arrested (perhaps mistakenly) along with a group of the faithful "on their way to blow up the Main Branch of the New York Public Library." *Before My Time* describes the period after Jim's arrest when he is visiting relatives who pull strings to keep him out of prison. This respite with the Quinn family gives him the opportunity to compare their values with those of his mother and father. His parents' "way" is certainly flawed, but nevertheless Jim returns to them, perhaps to become truly "the Cog" (as Shelley has called him) in an imperfect but familiar life pattern.

As a teenager, Seth Abraham Adler leaves New York City to make his fortune in Georgia, and a long portion of Richard Kluger's *Members of the Tribe* (1977) is devoted to this young Northern Jew's attempt to adjust to life in the South during the last quarter of the nineteenth and the first quarter of the twentieth centuries. Although Jews live comfortably in Savannah, Seth's new home, the boy's faith is both openly and subtly challenged at every turn. While Seth abandons his observation of the dietary laws, he moderately maintains his beliefs, even in his most severe test. His employer, a wealthy Christian merchandiser, offers the youth a partnership if he will become a Protestant Christian. Seth's refusal marks his maturation and a major shift in his life, for he begins to read for the bar and finds his true vocation. Kluger's effective portrait reveals not only Seth's personal strengths and weaknesses but also the attitudes of and toward Southern Jews.

Though the portrait of George Bowlegs, in *Dance Hall of the Dead* (1973) by Tony Hillerman, is presented secondhand, it is vivid and touching. Witness to and suspect for the murder of his best friend, George flees, and his characterization is slowly pieced together by the protagonist, Lieutenant Joe Leaphorn, the police officer who is searching for the boy. While some people describe George as "crazy," another witness sees him as a potential saint, and it soon becomes clear that he has a great curiosity, especially about spiritual matters. A Navajo, he is studying the faith and practices of the Zuñis, hoping to "convert." Somewhat estranged from his Navajo traditions, on the fringes of white society, and not yet a part of the tribe to which he aspires, George is in a peculiarly lonely position: "Where was home for this boy who had hunted for heaven?" Hillerman succeeds remarkably well in his presentation of George's personality, the boy's search for faith, and the Indian cultures which influence him.

For other young males, ethical and moral questions must be faced without reference to a particular religious faith. Ethical standards inculcated by families or absorbed from the social consensus may be as flawed or may come to seem as false as those enforced by an established religious body, and so this dilemma—to retain old standards or to reject them—may seem equally severe. As with religious struggles, a youth may ultimately come to reaffirm old beliefs and behaviors, he may adopt new ones and reject the old, or he may act essentially negatively, casting off the old without finding anything new to set in its place.

A character whose original values are reaffirmed by his experience is Danny Masters of David Wagoner's *The Escape Artist* (1965). Those values, however, are decidedly negative. Danny is an aspiring magician, and the deception of his trade is also the code of his everyday behavior. Early in the novel we are told:

> He'd been a kind of thief since as early as he could remember, anyway, hadn't he? Doing things too fast to be caught, making cards and coins disappear, lying in the line of duty, pretending to look where he wasn't looking, pretending not to do what he was doing, getting into trouble deliberately so he could get out of it, wanting to break all the rules.

He steals a wallet which turns out to be filled with "hot" one-hundred-dollar bills and from then on the novel follows the twin motifs of his flight from his angry victim and his attempts to become a stage magician. He lives by his code of deception, never seeing any reason to behave otherwise. Intended as a comic novel, the book raises ethical questions to which it suggests no answers, and the end of the novel seems to show Danny prevailing because of his cleverness.

Two young men face challenges to their sense of values in Edwin Lanham's *Speak Not Evil* (1964). Billy Brownlow, son of a banker, is a decent young man, happily dating the high-school valedictorian. When he is introduced into a small group (including a high-school classmate) that engages in sex orgies, he is appalled. In his shock and horror, he and another boy engage in an act of vandalism: they ransack a house and do a great deal of damage. But Billy's ethical sense is strong, and he confesses his act, eager to try to make restitution. Another young man who is sorely tried but remains true to his own standards is Theo Littleton. Helping with the renovation work on an old house, he discovers a cache of old and valuable coins; after brief temptation, he turns them over to their rightful owners. This novel has several important teenaged characters, all of whom face crises of one sort or another during one brief summer, and most eventually come through as well as Billy and Theo; the novel both studies troubled youth and shows a number of these young people managing to reaffirm traditional values.

In Fred Chappell's *The Gaudy Place* (1973), Linn Harper is a high-school student who gets on well with his parents and teachers and is an avid reader, but when a serious, beery discussion of Camus prompts him to commit a useless crime, Linn spends a night in the local jail. The experience tests Linn's ethics and allows Chappell to contrast him with two other teenagers who make their livings on the streets, and also to show that all levels of society engage in one "con" or another.

Borden Deal's *The Least One* (1967) depicts a poor Southern white family during the Depression. Life is hard, but the family's, especially the mother's, values are firmly held: pride, honesty, independence, cleanliness, and hard work are the basis of her ethic, and she inculcates these virtues in her two sons. The most difficult lessons for the young protagonist deal with death, guilt, and responsibility and are connected with his search for identity, symbolized by his name. He is called simply "Boy," his father believing that a person should choose his or her own name, he stubbornly considering it his father's duty to name what he has created. At the novel's climax, a series of events (his father's and his own brushes with death, his sense of guilt at causing serious injury to his father, his having to shoot a favorite mule because its leg is broken) leads him to discover his own name. Though still little more than a child, he has achieved an adult's awareness of mortality, the capacity to acknowledge guilt, and the ability to go on living the best way he knows how. He has learned his parents' lessons and gone beyond them as a result of his own experiences.

David H. Brooks's *Gone Away* (1975) is the narrative of an unnamed boy about his older brother, Doug Harrison, and Doug's conflicts with their strict father, a proud and reserved man of conservative political and moral views whom they always refer to as the "old man." When Doug is expelled from his exclusive prep school, the father utterly rejects him, and as a result, Doug simply disappears. When the narrator finds him again, he has become a typical example of what his father would scorn as hippiedom: long-haired, bearded, living with a black girl, involved in social protest. But in a violent climactic scene, he behaves nobly, and the narrator is startled to realize that the father is now proud of him:

> The old man watched them and he got the whole scene at a glance. He could see that Doug was not a drug addict and that he knew about blacks and the modern world and all the stuff the old man is always having trouble with. I thought that because Suzette was black, fire and steam might shoot out of the old man's ears like an explosion through the portholes of a doomed luxury liner, but the old man smiled as Doug took Suzette's hand and turned to face him. He actually *smiled*.

Through harsh experience Doug has learned to exemplify in his own world the courage and honor his father values, and through observing both Doug and the father, the narrator becomes conscious of those same values.

For Earl Whitaker, narrator and protagonist of Jeff Fields's ambitious, comic, and moving *A Cry of Angels* (1974), ethical tests and lessons come from a variety of sources. The novel covers only about two years, but Earl learns a great deal and matures into a strong and wise young man. An orphan living with an aunt who keeps a sort of unofficial nursing home for elderly white people in the middle of a Georgia black ghetto, he must overcome persistent nightmares caused by memories of his near death in the fire that killed his parents. His closest friends are a black youth who works as clerk in a nearby store, an eccentric young architect whose ambition is to build cheap but imaginative housing for poor people, and a Lumbee Indian who is alternately Earl's caretaker and charge. From the observed experiences of Jayell Crooms, the architect (who has a disastrous marriage and a passionate love affair), and from his relationship with Em Jujohn, the Indian (who is sometimes violent and always crudely honest), he learns much about the human condition. When his aunt is forced to leave him, he manages to survive alone. Among his most important lessons is the necessity of both independence and responsibility. But ultimately it is the importance of dreams which he most urgently comprehends. Jayell had speculated that "maybe we're creatures with angels exiled in our souls, banished to this godawful existence. . . . and all those fancy frigging dreams we have are only the cries of those poor old angels, their screams in our animal minds." It is dreams, as Earl finally realizes in the novel's brief epilogue, that *"gave Jayell the courage to build his fantasy village, his place in a comformist world he couldn't accept. . . . That stirred Miss Esther [Earl's aunt] and a house of forgotten old people to do battle with time itself."* And it is such dreams which free Earl at the novel's conclusion to face a very uncertain future with courage.

In Robert Baylor's *To Sting the Child* (1964), Paul Adamic, at twenty-one, returning from World War II, relives his past in an attempt to find his identity and a meaning to his life. Values and standards—their sources and significance—seem an insolvable mystery. His memories are almost without exception painful: his mother's commitment to a mental hospital, his loveless family life, sexual failures and embarrassments, his many disappointments. He speaks almost boastfully of his "adolescent illusions of unhappiness," and wants to be persuaded of the falsity of his belief that "the individual can't make himself count for anything. . . . the individual is overwhelmed and defeated. He's a victim." But his mentor, the Old Gent, reminds him that "despair is easy. . . . it cannot be cast out any more than you can cast out your liver or your heart. . . . it can only be assuaged, never cured. Your belief in the sun rising, in the heart quickening, in the mind and the spirit reaching unanimity. . . . that's what life is." Both symbolic and naturalistic, the novel does not really prepare for its hopeful conclusion, and much of its prose is rather pretentiously philosophical.

A number of other subject-novelists postulate rather special challenges for their male adolescent characters. These are, in some cases, the result of peculiar family situations, in others of membership in special subcultures (specifically, gangs), and in still others of particular social forces or historical events. For young Jesse Watersmith, in Luke Wallin's *The Redneck Poacher's Son* (1981), the problem is the nature of his family's ethics and behavior—which he is sensitive enough to react against, despite his youth and his fear of his brutal father. Jesse has been taught by his father to love killing animals, to hate blacks, and particularly to despise the mill owner against whom the father had an old resentment. But Jesse loves the wild animals his father gleefully kills, and because of his hatred of the violence which so thoroughly characterizes his father, he is able to withhold judgment on the other subjects. Thus when he escapes to town, takes a job at the mill, and is befriended by a black man whom his father had particularly hated, he begins to build a new life for himself. His escape from his appalling background and his discovery of new possibilities of life and love and trust are the subject of this novel.

In *Rover Youngblood: An American Fable* (1969) by Thomas McAfee, Rover takes to the road, to escape from a difficult family situation and his pregnant girlfriend's marriage plans. During his journey, however, he discovers that flight sometimes raises more problems than it solves, for scalawags confront him frequently. Rover learns that demands are made on one's conscience and human sympathy wherever one goes, that almost anyone or anything (including religion) can be exploited, and that viciousness and trickery are prevalent almost everywhere. His escape has been no escape at all, for flight from home has not freed him from the society which his family reflected. *Rover Youngblood*, a picaresque novel, uses its protagonist's travels as a means of casting a comic eye on some aspects of Southern life.

The ethical conflict suffered by Miguel Campos, sixteen-year-old protagonist of Donna Hill's *Catch a Brass Canary* (1965, YA), is between the code of his Puerto Rican gang and the morality of the employees, both black and white, of the New York Public Library branch where he is a page. In his confusion, he thinks back over the attitudes of people who have been important to him in one way or another:

> What should he think? Everybody told him something different. The Snake said get your own back. Theodore said do right by society. Victoria said to be a fine person was what counted, but what did she know about the hard world? Carmen said be good, Miguelito. Frank told him he was all wrong for the library and Rupert said the library was all wrong itself. Mr. Jason said find a better way to get what you want out of life, but he had died before he said how.

The novel depicts well Miguel's struggles with himself, his ambitions, and his effect on those around him. A subsidiary but important theme is the conflict between a well-intentioned desire to prevent harm by destroying "dangerous" books and the librarians' duty to preserve the written word and protect freedom of expression.

Fourteen-year-old Ponyboy Curtis, narrator-protagonist of S. E. Hinton's *The Outsiders* (1967, YA), has, like Hill's Miguel, accepted his values and ethics from a gang. Through a concentrated series of events, which include three violent deaths, Ponyboy realizes the futility of his old values:

> What kind of world is it where all I have to be proud of is a repu-
> tation for being a hood, and greasy hair? I don't want to be a
> hood, but even if I don't steal things and mug people and get
> boozed up, I'm marked lousy. Why should I be proud of it? Why
> should I even pretend to be proud of it?

At the novel's end, he has gained a hard-won objectivity; the novel is both his plea for understanding of boys like himself and his first step toward making something of himself, toward participation in society.

Resistance to the civil rights movement as it affects one white family of the Deep South in 1957 is shown in Madison Jones's *A Cry of Absence* (1971), a novel of conflicting ethics and loyalties. Cam Glenn, at seventeen still striving to be what his mother, the novel's central character, wishes him to be, is the catalyst; misunderstanding her devotion to tradition and her southern heritage, he brutally murders a black man. Though the novel concentrates on the effect that knowledge of this fact has on his mother and elder brother, the portrait of Cam as a bigoted, tormented, and insecure young man is believable and effective. Unlike Jesse Watersmith (*The Redneck Poacher's Son*), Cam lacks the sensitivity to perceive the falsity and cruelty of the ethos of his environment; he does not even understand what is good in his family's background. His maturation fails.

The problem faced by Jeremy Wolf in Nat Hentoff's *I'm Really Dragged But Nothing Gets Me Down* (1968, YA) is what to do when he reaches the statutory age for registering for the draft. As he struggles to think through his political and moral obligations, he discusses his situation with friends of varying viewpoints, but he simply refuses to discuss it with his family. Only the options of seeking conscientious objector status or of refusing to register are seriously considered.

> O.K. Easy Way. 2S. Four years, maybe more. War would be over
> then, would have to be. Next war? Worry about that then. Less
> easy way, but not hard either. Become part of a Quaker meeting
> or something like that. Register and apply for C.O. They'd see
> through that. But it *was* real, he didn't want to kill. And with the
> right counseling, maybe he could make it. . . . I will not be part of
> their machinery. To what point though? So I'm locked away and
> then let out, and I won't have changed a thing. I'll have changed
> myself. How sure can you be of that? You could come out so
> scared of ever having to go back in again that you'd never take
> another chance all your life. On anything. How the hell did I get
> into this? Girls are sure lucky.

But by the end of the novel, he finds within himself the courage to face the potential consequences of refusing to register, though little is actually resolved. The novel sharply presents not only his dilemma, but the emotional cost to families caught up in the struggles of the late 1960s.

Though the main plot of Max Apple's *Zip: A Novel of the Left and Right* (1978) details narrator Ira Goldstein's late maturation, the key to the book is Jésus "Crab" Martinez Goldstein, a teenaged boxer. Jésus remains true to the communistic ideals taught him in childhood. He conspires to kidnap J. Edgar Hoover and hold the F.B.I. man hostage to promote a fight symbolic of the struggles between Third World peoples and whites, between revolutionaries and the establishment, between communists and capitalists. Apple's use of fantasy creates a character known only through Ira's comments and through fragments of Jésus' own propagandistic autobiography. While Ira's self-portrait is clear, Jésus' portrait is hazy but powerful, denoting the mainstream's unclear understanding and exploitation of many minorities.

Laura Z. Hobson and Al Hine have created two very different boys who each face dilemmas caused by their realization that they are special, different. For one, Hobson's Jeff Lynn, the recognition is a painful awareness of his sexual preference. For the other, Hine's Gooney Bird Musgrave, it is an awareness of special intellectual capabilities which give him great power over others.

Jeff Lynn realizes at seventeen that he is homosexual. Laura Z. Hobson's *Consenting Adult* (1975) deals sympathetically with his adolescent struggle against his sexual preference, a struggle that is finally resolved only when as an adult of thirty, a practicing physician, he decides to "come out" and join the battle for gay rights. The novel, however, is seen from his mother's point of view and primarily concerns her slow coming to terms with what her son is.

Gooney Bird Musgrave, a brilliant high-school boy in Al Hine's *Lord Love a Duck* (1961), comes from very ordinary middle-class and middle-American origins. But he early discovers he has abilities others lack and learns he does not fit easily into "their" world. He begins idealistically, desiring to control in order to rescue a few of those he cares about.

> As long as you had this comparatively tiny handful of objects to manipulate and command and move about the board, you could go on playing the rest of the game their way, because they'd never guess you had your own game going too, and your game contained the most important pieces. . . .
> If he could figure out where he wanted, what he wanted. . . .
> If anything was really important.
> You could play their game so much better than they could, and emerge with the inevitable and necessary money and then what?
> Build a huge castle somewhere surrounded by moats of biting fatal acid, and live there and think there with the handful of people you wanted to save. [italics in novel]

The ability to manipulate and control others is corrupting, and before very long, he is attempting to murder one of those he had earlier hoped to save. His other primary subject escapes his control, and thus he is defeated. The novel is basically comic and satiric, but at the same time it gives, in Gooney Bird, an interesting study in unbalanced genius.

Jeff (*Consenting Adult*) feels, for years, that society is against him and all those like him; social institutions generally are his enemy. Only after a long battle with himself is he able to find strength to work to change those social institutions, and this resolution occurs well into his adult years. Hobson thus suggests that for such a young man, the very special pressures put on him by a disapproving society may delay true acceptance of self and thus real maturation long past the end of adolescence. Gooney Bird (*Lord Love a Duck*), on the other hand, early gains a sense of power from his awareness of his specialness. He learns quickly how to bend social institutions and manipulate people to his own purposes. For him, there seems no hope that maturation will ever occur.

A final and profound lesson is learned by two boys in Ray Bradbury's poetic *Something Wicked This Way Comes* (1962). Bradbury describes two boys, Jim Nightshade and Will Halloway, as they confront evil, represented by a magical, seductive carnival which promises immortality at the cost of alienation from all social institutions, even from humanity itself. A contemporary treatment of the themes of the Faust and Wandering Jew legends, the novel depicts real boys whose love of life and adventure is joyously re-created; it takes them from initial glee in the unexpected arrival of the carnival, through growing terror as they gradually discover its supernatural characteristics, to their final escape from its enticements, aided by Will's father, their mentor. The novel works surprisingly well on a number of levels: as portraits of lively boys, as allegory, as fantasy, and as suspense story. The boys' growth in awareness, as they learn of time, death, and good and evil, is sensitively shown.

The conflict between appearance and reality, a universal theme in literature, is pervasive in the novels studied in this chapter. Social institutions and the methods used to train young males to work within those institutions—even the devices used by the young males themselves as they try to fit themselves for places within those institutions—often overtly present one set of beliefs and behaviors as desirable, although the reality is that another set actually works. Or, an ethos and way of life that claims to be solidly based in worthwhile values may in truth be basically destructive. Young men, no less than young women, must perceive these contradictions and struggle to their own resolutions in order to achieve maturity. Some, like Jesse Watersmith (*The Redneck Poacher's Son*) manage to do this against great odds. Others fail, like the campers in *The War of Camp Omongo*, because they believe and internalize the false values they are taught. Still others, more fortunate, are presented with sound, working institutions or manage to find mentors or friends who help them to make something of themselves (Zebul, in *Entering Ephesus*, for example, or Seth Adler, in *Members of the Tribe*). For some, like the boy in *Sounder*, a relationship with a pet may be the tie that connects him to something outside himself and thus ultimately makes possible his participation in human society.

The picture of society that emerges from these novels is not pleasant—economic and class structure, educational and religious institutions, competitiveness ingrained through sports and games, are all presented as inherently shallow or potentially destructive. But there are mitigating factors, and many young men manage to learn from their experiences in these areas and to emerge stronger and wiser into a promising adulthood.

CHAPTER XIII
Male Response to Settings

In many novels of male adolescence, the settings—in either time or place—come to be as important as other characters affecting the development of the young males. These settings vary widely, of course, in the sort of effect they have on the youths. Given the socially conditioned greater passivity of women than men in our society, it is not surprising that the settings of novels of male adolescence seem to place greater emphasis on violence within the setting or in the young person's response to that setting. Thus, novels that relate the urban environment to boys tend to depict a greater amount of violence and to show the boys actually participating in that violence or crime. While they may be victims, they are less often shown as passively accepting what comes to them than young women are. In general, then, these novels tend to support the generalization that males in our society have an active interaction with their environment, unlike females, who tend to be acted upon rather than acting.

But this does not imply that any particular setting can make a boy's adolescent years easy. Each kind of place and time presents its own problems—the material problems of the city, for example, or the physical work of the West—each in some way presents challenges to the boy trying to learn who he is and who he wants to be.

Although the picture of urban life which emerges from our subject-novels is pervasively negative and depressing, some ameliorating forces or conditions do arise. Some boys find support through family members or through the culture of their particular ethnic group. These moderating forces are not often strong enough to counterbalance the effects of the surrounding poverty and degradation, but some boys do manage to escape.

For example, life in the New Orleans black ghetto is colorfully depicted in early portions of Ann Fairbairn's *Five Smooth Stones* (1966). Young David Champlin, brought up by his loving grandfather, sees much of poverty and suffering and early learns to fear and distrust the few whites he meets. But his black community is warmly supportive, and its music becomes an important part of his life. Though he is able to escape the ghetto, its influence on his life is pervasive and leads to his eventual dedication to the cause of his people.

Also seen in complex fashion, with essential nostalgia for the boyhood which had been painful in many ways, is the Brooklyn of Gerald

Green's *To Brooklyn with Love* (1967). This novel reminds us that the testing of youth, torturous as it may have seemed at the time, may later come to seem valuable and even beautiful to the adult, if only because it was the testing that helped the young person find who he was and prove his worth. Here it is the tension between the urban chaos and the stubborn strength of the older generation's imported culture that both creates the test and helps him to survive it. When Albert Abrams takes his children to see his boyhood home in the Brownsville section of Brooklyn, he relives in memory the day during his twelfth year when he begins to achieve acceptance among the tough street kids of the Depression. The boys' games are reported in detail, as is the violence (between races, between gangs, within gangs, within families) of Albert's beloved street, Longview Avenue, a symbolic battleground and testing place of Albert's slowly emerging manhood.

> For Albert this was his last look at the street—*his* street—before bed. It was dreadful—yet he loved it. He loved it simply because it was there, there to torture him, challenge him, embarrass him, entertain him, arouse him, offer him the hot meat of life. Dirty, crowded, noisy, the horrid arena where he would always be Four-eyes, Sister Mary, The Doctor's Son, he loved it nonetheless.

To Brooklyn with Love is a tribute to the vanished era of European-immigrant parents and children struggling with a bewildering culture and a damaging economic period.

Also balancing a special ethnic culture against the evils of urban life is Bryant Rollins's 1967 novel *Danger Song* with its vivid, compelling portrait of the Roxbury section of 1960s Boston. For young Martin Williams, the neighborhood is both solace and danger. On his home streets, he is excited and nourished by the vigorous, exciting black life which surrounds him. He understands the rules of the streets and of his gang, the Pythons. At the same time, Roxbury constantly exposes him to danger, particularly when he walks into another gang's territory or when war breaks out between two teen factions. A further problem is, of course, Martin's impulse, stimulated by his family and by his own abilities, to get out of Roxbury and operate effectively in other, white, areas of the city. To be able to do so would mean wider social acceptance, freedom to use his intellect and his skills. Both many of his fellow blacks and many whites exert terrible pressure to keep Martin Roxbury-bound. The neighborhood, which almost becomes a character in this strong novel, is an excellent symbol of the systematic strangulation of one segment of American society by another.

Occasionally it is the resilience and good nature of the young person which help him to see his city as a basically good place, despite his observations of the meaner side of urban life. New York City, from Rockefeller Center, the United Nations, and the Plaza Hotel to Spanish

Harlem, is depicted in *You Can't Get There from Here* (1965) by Earl Hamner, Jr., in which a sixteen-year-old boy, Wes Scott, spends one day roaming the city, which he knows intimately, searching for his father. Poverty and the threat of danger are shown, but it is largely a good-natured city as Wes knows it; he helps people and animals along his way and generally finds friendliness in return.

Most depictions of adolescence in the city are more unrelievedly negative. Crime, pimping and prostitution, gang warfare, poverty, danger both physical and psychic—these surround the boy unfortunate enough to be forced to grow up in the city. The temptations and threats presented by these forces make particularly difficult the process of undergoing any sort of valid apprenticeship, and they force the boy to confront deep questions about the worth of human life when, by his observation, it seems so cheap. Physical sensation and worldly power are often the promises, while the reality is a narrow, grim, meaningless round of activity—and the contrast between promise and reality sometimes inspires desperate action. New York is the quintessential representation of all these aspects of the modern urban world, as shown by a number of novels.

For Archie Larsen, New York City is a brutal and destructive place where he is a potential victim. Jack Coutter dramatizes Archie's attitude in *The Concrete Wilderness* (1967) when the boy takes refuge from a gang attack in a passing car.

> Twenty fists were beating at the windows, a chain crashed against the windshield, shattering the glass in crazy patterns. The car was rocking. They were yelling, wild hoodlums. A girl's profanity shrilled amid the hoots and laughter. Hands, fists, beating the metal and glass; the din, the wild motion, everything was crazy.

Expelled from the car, the boy is saved by a wild dog he has befriended, and the experience confirms his hatred of the city, his love of the natural wilderness.

The lives of poor immigrants and second-rate artists in New York City are depicted in L. J. Davis's *Whence All But He Had Fled* (1968). The central character, Robert Probish, is a lost soul among other lost souls; he feels animosity for almost everyone he meets—Ukrainians, Puerto Ricans, his Jewish landlord, the girl he sleeps with, homosexuals, and other aspiring artists. Drug trips and a grotesquely wild party are among the experiences he undergoes in the course of the novel. His world is a New York with the bleakness and despair of Gorky and the harsh comedy of Gogol; the imported cultures are not able to function in a redemptive way for him as they had for Albert Abrams (*To Brooklyn with Love*).

Yet despite the rigors of a New York boyhood, some boys do manage to survive. Brooklyn in the early 1950s is the setting for Kenneth H. Brown's *The Narrows* (1970). A large number of boys and girls who at-

tend various high schools, both public and parochial, and who are involved in various neighborhood groups or gangs move in and out of its
pages. They have progressively wilder parties, engage in sexual experimentation (unconsummated, however), and proceed to ever more serious forms of theft (from petty shoplifting to breaking and entering to
stealing liquor to car-theft). Their fathers, while disapproving, generally
manage to get them off in their few brushes with the law. For the boys,
enlistment in the Marine Corps becomes a sign of manhood and the indication they have successfully weathered their stormy and peculiarly
urban adolescence.

Although New York City is the most frequent symbol for modern
American urban life with all its pain and degradation, the same phenomena may affect other boys in other places. Arkie, a teenaged crook,
is the embodiment of the grimy underside of Braceboro, North Carolina,
in Fred Chappell's *The Gaudy Place* (1973). About fifteen, he's long been
on his own, conning "johns" for a living. But Arkie is ambitious, and he
is also attracted to Clemmie, a teenaged prostitute. Thus, in an effort to
rise in the power structure of Gimlet Street, the red-light district, he offers himself as Clemmie's new pimp. Her reactions trigger events that
culminate in a foolishly violent act as Arkie tries to prove his manhood
and his control of Clemmie. Through Arkie's adventures, author Chappell deftly dramatizes the habits and codes of this tough urban underworld.

One city boy, half real and half the creation of his novel's protagonist, epitomizes the complexities of the process of maturing, wherever
that maturation takes place. Here the author relates a grim city background to an almost archetypal presentation of adolescence as a universal process. *Montgomery Street* (1978) by Mark Dintenfass is a series of
"notes" by film maker Stephen Mandreg toward his next project, a combination of notebook on his conception, journal of his personal life, and
the practical steps taken toward production of the film. The movie is to
depict the squalid Brooklyn street on which he grew up, using one day
in 1960 and centering the action around two characters, Max, an adult
who recognizes the drabness of his life, and Stevie Feuer, who is partially based on Mandreg himself.

> I was attracted [he writes] to Stevie, age fourteen, because for an
> adolescent change comes willy-nilly. He can't go on being the
> child he was; he has to come to terms with his freedom. Which is
> why teen-agers tend to be such irritable lunatics. The crisis of
> being forced to change. Will Stevie merely ride it out or take it
> in hand, make himself new? Panic or possibility? . . . Stevie is
> plunged into the anxiety of freedom. How much courage does he
> have; how much courage can I give him?

As Mandreg's jottings continue, he comes to know both himself and
Stevie better; the narrative method serves Dintenfass well, and he cre-

ates characters, studies the creative process, and examines the impact of time and place on his characters.

Occasionally an orphan becomes a symbol for modern rootlessness and alienation. The setting for Sol Biderman's *Bring Me to the Banqueting House* (1969) is a Jewish orphanage in Denver. There we observe David Unicorn, a sensitive and imaginative boy, as he grows from the age of six to fifteen. His schooling, his experiments with petty theft, his self-consciousness about living in an orphanage and about being Jewish, his fascination with his maturing body, and his sexual initiation are all described in this collection of episodes from his life. In some he is protagonist while in others he is primarily an observer, but taken together they show his change from an ignorant child to a restless teenager with knowledge of life's cruelties.

Another youth lacking family and home is shown, after the orphanage experience, in *Hang-up* (1968) by Sam Ross. At seventeen, Dave Grant has been released from the Chicago orphanage which has been his "home" and has arrived in California to attempt to realize his dream of fame and success as a rock guitarist. On the Sunset Strip, Dave falls in with Scotty Bannister, a rootless, destructive, twenty-three-year-old who is the incarnation of life on the Strip. Like life on the Strip, Scotty's life is part nightmare, part realistic horror story, and Dave is innocently drawn into sharing it for a few terrible days. An innocent witness when Scotty murders a teenybopper, Dave is suspected of being the killer and works to protect another young girl who joins Scotty's followers. The Sunset Strip is the key symbol of teens' dislocation and disassociation in *Hang-up*, and Dave's retreat from the area indicates some slim hope for the young man.

The city, then, is largely shown in these novels as a destructive place. The sensitive youth may well be destroyed by its oppressive evil and cruelty, while the boy who strives to conform—a strong impulse during adolescence—may be led into crime and a life of violence. Some survive, through their own strength and intelligence, because of the support given by family or culture, or, perhaps, simply through luck.

Few comparable treatments of suburbia exist, despite the actual growth of wealthy communities surrounding our cities and the flight from the city to its environs. One such study is John Cheever's indictment of upper-middle-class suburbia, *Bullet Park* (1969). Tony Nailles is firmly separated from his desires by parents and teachers who intend to do well by him. Eventually, he retreats into total passivity: "I still feel terribly sad. I feel as if the house were made of cards. . . . This is a nice house and I like it, but I feel as if it were made of cards." When his malaise is cured by the mysterious incantation of a guru, Tony's life is threatened by a neighbor. This time, Tony is saved by his father's efforts, but because his story appears among several tales of empty adult lives depicted in *Bullet Park*, there is little hope of Tony's achieving happiness or even contentment.

Suburbia, then, is here shown as an empty, meaningless world, quite unlike the violent world of the city, but no more nurturing. An escape from the city or from suburbia to a resort or vacation area may give a young person the opportunity to gain perspective and objectivity on his ordinary life. It may also give him the chance for experiences quite different from what he is accustomed to—experiences, therefore, especially enriching to his maturation process. Thus the holiday may encompass moments of discovery that crystallize experience and promise continued growth and increasing awareness.

Harvey Jacobs's *Summer on a Mountain of Spices* (1975) is a comic depiction of a Jewish resort in the Catskills in August, 1945, with a large number of characters, prominent among whom is fifteen-year-old Harry Craft. It is an amusing novel, but lacks significant analysis of Harry's maturation process. Two other vacation novels, by Marjorie Lee (*The Eye of Summer*) and Robert Kotlowitz (*The Boardwalk*), give more attention to the process of introspection and growing self-understanding that are made possible by this time away from ordinary life.

Spence, one of two central characters in Marjorie Lee's *The Eye of Summer* (1961), spends his summers with his cousin Connie on an island where his family has a summer home. We see him during the summers when he is eight, sixteen, and nineteen. Though Connie, two years older than he, has usually been the ringleader in their escapades, both have seemed too old, too cynical for their years. It is he who finally realizes the ultimately destructive nature of their closeness. He tells her,

> We're like little kids, afraid of the dark, wanting a lamp left on in the hall. And that's just what we've done. That world out there that's supposed to be so big and all lit up? We've made it our hall, our tiny, narrow, two-peopled hall. Well, I'm sick of sitting inside, damning everyone and damning ourselves, hoarding our misery like two holy saints, and loving every minute of it. . . . Face it, Connie: the biggest thing we ever discovered in our whole lives was our own lostness. Without that we'd have ended up without an excuse!

The novel's symbolism sometimes seems too obvious, even clumsy, but it does bring alive Spence and Connie and their sometimes tormented, sometimes happy companionship.

Throughout a family vacation in Atlantic City during the summer of 1939, Teddy Lewin, of Robert Kotlowitz's *The Boardwalk* (1977), ponders himself, his family, and their friends, gradually discovering a deeper understanding of many of the relationships affecting him. Teddy has led a sheltered life in a comfortable, Jewish section of Baltimore, and he sometimes believes that he is ill prepared for independence. "He was soft, he was sensitive. His skin was as thin as a piece of mica peeled to its last layer. He was vulnerable to everything, without emotional discretion; hidden at the bottom of his soul lay a dusty mound of unhealed wounds. Soft. He hated the mere sound of the word." A gifted pianist, Teddy is being shunted into a career by "family consensus," and he determines that he will take control over his own future, "be what he decided to be." But the future is symbolized by the onset of World War II, and Teddy's resolve and the quiet, even tone of the book are sharply and ironically undercut by the danger and uncertainty that the war threatens.

As the adolescent male comes to understand himself and what he wants from life, he must also come to understand his world so he can see how he can fit into it—or whether, perhaps, he wishes instead to reject it. Small towns present special problems. Unlike the city, in which the violence and evil are palpable, or suburbia, which makes its bland sameness all too evident, or the vacation retreat, which is clearly only a momentary escape from reality (so that its idyllic appearance, whether deceptive or not, doesn't really matter, except as it creates distance from a boy's true reality elsewhere), the small town may present a sham surface whose actuality must be penetrated. The placid surface of village life, as so many fiction writers have shown us, may cover dishonesty disguised as probity, sensuality masked by religiosity, intolerance hidden by insular good humor, ignorance covered over by pretenses to culture. To a youngster struggling with self-definition, the need to define also his home and understand some new truth about his people can be an especially difficult burden. Ironically, often just as a boy is beginning to learn the truth about himself, he must face the fact that what he thought the truth about his community is a lie.

Two novels set in New England make clear both the hypocrisy of the small town and its potentially damaging effects on adolescent males. The boys of Leah, New Hampshire, in 1942 and thereafter, are depicted by Thomas Williams in *Whipple's Castle* (1968) in a far from flattering way. The novel centers around the children of the Whipple family, who are sensitive, but other young men are predatory beings, particularly in their callous sexuality. The young men in general are either victims, of themselves or of the society, or victimizers.

As Sagamore, Connecticut, the setting for Edwin Lanham's *Speak Not Evil* (1964), prepares for its tercentenary celebration, a number of crises occur in the lives of its citizens, among them several young men. One is Earl Dexter, only slightly beyond his adolescence, who has just come to Sagamore in search of his father; another is Billy Brownlow, who is shocked to see beneath the placid surface of small-town life into a world of perverse sexuality; and a third is Theo Littleton, a carpenter's son who is sorely tempted by the discovery of a cache of old coins. All three young men learn much about the town and themselves during this pivotal summer, and all three are strengthened by their experiences. At the end of the novel, the town itself seems cleansed of much of its hidden hypocrisy and guilt, partly by an airplane crash that causes the death of a woman responsible for sex orgies, partly by an apocalyptic hurricane, which symbolically coincides with the long-planned celebration, but most importantly by the revelation of various sorts of truths which had previously been hidden.

Several novels of southern villages recount troubled adolescences which are ultimately successful, though here, too, reality and appearance are sometimes very different. A hamlet called Bugscuffle Bottoms, in an unnamed southern state in 1932, is the locale for Borden Deal's *The Least One* (1967). The village consists of seven houses, two privies, an artesian well, and the home of "Senator" Clayton, who owns it all. The novel clearly evokes time and place, re-creating the struggles of the family against both natural environment and economic system; these forces help to shape young Boy Sword and hasten him to an early maturity.

Another picture of small-town southern life, this time in 1915, is given by Manly Wade Wellman in *Not at These Hands* (1962). At nineteen, George Cobbett leaves his widowed mother on her tenant farm and goes to town to become a newspaperman. His benefactor, a powerful local figure and the owner of the farm, introduces him to the life of Portici, North Carolina, where he soon becomes both an observer and a participant in the social, religious, and political affairs of the community. His mistake is falling in love with his benefactor's daughter. The climax of the novel is George's trial and acquittal for his benefactor's murder. The novel is suspenseful, and George is likable. His idealism and naiveté are dispelled by his experiences, but he remains throughout an honorable young man.

Lighter in tone is an examination of a midwestern boyhood in Guy Daniels's *Progress, U.S.A.* (1968). The tension between appearance and reality appears here in comic form, in a kindly satire of the small town of Progress, Iowa, in the early 1930s. Timothy Abbot, the central character, is a lively, inventive, and mischievous boy, and his town is a less venal, humorously presented version of Sinclair Lewis's Gopher Prairie. This very funny book successfully pokes fun at an all-too-recognizable village and its inhabitants' foibles, even while making its characters, especially young Tim, believable and likable.

Entirely loving in its treatment of a rural upbringing is *Spencer's Mountain* (1961) by Earl Hamner, Jr., which exemplifies the need of the maturing adolescent to destroy that which has been most valuable to him in order to free himself from it. A dream of education, of moving into the great world, far from an isolated rural backwater, may also mean leaving behind a truly nurturing family and community. Thus entry into an urban world, desirable because of opportunities it offers, requires rejection of the place and people that had shaped the boy who now is capable of leaving them. And thus the treatment of a mythic boyhood may be nostalgic, loving, even regretful—and the farm world itself may come to seem a lost Shangri-La, to which the adult, having left, nevertheless would not choose to return. A rural, mountainous area in Virginia, home of sturdy, uneducated poor people, is the setting for *Spencer's Mountain*. The only industry is a soapstone quarry, and subsistence also depends on hunting and wresting what they can from the land. When Clay-Boy Spencer, eldest of a large family, finishes high school with the highest marks ever achieved there, his teacher suggests the possibility of a scholarship to college. No one in the family except Clay-Boy has a remote idea of what college is all about, but they are eager for him to have his chance at a better life, no matter what sacrifices may be required. Clay-Boy's desire is for the education for its own sake as well as for the opportunities it will offer him. When his scholarship application is denied, his disappointment is profound:

> The world had become for him a party he would never attend. Somewhere boys with not half the heart and mind and craving to learn and to do something with that learning would be accepted by colleges and they would accept it as their due. For Clay-Boy a window had been briefly opened into a world he had only dared to dream of and all he could see at that moment was that the window had been slammed shut in his face and would never open again.

The novel, episodic in structure, begins with Clay-Boy's first deer hunt and his lucky killing of a white deer which is taken as an omen that he is somehow marked as special and ends with his setting off for college, the city, and "the beckoning world." The loving relationships of the large family, their intimate relationships with the land, and their confidence in traditional moral values are both realistically and nostalgically depicted, even as the novel, by implication, shows the beginnings of the destruction of that way of life.

As for Clay-Boy, so for two other boys, a relationship with nature, specifically with a wilderness, becomes crucial. Both Brad Nichols (*Home Is the North*) and Tim Hood (*Cold River*) find in nature a crucible that tests their ingenuity and courage and teaches them survival. For Brad, the wilderness is home, but for Tim, an arena he had not really intended to enter. Still, for both, the experience is an enriching one, and each boy learns and grows a great deal as a result of his danger and pain.

Brad Nichols, of Walt Morey's *Home Is the North* (1967, YA), loves Alaska, his home territory, and refuses to consider the possibility that some years spent in Seattle might prove fruitful. A series of physical trials stemming naturally from the dangers of the Alaskan wilderness dramatize the boy's growing maturity and help to prepare him for the most important decision of his boyhood. Morey's fine unification of setting and motivation is one of the strongest qualities of *Home Is the North*.

In *Cold River* (1974) by William Judson, Tim Hood, thirteen, is taken by his stepfather and stepsister on an Adirondacks camping trip that turns tragic. A series of miscalculations and accidents leads to their being lost, and Mr. Allison's death leaves the children with only their own skills and ingenuity to rely on. Tim, a year younger than Lizzie, is less confident and less knowing, but under her guidance and with her encouragement, he gradually takes more and more responsibility and becomes better able to act on his own initiative. The novel is narrated, many years later, by Lizzie, who still takes pride in the closeness the two developed and in the rapid maturation which Tim underwent.

Distinguished from the previously discussed novels, which stress a particular type of environment, are those which describe a geographical area. The South and the West have been especially stimulating, perhaps because those regions have both had special literary traditions as well as very particular natural and social peculiarities (landscapes, customs, mixtures of peoples, historical events and forces) that impinge upon character and help to create recognizably different personality types. For authors studying young males at the moments in their lives when they are deciding who they are, these regional characteristics give special opportunities. For novels stressing the local color of the South, William Faulkner is paradigmatic; it is no accident that a number of these books echo or allude to his work.

The tobacco country of North Carolina in 1916 is the setting for Burke Davis's *The Summer Land* (1965, YA), a comic and episodic novel centering on the experiences of young Fax Starling, its fifteen-year-old narrator. He tells of coon hunts, of loading watermelons with corn liquor, and of horse trading (his older brother could trade on equal terms with Faulkner's Flem Snopes). A bookish boy who loves school and is small in stature compared to the rest of his family, he learns to fight but retains his basic sensitivity and good nature. The novel is vividly written, and Davis makes effective use of the imaginative language of his simple farmers.

Vinnie Williams's *Greenbones* (1967) begins in 1912, in rural Georgia, and follows Nin Rabun, its protagonist, through 1920. This picaresque novel describes the dirty roads, the small towns, the often ignorant and sometimes violent people Nin meets, first as he and his mother travel about preaching and huckstering, and then as Nin alone tries to establish a life free of his domineering parent. The language of the people and their vigor as well as Nin's own persistence and courage are conveyed by the novel's vital prose and vigorous dialogue.

William Price Fox's story of one southern summer, *Moonshine Light, Moonshine Bright* (1967), is ostensibly set in Columbia, South Carolina, and some scenes, particularly those early in the novel, are clearly urban, but the flavor of the book often seems rural. The novel follows the activities of two fourteen-year-old boys and depicts the cafés and hangouts they frequent, the hillbilly music they hear, and the people they meet—card sharks, bootleggers, petty criminals, short-order cooks, faith healers, and the like. Their main concerns are cars and building their bodies so they can go out for football, and their world seems a southern backwater.

Hortense Calisher's *False Entry* (1961) is more serious in tone. As a boy of fourteen, Pierre Goodman observes a deadly Ku Klux Klan foray. He is accompanied by his seventeen-year-old friend, Johnny Fortuna, who serves as the Klan's errand boy. The two read the Klan's rule book and the list of members; all of that material as well as Johnny's account of his duties remains extraordinarily clear in Pierre's memory, perhaps because on that night he sees behind the pleasant façade of his small Alabama town. Seven years later, in an episode that closes his adolescence, serving justice if not truth, Pierre testifies in a grand jury investigation of Klan activities. He not only tells what he knows, but also presents Johnny's account as if it were his own to incriminate the Klansmen. His testimony has tragic results which indicate that the town's violence and racism are not easily terminated.

A more favorable picture of southern boyhood is given by Terry Kay. Rural Georgia immediately after World War II is the beautifully realized setting of *The Year the Lights Came On* (1976). Kay's descriptions of the area, particularly the Big Gully and Black Pool Swamp, are detailed and vivid, but even more important is his evocation of southern attitudes:

> We did not question our father. . . . We had been taught to honor the adult privilege of silence. Be patient, we were told; be patient and you'll know soon enough. I think I understood even then that patience was the gift of the Southerner. If anything made a Southerner different, it was patience, and an instinct for the Right Time.

Clearly, in the judgment of its author, the novel describes children growing into adulthood shaped and defined by their sense of place.

While depictions of southern adolescence tend to emphasize a rural folk-culture, violent black-white racial relations, and a slow-paced, leisurely life, treatments of the West often emphasize the majestic grandeur of nature along with a complicated mix of ethnic relationships. One idealized view of a youth who is taught by nature and his few human associates to become a fine adult is set in the past. Young Tobin Shattuck, the narrator of Will Bryant's *The Big Lonesome* (1971), roams the Northwest of the 1860s in search of gold. His love of the land and its animals is stressed by the putative editor of his journals, who speaks of his "deep, indeed almost mystic, sense of identity with the land and with the elements and with the animals, wild or not, that ranged the country." Sometimes poetic, heavily symbolic, the novel is an exciting tale of a boy, his father, their Indian friends, and a bear cub. As a result of his experiences, Tobin becomes a responsible and loving man.

Set primarily in Colorado through the 1910s and 1920s, Hal Borland's *When the Legends Die* (1963) tells of the death of Indian culture through the experiences of one boy. It is a wrenching story of a Ute caught between the old ways of his people, which he is no longer able to follow after his parents die, and the ways of the whites, which he adopts with a desperate fury when his "brother"—a grizzly bear cub and all he has left from his former life—is taken from him. His changes of name reveal his progress: from "the boy"; to Bear's Brother, as he grows in Indian knowledge; to Thomas Black Bull, the baptismal name foisted on him at the reservation school; to Tom Black (nicknamed "Killer Tom" and "Devil Tom"), as a successful and brutal bronco rider. Only as a mature man, after almost dying and then returning to the area of his childhood and early youth, does he discover who he truly is and accept the name of Tom Black Bull. Occasionally sentimental, but often painful to read, especially in the sections dealing with his parents and his reservation days, the novel is both a sympathetic study in ethnic acculturation and an indictment of the American treatment of the Indian.

Rural New Mexico is the setting for Richard Bradford's depiction of the maturation of seventeen-year-old Joshua Arnold in *Red Sky at Morning* (1968). Transplanted from his native Alabama to New Mexico, this son of a Mobile shipbuilder and a shallow, socially prominent mother must learn to understand a very different society. His new friend Steenie, explaining the caste system, tells him, "We only recognize three kinds of people in Sagrado: Anglos, Indians and Natives. You keep your categories straight and you'll make out all right." In this neat classification, a black becomes an Anglo.

> That is, he's an Anglo unless you're differentiating between him and an Indian. Then he's "white." I admit he's awfully dark to be white, but that's the way it goes around here. You have to learn our little customs and folkways, or it's your ass. And if you've got any Texas blood in you, you'd better take "spik" and "greaser" out of your vocabulary. If there's a minority group at all around here, it's the Anglos.

Blessed by a sense of humor, Joshua is able to relate well to members of various groups—Spanish-speaking servants, an eccentric sculptor, and his Anglo and Hispanic schoolmates. Native ceremonies that mix pagan and Christian elements, the pride of the Hispanic "natives" in their old culture, the sexual activities and the pranks of healthy adolescents—all become part of his experience in this pivotal year, and all are related half comically and half tenderly by Joshua himself.

The effects of past times on young males are studied in a number of other novels. Some of these novels specifically relate their action to particular historical events, while others try primarily to convey the texture of their particular time and place. For this latter type, the power of social conventions and institutions in forming a young man, for good or for evil, is what is stressed. For example, a small North Carolina town, around the turn of the century, is the setting for Doris Betts's *The Scarlet*

Thread (1964). Thomas Allen, the middle of three children of a shop-keeper, learns of sex from the daughter of a poor mill worker and of violence through observing Ku Klux Klan activities. His father hopes he will become a lawyer, and at fifteen he is sent away to the university. Too immature and poorly prepared to handle the work, he returns home in defeat. Of the three children, he becomes the most apparently successful and well adjusted, but his marriage is a sham, his sexual relations with his wife being a series of rapes. Through Thomas Allen's experiences, Betts dramatizes the harrowing and even brutalizing effects of what was a seemingly normal southern small-town boyhood.

A favored theme, much more prominent in novels of male than female adolescence, is that of war. Females tend to be shown adapting to new situations, while males test their physical courage in battle. One seminal time of conflict is the Revolutionary War. In two novels Howard Fast looks at that war from different perspectives, stressing in both, however, the waste and cruelty of war.

In one study of hatred and war, *The Hessian* (1972), Howard Fast uses Hans Pohl, a sixteen-year-old Hessian drummer boy involved in the American Revolutionary War, as his central device. Hans is the only survivor of a massacre perpetrated by Connecticut patriots; he makes his escape and is aided by a Quaker family and by the embittered doctor who narrates the short novel. After his capture, he is tried and condemned to death. Never characterized as fully as the Americans whose lives he touches, he remains mostly symbol. But through him Fast poignantly depicts the cruel waste of war.

Fast's *April Morning* (1961, YA), set in Massachusetts in 1775, describes the day and a half in which fifteen-year-old Adam Cooper comes to manhood. Hastily mustered into the militia, whose members intend only to talk sense to the Redcoats, he is horrified to see his father and others brutally killed. Shock and terror give way to resolve, however, and he determines to defend his "home place," having "said farewell to a childhood, a world, a secure and sun-warmed existence and past that was over and done with and gone away for all time." Graphically realistic in its battle scenes, *April Morning* effectively conveys Adam—as boy and as man—as well as the experiences that change him.

Another "Red Badge of Courage" story set during the Revolutionary War is James Forman's *The Cow Neck Rebels* (1969, YA). Here sixteen-year-old Bruce Cameron is caught up in the fighting, between rebels on the one side and Tories and Hessians on the other, that occurs around his Long Island home. The brutality and suffering of battle, the blind hatreds caused by political enmities, the change of Bruce and other young people from thoughtless youth to haunted maturity, are all effectively depicted in this novel, which seems indebted to Howard Fast's *April Morning*, but is more complex in both plotting and theme.

Another group of historical novels shows a special indebtedness to

Mark Twain. Boys with Huckleberry Finn's blend of naiveté and worldly wisdom are shown in the West, meeting and surmounting varied obstacles, learning of corruption in this world, and trying always to find a better place. If Huck had set out "for the Territory," accompanied by a young woman who was in love with him instead of by a former slave, the result might have been something like David Wagoner's *The Road to Many a Wonder* (1974). In 1859, young Ike Bender runs away from his Nebraska home to search for gold in Colorado, where an older brother had preceded him. Milly Slaughter follows him and persuades him to marry her. Together the young people face many adventures along the trail, indomitably and with good humor always managing to come through. The novel gives a grittily realistic picture of life on the trail and of the varied sorts of people, often disreputable or threatening, that inhabit it. Its comic tone, controlled by Ike's sometimes naive but always practical narration, like its depiction of innocent, basically virtuous male adolescence meeting a corrupt world, keep it squarely in the Twain tradition.

Another comic treatment of the West by David Wagoner is *Where Is My Wandering Boy Tonight?* (1970). Set primarily in a small town in Wyoming in the 1890s, it depicts the pranks and adventures of two boys, Andrew Jackson Holcomb, Jr., son of the local judge, and Fred Haskell, a minister's son. The two high-spirited boys (especially Jackson, the protagonist and narrator) have, from the beginning, a relatively clear view of the corruption and hypocrisy of their world, but through such adventures as invading a brothel, they learn more about the depth of that corruption (Jackson discovers his father in the brothel with a naked prostitute on his lap). Cowboy life is also depicted, as the two boys, who do not even know how to ride horseback, try to take up that trade. Witty, often epigrammatic in style, the novel, like much of Wagoner's work, shows the clear influence of *Huckleberry Finn* in style, characterization, and theme.

Despite the fact that the Wagoner novels clearly show the violence and cruelty of the West, they represent primarily the lighter, comic side of the Twain tradition. A novel by Milton Bass reminds us of the darker side. The violence and squalor of the Old West are vividly depicted in *Jory* (1969). The title character, fourteen when the novel opens, witnesses his drunken father's death (kicked brutally in a saloon) and, in his own first act of violence, takes vengeance. Subsequently, on the trail from Kansas to Texas, he learns to handle guns and achieves a reputation as a killer, though vomiting and nightmares reveal his pain and guilt. He becomes involved in a Texas ranch war; as a result of these experiences, he asks himself, "Why did I have to go around killing people? It was carrying the guns that did it. If you didn't have a gun, you figured out some other way of doing things." He passes up the opportunity to settle down; like another Huckleberry Finn, he determines to go further west. His sexual initiation is a subordinate theme in this realistic portrayal of a boy's attempts to retain his humanity through brutalizing experiences. His understated narration conveys well his confusion, his frequent lack of full understanding, and his revulsion at much that he observes and does.

These three novels display the strong influence of *Huckleberry Finn*, its importance in defining the nature of much of American tradition and culture as well as its power in describing American male adolescence. The adolescent, in a time of flux in his own life, is particularly vulnerable to the strains and contradictions of the society he confronts. Like Huck, he observes society and tries to understand what he sees. The choices he makes regarding his society and his place in it are both crucial decisions for his own life and comments on the nature of his society.

Another method of combining adolescence with social comment is found in science fiction. Several writers have used the device of setting the adventures of their adolescent protagonists in a future that carries to their potential conclusions certain tendencies of our own day. Ben Bova's *City of Darkness* (1976, YA), set in the mid-1970s, examines possible consequences of certain social trends of the period. It takes sixteen-year-old Ron Morgan (an aspiring astronomer who rebels against his father's insistence that he pursue a business career) to New York City. There Ron finds a nightmare, a city abandoned by the prosperous, technically advanced world outside. Joining a gang, Ron experiences the easy sex and violence that make up this world. He comes to love these young people, and he realizes that people Outside are no less slaves to their governmentally orchestrated lives than are his new friends to their brutalizing environment and the struggle to stay alive. Bova uses Ron's dedication to his new cause as proof of his maturation, but the novel is simplistic in its social analysis, perhaps because it is intended for young adult readers. Ron resolves, "I'm going back Outside to change them. They know the City exists. They know the kids are in here, in this jungle, turning into animals. They know it, but they ignore it. So I'm going to change them. I'm going to rub their noses in the filth they've left behind them."

Author Nancy Bond uses a similar device in *The Voyage Begun* (1981, YA). In a bleak twenty-first-century world in which the environment has been disastrously altered, sixteen-year-old Paul Vickers moves to Cape Cod with his scientist father and conventional mother. He soon finds friends among the local people, whom his parents scorn, and comes to know well the now half-deserted area. His parents, especially his mother, represent yearnings for an easy but vanished past, while his new friends have made varied accommodations to the present in which they must live. Scavengers loot decaying areas, causing further destruction and loss of life. Paul becomes involved with a woman conservationist, her artist friend, an old man (once a shipbuilder, but relegated to a nursing home when his home on the docks is burned by scavengers), and a girl of eleven who is trying to help the old man. Through these relationships and his efforts to work with the proud and sensitive girl, Paul finds purpose in his life and achieves maturity. Bond's novel gives a grim picture of what our world could become as a result of thoughtless and unprincipled attempts at finding new sources of energy.

The power of environment is great, and the responses to the many American environments portrayed in our novels are multifarious. The picture is largely a grim one, however. Whether the writers of recent novels featuring male adolescents are concerned to depict a particular sort of environment (city, country, etc.), a region of the country, or a particular time, they are pessimistic more often than not. There are exceptions, of course, and some of the young men are nurtured and strengthened by their surroundings. Clay-Boy in *Spencer's Mountain* by Earl Hamner, Jr., and, though in more complex fashion, Albert of *To Brooklyn with Love* by Gerald Green exemplify boys who find much in their home places that is of value to them and to what they become. Many more youngsters, however, find their periods of adolescence to be painful and their introductions to the great world to be disillusioning. And for many, the result is either a lack of true maturation or a maturation achieved despite, not because of, their surroundings.

CHAPTER XIV
Males and Fate

Just as for a female adolescent, illness, disability, or death may present extreme challenges in an already difficult period of life, so also a male youngster may find himself severely troubled by physical or mental afflictions. Already vulnerable because of his need to define himself and to learn how he will relate to his society, even while he is struggling to free himself from past dependencies, he may find his own illness, mental or physical, an added burden almost too much to bear, a cruel stratagem of a heedless destiny. If illness suggests to him his own mortality, then the death, threatened or actual, of some loved one may absolutely shake his world and his sense of having any secure place in it. The threat of his own death may, of course, be even more crippling.

Our subject-authors repeatedly suggest that for adolescent males with the goal of acquiring social power and control as well as personal autonomy, the realization that no human being, not even the most capable, self-assured adult male, is truly autonomous or immune to fate can be cataclysmic. Learning to live bravely and fully in the face of this awareness is, of course, a crucial test imposed upon a good many boys. When this test becomes their major challenge (not a confrontation with illness, madness, or death as part of familial dissolution, for instance, but as an individual and solitary personal test), some youngsters are pushed to the limits of their abilities to cope, adjust, or merely endure. Those who do master these hard lessons, our authors suggest, achieve true manhood in the best sense of the term. They do not remain lost in a haze of confusion, anger, or despair.

One significant difference between recent treatments of female and male adolescents emerges: depictions of young women suffering psychosomatic illnesses are relatively common, while this theme is lacking in reference to males. Male adolescent characters suffer mental and emotional illness no less than females, but those illnesses do not affect their physical well-being. It is tempting here to speculate on the reasons for this difference: we may remind ourselves that the word *hysteria* comes from the Greek root signifying *womb*, thus implying that women are innately less able to control their emotions and more apt to incur emotional disabilities which will then interfere with their physical condition. For a male to suffer a psychosomatic illness would be an admission of weakness, more damaging, perhaps, than either a purely mental or purely physical ailment. When a male is ill, he is truly ill, either in mind or body, not suffering from a weakness that is merely neurotic, not truly organic or psychotic. Or so, at least, our society has tacitly assumed, and this contrast in treatments of female and male adolescents seems to reinforce that assumption.

Some treatments of adolescent males suffering from mental illness show the illness to be the result of various sorts of social or individual influences and others study the mental illness as a phenomenon in its own right. David W. Elliott (*Listen to the Silence*) and Don Carpenter (*Blade of Light*) study the causes of mental impairments of two pathetic and helpless youngsters, both deeply injured by a society that has no place for them.

Early in Elliott's *Listen to the Silence* (1969), the protagonist, Timmy, observes: "Time doesn't heal. It opens old wounds and starts new ones. Each one [person who has left him] took a hand, a foot or a piece of one year and forgot to give it back. The real hard thing is they never say good-bye, not ever; they just go." This comment, the result of years of shunting among foster homes, is also the theme for Timmy's confinement in the mental hospital where he is now housed. Elliott uses Timmy's first-person narrative to record the abandonment, brutalization, and sexual exploitation to which the boy is subjected. For Timmy, maturation means accommodation to a nightmare "reality" and perhaps a descent into madness disguised as sanity, for while Timmy's tone is detached and reportorial, the book's impact is bitter and ironic.

In long flashbacks, Don Carpenter, author of *Blade of Light* (1968), depicts Irwin Semple's appallingly isolated life as a despised, impaired, and unwanted illegitimate boy surrounded by a callous, alcoholic family. Scorned by his schoolmates, the butt of cruel pranks, and the despair of his teachers, the lonely boy persistently seeks the company of Harold Hunt, a young tough who exploits Semple to feed his own ego. When Semple becomes the tool for the humiliation of Harold's angry girlfriend, dreadful events are set in motion, and the result is Semple's eighteen-year incarceration in an asylum. *Blade of Light* dramatizes Semple's transformation from an ugly, simple, but hopeful youngster, who constantly relishes "the possibility that something would happen tonight, something exciting," into a man for whom we can expect nothing positive.

Other novels analyze youngsters already in the grip of mental illness. This device has been a frequent motif in suspense novels, for the character who is mentally unsound can easily be made to seem a danger to others. The threat of the irrational, contrasted to what seems healthily normal, can be used to create terror and suspense in the reader. One chilling suspense novel, dealing with the psychopathic thirteen-year-old Robert Reagan, his likable tool and classmate Stu Parker, his doting mother, and the stepfather he bitterly hates, is Fielden Farrington's *A Little Game* (1968).

Sandra Scoppettone's *Such Nice People* (1980) is a portrait of a seemingly ordinary adolescent boy who is speeding toward disaster. Tom Nash, the protagonist, while still capable of maintaining some semblance of normalcy, is actually deeply and dangerously in the grip of religious mania. Tom sees manifestations of SOLUDA, a group of extraordinary, godlike beings who speak to him, primarily through the voice of SOLA, whose every strand of purple hair becomes a "deadly poisonous snake" during Tom's visions. SOLA's most compelling comment, "AS LONG AS THEY LIVE, YOU WILL BE IMPURE," leads Tom to plan the mass murder of his family, an event scheduled for the Christmas season. Sandra Scoppettone often writes of adolescents' sexual problems, and dramatizations of Tom's "worship" make clear that his sense of corruption arises not only from his disappointment in his parents' standards, but, perhaps even more significantly, from his profound distrust of his own sexuality. Only his peculiar and tormenting faith keeps the lad from complete despair, and, ironically, his efforts to "save" himself destroy his family.

Unlike Scoppettone, who studies psychosis as it leads to disaster, Judith Guest (*Ordinary People*) examines a young man on his way back from insanity. Like many treatments of mental instability in young women (Joanne Greenberg's *I Never Promised You a Rose Garden*, for example, or John Neufeld's *Lisa, Bright and Dark*), Guest stresses the importance of supporting and nurturing others in the process from mental illness back to health.

Guest introduces Conrad Jarrett, protagonist of *Ordinary People* (1976), shortly after his release from a mental institution. Once suicidal, Con has made good progress toward health, but still feels full of guilt and instability. "Everywhere he looks there is competence and good health. Only he, Conrad Jarrett, outcast, quitter, *fuck-up*, stands outside the circle of safety, separated from everyone by this aching void of loneliness; but no matter, he deserves it." Con's slow further progress, aided by Berger, his psychiatrist; Cal, his father; and Jeannine Pratt, his friend, forms the main action of a plot that realistically explores the difficulty of assuming healthy personal responsibility in a complex and often inexplicable world.

A character study of a youngster who is *not* mentally unstable is also relevant here, precisely because that youngster's concern about his mental condition reveals how very crucial such problems can be. Mark Cooper is terribly afraid that he will eventually "go crazy," and that fear is a recurring motif in *The Caretaker* (1980, YA) by Arthur Roth. Mark's dread arises from his father's alcoholism (the son resolves to take good care of his body and avoid all bad habits, lest they undermine his sanity) and his mother's immaturity—she evades her problems through heavy smoking, a passionate interest in numerous soap operas, fantasies about the past, and impulse buying at yard sales, expenditures that the family can ill afford. When Mark survives his most terrible crises with his father and asserts himself with both Mr. Cooper and with a runaway girl he has befriended, he begins to realize that he really is very sane, very capable, and his eventual, hard-won ability to laugh at the idea of being thought eccentric marks his maturation.

Physical illness or disability is a less frequent theme than mental illness in works portraying males; it occurs most often in connection with the theme of death. A number of young men are presented coming to terms with the deaths of others who have been important in their lives. (For a full treatment of the theme of death of family members, especially as it affects familial relationships, see Chapter IX, "Males within Families.") Judith Guest's *Ordinary People*, for example, depicts Conrad Jarrett's attempts to accept his brother's death by drowning, an event so crucial in his life that it has completely upset his mental equilibrium.

Another novel using the death of family members as the crucial event that sets the course for the children's lives is Margaret Boylen's *A Moveable Feast* (1961). In this novel, five children (three boys and two girls) are orphaned by the almost simultaneous deaths of their parents. The novel tells of their growing up and gradually reveals both how they have been influenced by those deaths and what the surprising truth about them was. As a youngster, Farnham, the eldest, is a rebel and troublemaker, while Gidley is particularly bright and talented. Oliver ("Little Od") is the family angel; the most apparently affected by the loss of the parents, he survives for only two years. An unusual comic novel, *A Moveable Feast* is a parody of *Five Little Peppers and How They Grew*—and a complex study of appearances and reality as well.

From the beginning of Ralph Blum's *Old Glory and the Real-Time Freaks: A Children's Story and Patriotic Goodtime Book with Maps* (1972), Quintus Ells, seventeen, knows his dearly loved, eighty-one-year-old grandfather, whom he calls Bebe, has terminal cancer. One of the book's most touching passages comes when Quintus, at Bebe's request, introduces him to marijuana. The young man dreads Bebe's death; and he tries to practice in advance the agony the death will cause. Still, Quintus affirms life joyously, and his appreciation of Bebe and the good life he lives until the very end shows this member of the troubled peace-generation of the early 1970s to be a remarkably mature young man.

Two other novels study the impact on their protagonists of deaths outside the family circle. In *The Outsiders* (1967, YA) by S. E. Hinton, the gang is the most significant—indeed the only real—group in Ponyboy's life. Three deaths (two friends and one enemy) are crucial in the maturation of fourteen-year-old Ponyboy Curtis. All three of those who die had been gang members, and two die meaninglessly: Bob dies because he attacked Ponyboy, the only provocation being their membership in different gangs; Johnny, who killed Bob, dies heroically as a result of saving children from a burning building; Dallas, distraught and embittered by Johnny's death, provokes the police to shoot him after a robbery.

Ponyboy sees the waste of gang activities and is touched by Johnny's gallantry (which he likens to the heroism of Southern soldiers depicted in *Gone with the Wind*). The book itself becomes his attempt to help others understand their lives, and it is his own declaration of independence from the forces that had led to the early deaths of Bob and Dallas.

Hadley Norman, a famous woman poet, comes to live in Cromwell, New York, home of Steve Harper, the eighteen-year-old narrator and protagonist of Barbara Wersba's *The Country of the Heart* (1975, YA). Steve is an aspiring poet who has been deeply moved by her work; she is dying of cancer. Despite her often cruel treatment of him, they gradually become close: first as mentor and pupil, and then as lovers. Only after she has precipitated a quarrel that results in their estrangement and then left his town does he learn the nature and seriousness of her illness. His narrative, written five years later, is his attempt to sort out his emotions and to understand their relationship, so that forebodings of her death color the entire novel, a moving and poetic depiction of a talented and sensitive young boy struggling with his hopes and needs.

In the above novels, the youthful males have had to contend with the deaths of individuals who were close to them. In several other novels, death as an abstraction becomes a significant theme. Awareness of death is briefly treated in *No More Reunions* (1973) by John Bowers. In a crucial passage, the narrator comments on the early deaths of four young people. The death of a girl, the result of being thrown by a horse, affects him deeply, reminding him of the other deaths (one from rabies, one from leukemia, and one from drowning), and teaching him, as he says in another connection, that "nothing that is alive in this world— person as well as idea—is ever safe."

A preoccupation with death is central to the search for identity of sixteen-year-old Jolly Osment, protagonist of John Weston's *Jolly* (1965). His best friend's father owns a mortuary, and in one central episode, Jolly is permitted to observe the embalming process. Another pivotal scene, recalled in flashback, is Jolly's Memorial Day visit to a cemetery to search (fruitlessly, as it turns out) for his father's grave. These scenes, along with trips in the hearse with his friend to pick up bodies, foreshadow the novel's climactic moment: the accidental death of his friend and its macabre consequences. Only a week passes during the novel, but much happens to Jolly; his interest in death remains constant, and, while it has not deepened, his awareness certainly has become more immediate and personal by the end of the novel.

The greatest challenge of all, perhaps, is to face one's own death. Adolescents find it difficult to believe in the fact of their own mortality; Jolly's morbid fascination with death and decay is clearly evidence of his nascent recognition that he too must surely die. But for him that recognition remains more theoretical than real, for his own existence is not threatened. Other youthful protagonists, however, are shown in confrontation with the awful chance of their own end. David Marshall, for example, victim of kidnapping in Frank Herbert's *Soul Catcher* (1972), faces the possibility of his own death bravely and in the process crosses the threshold from boyhood to manhood.

A poignant story of a promising young prelaw student and eager tennis player who faces death is found in *May I Cross Your Golden River?* (1975, YA) by Barbara Corcoran (pseudonym, Paige Dixon). At eighteen, full of ambition and hope for the future, Jordan Phillips learns he has amyotrophic lateral sclerosis (Lou Gehrig's disease). We follow him and his family as he weakens toward death, managing in the interim to be best man at a brother's wedding and godfather to his sister's baby. This novel for older young people offers no easy comforts: Jordan rebels against his faith and is unable to accept the Christian faith of his brother-in-law, an Episcopal priest. But he meets his death with courage and dignity.

Illness and death confront us with some of the ultimate truths about our existence. Adolescents, still learning about the nature of themselves and their world, find those truths no easier to accept or to cope with than do adults. Thus, it is particularly stressful for a young person to have to face such difficult facts at the very time when he is having to face other difficult questions. If one is still learning who one is and where one belongs and what one wishes to do with one's life, it seems almost too much to bear to be asked also to realize that one is mortal, that one's body and mind are not invincible but very fragile, and that nothing in life can be counted on to be permanent. Some male adolescents, such as Quintus Ells in *Old Glory and the Real-Time Freaks* and Jordan Phillips in *May I Cross Your Golden River?*, confront these challenges with grace and courage. Others, such as Tom Nash in *Such Nice People*, find the threats too great to surmount and are destroyed. For none of them, even those who survive with integrity and strength, is the struggle easy.

Afterword

In our subject-novels, characters between the ages of twelve and nineteen are preoccupied with seven basic concerns: love and sexuality, family relationships, friendships, crises, social institutions, environment (setting), and fate. Aware of their developing bodies, intrigued with the sexual experimentation that their peers discuss, most adolescents invest vast amounts of their time and energy in pursuit of sexual partners. Simultaneously, their ties to family, friends, and social institutions—all crucial influences in their early development—are being tested, evaluated, redefined, perhaps broken. For many of these youngsters, the times or localities in which they live are major factors in their development, and for others, an implacable fate (usually in the form of illness, disability, or death) is the force that enlarges or crushes their spirits.

Two dominant motivations stemming from these basic concerns underlie fictional adolescents' conflicts, triumphs, and defeats: their vigorous efforts to emancipate themselves from parental control and their profound desire to establish themselves as independent, autonomous adults. To the young characters we have studied, adulthood seems almost synonymous with freedom, and their desire for both is intense. Almost always, their struggle for emancipation and autonomy generates or complicates the basic concerns to which our subject-authors direct their readers' attention. By far the vast majority of the novels studied here, then, depict adolescence as a period of tension and conflict, of testing and trial.

The fact that modern United States culture does not formally recognize (or ritualize) the most important initiatory experiences of its young in no way minimizes their importance or severity. Indeed, that fact may exacerbate the difficulty of youngsters' transitions between youth and maturity because for many the sudden, disquieting knowledge that adulthood does not mean absolute freedom but rather a new set of responsibilities and obligations is the most difficult lesson they must master. This lesson often goes hand in hand with a growing awareness that some adults never achieve maturity. Youngsters who refuse to give heed to these key insights are themselves doomed to be immature women and men, frustrated, unhappy, and dangerous to themselves and others, as are the protagonists of Cynthia Applewhite's *Sundays* (1979), Barry Beckham's *My Main Mother* (1969), and Charles Gorham's *McCaffrey* (1961).

For adolescent females, such as the protagonists of Toni Morrison's *The Bluest Eye* (1970) or Kitty Burns Florey's *Chez Cordelia* (1980), the often conflicting desires to be autonomous but also to be accepted and loved absolutely are endlessly perplexing and tormenting. Equally diffi-cult for adolescent males are society's twin demands that they exercise dominance and aggressiveness but also discharge human responsibility effectively and gracefully. Useful examples are the central characters of Chaim Potok's *The Chosen* (1967), John Nichols's *The Wizard of Loneliness* (1966), and Richard Bradford's *Red Sky at Morning* (1968). Expected to fulfill obligations and to undertake roles that their parents and mentors have found taxing (or impossible), these fictional youngsters are pushed to extremes of effort and stress.

The severity of their young characters' initiation tests and the high level of stress under which most fictional adolescents function tend to be reflected in the novels' tones, which are generally serious, sometimes oppressively grim, as in Marjorie Kellogg's *Like the Lion's Tooth* (1972) or Joseph Hansen's *Skinflick* (1979), for example. Other novels of adoles-cence, however, such as Fannie Flagg's *Coming Attractions* (1981) and William Faulkner's *The Reivers* (1962), are informed by vigorous hu-mor that underscores their young protagonists' troubles with marvelous irony even as it provides comic relief.

Just as the intensity of adolescents' experiences dominates the tone of these novels, so does it pervade all the classifications established by publishers and critics. Young adult novels, such as Mary Stolz's *The Noonday Friends* (1965), Paul Zindel's *The Pigman* (1968), and Alice Chil-dress's *A Hero Ain't Nothin' But a Sandwich* (1973), and popular adult novels such as Charles Portis's *True Grit* (1968), Sara Paretsky's *Indem-nity Only* (1982), or Jerome Weidman's *Last Respects* (1971), portray tests and trials as exacting as any depicted in such "high culture" novels as Jo-anne Greenberg's *Founder's Praise* (1976), John Knowles's *Peace Breaks Out* (1981), or Joyce Carol Oates's *A Garden of Earthly Delights* (1966). And always—no matter the tone or the classification of the novel—one or more of the seven basic concerns of their adolescent characters is cen-tral to the plot.

Happily, in fiction as in life, many of these adolescent characters pass their initiation tests with some degree of success; they learn to com-promise with childish visions of total autonomy, complete freedom, and utter happiness, and they undertake to live with some confidence and considerable courage in a "world of sweets and sours," where, as Poe reminds us, "our flowers are merely—flowers." These stringent les-sons, after all, are the vital challenges of adolescents' maturation jour-neys and the source of their compelling interest for readers and writers.

Part Three

Annotated Chart

All novels treated in this volume as well as others that portray adolescence are listed in this chart. Titles are grouped by year of publication and appear, within each group, in alphabetical order, according to author's last name. Bibliographical information refers to the first American edition; annotations, which follow the bibliographical material, are very brief summaries of plot and/or focus.

Setting

State names are indicated by latest postal abbreviations. Names of cities are indicated by conventional abbreviations when abbreviated. Only locations in the United States are identified. In the absence of state names, major regions are indicated as follows:

NewE—New England	W—West
CenA—Central Atlantic	WC—West Coast
E—East	NW—Northwest
N—North	M—Midwest
SE—Southeast	JNY—Journey (Traveling)
S—South	?—Unspecified
SW—Southwest	

Age

When characters' ages are not given in numerals, the following symbols apply: (when several adolescent characters are listed, ages are given for each)

b—birth	m—maturity
c—childhood	col—college years
a—adolescence	d—death
hs—high-school years	

Type of Novel

A—Allegory	LC—Local Color
C—Character Study	M—Novel of Manners
D—Mystery/Detection/Suspense	My—Mystic
E—Experimental	P—Picaresque
F—Fantasy	Q—Quest
Fab—Fable	SC—Social Criticism
G—Gothic	SF—Science Fiction
H—Historical	SoG—Southern Gothic
Ho—Horror	W—Western
I—Initiation	YA—Young Adult

Tone of Novel

C—Comic	Rea—Realistic
D—Didactic	Rom—Romantic
F—Fantastic	Sat—Satiric
I—Ironic	Sen—Sentimental
N—Naturalistic	Su—Surrealistic
Nos—Nostalgic	Sym—Symbolic
P—Psychological	

Reference

Roman numerals refer to chapter numbers. *Underscored* numerals indicate discussions in the chapter; others simply indicate subjects treated in the novel. (See also under the title in the Index.)

1961

Author/Title	Setting	Age	Type	Tone	Reference
Blanton, Margaret Gray. *The White Unicorn*. NY: Globus, 424pp. Maidie observes various results of love and grows toward acceptance of and commitment to life.	TN	9–16	I	Rea,Sym	II,V
Boylen, Margaret [Currier]. *A Moveable Feast*. NY: Random, 269pp. Five orphans are scarred by death of parents but four survive to become successful though eccentric adults.	M	c,a–m	I,D	C,Sym,I	II,XIV
Breuer, Bessie [Elizabeth]. *Take Care of My Roses*. NY: Atheneum, 184pp. Some incidents portray Via's reactions to tensions between her new stepmother and the Salters' long-term housekeeper, factors complicating her maturation.	?	hs	C	Rea	II
Calisher, Hortense. *False Entry*. Boston: Little, 484pp. Pierre Goodman, English born, never adjusts fully to life in the South; always seeking his identity, he assumes several roles.	AL	c–m	C	Rea	IX,XI, XIII
Carrighar, Sally. *The Glass Dove*. Garden City, NY: Doubleday, 347pp. Sylvia MacIntosh helps run a farm and an underground railway station during her romance.	OH	15–20	H	Rea	I,IV,VI
Clark, Dorothy Park. *See* McMeekin, Isabella McLennan, and Dorothy Park Clark					
Clark, L. D. *The Dove Tree*. Garden City, NY: Doubleday, 360pp. Haley Blair puzzles over the strain between himself and his son, Duncan, as father and son attempt to build new lives.	TX	14	C	Rea	IX

Davis, Christopher. *First Family*. NY: Coward, 253pp. Friendship of black boy and white girl grows, then falters as his family "integrates" prosperous white neighborhood.	M	12	C,SC	Rea,P	IV,XI
Deal, Babs H. *It's Always Three O'Clock*. NY: McKay, 334pp. Eileen Holder retains her love of life and courage through many sorrows, while her friends mostly fail.	AL	hs–m	C,I,M	Rea,P, Sym	III
DeCapite, Raymond. *A Lost King*. NY: McKay, 213pp. Young loser's attempts at self-fulfillment are complicated by tangled relationship with his father.	OH	hs–m	C	Rea,P	IX
Ehle, John. *Lion on the Hearth*. NY: Harper, 406pp. Kin King matures amid family squabbles and financial problems.	NC	5–col	I	Rea	IX
Fast, Howard. *April Morning*. NY: Crown, 184pp. Adam Cooper sees father killed in Revolutionary War skirmish and learns how to fight to protect his home.	MA	15	YA,H	Rea	IX,XIII, XIV
Fugate, Terence. *Drum and Bugle*. NY: Simon, 405pp. Carl Roundtree's military-school experiences are generally grim, sometimes demeaning, occasionally dangerous.	GA	hs	I	Rea	VIII,IX, XI, XII
Gallagher, Patricia. *The Sons and the Daughters*. NY: Messner, 348pp. Jill Turner moderates her idealistic dreams and learns of sex and suffering in bleak west Texas small town.	TX	17	SC	Rea	I,V,VI
Gorham, Charles. *McCaffrey*. NY: Dial, 245pp. Vincent McCaffrey becomes prostitute (as is his friend Doreen) in rebellion against family and church.	NYC	17,18	I	Rea	IV,IX,XI
Gover, Robert. *One Hundred Dollar Misunderstanding*. NY: Grove, 192pp. Various kinds of innocence lead to massive misunderstandings when J.C. Holland patronizes Kitten, a teenaged prostitute.	?	14	SC	C	IV

1961 (*continued*)

Author/Title	Setting	Age	Type	Tone	Reference
Grubb, Davis. *The Watchman*. NY: Scribner's, 275pp. Complex relationships with Jill and Cristi Alt revise Jason Hunnicutt's perceptions of good and evil.	WV	17,19,a	I	Rea	I,II,XI
Haines, William Wister. *The Winter War*. Boston: Little, 247pp. Reared by Indians, Lita Littleton is torn between two cultures, alien to both, in aftermath of Little Big Horn.	MT	a	H	Rea	VI
Hamner, Earl, Jr. *Spencer's Mountain*. NY: Dial, 247pp. After symbolic killing of a white deer, Clay-Boy, with help from large and loving family, wins chance for a college education.	VA	16	LC	Rea	VIII,XI, XIII
Hine, Al. *Lord Love a Duck*. NY: Atheneum, 367pp. Brilliant Gooney Bird Musgrave exerts control over beautiful Barbara Anne Greene, to manipulate the hostile world she represents.	IA	16–18	M,SC	Sat	I,II,V,VI, VIII,IX, XII, XIV
Holmes, Marjorie [Rose]. *Follow Your Dream*. Phila: Westminister, 186pp. Tracy Temple's summer job with veternarian, a step toward her chosen profession, is complicated by friendship, romance.	DC	hs	YA,I	Rea	I,III,V
Hood, Margaret. *Drown the Wind*. NY: Coward, 220pp. Shy Letty Peaslee is a suspect in murder case.	ME	16	D	Rea	IV
Hurst, Fannie. *God Must Be Sad*. Garden City, NY: Doubleday, 284pp. Shy girl, defenseless and vulnerable, marries her stepfather, and is ultimately tried for murder.	NYC	8–m	D	Sen	I,II
Kantor, MacKinlay. *Spirit Lake*. Cleveland: World, 957pp. Accounts of duties of several youngsters, terrors and rigors of life for young captives in Indian camps illuminate frontier story.	IA	c–a	H	Rea	VI,XIII

Lambert, Janet Snyder. *Forever and Ever.* NY: Dutton, 182pp. Sandra, Josie, and Tenny Campbell, who have always lived abroad, adjust to life in small U.S. town.	IN	10,15,18	YA	Rea	II,VI
Lawrence, Josephine. *The Amiable Meddlers.* NY: Harcourt, 253pp. Jenny Faler enriches the circle of her middle-aged, spinster guardians.	?	15	I	Rea	II,IV
Lee, Marjorie. *The Eye of Summer.* NY: Simon, 191pp. Connie and Spence, cousins, spend summers on island, develop closeness both nurturing and destructive.	?	10,18,21	I	P	II,VI,VII, VIII,XIII, XIV
Lloyd, Norris. *A Dream of Mansions.* NY: Random, 274pp. Hallie Jones's painful loss of romantic notions of the South leads to developing wisdom, maturation.	GA	12	I	Rea	VI
Longstreet, Stephen. *Gettysburg.* NY: Farrar, 342pp. Subplot recounting pro-Union Alice Gross's romance with Confederate soldier symbolizes continuity amid wartime disruption.	PA	17	H	Rea	I
McMeekin, Clark. *See* McMeekin, Isabella McLennan, and Dorothy Park Clark					
McMeekin, Isabella McLennan, and Dorothy Park Clark [pseud., Clark McMeekin]. *The Fairbrothers.* NY: Putnam's, 288pp. Zion Hobbs wins a place for herself with her reluctant adoptive family.	KY	13	H,I	Rea	II
Malvern, Gladys. *Wilderness Island.* Phila: MacRae, 190pp. Tensions between Indians and Dutch immigrants influence growth of Alida Evertsen.	NY	c–m	I	H	IV,VI
Ogilvie, Elizabeth. *Becky's Island.* NY: McGraw, 187pp. Vicky's efforts to secure good education for Becky's Island children speed her maturation.	ME	17	I,YA	Rea	V,VI

Author/Title	Setting	Age	Type	Tone	Reference
1961 (*continued*)					
Pangborn, Edgar. *The Trial of Callista Blake*. NY: St. Martin's, 304pp. During her trial for murder, Callista Blake comes to terms with herself and her needs.	E	19	D,C	Rea	IV
Price, Reynolds. *A Long and Happy Life*. NY: Atheneum, 195pp. Rosacoke Mustian's pregnancy forces her into realistic assessment of her dreams and expectations.	NC	a	C	Rea	I
Rikhoff, Jean. *Dear Ones All*. NY: Viking, 558pp. The five Timble sisters evaluate impact of one another, female family members, and social pressures on their lives.	IL	c–m	I,C	Rea	II
Ritner, Ann. *Seize a Nettle*. Phila: Lippincott, 245pp. Serious reverses—father's death, the Depression—cannot daunt vigorous Eugenia, Margaret, and Jessica Abernathy or their female mentors.	CO	a	C	Rea	II
Ross, Ivan T. *Requiem for a Schoolgirl*. NY: Simon, 243pp. Teacher Ben Gordon investigates suicide of pupil Laurie Mitchell, finding her motivation in her family life.	E	hs	D	Rea	II,VII
Siebel, Julia. *For the Time Being*. NY: Harcourt, 219pp. Bleak midwestern landscape and parents' attitudes and handicaps complicate maturation of Mitchell, Ann, and Nora Bemboy.	KS	a–m	C,I	Rea	II,VI,IX, XIII
Stolz, Mary. *Wait for Me, Michael*. NY: Harper, 148pp. Anny's love for a young writer who yearns for her mother complicates yet speeds her maturation.	NewE	15	YA	Rea	I,II
Taylor, Robert Lewis. *A Journey to Matecumbe*. NY: McGraw, 424pp. David Burnie's cross-South journey with mentors Uncle Jim and former slave Zeb entails adventure, racism, romance, danger, maturation.	JNY	a	H,SC	Rea	VIII,IX,XI

Entry	Setting	Age	Char.	Mode	Themes
Turngren, Ellen. *Hearts Are the Fields.* NY: Longman, 182pp. Susan, Paul, and Dan Enberg, offspring of headstrong Swedish immigrant father, struggle to find their own ways of life.	MN	16,18,20	YA,H	Rea	I,VI,XII,XIII

1962

Entry	Setting	Age	Char.	Mode	Themes
Abbey, Edward. *Fire on the Mountain.* NY: Dial, 211pp. Billy Starr and grandfather defend family ranch against government takeover.	NM	12	W,P	Rea	IX
Astor, Mary. *The Image of Kate.* NY: Doubleday, 331pp. Kate Martin's life is damaged by feelings of guilt and alienation.	CA	b-60	C	Rea	II
Auchincloss, Louis. *Portrait in Brownstone.* Boston: Houghton, 371pp. The lives of Ida Trask and Geraldine Denison, cousins, are forever complicated by competition for the same man.	NYC	a-m	M	Rea	I,II
Berriault, Gina. *Conference of Victims.* NY: Atheneum, 248pp. Dolores Lenci's need to be sexually entrancing leads her to a series of affairs with older men.	CA	17–22	C	Rea	I,VII
Borland, Barbara Dodge. *The Greater Hunger.* NY: Appleton, 406pp. Horticultural skill and courage enable Hetty Downing to succeed in Puritan Massachusetts, despite a broken love affair.	MA	18	H	Rea	I,VI
Bradbury, Ray. *Something Wicked This Way Comes.* NY: Simon, 317pp. Two boys and the father of one confront magical, evil carnival that alters time and promises immortality.	IL	14,14	F,A	Su,Sym	X,XII
Carleton, Jetta. *The Moonflower Vine.* NY: Simon, 351pp. Flashbacks reveal events in the adolescences of the Soames sisters, one featuring Jessica's early marriage.	MO	c–m	C,I	Rea	I
Daniels, Sally. *The Inconstant Season.* NY: Atheneum, 244pp. Peggy Dillon recalls happy youth in loving family and generally favorable circumstances.	NY	c–m	I	N,Rea,P	II,VI

1962 *(continued)*

Author/Title	Setting	Age	Type	Tone	Reference
Dornfeld, Iris. *Jeeney Ray.* NY: Viking, 188pp. Spastic girl, Jeeney Ray, treated as half-wit, finds identity and hope when proper diagnosis is made.	CA	a	C,I	P,Rea	VII
Douglas, Ellen. *A Family's Affairs.* Boston: Houghton, 442pp. Southern girl, through relationships with teacher and first sweetheart, learns of dangers and uncertainties of love.	MS,LA	b–m	C,I	Rea,P	I,V
Eclov, Shirley. *My Father's House.* NY: Harper, 181pp. The Morrisons' adjustment to three generations living in the same house is complicated by Lydia's love affair.	?	18	I	Rea	II
Faulkner, William. *The Reivers.* NY: Random, 305pp. Picaresque trip teaches Lucius Priest responsibility, initiates him into manhood.	MS,TN	11	P,I	Rea,C	IV,VIII, IX,X,XI, XII
Forbes, [Delores Florine] Stanton, and Helen Rydell [pseud., Forbes Rydell]. *They're Not Home Yet.* Garden City, NY: Doubleday, 189pp. When Lana and four schoolmates are kidnapped, she is forced to a maturity beyond her years.	?	12	D	Rea	IV
Fumento, Rocco. *Tree of Dark Reflection.* NY: Knopf, 528pp. Son of Italian immigrants, torn between sexual guilts and Roman Catholicism, puzzles over his father's mixed gentleness and brutality.	MA,NY	c–m	I	P,Rea	VIII,XII
Gipson, Fred. *Savage Sam.* NY: Harper, 241pp. Travis Coates escapes, joins dog, Savage Sam, and white settlers in pursuing his Indian captors, freeing other prisoners.	TX	15	YA,H	Rea	XII,XIII
Hill, Pati. *One Thing I Know.* Boston: Houghton, 93pp. Through knowing several young men, Francesca Hollins learns the imperfection and incompleteness of human relationships.	DC	16	YA,I	Rea,P	I

Entry	Location	Age			
Jackson, Shirley. *We Have Always Lived in the Castle.* NY: Viking, 214pp. Lives of Constance and Mary Catherine Blackwood irrevocably altered by crime in recent past.	?	18	D,SC	P	II,IV
Lauritzen, Jonreed. *The Everlasting Fire.* Garden City, NY: Doubleday, 474pp. Lives and loves of several nineteenth-century adolescents are complicated by tenets of, bigotry toward, Mormonism.	IL,IA	a	H,SC	Rea	I,V,VI, VIII,XIII
Lawrence, Josephine. *I Am in Urgent Need of Advice.* NY: Harcourt, 216pp. Amanda, sometimes resentful of loving parents, overcomes guilt caused by friend's death and proves self-reliant in an emergency.	CenA	14	M	Rea,C	II,VII
Osterman, Marjorie K. *Damned If You Do, Damned If You Don't.* Phila: Chilton, 397pp. Youthful glimpses of several members of German-Jewish immigrant Simon family illustrate social, economic assimilation or its lack.	NYC	c–m	C	Rea	II,V,IX, XII
Prokosch, Frederic. *The Seven Sisters.* NY: Farrar, 405pp. Episodes (in U.S. and abroad) contrast the moral, ethical, and social awareness of the seven Nightingale sisters.	MD	hs–m	Fab,A	Rea	II
Robbins, Harold. *See* Rubin, Harold					
Rogers, Garet. *The Jumping Off Place.* NY: Dial, 307pp. Caddy Bartholomew's father fixation and desire to be a poet complicate life at mental hospital.	S	13?	I	Rea	II,V
Rubin, Harold [pseud., Harold Robbins]. *Where Love Has Gone.* NY: Simon, 350pp. Estranged father returns when Dani is apprehended for killing her mother's lover.	CA	14	M	Rea,P	I,II,IV,V
Rydell, Forbes. *See* Forbes, [Delores Florine] Stanton, and Helen Rydell					

Author/Title	Setting	Age	Type	Tone	Reference
1962 (*continued*)					
Sandburg, Helga. *The Owl's Roost*. NY: Dial, 308pp. Various youngsters, male and female, perceive supportive and damaging aspects of adulthood during summer at beach resort.	MI	15,17,18	C	Rea	I,II,VIII
Sanguinetti, Elise. *The Last of the Whitfields*. NY: McGraw, 279pp. Narrator Felicia Whitfield's malapropisms enliven account of family life, social tensions, and her brother Arthur's awkward maturation.	GA	14,16	C,LC	Rea	II,VI
Stoutenburg, Adrien. *Window on the Sea*. Phila: Westminster, 158pp. Mollie Lucas's attraction to Kingsley Reynal complicates her affection for Glenn Jorgens, but broadens her horizon and aspirations.	San Francisco	16	YA	Rea	I
Swarthout, Glendon. *Welcome to Thebes*. NY: Random, 372pp. Sex scandal surrounding Carlie and town power brokers motivates adult male protagonist to settle an old score.	MI	14	C	Rea	I
Wellman, Manly Wade. *Not at These Hands*. NY: Putnam's, 320pp. Newspaperman George Cobbett kills his mentor (rumored to be his natural father) in self-defense, is tried and acquitted.	NC	19	LC	Rea	XIII
Wolff, Maritta [Martin]. *Buttonwood*. NY: Random, 343pp. Affection for Susie, his surrogate daughter, motivates subplot in study of protagonist Paul Maitland.	?	16	C	Rea	II
York, Carol Beach. *Sparrow Lake*. NY: Coward, 155pp. Dissolution of isolation and social snobbery imposed by her guardian aunts symbolizes Liddie Howard's maturation.	NJ	16	YA	Rea	I,II,III

1963

Citation / Annotation	Place	Age			
Barker, Shirley. *Strange Wives*. NY: Crown, 377pp. Christian girl loves and marries Sephardic Jew against background of prejudice and war.	RI	7–m	I,H	Rea	VI
Blechman, Burt. *The War of Camp Omongo*. NY: Random, 215pp. Randy Levine learns to be ruthlessly competitive at summer camp.	NY	13	M	Sat,Su,C	XII
Borland, Hal [Glen]. *When the Legends Die*. Phila: Lippincott, 288pp. Indian Thomas Black Bull searches for identity through life in old ways, on reservation, and as a bronco rider.	CO,NY, NY	2–m	C,I	Rea,Sym	XIII
Faasen, Neal. *The Toyfair*. NY: Simon, 186pp. Boy and two girls, truants from a hated school, go in search of boy's long-lost father.	MI, Chicago	13	P,SC	Rea	V,XI,XII
Hall, James Baker. *Yates Paul, His Grand Flights, His Tootings*. Cleveland: World, 281pp. Despite difficult relationship with his father, boy learns to control his fears but refuses to give up his fantasies.	Lexington, KY	13	I	C,P	IX,XII
Kubly, Herbert. *The Whistling Zone*. NY: Simon, 384pp. Various students and Little Crown, a midget evangelist, inform Professor Mawther's stint at a conservative university.	M	16	SC	Sat	V
Lambert, Gavin. *Inside Daisy Clover*. NY: Viking, 245pp. Talented, independent girl survives movie stardom, unrequited loves, early marriage, and motherhood with courage and humor.	CA,NY	c–m	C	P	V
Nathan, Robert. *The Devil with Love*. NY: Knopf, 200pp. Voluptuous Gladys Milhouser is bait and temptation in demon's attempt to snare souls.	?	17	A	Sat,F	V

Author/Title	Setting	Age	Type	Tone	Reference
1963 (*continued*)					
Parks, Gordon. *The Learning Tree.* NY: Harper, 303pp. Violence and tension, family supportiveness mark Newt Winger's initiation as black midwesterner.	KS	hs	I,SC	Rea	IX,X,XI, XIII
Reed, Meredith. *Our Year Began in April.* NY: Lothrop, 221pp. Linda Sutherland finds maturity amid family's mutual efforts to sustain her father's career as Methodist minister.	NH	11–16	YA	Rea	II,V
Stolz, Mary. *Who Wants Music on Monday?* NY: Harper, 264pp. Mother's influence and sibling tensions fall into perspective as Lotta and Cassie Dunne mature.	?	hs	YA	Rea	II
Tanner, Louise. *Miss Bannister's Girls.* NY: Farrar, 239pp. Lives of various graduates marked and sometimes damaged by false values of private girls' school.	NYC	hs-m	C,SC	Sat	IV,V
Updike, John. *The Centaur.* NY: Knopf, 302pp. Peter Caldwell's relationship to father informed by juxtaposition with Prometheus-Chiron myth.	PA	15	C, Fab	Rea	IX
Wier, Ester. *The Loner.* NY: McKay, 153pp. A homeless, nameless orphan, David finds a name and a home with sheep ranchers and learns trust and love.	MT	14	YA,I	Rea	XI,XIII
Wilson, Sloan. *Georgie Winthrop.* NY: Harper, 304pp. Charlotte Harkin, daughter of protagonist's old rival, seeks passion and fulfillment through seducing him.	NY	17	I	P	I
Witheridge, Elizabeth. *Never Younger, Jeannie.* NY: Atheneum, 150pp. Californian Jeannie's year on grandparents' farm opens her awareness, aids in her maturation.	MI	11	YA	Rea	II,VI

Wolff, Ruth. *I, Keturah*. NY: Day, 285pp. Reared in orphanage, Keturah Brown finds home with elderly couple, becomes nursemaid-companion in aristocratic estate, and finally becomes a "lady."	?	16–m	I	P	I,II,VI
1964					
Baylor, Robert. *To Sting the Child*. Indianapolis: Bobbs, 312pp. Returning from war, young man relives past in search for identity and purpose.	PA	b–m	C,I	N,Su,Sym	VIII,IX, XII
Betts, Doris. *The Scarlet Thread*. NY: Harper, 405pp. Troubled adolescence leads to escape, a secretly brutal marriage, or withdrawal into stonecarving for sister and two brothers.	NC	12–15	C,I	Rea,Sym, P	VI,XIII
Brace, Gerald Warner. *The Wind's Will*. NY: Norton, 264pp. In one summer, David Wayne's own sexual initiation and his father's adultery cause his maturation.	ME	18	I	Rea	VIII,IX, XII
Charyn, Jerome. *On the Darkening Green*. NY: McGraw, 244pp. Orphaned Nick Lapucci works in a peculiar home for wayward boys, where his wild adventures lead to his maturation.	NY	15–19	P	Su	XII
Clarke, Tom E. *The Big Road*. NY: Lothrop, 252pp. Family tension and the Depression turn Vic Martin into a hobo.	NW	17	P,I	Rea	IX,XII
Crawford, Joanna. *Birch Interval*. Boston: Houghton, 183pp. Jesse's family faces isolation and sustains losses, forcing her to early maturity.	PA	11	I	Rea	II
Cuomo, George. *Bright Day, Dark Runner*. Garden City, NY: Doubleday, 421pp. J.I. LeBlanche's relationships with father and foster father generate a long flashback.	NewE	15	C,I	Rea	I,IX
Curtiss, Ursula [Reilly]. *Out of the Dark*. NY: Dodd, 183pp. Libby Mannering and Kit Austen's prank phone calls endanger themselves and motivate murder.	NM	14,14	D	Rea	IV

Author/Title	Setting	Age	Type	Tone	Reference
1964 *(continued)*					
Disney, Doris Miles. *The Hospitality of the House.* Garden City, NY: Doubleday, 183pp. Visit to pen pal becomes kidnapping for Mandy O'Brien.	NY	18	D	Rea	IV
Downey, Harris. *The Key to My Prison.* NY: Delacorte, 192pp. Delia Wright describes events and people who have led her to decision to commit suicide.	LA	17,19	C	P,Sym	I,III,VII
Farrell, James T[homas]. *What Time Collects.* Garden City, NY: Doubleday, 421pp. Unwise marriage to sexist, alcoholic Zeke threatens Anne Duncan Daniels's ambitions and maturation.	M	19	SC,I	Rea	I
Friedman, B. H. *Yarborough.* Cleveland: World, 374pp. Prodigy centers his life around bridge, sex, drugs, and one intimate friend.	NY	b–m, 13–m	C	Rea,P	VIII,X,XI, XII
Gover, Robert. *Here Goes Kitten.* NY: Grove, 184pp. J.C. Holland and Kitten again triumph clumsily over misunderstanding and misadventure.	?	17	C	C	IV
Grau, Shirley Ann. *The Keepers of the House.* NY: Knopf, 309pp. Abigail Howland's entire life is shadowed and altered by bigoted attitudes toward race.	S	11–m, b–m	C,I	Rea	II,IV
Green, Hannah. *See* Greenberg, Joanne					
Greenberg, Joanne [pseud., Hannah Green]. *I Never Promised You a Rose Garden.* NY: Holt, 300pp. Deborah Blau works from insanity toward mental health and self-acceptance.	M	16–19	C	Rea	II,III,VII
Hoffenberg, Mason. *See* Southern, Terry, and Mason Hoffenberg					

Kaufman, Bel. *Up the Down Staircase*. Englewood Cliffs, NJ: Prentice, 340pp. Beginning teacher Sylvia Barrett's painful initiation experiences include her near rape by one student, suicide attempt of another.	CenA	hs	SC	Rea	V,XII
Kenton, Maxwell. *See* Southern, Terry, and Mason Hoffenberg					
Lambert, Christine. *See* Loewengard, Heida Huberta Freybe					
Lanham, Edwin. *Speak Not Evil*. NY: Farrar, 591pp. As town prepares for tercentenary celebration, five young people undergo crucial maturing experiences.	CT	18?	I	Rea,P	*I,VI,XII, XIII*
Loewengard, Heida Huberta Freybe [pseud., Christine Lambert]. *A Sudden Woman*. NY: Atheneum, 278pp. Love of mother and daughter for the same man disrupts their relationship, but ultimately strengthens all three.	NY	17	I	Rea,P	*I,II*
Miller, Heather Ross. *The Edge of the Woods*. NY: Atheneum, 118pp. Anna Marie recalls *very* brief but significant memories of her grandparents to explain her troubled adulthood.	NC	c–m	I	Rea	II
Pitkin, Dorothy. *Sea Change*. NY: Pantheon, 250pp. Romance, physical changes, and choice of a career mark Vicky Harbison's transition into adulthood.	NewE	15	YA,I	Rea	I,V
Reed, Kit. *At War As Children*. NY: Farrar, 278pp. Denise McLeod looks back upon her peripatetic youth seeking understanding of her life choices, particularly religious ones.	various	c–a	C,I	Rea	V
Richter, Conrad. *The Grandfathers*. NY: Knopf, 180pp. Markedly different from her putative kin, Chariter Murdoch develops emotional ties to unacknowledged true grandfather during crucial maturation period.	MD	15	C,I	Rea	I,II
Robertson, Don. *A Flag Full of Stars*. NY: Putnam, 511pp. One subplot portrays Barbara Oesterreicher's pregnancy and consequent marriage.	various	hs	C,SC	Rea	I

Author/Title	Setting	Age	Type	Tone	Reference
1964 (*continued*)					
Sanguinetti, Elise. *The New Girl*. NY: McGraw, 272pp. Felica Whitfield withstands loneliness and snobbery while adjusting to boarding school, risks much to aid friend.	VA	15	C,I,LC	Rea	III,V
Southern, Terry, and Mason Hoffenberg [pseud., Maxwell Kenton]. *Candy*. NY: Putnam, 224pp. Candy's attitudes and sexual exploits, intended as satiric examination of contemporary scene.	JNY	17	C	C,SC	I
Taylor, Robert Lewis. *Two Roads to Guadalupé*. NY: Doubleday, 428pp. Mexican War adventures of soldiers Sam and Blaine Shelby (brothers) and Angeline Hughes include disguise, injury, captivity, abuse.	JNY	a	P,H	Rea	I,V,VIII, XII
Topkins, Katherine. *Kotch*. NY: McGraw, 190pp. Both elderly Kotch and his informally acquired pregnant charge, Erica, fruitlessly imagine happy but differing results from their relationship.	CA	15	C	Rea	II
Walter, Eugene. *Love You Good, See You Later*. NY: Scribner's, 183pp. Margaret Bergeron's competition with her grandmother for attentions of a man is only one family eccentricity explored here.	AL	hs	C,M	Rea	I,II
1965					
Allen, Elizabeth. *The Loser*. NY: Dutton, 128pp. Deirdre expands awareness of self and world by dating unsuitable boy.	SW	16,15	YA	Rea	I,II
Armstrong, Charlotte. *The Turret Room*. NY: Coward, 253pp. Boy, trying to see son (fruit of brief marriage to spoiled rich girl), is suspected of murder.	CA	a–m	D	Rea,P	V,VIII

Entry	Place				
Chappell, Fred. *The Inkling.* NY: Harcourt, 153pp. Jan Anderson and his retarded sister, Timmie, grow to adolescence in a grim, unnatural atmosphere.	NC	16,a	C	Su	*I,VII,IX*
Cormier, Robert. *Take Me Where the Good Times Are.* NY: Macmillan, 213pp. Annabel Lee Jones, mentally handicapped, helps precipitate crisis in life of aged protagonist.	?	14	C	Rea	III,VII
Davis, Burke. *The Summer Land.* NY: Random, 242pp. Participating in and observing family and social activities in rural setting, Fax Starling learns courage.	NC	15	I,YA	Rea,C	XII,XIII
Dornfeld, Iris. *Boy Gravely.* NY: Knopf, 213pp. Boy Gravely, self-taught musical genius, despite bleak background, becomes famous and controversial composer.	CA,NY, IL,NYC	5–m	C,P	Rea,P	XII,XIV
Drexler, Rosalyn. *I Am the Beautiful Stranger.* NY: Grossman, 185pp. Diary follows girl's struggle toward maturation, including period of sexual promiscuity.	NYC	13–16	C,I	Rea,P,C	*I*
Echard, Margaret. *I Met Murder on the Way.* Garden City, NY: Doubleday, 240pp. Betsy Foster and Bryn Pomeroy are key witnesses in solution to murder of their relatives.	KY	14,15	D	Rea	I,IV
Fikso, Eunice Cleland, C. F. Griffin]. *The Impermanence of Heroes.* Phila: Chilton, 185pp. Jessica and Brock Brewer come of age through their friendship with an abrasive Korean War veteran.	NewE	11–12, 12–13	I	Rea	I,II,III, V,VI
Friedman, Sanford. *Totempole.* NY: Dutton, 411pp. Middle-class Jewish boy, through family influences and summer-camp experiences, becomes alienated from self and is healed by homosexual relationships.	NYC,ME	2–m	I	Rea,P	VIII,IX, XII
Griffin, C. F. *See* Fikso, Eunice Cleland					
Grossman, Alfred. *Marie Beginning.* NY: Doubleday, 216pp. Marie Svobodna schemes and manipulates to achieve power and position.	NYC	18?	C	Sat	V

Author/Title	Setting	Age	Type	Tone	Reference
1965 *(continued)*					
Hamner, Earl, Jr. *You Can't Get There from Here.* NY: Random, 242pp. Wes Scott's day-long odyssey in search for his father takes him through a series of comic adventures.	NYC	16	Q	C	IX,XIII
Hentoff, Nat. *Jazz Country.* NY: Harper, 146pp. Tom Curtis, white, achieves acceptance by black jazz musicians through his talent and dedication to the trumpet.	NYC	16	YA,SC	Rea,P	XI,XII
Hill, Donna. *Catch a Brass Canary.* Phila: Lippincott, 224pp. Miguel Campos meets discrimination against Puerto Ricans, but grows through job at library and frees self from gang.	NYC	16	YA,I	Rea,P	XI,XII, XIII
Kelley, William Melvin. *A Drop of Patience.* Garden City, NY: Doubleday, 237pp. Ludlow Washington adjusts to life outside an institution for the blind.	S,NYC	16	P,I	Rea	XII
Lockridge, Richard. *The Empty Day.* Phila: Lippincott, 349pp. Elderly Martin Brent remembers his youth: irresponsible father and feckless family, sexual encounters, and early journalistic experience.	NYC	10–m	I	P	IX,XII
Mezvinsky, Shirley. *The Edge.* NY: Doubleday, 210pp. Flashbacks into Lois Marks's adolescence illuminate her adult attitudes and behavior.	MI	c–m	C	Rea	I,II
Meader, Stephen W. *A Blow for Liberty.* NY: Harcourt, 187pp. Jed Starbuck, a "bound boy," manages to aid Revolutionary cause while obeying Quaker conscience.	NJ	16	YA,H	Rea	XII
Richardson, Vokes. *Not All Our Pride.* NY: Braziller, 276pp. Traditional southern family's values and expectations affect lifelong bond between Hugh Alexander and Julie, his cousin, buddy, lover.	TN	a	C,SC	Rea	I,VIII,IX

Entry	Location	Age	Category		Themes
Schoonover, Shirley. *Mountain of Winter.* NY: Coward, 256pp. Ava Knuutinen's heritage enriches and sometimes complicates her maturation, recounted against backdrop of Finnish-American customs.	M	c–m	C,LC	Rea	I,II
Sprague, Gretchen. *A Question of Harmony.* NY: Dodd, 271pp. Jeanne Blake confronts strained friendships, dating problems, racism, and an important career decision.	M	16–17	YA,I	Rea	I,III,IV,V
Stolz, Mary. *The Noonday Friends.* NY: Harper, 182pp. Davis twins learn acceptance and family supportiveness despite pressures and duties imposed by father's inability to work.	NY	15	YA	Rea	II,IX
Updike, John. *Of the Farm.* NY: Knopf, 173pp. Visit to family farm reveals shifting, complex relationships between protagonist Joey Robinson, his stepson Richard, wife, mother.	PA	11	C	Rea	IX
Wagoner, David. *The Escape Artist.* NY: Farrar, 244pp. Danny Masters, gifted magician, seeks career as a performer and flees an enemy for three wild days.	M	16	P	C	XII
Westheimer, David. *My Sweet Charlie.* Garden City, NY: Doubleday, 255pp. Pregnant, alone, ignorant, and bigoted, Marlene Chambers finds refuge, friendship, and support with a Northern black attorney, also a fugitive.	S	17	I	Rea	IV
Weston, John. *Jolly.* NY: McKay, 246pp. Jolly Osment's preoccupations with sex and death are both brought to crisis during one eventful week.	AZ?	16	I	Rea	VIII,XIV
Williams, John. *Stoner.* NY: Viking, 278pp. His wife's destructive efforts to dominate daughter Grace complicate life of protagonist William Stoner.	MO	hs	C	Rea	II
Winter, Alice. *The Velvet Bubble.* NY: Morrow, 221pp. Dorrie Lawson's obsessive love for her father leads to disaster.	M?	14	D,C	P	II

Author/Title	Setting	Age	Type	Tone	Reference
1965 *(continued)*					
Wojciechowska, Maia. *A Kingdom in a Horse.* NY: Harper, 143pp. Through love for a horse, David Earl learns responsibility and overcomes his estrangement from his father.	VT	12–13	YA	P	XII
Wolff, Ruth. *A Crack in the Sidewalk.* NY: Day, 282pp. Linsey Templeton, from large, poor, loving family, finds success and eventually love through her singing.	KY?,OH	13–19	I,YA	Rea	V
1966					
Barrett, Mary Ellin. *Castle Ugly.* NY: Dutton, 255pp. In two flashbacks, Sally Courtland relives youthful knowledge of adult infidelities and resulting violent deaths.	NY	11	I	Rea	I,II
Caidin, Martin. *Devil Take All.* NY: Dutton, 382pp. Terri Bradshaw is kidnapped, raped, and terrorized in an intricate plot for an exotic ransom.	CA	19	D	Rea	VII
Clarke, Mary Stetson. *The Iron Peacock.* NY: Viking, 251pp. Orphaned, aristocratic Joanna Sprague adjusts to life as a bond servant in the Bay Colony.	MS (Bay Colony)	16	YA,H	Rea	II,V,XII
Fairbairn, Ann. *Five Smooth Stones.* NY: Crown, 756pp. Born into poverty, race discrimination, and love, David Champlin achieves success, but retains dedication to black people.	LA,OH	b–m	SC	Rea	VIII,XII,XIII
Hill, Weldon. *See* Scott, William R.					
Jaffe, Rona. *The Cherry in the Martini.* NY: Simon, 190pp. Unnamed narrator nostalgically recalls childhood and adolescence in apparently autobiographical sketches.	NYC	c–m	I	P	I,V
Madison, Arnold. *Danger Beats the Drum.* NY: Holt, 191pp. Danger mixes with vacation fun as Bob Carsten helps break a drug ring and thus salvages his own reputation.	NY	16	YA,D	Rea	IV

Morressy, John. *The Blackboard Cavalier.* Garden City, NY: Doubleday, 209pp. Humorously realistic classroom scenes, brief sketches of students' personalities, conflict over final grade complicate English teacher's first year.	?	hs	C	Rea	XIII
Nichols, John. *The Wizard of Loneliness.* NY: Putnam, 317pp. Wendall Oliver's difficult adjustment to extended family teaches him to perceive people fairly, even to trust others.	VT	c	C,I	Rea	IX
Oates, Joyce Carol. *A Garden of Earthly Delights.* NY: Vanguard, 440pp. Abuse by migrant-worker father, unrequited love, and calculated marriage during adolescence shape Clara's arid life, son Swan's tragedy.	S	c–m,c–a	C,I,SC	Rea	I,II,IX,XI
Olsen, Paul. *Country of Old Men.* NY: Holt, 248pp. Martha Nowell's affair reawakens old animosities, incites violence, forever changes the lovers.	NewE	17	SC,C	Rea	I
Patterson, Mary. *The Iron Country.* Boston: Houghton, 403pp. Friendship, love, war, violence, and death all affect John Moore and Maxine Johnson, two important characters.	MN	hs	I	Rea	I,III,VII,X
Patterson, Sam[uel H.]. *A Nickel's Worth of Ice.* NY: Knopf, 296pp. Carey Niven's initiation requires awareness, evaluation, sometimes acceptance of evil in adults important to him.	VA	13	C,I,SoG	Rea	VIII,IX, XII
Price, Reynolds. *A Generous Man.* NY: Atheneum, 275pp. Milo Mustian's initiation into adulthood includes ritual search, trials; Lois Provo's includes trials, self-discovery.	NC	15,16	C,I,Fab	Rea	II,VI,VIII
Richert, William. *Aren't You Even Gonna Kiss Me Good-by?* NY: McKay, 247pp. Chronicle of Jimmy Reardon's sometimes funny, sometimes silly, sometimes questionable romantic and money-making ventures.	IL	17	I	C	VIII,X

Author/Title	Setting	Age	Type	Tone	Reference
1966 (*continued*)					
Richter, Conrad. *A Country of Strangers*. NY: Knopf, 169pp. Reared by Indians, Stone Girl (Mary Stanton) finds only grief and alienation when returned to her parents' home.	PA	a–m	H	Rea	I,II,VI
Ritter, Margaret. *Simon Says*. Boston: Little, 248pp. Diana Braden struggles to come to terms with her parents, her mentor, a career, marriage, and motherhood.	NY	a	I	Rea	I,II,V
Robertson, Don. *The Sum and Total of Now*. NY: Putnam, 251pp. Morris Bird III puzzles over adult pettiness in face of grandmother's terminal illness, retains optimism.	OH	13	I	Rea	IX
Rodman, Bella. *Lions in the Way*. Chicago: Follett, 238pp. Black and white students are caught up in violence instigated by outsiders as high school is desegregated.	TN	16	YA,H	Rea	XII
Scott, William R. [pseud., Weldon Hill]. *Rafe*. NY: McKay, 342pp. Vulnerable and resentful, Rafe Layton wins respect by bravery and resourcefulness during flash flood.	OK	11	YA,I	Rea,P	VIII,XIII
Sherburne, Zoa. *Girl in the Mirror*. NY: Morrow, 190pp. Both major problems—the deaths of her parents, acceptance of a stepmother—and minor—being overweight—distress Ruth Ann Callahan.	?	16	YA	Rea	II
Susann, Jacqueline. *Valley of the Dolls*. NY: Random, 442pp. One plot line details talented Neely O'Hara's struggle for happiness and stardom, her dependency on drugs.	NY	c–a	C	Rea	IV,VI
Walker, Margaret. *Jubilee*. Boston: Houghton, 497pp. Uncertainties, humiliations, and the destructiveness of life as a slave are recounted in Vyry's story of unacknowledged daughterhood, love, marriages.	GA,AL	c–m	H,SC	Rea	I,II,IV

Entry	Location	Age	Code	P/Rea	Refs
Wells, Tobias. *A Matter of Love and Death.* Garden City, NY: Doubleday, 191pp. When her guardians are killed, Judy Carter is immediately suspected and tells conflicting lies.	Boston	19	D	P	V
Whitney, Phyllis A. *Columbella.* Garden City, NY: Doubleday, 306pp. Tensions between Leila Drew and her mother complicate relationship with Leila's tutor, protagonist Jessica Abbott.	Virgin Is.	14	C	Rea	II
Wilkinson, Sylvia. *Moss on the North Side.* Boston: Houghton, 235pp. Falling in love helps Cary, a half-blood Cherokee, come to terms with heritage, loss of father, disdain for mother.	S	14	I,C	Rea	I,II
Wilner, Herbert. *All the Little Heroes.* Indianapolis: Bobbs, 487pp. Gang teaches dying physician about life.	Brooklyn	12–16	SC	P	XI
Wojciechowska, Maia. *The Hollywood Kid.* NY: Harper, 165pp. Bryan Wilson, son of beautiful film star, is reconciled with mother and overcomes hatred of self and the world.	CA	15	YA	P	XIII
1967					
Aaron, Chester. *About Us.* NY: McGraw, 239pp. Benny Kahn matures through the Depression and into World War II amid poverty and tragedy.	PA	8–20	I	Rea	IX,XI
Baxt, George. *A Parade of Cockeyed Creatures; or, Did Someone Murder Our Wandering Boy?* NY: Random, 209pp. Boy's disappearance leads policeman to reconstruct his tormented life and motivation. Never seen, Tippy becomes very real.	NYC	17	D	Rea	IX
Clarke, Mary Stetson. *The Limner's Daughter.* NY: Viking, 255pp. Amity Lyte makes a new life for her father and brother by establishing an inn.	MA	16	YA,H	Rea	II,V

1967 *(continued)*

Author/Title	Setting	Age	Type	Tone	Reference
Colman, Lonnie [William Lawrence]. *King.* NY: McGraw, 177pp. Two boys and a dog find refuge and mild adventure with foster parents.	GA	15,a	I	Rea	IX
Couffer, Jack. *The Concrete Wilderness.* NY: Meredith, 212pp. Nature-loving Archie Larsen and Wolf, a wild dog, face city life and laws.	NYC	13	I	Rea	IX,X,XII, XIII
Deal, Borden. *The Least One.* Garden City, NY: Doubleday, 360pp. Son of stubborn, proud, and poor southern whites learns of death, guilt, and responsibility as he finds his identity.	S	12	I	Rea,Sym, P	IX,XII, XIII
Duhrssen, Alfred. *Memoir of an Aged Child.* NY: Holt, 184pp. Nameless narrator presents scenes from his growing up, including parents' divorces, private schooling, and first love affair.	?	c–m	I	Su,Sym	VIII,IX, XII
Fox, Paula. *Poor George.* NY: Harcourt, 220pp. Dropout invades the home of a teacher, triggering changes in his life.	NY	17–18	C	Rea,P	XI
Fox, William Price. *Moonshine Light, Moonshine Bright.* Phila: Lippincott, 383pp. Boys' search for perfect car leads them into petty crime, including bootlegging.	SC	14,14	LC	C	XII,XIII
Gates, Natalie. *Hush, Hush Johnson.* NY: Holt, 175pp. Mindy Johnson becomes the innocent pawn of Russian spies.	NJ	18	D	C	IV
Green, Gerald. *To Brooklyn with Love.* NY: Trident, 305pp. Albert Abrams fights his parents' protectiveness and his sissified reputation among tough street kids.	NYC	hs	I,M	Rea	XIII

Herrick, William. *The Itinerant*. NY: McGraw, 228pp. Of radical Jewish background, Zeke Gurevich observes or participates in most social causes of 1920s and 1930s.	NYC,JNY	6–m	P,SC	Sat,Rea	VIII,XII, XIII
Hinton, S. E. *The Outsiders*. NY: Viking, 188pp. Through three deaths, narrator Ponyboy Curtis, gang member, learns futility of hatred and pleads for understanding of boys like him.	OK	14	YA,I,SC	Rea,P	IX,XI,XII, XIII,XIV XIII,XIV
Mailer, Norman. *Why Are We in Vietnam?* NY: Putnam, 208pp. Hunting trip anticipates D.J.'s coming tour of duty in Vietnam, suggesting both traditional and contemporary male initiation rites.	AK	18	SC,I	Rea	XII,XIII
Marshall, Catherine. *Christy*. NY: McGraw, 496pp. Christy Huddleston, idealistic, stubborn, and naive, spends a year as a teacher in a mountain mission school.	TN	19	LC,I	Rea,P	V,VI
Morey, Walt. *Home Is the North*. NY: Dutton, 223pp. Orphaned at fifteen, Brad finds a new family, earning their respect and the right to make key decisions.	AK	15	YA,I	Rea	IX,XII, XIII
Perrin, Ursula. *Ghosts*. NY: Knopf, 253pp. Adult Eleanor Munson reflects upon a key adolescent choice—to attend college—in attempt to understand its full ramifications.	NY	c–m	C,I	Rea	V,VI
Potok, Chaim. *The Chosen*. NY: Simon, 284pp. Danny, groomed to succeed his Hasidic Rabbi father, and Reuven, son of a Talmudic scholar, confront their heritages and ambitions.	NY	hs	I	P	IX
Reed, Kit. *The Better Part*. NY: Farrar, 208pp. Jealous of father's commitment to girls' correctional institution he supervises, Martha Ewald rebels (and matures) by helping inmate escape.	?	a	C	Rea	II
Richardson, Anne. *Digging Out*. NY: McGraw, 181pp. Adult Laura Smith recollects several family members' histories, trying to understand their attitudes toward one another, Judaism, and America.	NYC	c–m	C	Rea	II,V

Author/Title	Setting	Age	Type	Tone	Reference
1967 *(continued)*					
Rollins, Bryant. *Danger Song*. Garden City, NY: Doubleday, 280pp. Lives of Arla McMahon and Martin Williams illustrate societal and racial repression.	Boston	hs	I	Rea	*II,VIII,IX, XI,XIII*
Rosenberg, Jessie. *Sudina*. NY: Dutton, 236pp. Sudina Wraith Howell's obsessive sense of herself as evil and dangerous nearly destroys her.	S	13	C	Rea	VII
Roth, Philip. *When She Was Good*. NY: Random, 306pp. Much of Lucy Nelson's uneasiness with demands of father, husband, society stem from attitudes and choices established during adolescence.	M	c–m	C	Rea	I,II
Salas, Floyd. *Tattoo the Wicked Cross*. NY: Grove, 351pp. Aaron D'Aragon's cycle of crime-reform school-crime prevails over efforts of family, girlfriend Judith.	CA	15	SC	Rea	VIII,IX,XI
Samuels, Gertrude. *The People vs. Baby*. Garden City, NY: Doubleday, 292pp. Josephine Delia ("Baby") Gomez's futile attempts to escape her drug-, gang-, and crime-infested life are based on fact.	NYC	hs	SC	Rea	II,IV
Sandburg, Helga. *The Wizard's Child*. NY: Dial, 260pp. Her father's wishes and his skill with folk magic sharply affect Marn Coomb's pregnancy, her choice of mate.	NC	17	C,LC	Rea	I,II,III
Sherburne, Zoa. *Too Bad about the Haines Girl*. NY: Morrow, 191pp. Melinda Haines confronts the now familiar theme of problems facing a pregnant teenager.	?	hs	YA	Rea	I
Speare, Elizabeth George. *The Prospering*. Boston: Houghton, 372pp. Elizabeth Williams's life and interests illuminate story of Stockbridge Indian mission.	MA	c–m	H	Rea	V,VI

Stuart, Jesse. *Mr. Gallion's School.* NY: McGraw, 337pp. Former principal returns to troubled rural high school, in attempt to save it.	KY	hs	M	D	XII
Welles, Patricia. *Babyhip.* NY: Dutton, 256pp. Precocious intellectually and sexually, aggressive verbally, rebellious against the middle class and the Midwest, Sarah Green follows her fiancé to Harvard.	MI,MA	16	P,I	C	I,IV
West, Jessamyn. *Leafy Rivers.* NY: Harcourt, 310pp. Leafy Rivers's marriage, maturation journey, and love affair reveal her growth.	IN,OH	c–a	H,I	Rea	I,V
Wilkinson, Sylvia. *A Killing Frost.* Boston: Houghton, 216pp. A life divided between school and the swamp forest teaches Ramona Hopkins about life and her own special background.	NC	13	LC	Rea	VI
Williams, Vinnie. *Greenbones.* NY: Viking, 244pp. Yearning for education, Nin Rabun is tricked into becoming wandering evangelist and travels backwoods Georgia with his overpowering mother.	GA	12–20	P	C	XII,XIII

1968

Baker, Elliott. *The Penny Wars.* NY: Putnam's, 255pp. Familial and personal crises complicate the initiation of urban Tyler A. Bishop in 1939; novel mixes the comic and painful.	NY	16	C,I	C,Rea	VIII,IX,XIII
Baldwin, James. *Tell Me How Long the Train's Been Gone.* NY: Dial, 484pp. Successful bisexual black actor recalls youth in Harlem, adored older brother, and theatrical apprenticeship.	NYC	10–39	I,SC	Rea,Sym,P	VIII, XI, XII
Benchley, Nathaniel. *Welcome to Xanadu.* NY: Atheneum, 304pp. Ignorant girl, kidnapped by madman, uses her wits to survive but also learns much from her captor.	NM	16	C	Rea,C	IV

Author/Title	Setting	Age	Type	Tone	Reference
1968 *(continued)*					
Bradford, Richard. *Red Sky at Morning*. Phila: Lippincott, 256pp. Against background of war, Joshua Arnold forms new friendships and accepts new responsibilities—his coming of age.	NM	17	I	Rea	*IX,X,XIII*
Caldwell, Erskine. *Summertime Island*. NY: World, 183pp. Steve Henderson learns about racism on fishing trip.	TN	15	I	Rea	*VIII,XI*
Carpenter, Don. *Blade of Light*. NY: Harcourt, 181pp. Harold Hunt, Irwin Semple, and Carole Weigandt's bizarre youthful triangle results in both immediate and future tragedy.	?	hs	C	Rea	*I,X,XIV*
Chappell, Fred. *Dagon*. NY: Harcourt, 177pp. Mina Morgan symbolizes decadence in modern American society.	S	16	SC	Su	*IV*
Cozzens, James Gould. *Morning, Noon, and Night*. NY: Harcourt, 408pp. Several brief flashbacks depict Henry Dodd Worthington's social, sexual, and philosophical development.	E	c–60	C,M	Rea	*VIII,IX*
Culp, John H. *A Whistle in the Wind*. NY: Holt, 281pp. Cesre and Roderick grow up and marry in a camp for Indians' captives.	TX	8–a	H	Rea	*II,VIII*
Daniels, Guy. *Progress, U.S.A.* NY: Macmillan, 214pp. Depression-era small town is setting for lively boy's adventures and misadventures.	IA	a	M	Sat,C	*XIII*
Davis, L. J. [Lawrence J.]. *Whence All But He Had Fled*. NY: Viking, 247pp. Alienated Robert Probish unsuccessfully seeks identity in New York melting pot.	NYC	18	C	Rea,C	*XI,XIII*

Disney, Doris Miles. *Voice from the Grave.* Garden City, NY: Doubleday, 190pp. Disappearance of two boys while on fishing trip leads to mystery.	ME	17,17	D	Rea,P	XI
Farrington, Fielden. *A Little Game.* NY: Walker, 150pp. Brilliant but psychopathic boy rules friend with fear and engages in murder "games."	E	13,13	D	Rea	XIV
Hentoff, Nat. *I'm Really Dragged But Nothing Gets Me Down.* NY: Simon, 127pp. Despite distraught father's inability to understand, Jeremy Wolf resolves to resist the draft.	NYC	17	SC,YA	Rea,P	IX,XII
Hunter, Evan. *Last Summer.* Garden City, NY: Doubleday, 256pp. Sexuality and thoughtless cruelty occur in Peter's, David's, and Sandy's treatment of each other, pet seagull, and Rhoda.	NewE	a	I	Rea,Sym	I,IV,V, VIII,X
Hunter, Kristin. *The Soul Brothers and Sister Lou.* NY: Scribner's, 248pp. Racial persecution, a death, and her musical talent contribute to Louretta Hawkins's maturation.	NY	14	I,YA	Rea	III,V,XI
Kirkwood, James. *Good Times/Bad Times.* NY: Simon, 348pp. Peter Kilburn is driven to murder by misapprehension of his friendship with Jordan Legier.	NH	18	C,I	Rea	VIII,X,XII
Leigh, James. *Downstairs at Ramsey's.* NY: Harper, 250pp. After seducing her foster father, Delilah reports him to police when he refuses to marry her.	CA	14–15	I	Rea,P	I
Macdonald, Ross. *See* Millar, Kenneth					
McGraw, Eloise Jarvis. *Greensleeves.* NY: Harcourt, 311pp. Shannon Lightley successfully defines her career goals.	OR	18	YA,C,I	Rea	V
Millar, Kenneth [pseud., Ross Macdonald]. *The Instant Enemy.* NY: Knopf, 237pp. Runaway Sandy Sebastian's criminal activity thwarts detective Lew Archer, symbolizes social decay.	CA	hs	D	Rea	II,IV

Author/Title	Setting	Age	Type	Tone	Reference
1968 (*continued*)					
Portis, Charles. *True Grit*. NY: Simon, 215pp. Mattie Ross faces danger and death while recruiting help and then avenging father's murder.	AR,OK	14	I,W,H	Rea	II,III,IV
Rickett, Frances. *A Certain Slant of Light*. NY: Putnam's, 320pp. Supportive female family members help Angel Crowley confront the wickedness and value the decency in various adults' behavior.	IN	a	I,C	Rea	II
Ross, Sam. *Hang-up*. NY: Coward, 222pp. Grim teen life on Sunset Strip affects Sherry Loomis and Dave Grant, kills Martha Carson.	CA	15	D,SC	Rea	II,XIII
Tomerlin, John. *The Fledgling*. NY: Dutton, 188pp. By learning to fly, Rich Newman gains confidence and overcomes personal problems.	KS	17	YA,I	Rea,P	IX,XII
Williams, Thomas. *Whipple's Castle*. NY: Random, 535pp. Children of embittered, crippled father mature through varied wartime and postwar experiences; tragic climax destroys one of them.	NH	a	I	Rea	I,II,IV,VI, VIII,IX, XI,XIII
Zindel, Paul. *The Pigman*. NY: Harper, 182pp. John and Lorraine betray trust and friendship of an old man and face severe guilt.	NJ	hs	YA,I	Rea	III,XIII
1969					
Armstrong, William H. *Sounder*. NY: Harper, 116pp. Black lad helps sustain family and seeks education during father's imprisonment.	GA	10–16	YA,I	Rea	IX,XII
Barrett, B. L. *Love in Atlantis*. Boston: Houghton, 182pp. Comic and nostalgic recollection of sexual awakening of innocent, ignorant young girl.	CA	14	I	Rea	I

Bass, Milton R. *Jory*. NY: Putnam's, 256pp. Jory learns of sex, violence, and death, becomes a killer, and learns to direct his own life.	KS,JNY, TX	15	I,W	Rea	VIII,IX, XII,XIII, XIV
Beckham, Barry. *My Main Mother*. NY: Walker, 214pp. In long flashback, Mitchell Mibbs explains why he killed his mother, whom he both loved and hated.	ME,NYC, RI	a	C,I	Rea	IX,XI,XII
Biderman, Sol. *Bring Me to the Banqueting House*. NY: Viking, 284pp. David Unicorn, growing up in Jewish orphanage, learns about himself and life through both observing and participating.	CO	6–15	I	Rea,C	XIII
Caldwell, Erskine. *The Weather Shelter*. NY: World, 190pp. Mulatto Jeff Bazemore's white father helps him escape being lynched.	TN	12–17	I	Rea	VIII,IX
Cheever, John. *Bullet Park*. NY: Knopf, 245pp. Tony Nailles experiences alienation in seemingly pleasant suburbia.	E	hs	SC	Su	XIII
Cleaver, Bill. *See* Cleaver, Vera, and Bill Cleaver					
Cleaver, Vera, and Bill Cleaver. *Where the Lilies Bloom*. Phila: Lippincott, 174pp. At fourteen, orphaned Mary Call Luther assumes responsibility for her three siblings.	NC	14	YA,I,C	Rea	II
Connell, Evan. *Mr. Bridge*. NY: Knopf, 369pp. Relationships of Ruth, Carol, and Douglas Bridge with their father help reveal his character.	KS	hs	C	Rea	III,IX
Elliott, David W. *Listen to the Silence*. NY: Holt, 279pp. Timmy accommodates to mental hospital.	?	14	I	P	XIV
Forman, James. *The Cow Neck Rebels*. NY: Farrar, 272pp. Amid horrors of war, boy matures and learns to value freedom.	NY	16	YA,H	Rea	XIII
Koch, Stephen. *Night Watch*. NY: Harper, 212pp. David Fontana and his sister, Harriet, turn to one another after sexual experiments with others.	NY	hs	E	Su	I,II,VIII, IX

Author/Title	Setting	Age	Type	Tone	Reference
1969 (*continued*)					
Lafore, Laurence. *Nine Seven Juliet*. Garden City, NY: Doubleday, 300pp. Amateur detection, flying lessons, and romance normalize crippled Richie's attitudes, behavior.	?	hs	D	Rea	VIII,XI, XIV
McAfee, Thomas. *Rover Youngblood: An American Fable*. NY: Baron, 208pp. Rover Youngblood undertakes traditional maturation journey.	AL,JNY	16	P,I	Rea	I,II,IX,X, XII
Means, Florence Crannell. *Our Cup Is Broken*. Boston: Houghton, 229pp. Adopted and educated by whites, Sarah, a Hopi, discovers that readjustment to Hopi life is supremely difficult.	E,W	8–20	YA,SC,H	Rea	I,II,IV
Neufeld, John. *Lisa, Bright and Dark*. NY: Philips, 125pp. Three friends try to stop Lisa's descent into madness as her parents refuse to confront the problem.	NY	15,16	C	P	VII
Oates, Joyce Carol. *them*. NY: Vanguard, 508pp. Grim histories of Loretta Bottsford Wendall Furlong and her children, Maureen and Jules Wendall, illustrate modern urban life.	Detroit	c–m	C,I,SC	Rea	I,IV,VI, VIII
Tucker, Helen. *The Sound of Summer Voices*. NY: Stein, 256pp. Account of his mother's difficult adolescence explains Patrick Quincannon Tolson's puzzling status in relatives' home, may contribute to his maturation.	S	12	C,I	Rea	IX
Ware, Clyde. *The Innocents*. NY: Norton, 240pp. Old prospector and abandoned girl, called Doe, form loving symbiotic relationship until threatened by outlaws.	SW	6?–19?	W	Rea	VI
Waugh, Hillary. *The Young Prey*. Garden City, NY: Doubleday, 206pp. Virgie Hall's death during junket to New York City motivates police investigation.	NYC	15	D	Rea	IV

1970

Entry	Place	Age			
Adelman, Robert H. *The Bloody Benders.* NY: Stein, 247pp. Bradley Fisher recounts his infatuation with Kate Bender, leader of her family of murderers and thieves.	KS	17,19	H,I,D	Rea	*IV,VIII*
Arnow, Harriet Simpson. *The Weedkiller's Daughter.* NY: Knopf, 372pp. Susan Schnitzer keeps a large part of her life secret from her bigoted parents.	Detroit	15	C	Rea	*II,III,V*
Brown, Kenneth H. *The Narrows.* NY: Dial, 277pp. Middle-class boys and girls in Brooklyn engage in wild parties, experiment with theft, and emerge relatively whole.	NYC	14–18	I	Rea	*VIII,X, XI,XII, XIII*
Burke, James Lee. *To the Bright and Shining Sun.* NY: Scribner's, 241pp. Perry James tries to support family and better himself during coal strike and attendant violence.	KY	16	SC,C	N	*XII*
Dizenzo, Patricia. *Phoebe.* NY: McGraw, 120pp. High-school senior Phoebe Altman is frightened and confused by her pregnancy.	?	16	YA	D,Rea,P	*I*
Drexler, Rosalyn. *One or Another.* NY: Dutton, 167pp. Affair of high-school student and teacher's wife is disturbing to both.	NYC	17	C,F	C,Su	*VIII*
Estes, Winston M. *Another Part of the House.* Phila: Lippincott, 255pp. Larry Morrison learns that even death and dishonesty cannot shake his family's stability.	TX	10	I	Rea	*IX,XI*
Fall, Thomas. *See* Snow, Donald Clifford					
Goddard, J. R. *The Night Crew.* Boston: Little, 186pp. A state fire-crewman cowboy survives his first major fire.	CA	18	I	Rea	*XII*
Hansen, Joseph. *Fadeout.* NY: Harper, 187pp. Brief affair with Anselmo mitigates investigator-protagonist Dave Brandstetter's grief over lover's death; other adolescents complicate his current case.	CA	18	D	Rea	*VIII*

1970 *(continued)*

Author/Title	Setting	Age	Type	Tone	Reference
Horwitz, Julius. *The Diary of A.N.: The Story of the House on West 104th Street.* NY: Coward, 220pp. Bright, perceptive A.N. seeks to escape black ghetto and dependence on welfare through education.	NYC	hs	SC	N	I,II,IV,V,VII
Kennedy, Raymond. *Good Night, Jupiter.* NY: Atheneum, 244pp. Tom and Maxwell spend Christmas eve in extravagantly comic confrontation with death and sex.	NewE	hs	G	C	VIII,XIV
Kingman, Lee. *The Peter Pan Bag.* NY: Houghton, 214pp. Leaving boarding school and rebelling against her parents, Wendy Allardyce goes to Boston to live a free life with hippies.	MA	17	M	Sat	V
Meriwether, Louise. *Daddy Was a Number Runner.* Englewood Cliffs, NJ: Prentice, 208pp. Irrepressible Francie Coffin observes poverty, crime, bigotry, and hopelessness in Harlem during the Depression.	NYC	11–13	SC,C	Rea	VI
Michael, David J. *A Blow to the Head.* Boston: Houghton, 262pp. J. Roger Gaffrey's aloofness from fellow students precipitates tragedy for him and the narrator, Anthony "Pooch" Pansella.	WI?	hs,hs	I,C	Rea	IX,X,XI,XII,XIII
Morrison, Toni. *The Bluest Eye.* NY: Holt, 164pp. Pecola Breedlove is driven mad by racism, loneliness, and abuse.	M	a	SC,C	Rea	II,IV,VII
Nathan, Robert. *Mia.* NY: Knopf, 179pp. Mia, the corporeal manifestation of sedate, adult Emmeline Anderson's youthful, adventurous spirit, complicates life of protagonist Robert Nathan.	NewE	15?	F	F,Sat	I

Robertson, Don. *The Greatest Thing That Almost Happened.* NY: Putnam, 248pp. Leukemia forces Morris Bird III, preoccupied with basketball and love, to learn a new heroism in face of death.	OH	17	C,I	Rea	XIV
Sarton, May. *Kinds of Love.* NY: Norton, 464pp. Romance between Cathy and Joel is key subplot in novel focusing on the elderly.	NH	15	M,SC	Rea	II,VI
Shaw, Irwin. *Rich Man, Poor Man.* NY: Delacorte, 629pp. Competitiveness, rebellion, and sibling rivalry mark adolescences of Rudy, Tom, and Gretchen Jordache.	NY	c–m	C,I	Rea	II,IX
Snow, Donald Clifford [pseud., Thomas Fall]. NY: McCall, 312pp. *The Ordeal of Running Standing.* Constant tensions between Kiowa, Cheyenne, and "white" cultures complicate lives of Running Standing (Joe) and Crosses-the-River (Sara Cross).	OK,PA	a–m	H,I,C,SC	Rea	I,V,VIII,XII
Turner, Steven. *A Measure of Dust.* NY: Simon, 190pp. Characters of naive Mark Torrance and sexually active Geraldine Wester revealed in good part through their relationship.	MS	13,14	C,I	Rea	I,VIII
Tyler, Anne. *A Slipping Down Life.* NY: Knopf, 214pp. Evie Decker's bland home life, her fascination with and marriage to rock musician, and her pregnancy contribute to maturation.	NC	17	C	Rea	I,II
Vasquez, Richard. *Chicano.* Garden City, NY: Doubleday, 376pp. Lives of various Sandoval family members celebrate Mexican-American heritage and reveal discrimination against them.	Los Angeles	hs	SC	Rea	IV,VI,XI,XIII
Wagoner, David. *Where Is My Wandering Boy Tonight?* NY: Farrar, 255pp. Andrew Jackson Holcomb, Jr., judge's son, and Fred Haskell, minister's son, discover corruption of fathers and town during wild adventures.	WY	17,17	H	C	X,XIII

Author/Title	Setting	Age	Type	Tone	Reference
1970 *(continued)*					
Weidman, Jerome. *Fourth Street East.* NY: Random, 239pp. Benny Kramer recalls incidents from his childhood and youth among immigrant Jews on New York City's Lower East Side.	NYC	7–m	LC	Rea	XIII
Welty, Eudora. *Losing Battles.* NY: Random, 436pp. Ella Fay Renfro complicates life of brother Jack; both contribute to portrait of 1930s southern extended family.	MS	16	LC,C,I	Rea	II,VI,IX, XIII
Wersba, Barbara. *Run Softly, Go Fast.* NY: Atheneum, 205pp. Death of father, whom he loved and hated, prompts David Marks to try to understand his father and himself.	NYC	c–19	YA,C	P	VIII,IX,X, XII
Wilson, Sloan. *All the Best People.* NY: Putnam's, 510pp. The childhoods and courtship of Caroline Stauffer and Dana Campbell make for difficult adjustments in their marriage and adult lives.	NY,MA	c–m	I	Rea	I,VIII
Young, Al. *Snakes.* NY: Holt, 149pp. MC Moore, ghetto youth, experiments with life, finds greatest joy—and future—in music.	MI	hs,hs	I	Rea	VIII,XI, XII
Zindel, Paul. *I Never Loved Your Mind.* NY: Harper, 181pp. Dropouts Yvette and Dewey discover that sexual attraction and dissatisfaction with society are inadequate bases for union.	NJ,NY	hs	YA	Rea	I,VIII
1971					
Abbey, Edward. *Black Sun.* NY: Simon, 159pp. Sandy MacKenzie has affair with older man.	SW	19	C	Rea	I
Athas, Daphne. *Entering Ephesus.* NY: Viking, 442pp. Irene, Urie, and Loco Poco Bishop, daughters of eccentric parents, seek education and experience in southern university town.	GA	a	I	Rea	I,II,V, VIII,XII

Atwell, Lester. *Life with Its Sorrow, Life with its Tear.* NY: Simon, 414pp. Paul Forrest discovers the strengths and weaknesses of the maternal relatives who rear him.	NY	hs	C	Rea	IX
Berkley, Sandra. *Coming Attractions.* NY: Dutton, 212pp. Bright, aspiring starlet, growing up in Hollywood, finds life quite different from the movies.	CA	4–17	M	Sat	I,V,VI
Blatty, William Peter. *The Exorcist.* NY: Harper, 340pp. Regan MacNeil, victim of literal satanic possession, has her demon exorcised by Roman Catholic priest.	DC	11	D	Rea	V
Brautigan, Richard. *The Abortion: An Historical Romance, 1966.* NY: Simon, 226pp. Alienation of beautiful girl and older lover is dissipated by their affair, which includes an abortion.	CA	19	F	Rea	I
Bryant, Will. *The Big Lonesome.* Garden City, NY: Doubleday, 352pp. Tobin Shattuck meets adventures while wandering in West with father and grizzly bear cub.	CA,OR	a	W,I,H	Rea,Sym	XII,XIII
Chute, B. J. *The Story of a Small Life.* NY: Dutton, 208pp. Mig fancies himself a rising "operator" on his slum street, resisting responsibility for Anna, his clinging, pregnant girlfriend.	NYC	15?,17	SC	Rea	I,VIII
Covert, Paul. *Cages.* NY: Liveright, 181pp. Gossip and tragedy destroy the warm friendship between Bob Ward and Eric Mathews.	PA	14–15	I	Rea	I,IX,X
Dizenzo, Patricia. *An American Girl.* NY: Holt, 148pp. Middle-class daughter of alcoholic mother and ineffectual father records minutiae of her daily life.	NJ	hs	C,SC	Rea,P	II,IV,V
Dunn, Katherine. *Truck.* NY: Harper, 217pp. Alienated Jean ("Dutch") Gillis runs away to join friend who also hates middle-class life and values.	OR,CA, JNY	15	C	Su	IV

1971 (*continued*)

Author/Title	Setting	Age	Type	Tone	Reference
Gallagher, Patricia. *Summer of Sighs*. NY: Avon, 288pp. Pregnant by son of mother's lover, Nina Bradley learns of parental affair and commits suicide.	S	17	I	Rea	I,II,V
Grossbach, Robert. *Someone Great*. NY: Harper's, 205pp. Brief passages contrast his parents' dreams for Stuie with the dreary reality of his adulthood.	NYC	c–m	C,I	Rea	IX
Hale, Nancy. *Secrets*. NY: Coward, 126pp. Writer nostalgically remembers Boston childhood and youth spent with four friends, two boys and two girls.	Boston	c–m	C	N	III
Hayes, Joseph Arnold. *Like Any Other Fugitive*. NY: Dial, 446pp. Family problems prompt Laurel Taggart to join fugitive B.C. Chadwick in maturation journey and eventual marriage.	JNY	17	I	Rea	V
Herlihy, James Leo. *The Season of the Witch*. NY: Simon, 383pp. Commune represents escape, rebellion, and testing-ground for Gloria Random and John McFadden, fugitives from family and the draft.	JNY,NYC	hs,19	C,P,I	Rea	II,XII
Higgins, Colin. *Harold and Maude*. Phila: Lippincott, 145pp. Harold Chasin's friendship and affection for aged Maude (Countess Mathilde Chardin) ends his "suicide attempts," counteracts mother's destructiveness.	?	19	SC,I	C,I	IX,X
Jones, Madison. *A Cry of Absence*. NY: Crown, 280pp. Cam Glenn, in misguided attempt to live up to mother's standards, participates in ugly racial incidents.	S	17	SC	Rea,P	XII

Killens, John Oliver. *The Cotillion; or, One Good Bull Is Half the Herd.* NY: Trident, 256pp. Account of Yoruba Lovejoy's reluctant participation in debut party held for young blacks allows for biting social criticism.	NYC	18	SC	C	I,II,IV
Lewin, Michael Z. *Ask the Right Question.* NY: Putnam's, 190pp. Eloise Crystal requests investigation of her true parentage, complicates detective's pursuit of the case.	IN	15	D	Rea	II
Lieberman, Herbert. *Crawlspace.* NY: McKay, 306pp. Richard Atlee, alienated and embittered, finds a haven with an elderly couple but gradually becomes both help and menace.	N	18?	D	P	XI
Macdonald, Ross. *See* Millar, Kenneth					
Millar, Kenneth [pseud., Ross Macdonald]. *The Underground Man.* NY: Knopf, 272pp. Susan Crandall's nightmare flight with her kidnapped victim, little Ronnie Broadhurst, sets detective on her trail.	CA	19	D	Rea	II,IV
Raucher, Herman. *A Glimpse of Tiger.* NY: Putnam's, 222pp. Janice ("Tiger") McAllister pays dearly for terminating affair with Luther, a fellow dropout.	NYC	19	C	Rea	I,V,VIII,XII
Raucher, Herman. *Summer of '42.* NY: Putnam's, 251pp. Sexual experimentation of Hermie, Oscy, Benjie, Gloria, Miriam, and Aggie marks boys' maturation in story evoking early 1940s.	NewE	15	C,M	Rea	VIII,X,XIII
Reeve, F. [Franklin] D. *The Brother.* NY: Farrar, 307pp. Will and David Spencer, scarred by aloof, demanding parents, find only tragedy, despite efforts of women who love them.	VT	c-m	I,M	Rea	VIII,IX
Stolz, Mary. *By the Highway Home.* NY: Harper, 194pp. Catty's ability to cope with economic uncertainty, relocation of family, and brother's death symbolized by beginning of first love affair.	VT	13	YA	Rea	II

Author/Title	Setting	Age	Type	Tone	Reference
1971 *(continued)*					
Updike, John. *Rabbit Redux*. NY: Knopf, 407pp. Entanglement of Harry "Rabbit" Angstrom and his young son, Nelson, with Jill Pendleton, 1960s rebel, leads to reassessment, tragedy.	PA	13,18	SC,C	Rea	I,IX,X
Weidman, Jerome. *Last Respects*. NY: Random, 372pp. Benny Kramer, inspired by mother's death, continues recalling New York boyhood among a mixture of cultures.	NY	14–m	LC	Rea	XIII
1972					
Blum, Ralph. *Old Glory and the Real-Time Freaks: A Children's Story and Patriotic Goodtime Book with Maps*. NY: Delacorte, 206pp. On marijuana, Quintus Ells writes life-affirming journal while awaiting grandfather's death.	CT	17	C	Rea,Su,P	VIII,XI, XIV
Colter, Cyrus. *The Rivers of Eros*. Chicago: Swallow, 219pp. Addie's affair with a married man precipitates tragedy.	Chicago	16	C,I	Rea	I,II
Ellis, Mel. *This Mysterious River*. NY: Holt, 208pp. Hammond Drumm endeavors to earn ten dollars to replace money he has stolen from church collection plate.	WI	12	YA,I	Rea	XII
Eyerly, Jeannette. *Bonnie Jo, Go Home*. NY: Lippincott, 141pp. Bonnie Jo Jackson overcomes a number of difficulties to have an abortion.	NYC	17	YA	Rea	I
Fair, Ronald. *We Can't Breathe*. NY: Harper, 216pp. In Chicago ghetto, black lad observes injustice and violence and strives to become a writer.	IL	9–14	SC	N	VIII,XI, XII,XIII
Fast, Howard. *The Hessian*. NY: Morrow, 192pp. The only survivor of a massacre, wounded drummer boy is tried and condemned to death by American patriots.	CT	16	SC	Rea,D	XIII

Entry	Place				
Friedman, Alan. *Hermaphrodeity: The Autobiography of a Poet.* NY: Knopf, 426pp. Social and sexual confusion of Millie/Willie Nieman, a hermaphrodite, used to attack sex-role stereotyping, examine role of poet.	CenA, NewE	c–m	SC,Fab	Sat	I
Gilbert, Julie Goldsmith. *Umbrella Steps.* NY: Random, 181pp. Protagonist Prudence Goodrich and Lolly Spitz, friends, are changed by affair each conducts with the other's father.	NYC	16–17	C,I	Rea	I,III
Gould, Lois. *Necessary Objects.* NY: Random, 275pp. Jill, Cathy, and Jason, cousins, demonstrate their parents' inability to love.	NYC	14,18,15	M	Rea	II,IX
Green, Hannah. *See* Greenberg, Joanne					
Greenan, Russell H. *The Queen of America.* NY: Random, 214pp. Ignacio Never's life becomes a nightmare under the influence of his psychotic father and Betsy March, a young killer.	Boston	14,16	Ho	Rea	XI
Greenberg, Joanne [pseud., Hannah Green]. *The Dead of the House.* NY: Doubleday, 180pp. The long central section recounts Vanessa Nye's awakening to young womanhood as she reports her family history.	OH	c–m	C,M	Rea	II
Harington, Donald. *Some Other Place. The Right Place.* Boston: Little, 462pp. Theories of reincarnation and attempts to learn ancestor's history complicate and illuminate love between Diana Stoving and Day Whittacker.	E	hs	F,H	Rom	I
Herbert, Frank. *Soul Catcher.* NY: Putnam's, 250pp. When kidnapped, David Marshall achieves manhood (shown by sexual initiation, survival in wilderness, brave facing of death) but retains innocence.	WA	13	C,I	P,Sym	VIII,XI,XIV
Hill, Weldon. *See* Scott, William R.					

Author/Title	Setting	Age	Type	Tone	Reference
1972 (*continued*)					
Holland, Isabelle. *The Man without a Face*. Phila: Lippincott, 158pp. While being coached for prep school exam by dis-figured man, Charles Norstadt learns to balance freedom and responsibility.	NewE	14	YA,I	Rea,P	IX,XI,XII
Hotchner, A. E. *King of the Hill*. NY: Harper, 240pp. Aaron's adventures intended as comic, quasi-nostalgic portrait of hardscrabble survival during Depression.	MO	hs	I	C	XIII
Kazan, Elia. *The Assassins*. NY: Stein, 377pp. Juana de Flores's experiments with drug scene and sex impel her father to murder her lover.	NM	17	SC	Rea	IV
Kellogg, Marjorie. *Like the Lion's Tooth*. NY: Farrar, 147pp. A number of abused children struggle to adapt to life in a children's home.	NY	a	P,I	Rea	II,IX,X
Kerr, M. E. *See* Meaker, Marijane					
Meaker, Marijane [pseud., M. E. Kerr]. *Dinky Hocker Shoots Smack*. NY: Harper, 198pp. Susan (Dinky) Hocker resorts to angry, dramatic plea for help to gain attention and sup-port of family, friends.	NYC	a	YA,SC,C	Rea	II,III,IV
Mountzoures, H. L. *The Bridge*. NY: Scribner's, 373pp. Philip Neros's life story depicts immigrant experience, his own difficult maturation, strains imposed on family by mother's mental illness.	CT	c–m	I	Rea	VIII,IX
Newlove, Donald. *Leo & Theodore*. NY: Sat. Rev., 341pp. Siamese twins, joined at hip, meet adversities and joys of life, usually courageously and with great good humor.	NY	c–m	C	P	XIV

O'Brien, Robert C. *A Report from Group 17*. NY: Atheneum, 210pp. Kidnapping of Allison leads to defeat of spy ring.	VA	12	D	Rea	IV
Peck, Richard. *Don't Look and It Won't Hurt*. NY: Holt, 173pp. Child of a working mother and an estranged father, Carol Patterson assumes considerable family responsibility.	M	15	YA,C	Rea	II
Rechy, John. *The Fourth Angel*. NY: Viking, 157pp. Toughened by incestuous rape at eleven, Shell leads three friends in drug and sex orgy.	TX	a	SC,C	Rea	I,IV,VIII, XI
Savage, Elizabeth. *Happy Ending*. Boston: Little, 308pp. Maryalyse Tyler and Bud Romeo fall in love under the protection of their elderly mentors and employers, the Russells.	MT	19	C	Rea	I,II
Scott, William R. [pseud., Weldon Hill]. *Jefferson McGraw* N.Y.: Morrow, 248pp. In one eventful summer, Jeff observes life and death and learns much about himself.	OK	12	I	Rea,C, Nos	XIII
Seelye, John. *The Kid*. NY: Viking, 119pp. Violence and deception in western cattle town contribute to revelation that Blondie, supposedly male, is female.	WY	a	W,H,LC	C	III,VI
Shulman, Alix Kates. *Memoirs of an Ex-Prom Queen*. NY: Knopf, 274pp. Failed marriages and infidelities cause Sasha Davis to recall her privileged and troubled adolescence.	OH,NY, MA	c–m	I,P	P	I
Stallworth, Anne Nall. *This Time Next Year*. NY: Vanguard, 288pp. Florrie Birdsong's stubborn immaturity stems from observing parents' struggle with their dreams and Depression-era economic reality.	AL	15	C	Rea	II
Stolz, Mary. *Leap before You Look*. NY: Harper, 259pp. During the year of her parents' divorce, Janine ("Jimmie") Gavin also faces other major—and some minor—adjustments.	NJ	14	YA	Rea	II

Author/Title	Setting	Age	Type	Tone	Reference
1972 (*continued*)					
Weesner, Theodore. *The Car Thief.* NY: Random, 370pp. Thief and truant, Alex Houseman spends time in juvenile detention, flounders in school, and is marked by father's suicide.	MI	16	I	Rea	IX,XI,XII
Yglesias, Rafael. *Hide Fox, and All After.* Garden City, NY: 203pp. Gifted actor and writer, Raul Sabas finds school unchallenging, a distraction from his real work.	NYC	14	C	P	XII
1973					
Bowers, John. *No More Reunions.* NY: Dutton, 224pp. Experimenting with sex and sports, Boney learns of death and matures into readiness to leave his small home town.	TN	hs	I	C,Rea,N	VIII,XII, XIV
Calisher, Hortense. *Eagle Eye.* NY: Arbor, 249pp. Flashbacks depict the development of Bunty Bronstein and of his upwardly mobile parents.	NYC	11–21	C	P	IX
Chappell, Fred. *The Gaudy Place.* NY: Harcourt, 178pp. The lives of Clemmie, a prostitute; Arkie, a con man; and Linn, a student, cross one another and the law.	NC	a	SC	Rea	IV,XII, XIII
Childress, Alice. *A Hero Ain't Nothin' But a Sandwich.* NY: Coward, 126pp. Friends and relatives try to help Benjie Johnson kick the drug habit.	NYC	13	YA,SC	Rea	IX,X,XI, XIII
Coffey, Marilyn. *Marcella.* NY: Charterhouse, 240pp. Marcella Colby prays for capacity to control the urge to masturbate.	KS	12–16	I	Rea	V
Coleman, Lonnie. *Beulah Land.* Garden City, NY: Doubleday, 495pp. Brief but important adolescent episodes figure in the antebellum lives of black and white extended plantation families.	GA	a	H	Rea	II

Entry	Location	Age	Category	Rea,Sym	Roman
Foster, Alan S. *Goodbye, Bobby Thomson! Goodbye, John Wayne!* NY: Simon, 190pp. Football player learns to reject American sports and military heroes as his role models.	NJ,NY,OH,PA	18–m	I,SC	Rea,Sym	XII
Gallagher, Patricia. *The Thicket.* NY: Avon, 256pp. With her Indian sweetheart and her brother's lover, Beth Hall is lost in wilderness and faces death while awaiting rescue.	TX	16	C,LC,SC	Rea	I,V,VI
Gardner, John [Champlin]. *Nickel Mountain.* NY: Knopf, 312pp. Callie Wells's unlikely marriage to protagonist Henry Soames both enhances and encumbers their lives.	NY	16	C	Rea	I
Greene, Bette. *Summer of My German Soldier.* NY: Dial, 230pp. Patty Bergen shelters an escaped German prisoner of war during World War II.	AR	12	YA,H,SC	Rea	II,III,IV
Guthrie, Alfred B., Jr. *Wild Pitch.* Boston: Houghton, 224pp. Jason Beard, an unofficial deputy, helps his hero, the sheriff, solve a murder case.	NW	17	D	Rea	XII
Guy, Rosa. *The Friends.* NY: Holt, 203pp. The lives of two Harlem girls, Edith Jackson, American-born, and Phyllisia Cathy, West Indian, are contrasted.	NYC	14,14	YA,C	Rea	II,III,IV
Harris, Marilyn. *Hatter Fox.* NY: Random, 241pp. Young doctor tries to reclaim Hatter Fox, an angry, bitter, sometimes violent Navajo.	NM	hs	C,SC	P,N	IV
Hillerman, Tony. *Dance Hall of the Dead.* NY: Harper, 166pp. Ernesto Cata, a Zuñi Indian, is a murder victim; George Bowlegs and Susanne are suspects.	NM	12,14,18	D	Rea	IV,XII
Hough, John [T.], Jr. *A Two-Car Funeral.* Boston: Little, 216pp. Political corruption permits brutal mistreatment of Stewart Browne, Raymond Karras, and "Kentucky" Danovic in "guidance center."	MA	15,15,15	SC	N,P	VIII,XI,XII

Author/Title	Setting	Age	Type	Tone	Reference
1973 (*continued*) Kerr, M. E. *See* Meaker, Marijane					
Logan, Jane. *The Very Nearest Room.* NY: Scribner's, 249pp. Chief caretaker of invalid mother and two siblings, Lee Kramer struggles for personal maturity to match her adult responsibilities.	NC	15	I	Rea	II
MacDougall, Ruth Doan. *The Cheerleader.* NY: Putnam's, 288pp. Henrietta Snow's sexual, social, and intellectual development in 1950s.	NH	hs	C,I	Rea	I,V,VI,VIII
Meaker, Marijane [pseud., M. E. Kerr]. *If I Love You, Am I Trapped Forever?* NY: Harper, 177pp. Alan Bennett experiences disappointment in love and a difficult reunion with his long-absent father.	NY	hs	C,I,YA	Rea	VIII,IX,XII
Morris, Willie. *The Last of the Southern Girls.* NY: Knopf, 287pp. Flashbacks to her Arkansas girlhood explain Carol Hollywell, an atypical Southern Belle.	DC	c–m	C	Rea	VI
Morrison, Toni. *Sula.* NY: Knopf, 174pp. Sula Peace and Nel Wright grow up diminished by parental error and racism.	OH	c–m	SC,C	Rea	II,III,IV
Murray, Michele. *The Crystal Nights.* NY: Seabury, 310pp. Elly Joseph's reluctance to accept relatives, refugees from Nazi Germany, intensifies growing pains, complicates family life.	CT	14–16	YA,I	Rea	II,VI
Neufeld, John. *For All the Wrong Reasons.* NY: New Am., 220pp. Wed because they expect a child, Tish and Peter react very divergently to responsibilities and strains of marriage, parenthood.	?	hs	I	Rea	I,VIII,XIV

Ogburn, Charles. *Winespring Mountain.* NY: Morrow, 252pp. Herself blind, Letty Shepherd nevertheless teaches Wick Carter to perceive beauties of coal country; growing awareness parallels growing love.	WV	17	SC,C	Rea	I,VII, VIII,XII
Price, Nancy. *A Natural Death.* Boston: Little, 376pp. Relationships between youthful mistress, "Buck Algrew," and slaves, Joan and Will Kind, portray destructive impact of slavery on all parties.	SC	17,15	H,SC	Rea	I,IV
Sarton, May. *As We Are Now.* NY: Norton, 134pp. Lisa Thornhill offers moments of humanity and relief to elderly protagonist, an inmate of a dreadful nursing home.	NewE	hs	C	Rea	III
Schaeffer, Susan Fromberg. *Falling.* NY: Macmillan, 307pp. Adult Elizabeth Kamen contemplates brief scenes of her youth to earn independence from, respect for, her family.	NY,IL	c–m	C,I	Rea	II
Smith, Lee. *Fancy Strut.* NY: Harper, 329pp. Various youngsters participate in preparations, including a queen contest, for town's centennial festival.	AL	hs	SC	Rea,C	VI
Thomas, Audrey. *Songs My Mother Taught Me.* Indianapolis: Bobbs, 200pp. Difficult, demanding work helps Isobel Cleary gain control over her reactions to oppressive, neurotic family.	?	hs–m	C	Rea	II
Uhnak, Dorothy. *Law and Order.* NY: Simon, 512pp. Portraits of youthful members of O'Malleys, traditionally a family of police officers, contribute to study of NYPD.	NYC	c–m	C,SC,D	Rea	IX,XII, XIII

Author/Title	Setting	Age	Type	Tone	Reference
1974					
Baker, Elliott. *Unrequited Loves.* NY: Putnam's, 239pp. The coming of age of talented Elliott, shown through crucial, interlocking episodes.	NY,IN	9–22	C	C	VIII,IX, XII
Cassill, R. V. *The Goss Women.* Garden City, NY: Doubleday, 464pp. Tamisan's belief that her sexuality is her identity is confirmed by experiences with various Goss family members.	NYC	12–13	SC	Rea	I
Clements, Bruce. *I Tell a Lie Every So Often.* NY: Farrar, 149pp. Henry and Clayton Desant attempt to rescue a cousin from Indians.	MO	14,hs	YA,H,C	Rea	IX,XI
Cormier, Robert. *The Chocolate War.* NY: Pantheon, 253pp. Jerry Renault resists social pressure and physical punishment to stand up against a gang.	NewE	hs	YA,I	Rea	XII
Deal, Babs H. *The Reason for Roses.* Garden City, NY: Doubleday, 276pp. Spencer Howard remembers activities with cousins during important girlhood summer, attempting to understand why she has survived.	AL	hs	I	N,P	II,VI
Fields, Jeff. *A Cry of Angels.* NY: Atheneum, 383pp. Orphaned Earl Whitaker retains his dreams while learning of independence and responsibility by observing and relating to others.	GA	13–15	I	Rea,C	IX,XI,XII
Gerber, Merrill Joan. *Now Molly Knows.* NY: Arbor, 263pp. Molly's maturation process is depicted in terms of her sexual development.	NYC,FL	c–m	C,I	Rea	I
Heller, Joseph. *Something Happened.* NY: Knopf, 565pp. Unhappy, unnamed daughter of narrator complicates her own and parents' lives, echoes their shortcomings.	E	15	SC,C	Rea	II

Entry	Location				
Howard, Maureen. *Before My Time*. Boston: Little, 241pp. Visit of young relative, Jim Cogan, causes protagonist Laura Quinn to reexamine herself, her past, her marriage, his family.	Boston, NYC	17,12,12	C	Rea	II, VIII, IX, XI, XII
Johnson, Charles. *Faith and the Good Thing*. NY: Viking, 196pp. Faith Cross's quest for security leads only to sexual abuse, prostitution, despair.	Chicago	18	SC,C	Rea	IV
Johnson, Mendal W. *Let's Go Play at the Adams'*. NY: Crowell, 282pp. Five youngsters imprison, rape, torture, and kill babysitter in what begins as a game, then turns serious.	MD	10,17,hs	I,H	Rea,P	IV, V, VIII, XI, XII
Judson, William. *Cold River*. NY: Mason, 213pp. Lizzie and Tim, stranded in woods during winter storm, survive and mature.	NY	14,13	I	Rea	II, VI, VII, IX, XIII, XIV
Kavanagh, Paul. *Not Comin' Home to You.* NY: Putnam's, 220pp. Fact-based account of Betty Marie Dienhardt and drifter Jimmie John Hall's cross-country crime spree.	JNY	15	D	Rea	IV
Kerr, M. E. *See* Meaker, Marijane					
Lurie, Alison. *The War between the Tates*. NY: Random, 372pp. Matilda Tate resents the threatened breakup of her parents' marriage.	NY	13	M	Rea	II
Lyle, Katie Letcher. *Fair Day, and Another Step Begun*. Phila: Lippincott, 157pp. Pregnant after a brief encounter, Ellen Burd follows her lover, certain he will love her when he understands her love.	VA,TN	16	YA,F	Sym,P	I
Madden, David. *Bijou*. NY: Crown, 500pp. Lucius Hutchfield's family, first love, job, and fascination with movies all complicate his life.	TN	a	I	Rea	VIII, IX, XI, XII

Author/Title	Setting	Age	Type	Tone	Reference
1974 (*continued*)					
Mathis, Sharon Bell. *Listen for the Fig Tree.* NY: Viking, 175pp. Christmas and Kwanza celebrations help Muffin to mature, reaffirm her heritage, cope with blindness, understand her mother.	NYC	16	YA,C,I	Rea	II,VII
Meaker, Marijane [pseud., M. E. Kerr]. *The Son of Someone Famous.* NY: Harper, 226pp. Adam Blessing adopts another name and flees to Vermont to escape the shadow of his famous father.	VT	16	YA,C	Rea	VIII,IX,X
Rushing, Jane Gilmore. *Mary Dove: A Love Story.* Garden City, NY: Doubleday, 209pp. Parents' remembered biases and extreme isolation complicate Mary Dove Pardue's frontier romance.	TX	a	H,I	Rea	I,VI
Scoppettone, Sandra. *Trying Hard to Hear You.* NY: Harper, 264pp. Tragedy results when Camilla Crawford and her crowd learn of good friend Jeff Grathwohl's homosexuality.	NY	16,hs	I	Rea	I,III,VIII,X
Seton, Cynthia Propper. *The Half-Sisters.* NY: Norton, 213pp. Early adolescent relationship of Billie and Erica affects later development of each.	E	11–m	I,C	Rea	II
Stein, Sol. *Living Room.* NY: Arbor, 309pp. Adult Shirley Hartman's brilliant career and personal problems are affected by childhood and adolescent learning experiences.	NY	c–m	C	Rea	V
Vliet, R. G. *Rockspring.* NY: Viking, 120pp. Kidnapped by Mexican bandits, Jensie survives and, much changed by her suffering, is eventually returned home.	TX	14	H	Rea,P	VI
Wagoner, David. *The Road to Many a Wonder.* NY: Farrar, 275pp. Ike Bender, with spunky and assertive bride Milly, has many adventures while traveling west to search for gold.	NE,CO	a,15	P	C	I,VIII,XIII

1975

Berger, Thomas. *Sneaky People*. NY: Simon, 315pp. Fascinated by sex, Ralph Sandifer lives his own life, little concerned with hypocrisies around him.	?	15	I,M	C,Rea	VIII
Bernays, Anne. *Growing Up Rich*. Boston: Little, 343pp. Sudden deaths of mother and stepfather force Sally Stern to make enormous adjustments, establish her own identity, reevaluate her past.	MA	15	C,I	Rea	II,V
Blume, Judy. *Forever*. Scarsdale, NY: Bradbury, 199pp. Katherine Danziger learns that her first love is not necessarily her last or only love.	NY	hs	I,YA	Rea	I
Boyd, Shylah. *American Made*. NY: Farrar, 407pp. A difficult home life and sexual activity define Shylah Dale's adolescence.	FL,NY	c–m	C,I	Rea	I
Boyle, Kay. *The Underground Woman*. Garden City, NY: Doubleday, 264pp. Melanie Gregory's commitment to her commune is compared to the Persephone myth.	CA	19	C,SC	Rea	V
Brooks, David H. *Gone Away*. NY: Harper, 232pp. Two brothers learn independence and self-reliance in reacting to and rebelling against strict father and his values.	CT	hs	I	Rea,P	IX,XII
Coleman, Lonnie [William Lawrence]. *Orphan Jim*. Garden City, NY: Doubleday, 204pp. Trudy Maynard reluctantly undertakes the care of her young brother after mother's death and father's desertion.	S	13	C,P,I,SC	Rea	II,IV,V
Corcoran, Barbara [pseud., Paige Dixon]. *May I Cross Your Golden River?* NY: Atheneum, 262pp. Intelligent and athletic boy faces death from Lou Gehrig's disease.	CO	18	YA,I	Rea,P, Sym	XIV
Dixon, Paige. *See* Corcoran, Barbara					

Author/Title	Setting	Age	Type	Tone	Reference
1975 (*continued*)					
Finch, Phillip. *Haulin'*. Garden City, NY: Doubleday, 225pp. Two truck drivers become involved with a number of people, including a beautiful runaway girl.	JNY	18	C	Rea	I
Gores, Joe. *Hammett*. NY: Putnam's, 251pp. Plot contrasts Goodie Owens (20), who escapes from, and Crystal Tam, who succumbs to, underworld life in San Francisco.	San Francisco	15	D	Rea	IV
Hinton, S. E. *Rumble Fish*. NY: Delacorte, 122pp. Rusty-James idolizes older brother, the toughest boy around, but attempts to emulate him end in disaster.	?	14,17	YA,I	Rea,P	XI
Hobson, Laura Z. *Consenting Adult*. Garden City, NY: Doubleday, 256pp. Jeff Lynn's recognition of his homosexuality brings shame and creates family tensions, but he and family eventually accept it.	NY,CT, CA	17–30	SC	Rea,P	VIII,IX, XII
Jacobs, Harvey. *Summer on a Mountain of Spices*. NY: Harper, 333pp. Harry Craft, his family, and many others spend last summer of World War II at Jewish resort.	NY	15	M	C	VIII,XIII
Maling, Arthur. *Bent Man*. NY: Harper, 227pp. Father's efforts to protect him from criminals leads Steve Livingston to reassess life-style, standards, goals.	Chicago	19	D	Rea	VIII,XI
O'Brien, Robert C. *Z for Zachariah*. NY: Atheneum, 249pp. Ann Burden, survivor of nuclear holocaust, copes with life alone, then with complications generated by John Loomis, another survivor.	NY?	16	SF	Rea	V
Price, Reynolds. *The Surface of Earth*. NY: Atheneum, 491pp. Adolescent wife and mother Eva Kendal abandons her difficult marriage because of father's persuasion, guilt over mother's suicide.	NC,VA	16	C,I	Rea	I,II

Citation	Place				
Roe, Judy. *The Same Old Grind.* Milbrae, CA: Les Femmes, 223pp. Zehyah (Roberta Lattimore), a black, and Elly Mae, a poor white, seek identities while working as strippers.	W	hs	M,SC	Rea,C	V
Seton, Anya. *Smouldering Fires.* Garden City, NY: Doubleday, 159pp. Dowdy, introverted Amy Delatour, reliving her Acadian ancestress' tragic experiences, is eventually released from her obsession by an understanding teacher.	CT,LA	16	D,H	Rom,P	VI
Wersba, Barbara. *The Country of the Heart.* NY: Atheneum, 115pp. Aspiring poet Steve Harper forces his way into the life of a leading woman poet who is dying of cancer.	NY	18	YA,I	P	VIII,XII, XIV
West, Jessamyn. *The Massacre at Fall Creek.* NY: Harcourt, 373pp. Hannah Cape's maturation parallels that of her frontier community.	IN	17	I,H	Rea	I,VI
1976					
Alther, Lisa. *Kinflicks.* NY: Knopf, 503pp. Adult Virginia Babcock Bliss relives her youth in memory, while seeing mother through terminal illness.	TN,MA	c–m	C,I	Rea	I
Bova, Ben. *City of Darkness.* NY: Scribner's, 150pp. Ron Morgan, in a future city of violent youth gangs, adopts goal of working for social change.	NYC	16	SF,YA	N	XII,XIII
Cahill, Susan. *Earth Angels.* NY: Harper, 213pp. Martha Girling-hausen explores parochial schools, sex, and a vocation as a nun.	NYC	c–m	C	Rea	V
Gould, Lois. *A Sea-Change.* NY: Simon, 163pp. Diane Waterman survives severe tests in mythic maturation journey.	CenA	13	L,A	My	II
Gray, Francine Du Plessix. *Lovers and Tyrants.* NY: Simon, 316pp. Brief but effective chapter details Stephanie's female friendships.	NYC	a	I	Rea	III

1976 *(continued)*

Author/Title	Setting	Age	Type	Tone	Reference
Greenberg, Joanne. *Founder's Praise.* NY: Holt, 328pp. Edgar Kornarens exploits the religious sect his family has founded.	CO	hs	I,SC	Rea	X,XII
Guest, Judith. *Ordinary People.* NY: Viking, 263pp. Conrad Jarrett painfully recovers from mental illness and family tragedy.	Chicago	17	I	Rea	VIII,IX,X, XIV
Guy, Rosa. *Ruby.* NY: Viking, 217pp. Ruby Cathy and Daphne Duprey conduct a secret love affair.	NYC	18,19	YA,C	Rea	I,IV,V
Hahn, Harriet. *The Plantain Season.* NY: Norton, 207pp. During crucial year, bright, insecure girl declares independence and gains sense of worth, partly through sexual encounters.	NYC	17	I	Rea,P	I,VII
Hauser, Marianne. *The Talking Room.* NY: Fiction Collective, 156pp. Obese and pregnant, B observes the erratic behavior of her mother, J, and the possessiveness of V, the mother's lesbian lover.	NY	13	E	Su	I
Hill, Deborah. *This Is the House.* NY: Coward, 411pp. Milly Deems marries to gain financial security and social mobility.	MA	c–m	H	Rom	I
Kay, Terry. *The Year the Lights Came On.* Boston: Houghton, 288pp. The advent of the Rural Electrification Administration creates new pressures and alliances among Colin Wynn's circle.	GA	a	I	Rea	VIII,IX,X, XI,XIII
Kotker, Zane. *A Certain Man.* NY: Knopf, 367pp. Arley Minor chooses a career in the Christian ministry and trains for his vocation.	CT	c–m	C,I	Rea	XII

Majerus, Janet. *Grandpa and Frank*. Phila: Lippincott, 192pp. Sarah MacDermott, aided by Joey Martin, protects her grandfather's control over the family farm.	IL	12	I,P	Rea	II,VI,X
Mojtabai, A. G. *The 400 Eels of Sigmund Freud*. NY: Simon, 258pp. Intellectual, emotional, and social pressures complicate participation in summer science worksh-op for Naomi Heschel and other gifted students.	NY	15	SC	Rea	III,V,VII
Nissenson, Hugh. *My Own Ground*. NY: Farrar, 182pp. Russian-Jewish immigrant, Jake Brody, survives in slum world of pimps, prostitutes, poverty, and arguments over Russian revolutionary politics.	NYC	15	I,SC	Rea,P	VIII,XI, XII,XIII
Peck, Richard. *Are You in the House Alone?* NY: Viking, 156pp. While dating Steve Pastorini, an "unsuitable" boy, Gail Osburne is terrorized and raped by socially prominent Phil Lawver.	CT	hs	YA,D	Rea	IV
Robbins, Tom. *Even Cowgirls Get the Blues*. Boston: Houghton, 365pp. Sissy Hankshaw's development is complicated and enhanced by her enormous thumbs and bizarre mentors encountered on maturation journey.	VA,JNY, W	15–m	F,SC,C	C	I,III,V
Rosen, Winifred. *Cruisin for a Bruisin*. NY: Knopf, 150pp. Family tension and sexual experimentation mark Winnie Simon's maturation.	NY	13	I,C,YA	Rea	I
Rothweiler, Paul R. *The Sensuous Southpaw*. NY: Putnam's, 253pp. Jeri "Red" Walker's initial season as a major league baseball player also forces her confrontation with bias, sexuality, fame.	JNY	18	C,YA	Sat	I,V
Walker, Alice. *Meridian*. NY: Harcourt, 228pp. Chapters devoted to Meridian Hill's girlhood effectively describe the exhaustive tension of Civil Rights movement.	S	c–m	I	Rea	V

Author/Title	Setting	Age	Type	Tone	Reference
1976 (*continued*)					
Yates, Richard. *The Easter Parade.* NY: Delacorte, 299pp. Adolescent romances and the relationship between sisters Sarah and Emily Grimes affect their adult lives.	NY	a–m	C	Rea	I,II
Yglesias, Rafael. *The Work Is Innocent.* Garden City, NY: Doubleday, 156pp. Richard Goodman finishes and publishes first novel, loses virginity, and comes to terms with his intellectual and political family.	NYC	15–16	I	P	VIII,XII
Zindel, Paul. *Pardon Me, You're Stepping on My Eyeball!* NY: Harper, 262pp. Disturbed "Marsh" Mellow and alienated Edna Shinglebox find friendship and a chance to be honest with each other.	NY	15	YA,C,I	Rea	III,IV,V, VIII,X,XII
1977					
Blackwood, Caroline. *The Stepdaughter.* NY: Scribner's, 96pp. Fat, withdrawn Renata innocently precipitates family dissolution.	NYC	13	C,D	P,Rea	II
Bredes, Don. *Hard Feelings.* NY: Atheneum, 377pp. Obsessed with sex, Bernie Hergruter must also confront sadistic enemy.	NY,JNY, OH	16	I	Rea	VIII,XI, XII
Broughton, T. Alan. *A Family Gathering.* NY: Dutton, 184pp. Boy observes near break-up of his family, triggered by father's loss of job leading to infidelity and attempted suicide.	VA	12	I,C	Rea,P	VIII,IX
Calisher, Hortense. *On Keeping Women.* NY: Arbor, 325pp. One long episode centers on four siblings' responses to family tensions.	NY	a	C	Rea	II,IX

Cormier, Robert. *I Am the Cheese.* NY: Pantheon, 233pp. Gangland execution precipitates Adam Farmer's mental breakdown.	NewE	14	YA,D	P	III,IX,XIV
Gordon, R. L. *The Lady Who Loved New York.* NY: Crowell, 277pp. Flashbacks reveal Alice Barrington's relationships with her upper-class parents and their turn-of-the-century restrained, formal life.	NYC	c–m	C	Rea	II
Hamill, Pete. *Flesh & Blood.* NY: Random, 276pp. Despite violent temper, prison term, and incestuous affair with mother, Bobby Fallon becomes boxing contender.	NY	18–20	I,SC	N	VIII,IX, XI,XII
Hassler, Jon. *Staggerford.* NY: Atheneum, 341pp. A secondary character, tormented Beverly Bingham, is the innocent, indirect cause of her adored teacher's death.	MN	18	C	Rea,Sat	II,V
Hoffman, Alice. *Property Of.* NY: Farrar, 248pp. Unnamed narrator obsessively loves gang leader but manages to avoid drug addiction and to maintain own identity.	NYC	17	I,SC	Rea,P	I,IV,VI
Houston, James A. *Ghost Fox.* NY: Harcourt, 302pp. Conflicts between whites and Indians, her captivity, and subsequent marriage to an Indian compel Sarah Wells's evaluation of both cultures.	Frontier	17	H,YA	Rea	I,IV,VI
Klein, Norma. *It's OK If You Don't Love Me.* NY: Dial, 202pp. Jody Epstein's sexual freedom startles, puzzles, angers, and delights Lyle, her new boyfriend.	NYC	17	YA,C,I	Rea	I,II,VI, VIII
Kluger, Richard. *Members of the Tribe.* Garden City, NY: Doubleday, 471pp. The challenges and support offered to Seth Adler reveal the status of southern Jews at the turn of the century.	GA	c–m	C,SC	Rea	XII,XIII
Kotlowitz, Robert. *The Boardwalk.* NY: Knopf, 275pp. Teddy Lewin's last pre–World War II vacation marks the end of his childhood.	MD	14	C,I	Rea	XII,XIII

Author/Title	Setting	Age	Type	Tone	Reference
1977 *(continued)*					
Lee, Joanna. *I Want to Keep My Baby.* NY: New Am., 166pp. Deserted by boyfriend, Sue Ann Cunningham tries to make it alone with her baby, despite financial and emotional problems.	Los Angeles	15	YA	P	I
Lowry, Beverly. *Come Back, Lolly Ray.* Garden City, NY: Doubleday, 230pp. Despite humble origins, Lolly Ray Lasswell, gifted baton twirler, has special place in class-conscious southern town.	MS	hs	C,LC	Rom,Sat	V,VI
Marshall, Alexandra. *Gus in Bronze.* NY: Knopf, 242pp. Protagonist Gus Kaligas affirms her life—and teaches her teen-aged daughters and others to do so—as she faces death.	NY	hs	C,I	Rea	II
Morrison, Toni. *Song of Solomon.* NY: Knopf, 337pp. Brief glimpses of Milkman Dead's youth and a lyrical flashback into Pilate Dead's adolescence illuminate their maturations.	MI	c–a	C,P,I	Rea	II,IX
Offit, Sidney. *What Kind of a Guy Do You Think I Am?* Phila: Lippincott, 160pp. Despite sharply differing goals and attitudes, Hilary and Ted find some stability through their decision to live together.	NY	18	YA,C	Rea	I,VIII,XII
Rabe, Berniece. *The Girl Who Had No Name.* NY: Dutton, 149pp. Girlie Webster must overcome father's rejection, and unravel secret of her birth, problems intensified by mother's death.	MO	12	C,M	Rea	II
Stallworth, Anne Nall. *Where the Bright Lights Shine.* NY: Vanguard, 314pp. Father's desertion and mother's obsessiveness scar and limit life choices of Maribeth, Lee Rose, and Jo Anna Berryhill.	AL	a–m	C	Rea	I,II

1978

Entry	Place	Age		Mode	
Adams, Alice. *Listening to Billie.* NY: Knopf, 215pp. Catherine Quarles complicates late maturation of her mother, Eliza, the protagonist.	CA	c–a	C	Rea	II
Andrews, Raymond. *Appalachee Red.* NY: Dial, 283pp. Baby Sweet's (and briefly, others') sexual, social, religious experiences illuminate saga of the title character, of changing black life.	GA	c–m	SC	Rea	I,IV
Apple, Max. *Zip: A Novel of the Left and the Right.* NY: Viking, 183pp. Jésus Martinez turns his boxing career into political protest.	Detroit	18	F	F	XII
Brown, Rita Mae. *Six of One.* NY: Harper, 310pp. Histories of Julia Ellen ("Juts") and Louise ("Wheezie") Huntzenmeier reflect sibling love and rivalry, the influence of women surrounding them.	PA,MD	c–m	C,SC	Rea,C	I,II,III
Brown, Wesley. *Tragic Magic.* NY: Random, 169pp. Very brief flashbacks to his youth and deadly encounter with street kids help Melvin Ellington define his manhood.	NYC	c–m	C,SC	Rea	XI
Caldwell, Joseph. *In Such Dark Places.* NY: Farrar, 229pp. David Stokes, urban waif, seeks home and some level of security.	NYC	13	A	Rea	IX
Carroll, James. *Mortal Friends.* Boston: Little, 607pp. Various youngsters, especially his grandson, complicate and illuminate protagonist Colman Brady's Irish-immigrant experiences.	Boston	c–m	C,SC	Rea	IX,XIII
Dintenfass, Mark. *Montgomery Street.* NY: Harper, 175pp. Film maker plans movie based on scene of his youth and creates two characters, one adult and one adolescent.	NYC	14	C	Rea,P	XIII
Duncan, Lois. *Killing Mr. Griffin.* Boston: Little, 243pp. Plot to frighten hated teacher unexpectedly turns serious for five teenagers.	NM	16,17	YA,D	Rea,P	IV,V,XI,XII

1978 (*continued*)

Author/Title	Setting	Age	Type	Tone	Reference
Guy, Rosa. *Edith Jackson.* NY: Viking, 187pp. Orphaned Edith Jackson attempts to keep her sisters together as a family and to find romance.	NY	17,18	YA,C,I	Rea	I,II
Irving, John. *The World According to Garp.* NY: Dutton, 437pp. Saga of protagonist Garp and of various young women who influence him reflects social change.	E	c–m	SC	C	VIII,IX
Jones, Craig. *Blood Secrets.* NY: Harper, 199pp. Father's secretiveness, distrust, and excessive concern for daughter creates marital discord and motivates crime.	MI	hs	C,D	Rea	II
Lowry, Beverly. *Emma Blue.* Garden City, NY: Doubleday, 231pp. Illegitimate, alienated Emma Blue Lasswell matures by redefining wayward mother's influence.	MS	16	C,LC,SC	Rea	I,II,VI
Pilcer, Sonia. *Teen Angel.* NY: Coward, 262pp. Tough, funny, gifted Sonny Palovsky's discovery that leadership of a prominent gang is unsatisfying signals her maturation.	NYC	14	C,SC	Rea,C	I,IV
Robinson, Jill. *Perdido.* NY: Knopf, 431pp. Susanna Howard's attempts to clarify family ties and establish her independence are complicated by rejection, bad marriage, and filmdom glitter.	Hollywood	14–m	I,SC	Rea	I,II,VI
Savage, Elizabeth. *The Girls from the Five Great Valleys.* Boston: Little, 240pp. Five friends, Hilary, Amelia, Doll, Kathy, Janet, grow up and apart because of family responsibilities, ambitions, economic pressures.	MT	hs	I	Rea	I,II,III
Schaeffer, Susan Fromberg. *Time in Its Flight.* Garden City, NY: Doubleday, 782pp. Panoramic novel of family life focuses upon several teenagers as author explores constancy and mutability of love.	NewE	c–m	H	Rea	II

Scoppettone, Sandra. *Happy Endings Are All Alike*. NY: Harper, 202pp. The rape of Jaret Tyler leads to revelation of her affair with Peggy Danziger.	?	hs	I,YA	Rea	I,II,XI
Shulman, Alix Kates. *Burning Questions*. NY: Knopf, 361pp. Independence and spunkiness fostered during adolescence strengthen Zane Indiana to meet challenges of adulthood.	IN,NY	a–m	C,I	Rea	II
Yates, Richard. *A Good School*. NY: Delacorte, 178pp. William Grove recalls prep-school days as central to his character development.	CT	15–m	C,M	Rea	XII
Zindel, Paul. *The Undertaker's Gone Bananas*. NY: Harper, 239pp. Riddled with phobias, Lauri nevertheless sees Bobby through his troubles; he "cures" her fears as they solve mystery.	NJ	hs,15	YA,D	Rea	III,X
1979					
Applewhite, Cynthia. *Sundays*. NY: Avon, 204pp. Cha'Lou Moonlight is torn between awakening sensuality and Bible Belt religion.	MO	a	I,C	Rea	III,V,VI
Bridgers, Sue Ellen. *All Together Now*. NY: Knopf, 238pp. One summer's experiences—baseball, friendship with retarded man, a wedding—help tomboyish Casey Flanagan mature.	NC	12	YA,I	Nos	III,V,VI
Butler, Octavia E. *Kindred*. Garden City, NY: Doubleday, 264pp. Rufe, a slaveholder, Alice, a free black, and Carrie, a slave, demonstrate insidiousness of systematic slavery to time-travelers Dana and Kevin.	MD	c–m	SF,H,I	Rea	I,IV,VIII IX,XI
Canby, Vincent. *Unnatural Scenery*. NY: Knopf, 274pp. In many flashbacks, adult Marshall Lewis Henderson assesses his family, physical disability, marriages, values.	VA	c–m	C	Rea	IX,XII
Childress, Alice. *A Short Walk*. NY: Coward, 333pp. Moments in adolescence of Cora James reveal the racism, sexism, and poverty she has overcome.	SC,NY	c–m	C,SC	Rea	II,IV

1979 *(continued)*

Author/Title	Setting	Age	Type	Tone	Reference
Cormier, Robert. *After the First Death.* NY: Pantheon, 233pp. The hijacking of a busload of children is a turning point in the lives of three teenagers.	NewE	hs	C,YA,D	Rea,P	IV,IX,XI
Culin, Charlotte. *Cages of Glass, Flowers of Time.* Scarsdale, NY: Bradbury, 316pp. Child of divorced alcoholics, victim of abuse, Claire finds strength through art, friendship, love.	S	14	YA,C	Rea	I,II,III
Cummings, Betty Sue. *Now, Ameriky.* NY: Atheneum, 175pp. Brigid Ni Clery, driven by potato famine, transplants her dream of land ownership from Ireland to New World.	NY	19	YA	Rea	II
Duncan, Lois. *Daughters of Eve.* Boston: Little, 239pp. Justified resentments against sexism and discrimination lead members of a high-school sorority to excessive, even violent, retaliation.	MI	hs	YA,SC	P,Rea	V
Goldman, William. *Tinsel.* NY: Delacorte, 342pp. Flashbacks reveal adolescent roots of problems exacerbated when Patsy Higgins, Ginger Abraham, and Noel Garvey become involved in "major" film.	Hollywood	c–m	SC,C	Rea	I,II,III,V, VI,VII, VIII,X,XI
Gutcheon, Beth. *The New Girls.* NY: Putnam's, 347pp. Five alumnae reassess boarding-school experience, their friendship, their families, and themselves during class reunion.	NewE	a–m	C,I	Rea	I,II,III,V
Hansen, Joseph. *Skinflick.* NY: Holt, 194pp. Charleen Sims's involvement in crime, porno films, and murder sets detective on her trail.	CA	a	D	Rea	IV
Hardwick, Elizabeth. *Sleepless Nights.* NY: Random, 151pp. One segment recounts Elizabeth's unaccountable, destructive movement into prostitution.	KY,MA, NY,ME	a	C	Rea	IV

Citation	Location	Age			
Harnack, Curtis. *Limits of the Land*. Garden City, NY: Doubleday, 232pp. Sheila's turbulent adolescence is subplot and symbol in story of father's search for ideal rural life.	IA	a–m	C,I	N	II,VI
Hoffman, Alice. *The Drowning Season*. NY: Dutton, 212pp. Esther the Black reassesses relationship with grandmother, Esther the White, comes to terms with family history, father's suicide, and adulthood.	NY	18	C,I	Rea	II,VIII
Johnson, Sandy. *The CUPPI*. NY: Delacorte, 255pp. Runaways Freddie Charles and Winter Richards become involved in child-prostitution ring, while Donnie Wood is used as decoy by police.	NYC	12,12,12	SC	Rea	IV
Leffland, Ella. *Rumors of Peace*. NY: Harper, 389pp. Impact of World War II affects every attitude, many events of Suse Hansen's adolescence.	CA	11–15	C,I	Rea	II,III,IV,V
McConkey, James. *The Tree House Confessions*. NY: Dutton, 214pp. Peter recollects moments of youth, seeking perspective on deaths of loved ones, his own life-choices.	KY	c–m	C	Rea	VIII,IX
Nixon, Joan Lowery. *The Kidnapping of Christina Lattimore*. NY: Harcourt, 179pp. Christina learns independence when her kidnappers attempt to implicate her in their crime.	TX	hs	D,YA	Rea	II,IV
Price, Nancy. *An Accomplished Woman*. NY: Coward, 288pp. Her foster father's painstaking care lays groundwork for Catherine Buckingham's glittering façade, empty heart.	MI,IA	c–m	C	Rea	II
Southerland, Ellease. *Let the Lion Eat Straw*. NY: Scribner's, 181pp. Key segment depicts Abeba Williams's adolescent confrontation with problems—poverty, racism, incest—that also haunt her adulthood.	NC,NY	c–m	C,SC	Rea	II,IV

Author/Title	Setting	Age	Type	Tone	Reference
1979 (*continued*)					
Spencer, Scott. *Endless Love.* NY: Knopf, 417pp. David Axelrod's romantic fixation upon Jade Butterfield incites an affair, conflict, tragedy, punishment, and, ultimately, sharply diminished future.	Chicago	17,16	C	Rea	I,II,VIII
West, Jessamyn. *The Life I Really Lived.* NY: Harcourt, 404pp. Orpha Chase's relationships with parents and youthful marriage reveal violence and tragedy beneath seemingly placid surface.	KY,CA	c–m	C	Rea	I,II
1980					
Arrick, Fran. *Tunnel Vision.* Scarsdale, NY: Bradbury, 167pp. Family and friends try to comprehend and accept Anthony Hamil's suicide.	NY	15	YA	P	XIV
Bach, Alice. *Waiting for Johnny Miracle.* NY: Harper, 240pp. Identical twins Becky and Theo Maitland face separate challenges when Becky develops cancer.	NJ	hs	YA	P	II,VII
Bambara, Toni Cade. *The Salt Eaters.* NY: Random, 295pp. After suicide attempt, Velma Henry—and her "Healer" Minnie Ransom—reassess their girlhoods, the people who influenced them, black experience.	GA	c–m	C,SC	Rea	I,II
Beattie, Ann. *Falling in Place.* NY: Random, 342pp. Mary's school problems and unrealistic concept of "real" life form one of many subplots.	CT	hs	M	Rea	II,V
Burke, Alan Dennis. *Fire Watch.* Boston: Little, 386pp. Racism, violence, apathy among students and faculty at John Quincy Adams High School heighten security officer Peter Lyons's midlife crisis.	CenA	hs	C,SC	Rea	V,VII

Cheatham, K. Follis. *Bring Home the Ghost.* NY: Harcourt, 288pp. Master-slave relationship of Tolin Cobb and Jason becomes friendship; but after many trials, Jason wins complete freedom.	AL,JNY	12–m, 10–m	Q	Rea	X
De Vries, Peter. *Consenting Adults; or, The Duchess Will Be Furious.* Boston: Little, 221pp. Innocent Columbine contrasts with wilder neighbor, Peachum, whom she is to marry.	IL	c–a	C	Sat	I
Doty, Carolyn. *A Day Late.* NY: Viking, 232pp. Pregnant, abandoned, and frightened, Katy Daniels hitchhikes home with salesman Sam Batinovich, who is mourning death of daughter.	JNY,W	17	P	Rea	I,III
Florey, Kitty Burns. *Chez Cordelia.* NY: Seaview, 296pp. Cordelia Miller survives academic problems, family tension, broken marriage, and difficult career choice.	CT	c–m	C,I	Rea	I,II,V
Higgins, George V. *Kennedy for the Defense.* NY: Knopf, 225pp. Heather Kennedy represents the decent world which counterbalances the professional world of her father, the protagonist, a criminal lawyer.	MA	13	C	Rea,C	II
Hogan, William. *The Quartzsite Trip.* NY: Atheneum, 306pp. Various male and female high-school students represent American stereotypes.	OK	hs	SC	Rea	V,XI
Hunt, Irene. *Claws of a Young Century.* NY: Scribner's, 292pp. Ellen Archer's determined struggles, defeats, and successes as daughter, wife, mother, and worker exemplify those of many early-twentieth-century feminists.	M	17	C,SC,H	Rea	I,II,V
Jones, Douglas C. *Elkhorn Tavern.* NY: Holt, 311pp. Confederate Calpurnia Hasford's love for Union soldier complicates difficulties she, her mother, and her brother Roman face during Civil War.	W	17,15	H	Rea	I,XII

Author/Title	Setting	Age	Type	Tone	Reference
1980 (*continued*)					
Josephs, Rebecca. *Early Disorder*. NY: Farrar, 185pp. Hidden anxieties trigger Willa Rahv's severe case of anorexia nervosa.	NY	15	C	Rea	*VII*
Kallen, Lucille. *C.B. Greenfield: The Tanglewood Murder*. NY: Wyndham, 222pp. Jenny Springer must assume responsibility and behave maturely when past deeds affect her mother's present behavior.	MA	hs	D	Rea	II
Kaplan, Johanna. *O My America!* NY: Harper, 286pp. Mary Slavin reviews her past, seeking understanding of her complex father, their extended family, and her own identity.	NY	c–m	C	Rea	I,II
Kennedy, Raymond. *Columbine*. NY: Farrar, 378pp. Bewitching Columbine Kokoriss willfully courts protagonist Henry Flynn, complicating his life, altering, perhaps permanently diminishing, her own.	MA	13	C	Rea	I
Klein, Norma. *Breaking Up*. NY: Pantheon, 207pp. Romance, redefinition of friendship, discovery of her mother's lesbianism, and the consequent custody battle complicate Alison Rose's summer.	NY,CA	15	YA,C,I	Rea	I,II,III
Leavitt, Caroline. *Meeting Rozzy Halfway*. NY: Seaview, 294pp. Rozzy Nelson's mental illness affects her younger sister, Bess.	MA	c–m	I,C	Rea	II,*VII*
Morris, Wright. *Plains Song: For Female Voices*. NY: Harper, 229pp. Great Plains setting, Cora's pragmatic early marriage, and her consequent accommodations during adulthood influence lives of her daughter and nieces.	NE	a–m	H,C	Rea,P	I,II,VI
Pelletier, Louis. *See* Snyder, Anne, and Louis Pelletier					

Pfeffer, Susan Beth. *About David*. NY: Delacorte, 167pp. Lynn's journal recounts stages of grief and the struggle to understand motives of best friend, David, a murderer-suicide.	E	17	YA,C	Rea	III,IV,VII
Robinson, Marilynne. *Housekeeping*. NY: Farrar, 219pp. Relatives' deaths and self-absorption complicate development of Ruth and Lucille, who must choose between rebellion and surrender to family eccentricities.	WA	c–m	I	Rea	II,VII
Rogers, Thomas. *At the Shores*. NY: Simon, 284pp. Jerry Engel and Rosemary Ingleside's love affair illustrates his pre-occupation with sexual fantasy, her willing submissiveness, their immaturity.	Chicago	hs	C,I	Rea	I,VIII
Rossner, Judith. *Emmeline*. NY: Simon, 331pp. Seduced by older man, teenaged factory hand Emmeline Mosher becomes pregnant, relinquishes her child, suffers dreadful lifelong repercussions.	NewE	13–m	C,SC,H	Rea	I,II,V
Roth, Arthur. *The Caretaker*. NY: Four Winds, 216pp. Coping with father's alcoholism and with runaway Pam Sheehy helps Mark Cooper mature.	NY	17	YA,I	Rea	I,IX,XIV
Schneider, Nina. *The Woman Who Lived in a Prologue*. Boston: Houghton, 479pp. Aged and ill, Ariadne Arkady reviews her youth, searching for understanding of her limitations and considerable strength.	NY	c–a	C	Rea	I,II
Scoppettone, Sandra. *Such Nice People*. NY: Putnam's, 284pp. Tom Nash's mental breakdown imposes tragedy upon already troubled family.	PA	17	C,SC	Rea	IX,XI,XII,XIV
Segal, Erich. *Man, Woman, and Child*. NY: Harper, 244pp. Jessica Beckwith's maturation is accelerated and complicated by discovery that supposed guest is half-brother.	Boston	12	C,I	Rea	II

Author/Title	Setting	Age	Type	Tone	Reference
1980 (*continued*)					
Settle, Mary Lee. *The Scapegoat.* NY: Random, 278pp. Unionization wars affect lives, welfare, attitudes of Mary Rose, Althea, and Lily Lacey, mine-owner's daughters.	WV	15,16,18	I,SC	Rea	II,V
Smith, Lee. *Black Mountain Breakdown.* NY: Putnam's, 228pp. Lives of Crystal Spangler, Agnes McClanahan are contrasted, as influenced by families, community, personal expectations, strengths, and weaknesses.	VA	c–m	C,SC	Rea	I,II,III
Snyder, Anne, and Louis Pelletier. *Counter Play.* NY: New Am., 166pp. Brad Stevens's carefully structured world teeters when parents and fellow students discover that Alex Prager, his best friend, is gay.	CA	hs,hs	YA	Rea	XII
Tolan, Stephanie S. *The Last of Eden.* NY: Warne, 154pp. Students in boarding school experience rivalries, jealousies, and malice, but most are strengthened as a result.	MI	15	YA,I	Rea,P	I,III,V
Valin, Joseph. *The Lime Pit.* NY: Dodd, 245pp. Disappearance of Cindy Ann Evans incites investigation, reveals her as victim and victimizer.	OH	16	D	Rea	I,IV
Wolitzer, Hilma. *Hearts.* NY: Farrar, 324pp. Cross-country trek slowly reconciles Robin Reismann to father's death, mother's abandonment, stepmother's affection.	JNY	13	P	Rea	II,VII
Zindel, Paul. *The Pigman's Legacy.* NY: Harper, 183pp. In sequel to *The Pigman*, Lorraine and John support another elderly, dying friend, assuage old guilts, and discover romance.	NJ	hs	YA	Rea	I,III,VIII,X
1981					
Alther, Lisa. *Original Sins.* NY: Knopf, 592pp. The lives of Emily, Sally, Jed, Raymond, and Donny exemplify modern southern values, mores, concerns.	TN,NYC	c–m	I	Rea	I,VI,VIII

	State	Age	Category		Chapters
Belden, Wilanne Schneider. *Mind-Call*. NY: Atheneum, 246pp. Tallie leads a group of talented, precognitive youngsters in campaign against evil.	?	15	YA,SF	Rea	IV
Blume, Judy. *Tiger Eyes*. NY: Bradbury, 206pp. Father's violent, meaningless death stuns Davey Wexler, her mother, and brother, but gradual recovery follows.	NJ,NM	15	YA	P	II,VII
Bonanno, Margaret Wander. *Callbacks*. NY: Seaview, 282pp. Jimmy, a black runaway, and Claire, her rebellious daughter, complicate Alice Antonelli's mid-life crisis and force her to examine values.	NY	18,16	C,I,SC	Rea	II,XI
Bond, Nancy. *The Voyage Begun*. NY: Atheneum, 319pp. Paul Vickers finds purpose and companionship in aiding young girl and old man.	MA	16	SF,YA	Rea	XIII
Bunker, Edward. *Little Boy Blue*. NY: Viking, 301pp. Alex Hammond's destructive entrapment on the "classic institutional treadmill" hardens him, propels him further into criminality.	CA	14	C,SC	Rea	XI
Childress, Alice. *Rainbow Jordan*. NY: Coward, 142pp. Through varied, often troubled relationships, Rainbow Jordan learns of love and loss.	?	14	I	P	VI
Dew, Robb Forman. *Dale Loves Sophie to Death*. NY: Farrar, 217pp. Brief but telling flashbacks and memories of her youth enlarge Dinah Howells's self-awareness and grasp of human condition.	OH	c-m	C	Rea	II,III
Elfman, Blossom. *The Return of the Whistler*. Boston: Houghton, 163pp. Disaffected, bored, unhappy students' pranks incite near-tragedy, force them to face responsibility.	CA	a	YA	Rea	III,V,VII
Flagg, Fannie. *Coming Attractions: A Wonderful Novel*. NY: Morrow, 320pp. Economic insecurity, family quarrels, and keen ambition influence Daisy Fay Harper's maturation.	MS	12–17	I	Rea,C	III,V,VI

Author/Title	Setting	Age	Type	Tone	Reference
1981 *(continued)*					
Gallagher, Patricia. *All for Love.* NY: Avon, 391pp. Jacintha Howard loves married guardian, but weds corrupt businessman and bears son to guardian, with whom she finally finds happiness.	NYC	17–m	H	Rea	VI
Greenberg, Joanne. *A Season of Delight.* NY: Holt, 244pp. Brief glimpses of adolescences of Grace Dowden and her daughter, Miriam, illuminate Grace's adulthood.	PA	c–m	C	Rea	V
Hall, Lynn. *The Horse Trader.* NY: Scribner's, 121pp. Karen Kohler buys and cares for a horse, cements relationship with mother, learns about love.	CO	15	I	Rea	I,II,V
Hunter, Evan. *Love, Dad.* NY: Crown, 407pp. Leslie Croft's rebelliousness and immaturity drive her to flight, wound her father, damage her parents' marriage.	CT	16	C,SC	Rea	II
Hunter, Kristin. *Lou in the Limelight.* NY: Scribner's, 296pp. Louretta Hawkins finds first stages of career as pop and soul singer difficult, even dangerous.	NYC,JNY	15–16	YA,C	Rea	I,II,III,IV,V
Irving, John. *The Hotel New Hampshire.* NY: Dutton, 401pp. Franny's sexual adventures and misadventures, including rape and affair with brother John, complicate Berry family life.	NH,NY,ME	c–m	SC	Rea	II,IV
Kerr, M. E. *See* Meaker, Marijane					
Klein, Norma. *Domestic Arrangements.* NY: Evans, 285pp. Rusty Engleberg will survive intact, though film stardom, an adolescent affair, and parents' differing values strain family stability.	NYC	14	C,I	Rea	I,II,V

Author, Title, and Annotation	Place	Age	Category	Type	Themes
Knowles, John. *Peace Breaks Out.* NY: Holt, 193pp. Clashes between private-school students, super-patriot Wexford and Hitler-admirer Hochschwender, escalate to violence and death.	NH	hs	C,SC	Rea	XI,XII
Lorimer, L. T. *Secrets.* NY: Holt, 192pp. Maggie Thompson explains why her minister-father committed suicide.	CA	16	I,YA	Rea,P	II,VII
MacDougall, Ruth Doan. *The Flowers of the Forest.* NY: Atheneum, 275pp. Glimpses into lives of several adolescents in Livingston and MacLorne families describe women's lot in latter nineteenth century.	NH	c–m	I	Rea	I
Maynard, Joyce. *Baby Love.* NY: Knopf, 244pp. Pregnancy, motherhood, eating disorders, alcohol dependency, rejection, marital troubles, and other problems variously beset Jill, Wanda, Sandy, Tara, Ann.	NH	hs	SC,C	Rea	I,II,III,VIII
Meaker, Marijane [pseud., M. E. Kerr]. *Little Little.* NY: Harper, 183pp. Little LaBelle, a dwarf, copes with suitors Sidney Cinnamon and Knox Lionel and with social bias.	NY	hs	C,SC	Sat	I,VII
O'Donnell, Lillian. *The Children's Zoo.* NY: Putnam's, 209pp. Led by Bud Stucke, a gang of elitist teenagers (symbols of American social decay) vandalize and kill.	NYC	hs	D	Rea	IX,X,XI
Peck, Richard. *Close Enough to Touch.* NY: Delacorte, 133pp. Friendship between Matt Moran and Margaret Chosen helps each cope with various problems: death, family disruption, disappointment.	?	hs	YA,C,I	Rea	VIII,X,XIV
Savage, Thomas. *Her Side of It.* Boston: Little, 299pp. Protagonist recalls Liz Phillips's accounts of her youth in sad tribute to her brave, unsuccessful search for fulfillment.	M	c–m	C	Rea	II
Schwartz, Lynne Sharon. *Balancing Acts.* NY: Harper, 216pp. Reluctantly, sometimes unwittingly, aged Max Fried teaches young friend Alison Markman that adult loneliness and compromises are inevitable and bearable.	NY	12–13	C,I	Rea	III

1981 (*continued*)

Author/Title	Setting	Age	Type	Tone	Reference
Shaw, Irwin. *Bread upon the Waters.* NY: Delacorte, 438pp. Carolyn Strand (white) behaves heroically; Alexander Rollins (black) strives to achieve, while Jesus Romeno (Puerto Rican) becomes alienated.	NYC	17	C	Rea	II,V
Shulman, Alix Kates. *On the Stroll.* NY: Knopf, 301pp. Robin Ward's dangerous, dreary sojourn on "the Stroll" (New York City's Times Square area) illustrates the life of adolescent prostitutes.	NYC	16	SC	Rea	III,IV
Voight, Cynthia. *Homecoming.* NY: Atheneum, 312pp. As surrogate parent for younger siblings, Dicey Tillerman faces grave responsibilities and makes difficult choices.	JNY	13	I	Rea	II
Wallin, Luke. *The Redneck Poacher's Son.* Scarsdale, NY: Bradbury, 245pp. Jesse Watersmith escapes his crude, violent father and eventually learns to stop hating.	AL	16	I	P	IX,XII
Yglesias, Helen. *Sweetsir.* NY: Simon, 332pp. On trial for killing husband, Sally Sweetsir worries about daughter Laura's romance, which parallels Sally's youthful mistakes.	ME	16	C	Rea	I,II
Zacharias, Lee. *Lessons.* Boston: Houghton, 342pp. Flashbacks recount Janie Hurdle's love of music, her devastating affair, and destructive marriage.	IN	c–m	I	Rea	I,II,V,VI
Zindel, Paul. *The Girl Who Wanted a Boy.* NY: Harper, 148pp. Sibella Cametta's uneasiness about her intellectual prowess and her unrequited crush complicate and aid her maturation.	NY	15	C,LYA	Rea	I

1982

Guest, Judith. *Second Heaven.* NY: Viking, 320pp. Cat Holzman's efforts to help abused teenager Gale Murray complicate and illuminate her life.	MI	16	C,I	Rea	IX
Hoffman, Alice. *White Horses.* NY: Putnam, 254pp. Fabulistic dreams inform Teresa's difficult maturation, complicated by fascination with mythic romantic heroes and fixation on older brother, Silver.	CA	a	I,Fab	P	I,III,IX,XII
Kanin, Garson. *Cordelia?* NY: Arbor, 236pp. Actor Alan Standish discovers bizarre, secret circumstance behind youngest daughter's disinterest in theater.	E	18	C	Rea	II,V
Langton, Jane. *Natural Enemy.* New Haven: Ticknor, 282pp. Murder and competition for attention of the "older woman" he loves complicate and accelerate John Hand's maturation.	MA	17	D	Rea	VIII,XII
Myers, James E. *Jones.* Springfield, IL: Lincoln, 200pp. Working with quality bird dogs facilitates orphan Jones's painful maturation amid Jonah-like trials.	IL	16	C,I,A	Rea	XII
Paretsky, Sara. *Indemnity Only.* NY: Dial, 244pp. Murder of collegian Peter Thayer also entangles and endangers his lover Anita McGraw and his younger sister Jill.	Chicago	14	D,SC	Rea	II,IV
Parker, Robert B. *Ceremony.* NY: Delacorte, 152pp. Prostitution constitutes April Kyle's rebellion against parents and society.	MA	hs	D	Rea	II,IV
Sanders, Lawrence. *The Case of Lucy Bending.* NY: Putnam's, 440pp. Various youngsters including Lucy Bending (a physical and emotional adolescent at age eight) illustrate contemporary upper-class decadence.	FL	8	SC	Rea	I,II

Author/Title	Setting	Age	Type	Tone	Reference
1982 (*continued*)					
Tesich, Steve. *Summer Crossing*. NY: Random, 373pp. Friendship between Daniel Price, Larry Misiora, and Billy Freund altered by love affairs, family and economic pressures, changing values, and time.	IN	hs–m	C,I	Rea	VIII,IX,X,XIII
Valin, Jonathan. *Day of Wrath*. NY: Congdon, 244pp. Robbie Segal's rebellion against mother's "middle-class legalized repression and sublimation through status" involves sexual exploitation, murder, symbolizes cultural decay.	OH	14	D	Rea	I,IV,XI
Walker, Alice. *The Color Purple*. NY: Harcourt, 245pp. Glimpses of several adolescents indicate the poverty, abuse, sexism, and racism over which they triumph, primarily by female bonding.	S	c–m	I,SC	Rea	I,II
Wilkinson, Sylvia. *Bone of My Bones*. NY: Putnam's, 272pp. Ella Ruth Higgins's notebook-journal-novel reflects painful childhood and adolescence and her artistic development.	NC	c–a	C,I	Rea	II,IV,V,VI

Index